J.L. VIVES

DE INSTITUTIONE
FEMINAE CHRISTIANAE

LIBER PRIMUS

SELECTED WORKS OF J.L. VIVES

GENERAL EDITOR

C. MATHEEUSSEN

EDITORIAL COMMITTEE

C. Matheeussen, President, Brussels
M. de Schepper, Brussels
C. Fantazzi, Windsor, Canada
E. George, Lubbock, Texas
J. IJsewijn, Louvain

VOLUME VI

J.L. VIVES

DE INSTITUTIONE
FEMINAE CHRISTIANAE

LIBER PRIMUS

J. L. VIVES

DE INSTITUTIONE FEMINAE CHRISTIANAE

LIBER PRIMUS

Introduction, Critical Edition, Translation and Notes

EDITED BY

C. FANTAZZI and C. MATHEEUSSEN

TRANSLATED BY

C. FANTAZZI

E.J. BRILL

LEIDEN · NEW YORK · KÖLN

1996

This book has been published with the financial support from the Ministerie van de Vlaamse Gemeenschap.

The paper in this book meets the guidelines for permanence and durability of the Committee on Production Guidelines for Book Longevity of the Council on Library Resources.

Library of Congress Cataloging-in-Publication Data

Vives, Juan Luis, 1492–1540.
   [De institutione feminae Christianae. English & Latin]
   De institutione feminae Christianae : liber primus / J.L. Vives ; introduction, critical edition, translation, and notes ; edited by C. Matheeussen, C. Fantazzi ; translated by C. Fantazzi.
     p. cm. — (Selected works of J.L. Vives, ISSN 0921–0717 ; v. 6)
   Includes bibliographical references and indexes.
   ISBN 9004106596 (alk. paper)
   1. Women—Early works to 1800. 2. Women—Education—Early works to 1800. 3. Virginity—Early works to 1800. I. Matheeussen, Constantinus. II. Fantazzi, Charles. III. Title. IV. Series: Vives, Juan Luis, 1492–1540. Selections, English & Latin. 1987 ; v. 6.
HQ1201.V54   1996
305.4—dc20
                            96–9824
                              CIP

Die Deutsche Bibliothek - CIP-Einheitsaufnahme

Vives, Juan Luis:
[Selected works]
Selected works of J. L. Vives / general ed. C. Matheeussen. – Leiden ; New York ; Köln ; Brill.
NE: Matheeussen, Constant [Hrsg.]; Vives, Juan Luis: [Sammlung]
Vol. 6. Vives, Juan Luis: De institutione feminae Christianae liber primus. – 1996
Vives, Juan Luis:
De institutione feminae Christianae liber primus : introduction, critical edition, translation and notes / J. L. Vives. Ed. by C. Matheeussen ; C. Fantazzi. Transl. by C. Fantazzi. Leiden ; New York ; Köln ; Brill, 1996
  (Selected works of J. L. Vives / Juan Luis Vives ; Vol. 6)
  ISBN 90–04–10659–6

ISSN 0921-0717
ISBN 90 04 10659 6

PRINTED IN THE NETHERLANDS

CONTENTS

ACKNOWLEDGMENTS

We gratefully acknowledge the assistance of the following individuals and organizations on both sides of the Atlantic: our fellow editors of the Selected Works of Juan Luis Vives—Marcus De Schepper, Edward George and Jozef IJsewijn—for their punctilious criticism and scholarly collaboration; David Viera for his advice in Catalan bibliography; Wendy Curtis and Diane Lane for their expert initial typing of the manuscript; Margie Prytulak for her patient retypings of the apparati; Philippa Matheson for her elegant and accurate typographics; the Katholieke Universiteit Brussel; the University of Windsor; the Ministerie van de Vlaamse Gemeenschap, Departement Onderwijs; the National Endowment for the Humanities; the Social Sciences and Humanities Research Council of Canada.

INTRODUCTION

Nous employons toutes sortes de moyens pour leur abattre le courage; les forces seroient égales, si l'éducation l'étoit aussi. (We use every kind of stratagem to demoralize them [women]; their powers would be equal to ours if their education were also.)

Montesquieu, *Lettres persanes*, XXXVIII

I. PREFATORY REMARKS

The main objective of this edition, as with all of those in the *Selected Works of Juan Luis Vives*, is to provide an accurate text, expurgated of errors and equipped with the necessary scholarly appurtenances, together with a faithful translation into English, accompanied by some additional historical notes to supplement the *apparatus fontium* of the Latin text. In the case of the *De institutione* the final text authorized for publication by Vives differs greatly from the first edition, so that a critical edition affords new insights into the evolution of the text. In matters of orthography we follow the model of the *Thesaurus Linguae Latinae* with certain allowances for the idiosyncrasies of sixteenth-century Latin spelling.

The English translation of this text has long been a desideratum for those who would wish to know Vives' thoughts on the subject of the education of women but might find his eclectic Latin too difficult to decipher. This is the first time that the integral text of the treatise has been translated into English.[1] All other translations were based on the first, unrevised edition, including the Tudor translation of Richard Hyrde, partially reproduced in Foster Watson's *Vives and the Renascence Education of Women* (New York, 1912), no longer in print and not readily accessible. His text is selective and not based on an authoritative edition of Hyrde. A much more reliable source for this translation is a dissertation by Ruth Kuschmierz (University of Pittsburgh, 1961). A definitive, commented edition of Hyrde's *The Instruction of a Christen Woman* is promised by a group of scholars.

It is not our purpose to enter into the Renaissance or contemporary *querelle des femmes*, but merely to present this important text to the interested reader in a modern scholarly edition with minimal interpretative commentary. A

---

[1] A Spanish version of the whole text has recently been published under the auspices of the city of Valencia, Juan Luis Vives, *De institutione feminae Christianae* 'La formación de la mujer Cristiana,' Introducción, traducción y notas por Joaquín Beltrán Serra (Valencia, 1994). This is a much more accurate version than that of Lorenzo Riber in Juan Luis Vives, *Obras completas* I (Madrid, 1947), pp.785–1178.

second volume containing the second and third books of the treatise, on the
married woman and the widow, will follow punctually.

II.   CIRCUMSTANCES OF COMPOSITION

At the beginning of 1523 the fortunes and energies of the youthful Juan Luis
Vives were at a particularly low ebb. After the premature death of his princely
charge and patron, William of Croy, and the protracted trial, and eventual
execution, of his father before the Inquisition, his existence in Louvain
became very precarious and isolated. In addition, he had suffered the thinly
veiled rebuffs of Erasmus for the financial insuccess of the commentary on
the *City of God*, on which he had toiled to the point of physical and mental
exhaustion. Erasmus remonstrated with him over the excessive length of the
commentary and was also somewhat embarrassed at the poor sales because,
as he says, 'Froben took this business on under compulsion from me rather
than persuasion.'[2] In his preface to the Froben edition of September 1522,
Erasmus gives the book and its author rather faint praise. He states that he
will leave it to the reader to discover how much more learned commentary
it contains than previous editions, and he is very sparing in his praise of the
author, saying rather ungraciously: 'For Luis Vives has extolled my merits
far beyond what they deserve, with the result that it would be legitimate to
praise him in my turn even did he not deserve it.'[3] The dedication of the
work to Henry VIII met with little more success. Vives had outdone himself
in praise of the monarch's great virtues and erudition as the ideal recipient
of this treatise. The response from the Court of Greenwich, which did not
come until January of the following year, was polite and commendatory but
held forth no concrete promises, as this excerpt may indicate: 'But whereas it
pleased you to dedicate these commentaries unto our name, we cannot but
retaine a gratefull minde, and returne you great thankes: in that especially
your minde therein seemeth to manifest no vulgar love and observance
towarde us. Wherefore wee would have you perswaded that our favour and
good will shall never faile in your affaires, whatsoever occasion shall be
offered that may tend to your availe.'[4]

In the midst of his complaints to Erasmus, however, about the labors
of the *Commentary* he does mention in passing, in a letter from Louvain, 15
August, 1522 (Ep. 1306, CWE 9, p.162), that he had already begun another
book, presumably the *De institutione*. On April 5, Easter Sunday, of 1523, the

---

[2] Ep. 1531, CWE 10, p.470. In the end, when the collection of all of Augustine's works
appeared under Erasmus' general editorship, all of Vives' commentary and preface were
omitted.

[3] Ep. 1309, 7 CWE 9, p.173.

[4] Saint Aurelius Augustine, *Of the Citie of God*, ed. J.L. Vives (London, 1620) 4 r.

book was completed, as the date of the prefatory letter to Queen Catherine makes clear, but because of difficulties in dealing with the financier and bookseller, Francis Birckmann, the book would not appear until January of the following year. Thus on 10 May, 1523, Vives gives vent to his feelings in two despairing letters, one to Cranevelt and one to Erasmus. To the Flemish statesman he writes that a kind of fatal calamity hangs over his destinies and a dark night obscures both his spirit and his purpose.[5] He is more guarded in his letter to Erasmus, making only vague references to the caprices of Fortune and talking more about financial transactions concerning the Augustine publishing venture. He also remarks in somewhat self-deprecating terms about the *De institutione* that it falls short of his intentions and that he has committed hundreds of 'full-grown mistakes' (*sexcentos soloecismos adultos*) in the writing. In rather crass terms he expresses the hope that the king (ὁ βασιλεύς) will not make any in the gift department (*in dando*).[6]

To both men Vives announces that he has determined to set out for Spain via England. We cannot know if he was serious in this intent, for he never returned to Spain. At any rate the trip to England turned out to be auspicious indeed and for some time to come his English sojourn afforded him that leisure for an untrammeled life of study that he so desired.[7] Concerning the book Vives repeats once again his dissatisfaction with it, including the title, in a letter to Cranevelt of 25 January, 1524, which date must have corresponded closely with the appearance of the work, since he remarks that it is now in the public domain. He blames the choice of the title on the publishers, who look to their own interests. Such titles, Vives complains, only serve to arouse envy among his enemies and disappointment to the average reader, who may find the book does not live up to its title. It is difficult to see what Vives found so objectionable in the title, which certainly seems to reflect the contents of the book very well and had been used as the title of other books on the subject of the education of women. Actually the treatise is multi-faceted, and cannot easily be summarized in a convenient title. Not only does it discuss the education of women in the three states of

---

[5] 'Tenebrae omnia et nox non in rebus maior quam in animo et consiliis meis, quae omnia adempta sunt mihi violentia molestiarum.' Henri de Vocht, *Litterae virorum eruditorum ad Franciscum Craneveldium* (Louvain, 1928) Ep. 56, p.141.

[6] CWE 10, Ep. 1362, p.14.

[7] As early as 1521 Vives had expressed this fervent desire to his most trusted confidante, Cranevelt, in a letter now brought to light once again in the *Litterae ad Craneveldium Balduinianae*, Ep. 91, *Humanistica lovaniensia* 44 (1995), pp.16–17: 'Ocium ad perficiendum quod institui, nempe opera studiis nec iniucunda nec (ut spero) inutilia, tum etiam nec Christo ingrata, vitam compositam et si quid est in rebus humanis certi, certam, tranquillam, honestam, sanctam et si hoc verbum ire sine invidia potest, qualem ingenium meum decet, semotam a puerilibus ineptiis, a μικρολογία absque invidiolis, absque obtrectatiunculis, quae me plus conficiunt quam ullus studiorum labor, quod est ingenii mei pabulum saluberrimum.'

life—unmarried woman, wife and widow—but it also addresses the social status of women in general, the Church's doctrine on the sacrament of matrimony and the moral instruction of womankind. Writing to Cranevelt once again on 1 May, 1524,[8] Vives returns to a discussion of the recently issued book and comments on several typographical errors that Cranevelt had pointed out to him (these will be signalled in the *apparatus criticus*), and also defends certain linguistic usages with examples from classical writers.

In October of that same year, 1524, at the express wish of the Queen, Vives produced a brief manual outlining a course of study to be followed by Princess Mary, the *De ratione studii puerilis*, which is composed of two letters, one for the Princess and another for Charles Mountjoy, son of William Mountjoy, the Queen's Chamberlain.[9] In writing this practical outline Vives was perhaps tacitly aware that Mary, sole heir to the throne, might some day be destined to rule. The books he counsels for her study are much more oriented to government than those recommended in the *De institutione*: dialogues of Plato relating to the government of the state, More's *Utopia*, and Erasmus' *Institutio Christiani principis*. In addition to the Scriptures and the Fathers of the Church he would have her learn the secular wisdom of the *Distichs of Cato*, the *Mimes* of Publilius and the *Sentences of the Seven Sages* collected by Erasmus. As a true pedagogue Vives first gives practical instruction in the learning of the parts of speech and syntax and advocates the learning of Latin conversation in company with three or four other fellow students. From her own reading the Princess should copy down sententious sayings in a notebook for memorization. At about the same time Vives put together a collection of mottoes and devices for the use of the Princess, which he entitled the *Satellitium vel Symbola*, to serve as a 'mystical guard' over her person. Yet another instructional book came from Vives' pen during this period, the *Introductio ad sapientiam*, a work that attained immense popularity, with one hundred editions in Latin and various languages appearing before 1600. All three books were first published by Pieter Martens in Louvain, 1524. Other scholars also contributed to Mary's education, Thomas Linacre with a *Rudimenta grammatikes* (in English), 1524, and Giles Duwes with an *Introductorie for to lerne to rede, to pronounce and to speke French trewly*, also 1524.

---

[8] De Vocht, Ep. 91, pp.274-276.

[9] There is extant in the Cotton Library of London a touching letter from Catherine to her daughter, in which she expresses her solicitude for Mary's program of study: 'As for your writing in Lattine I am glad that ye shall chaunge frome me to Maister Federston, for that shall doo you moche good to lerne by him to write right. But yet some tymes I wold be glad when ye doo write to M.F. of your own enditing, when he hathe rede it that I may se it. For it shal be a grete comfort to me to see you kepe your Latten and fayer writing and all.' Henry Ellis, *Original Letters Illustrative of English History* (London, 1824), vol. II, pp.19-20.

Mary did not disappoint her mentors. There is a copy of her translation of a prayer of Thomas Aquinas in the British Library done at the age of twelve.[10] Erasmus in 1529 praises her composition of fine Latin epistles.[11] Moreover, a member of a French embassy to the King's court in 1527 relates that she spoke in Latin, Italian and French and played the virginal.[12]

After a long silence, which made Vives wonder about their scholarly friendship, Erasmus wrote Vives a brief letter from Basel on 29 May, 1527. In response to Vives' inquiry about what he thought of his most recent writings, Erasmus gives his frank opinion: 'Your writings have my enthusiastic approval, especially what you have written about marriage. But you strive after extemporaneousness, which in your case, to be sure, is more successful than the most minute care exercised by a great many writers. If, however, you would be willing to restrain your ardor and adapt yourself more to the opinion of the reader, for whom the play is being performed, then certain elements would be a little less harsh.'[13] Erasmus then goes on to talk more specifically and more bluntly about Vives' views on marriage, which will be discussed in the next volume. In closing Erasmus states: 'You have my opinion, but it is one on which you in turn are free to have yours; you should at least appreciate my compliance with your wish, as it was you who asked it of me.'

Vives did not take kindly to the proffered criticism. After the usual polite formalities in his reply of 20 July, 1527, he reverts once again to his excuse about being worn out from his work on Augustine but still determined to produce something for the Queen. 'Consequently' he says, 'there was no time to polish the style if indeed I could have polished it, however much I tried. Then I took into account those for whom I was writing, namely, women, and especially the one to whom I was dedicating it. I thus adopted a plainer style so that it would be understood by the one for whom I was composing the work and whose approbation I sought … A good number of people have expressed their enthusiastic approval of the simple and unaffected style of the work; at least that is what they said.' A little further on, gathering more courage, as it were, Vives blurts out: 'Now that I have transgressed the bounds of modesty, I may be allowed to be well and truly shameless.' He then launches into a spirited defense of his treatment of women in the book, and answers all of Erasmus' critiques, especially those concerning marriage, which is the subject of the second book. It is strange that Erasmus never

---

[10] British Library, Royal MS 17 CXVI

[11] Allen, Ep. 2023

[12] British Library, Additional MS 12, 192, ff. 42–89. Cf. David Loades, *Mary Tudor, A Life* (London, 1989), pp.32 ff.

[13] These translations are my own and will appear in volume 14 of *The Complete Works of Erasmus* (University of Toronto Press).

alludes to the fact that he had himself the year before written a treatise on that same subject for the same Queen Catherine, which he had begun two years earlier, as he says at the beginning of his prefatory letter (Allen, Ep. 1727).[14] As for the Queen, she certainly would not have been flattered to know that the style had to be simplified for her more ready comprehension. All in all, Vives seems to have been very apprehensive about the fortunes of this book.

Encouraged by the unexpected success of the previous volume, Vives embarked upon a sequel to it on the duties of the husband in response to the interests of various friends, including Alvaro de Castro, a merchant from Burgos with whom he shared a residence in London in the latter part of 1524. He began work on it in the next year and probably finished it in a short time, for it bears the marks of hasty composition. It was written at first in Spanish, as we learn from the preface, since de Castro could not read Latin. The work is dedicated to Juan Borja, duke of Gandía, near Valencia. In the fourth chapter of this second treatise Vives returns to the education of women in much the same terms as he had adopted in the *De institutione*. The woman is to be denied access to those liberal arts that deal more with the man's world—dialectic, history, mathematics and politics. She will occupy herself rather with those books that will improve her morals and give her serenity of spirit. Once again Vives concedes that the female sex is not wicked by nature and ridicules those who are of that opinion, but in pessimistic tones he sees all humanity as drawn towards evil, a condition that can be remedied in part by good reading. To that end she should read books of piety, the Scriptures and lives of the saints, but also works of philosophy of Plato, Cicero, Seneca and Plutarch that treat of moral conduct. On the other hand she should not interest herself in the more abstruse regions of theology.

III.   EDITIONS AND CONSTITUTION OF THE TEXT

These are the editions consulted for the elaboration of the text:

H = IO. LODO / VICI VIVIS. VALENTINI / De institutione foeminae Christianae, ad / Sereniss. D. Catherinam Hispanam, Angliae / Reginam, libri tres, mira eruditione, ele / gantia, brevitate, facilitate, plane aurei, pi / etateque & sanctimonia, vere Christiani, / Christianae in primis Virgini, deinde Maritae, postremo Viduae, novo / instituendi argumento / longe utilissi / mi.
Antverpiae apud Michaelem Hillenium Hooch / stratanum. In intersignio Rapi excusum, / Impensis vero honesti viri Francisci / Byrckman, Civis Coloniensis. / Anno M.D.XXIIII.

---

[14] It is interesting to note that Erasmus, too, apologizes for the flat and stilted character of the style of the piece. The more technical character of Erasmus' essay on the sacrament of matrimony will be discussed in the next volume.

W = IOANNIS / LODOVICI VIVIS VALENTI / ni de Institutione foeminae Christia / nae ad Inclytam D. CATHARI / NAM Hispanam, An / gliae Reginam, Li / bri tres. Ab auctore ipso recogniti, au / cti, & reconcinnati. / Una cum rerum & verborum diligentissimo / INDICE. / BASILEAE / M.D.XXXVIII.
Colophon: BASILEAE, PER RO / BERTUM VVINTER, MENSE / AVGUSTO, ANNO / M.D.XXXVIII.

W² = IOANNIS / LUDOVICI VIVIS / VALENTINI / DE OFFICIO MARITI / Liber unus. / DE INSTITUTIONE FOE / MINAE Christianae / Libri tres. / DE INGENUORUM ADO / lescentum ac puellarum Insti / tutione Libri duo. / Omnes ab autore recogniti, aucti ac re- / concinnati, una cum rerum ac verborum locupletissimo Indice. pp.187–576
Colophon: BASILEAE / IN OFFICINA ROBERTI / VVINTER ANNO M. / DXXXX mense / Septembri.

IOANNIS / LUDOVICI VIVIS / VALENTINI, / DE OFFICIO MARITI / Liber Unus. / DE INSTITUTIONE FOE / minae Christianae / Libri tres. / DE INGENUORUM ADO / lescentum ac puellarum Insti / tutione Libri duo. / Omnes ab autore postremo recogniti, aucti / ac reconcinnati; una cum locuplete / rerum ac verborum Indice. BASILEAE, per Io- / annem Oporinum. (s.d.) pp.176–533.

B = Io. Lodovici Vivis Valentini opera, in duos distincta tomos: quibus omnes ipsius lucubrationes, quotquot umquam in lucem editas voluit, complectuntur: praeter commentarios in Augustinum De civitate Dei, Basileae, apud N. Episcopium, 1555, vol. II, pp.650-759.

V = Joannis Ludovici Vivis Valentini, opera omnia, distributa et ordinata in argumentorum classes praecipuas a Gregorio Majansio. Valentiae edetanorum, Monfort, 1782–1790 [London, Gregg Press, 1964], vol. IV, pp.65–301.

There exists another undated edition, published at Basel, which has the same title as the preceding, but does not bear the name of Oporinus.
    Despite some rather minor errors the Hillen edition, as in previous texts of Vives in this series, including mine of *De conscribendis epistolis*, is an accurate text and in many cases the sole witness of what is clearly the correct reading: *et*, (p.14, line 20); *habebat* (p.60, line 1); *in ipsis* (p.66, line 13); *non* (p.72, line 9); *Democrates* (p.90, line 19); *mutet* (p.98, line 17); *comat se* (p.98, line 20); *virgines* (p.118, line 13); *acciperet* (p.120, line 4); *nullum* (p.148, line 9); *nudare* (p.154, line 16); *strepitur* (p.154, line 18); *iudicent* (p.168, line 27).
    In many other instances the correct reading of **H** is also preserved either in **W**, **W²**, or, less often, in **B**. When such a reading is omitted or changed in

W or **B**, it is reproduced in Majansius. At other times, however, Majansius recovers a reading of **H** that Vives had definitely wished to be expunged, as the opening sentence of Chapter 7, and, as will be seen in the succeeding volume, the opening chapter of Book II. Several times **W** alone of all the editions has the correct reading: *maritas* (p.60, line 27); *dicat* (p.62, line 6); *intolerabilia* (p.70, line 16); *opera bona* (p.76, line 2); *administram* (p.172, line 11). Otherwise it is supported by the reading of **W²**, Basel s.d. or Oporinus. There is only one case in which **W²** has a correct reading not found in any other edition: *meret* (p.170, line 23), which is probably a correction of the editor.[15] Basel s.d. and Oporinus are of no importance in the constitution of the text since they are based either on **W** or **W²**, and introduce no independent readings of their own. The 1555 *Opera omnia* often follows Oporinus and may be based on it, but it contains many banal errors of its own devising, many of which are then reproduced in **V**. Majansius also contains a considerable number of false readings and typographical errors present in none of the previous editions. Both Basel 1555 and Majansius make corrections of obvious misprints in the textual tradition, sometimes concording in the correction, sometimes independently one of the other. In one passage Majansius corrects the inflections of nouns to accord with the sense, a correction which we have accepted (p.174, lines 11–12).

The text is thus based on **W**, the Basel edition that Vives himself revised for publication, corrected from various other editions when it is obviously in error.

IV. TRANSLATIONS

First to appear of the numerous translations into the vernacular languages is that into Castillian: *Instrucción de la muger Christiana ... traduizido aora nuevamente de latin en romance por Juan Justiniano criado del Excelentissimo señor duque de Calabria, derigido a la Serenissima reyna Hermana mi señora*, Valencia 1528. The translator was actually an Italian, Giovanni Giustiniani, in the service of Don Fernando of Aragon, Viceroy of Valencia and Germana de Foix, but very well versed in the Castillian tongue. He says in the preface that he wishes to make this '*lectura tan buena*' available to all women of Spain since even foreign lands have been able to enjoy it. He is aware that it has already been translated into English by the royal treasurer at the behest of the Queen herself, and has heard that a French translation already exists. From the first the translator alerts the reader that he has taken the liberty of adding things not present in the original. An interesting example of this is the addition of further reading material for young

---

[15] The active rather than the deponent form of the verb *mereo* is preferred with the noun *stipendia* (cf. OLD *mereo* 2.).

women to the list provided by Vives in Chapter 5 of the treatise. Justinian adds for those who cannot read Latin the letters of Saint Catherine of Siena, translations of Boethius and Gregory, Petrarch's *De remediis utriusque fortunae* and '*el Cartujano*,' i.e., the Carthusian, Ludolphus of Saxony, whose popular *Vita Christi* had been translated both into Catalan and Castillian before 1500. He recommends especially Erasmus' *Enchiridion militis christiani*, which had just appeared in that same year in Valencia from the same printer of the *Instrucción*, Jordi Costilla. A year later a corrected version by an unknown author was published in Alcalá. In the preface, once again addressed to Doña Germana, the anonymous translator declares that he had to re-translate many passages and add several chapters that had been omitted for some unknown reason. There followed numerous other editions of Justiniano: Seville, 1535; Zaragoza, 1539, 1545, 1555; Zamora, 1539; Valladolid, 1584.[16]

It is altogether fitting that the English translation of Vives' treatise should proceed from the More household. More himself had been elaborating a version of it when he learned from Richard Hyrde, who had recently entered his services as a tutor, that he had completed his own translation. Hyrde mentions in his preface to the Queen that he showed his work, which he had done in secret, to his good master, who confided to him that he had begun it himself thinking that it would have procured great pleasure to the Queen in her zeal for the virtuous education of womankind in her realm. Hyrde's ideas on the education of women were even more forceful than those of More himself, as can be seen in his preface to Margaret Roper's translation of Erasmus' meditations on the Lord's prayer, *Precatio dominica in septem portiones*, published in 1524.[17]

It may reasonably be conjectured that Vives discussed the problem of women's education at More's estate in Chelsea, where he must have been a guest from time to time. The translator reserves great praise for the book saying: 'I verily believe there was never any treatis made, either furnisshed with more goodly counsayles, or sette out with more effectuall reasons, or garnysshed with more substanciall authoritees, or stored more plentuously of convenient examples, nor all these thynges together more goodly treated and

---

[16] An interesting historical analysis of the two versions of the Castillian translation is given in Joan Fuster, 'Joan Lluis Vives i València, 1528,' *Llibres i problemes del renaixement* (Valencia, 1985), pp.9–48.

[17] The translation and Hyrde's preface are available in R.C. Demolen, *Erasmus of Rotterdam, A Quincentennial Symposium* (New York, 1971), pp.93–104. Hyrde is especially vitriolic towards those who think that learning is dangerous for women: 'And where they fynde faute with lernyng bycause they say it engendreth wytte and crafte, there they reprehende it for that that it is moost worthy to be commended for, and the whiche is one singuler cause wherfore lernyng ought to be desyred, for he that had lever have his wyfe a foole than a wyse woman I hold hym worse than twyse frantyke.' p.100.

handeled, than maister Vives hath done in his boke.'[18] He does justice to the
original, accommodating the difficult Latin of Vives into a clear and vigorous
English, which he submitted to the inspection of More for approval and
correction. Some of Vives' more severe strictures against female adornment
in the first book are omitted and the long diatribe of Isaiah that Vives quotes
in this regard is abbreviated. At other times he adds a phrase or two for the
sake of rhythm or clarity, and like the Castillian translator, Justiniano, makes
additions and deletions to the list of romances forbidden by Vives, inserting
such English examples as Parthenope of Blois, Ipomedon, Guy of Warwick
and Bevis of Hampton.

The elaborated title of Hyrde's translation reads:

> A very frutefull and pleasant boke called the INSTRUCTION OF A CHRIS-
> TEN WOMAN, made fyrst in Laten, and dedicated unto the quenes good
> grace, by the right famous clerke mayster Lewes Vives, and turned into
> Englysshe by Rycharde Hyrd. Whiche boke who so redeth diligently shal have
> knowledge of many thynges, wherein he shal take great pleasure, and specially
> women shall take great commodyte and frute towarde the encreace of vertue
> and good maners.

The last phrase is to be interpreted in modern English as good morals, and
this is indeed the primary intention of Vives' treatise. The *Instruction* went
far in propagating Vives' educational ideas in England, becoming the most
popular conduct book for women during the Tudor period and beyond. It
went through nine known editions, all from the printer, Thomas Bertelet.
The first edition antedates his appointment as *regius impressor*, which was
given to him on 15 February, 1530. Since he opened shop in August 1528,
the first undated edition must be either 1528 or 1529.[19] In any case the work
was published posthumously, for Richard Hyrde died in Italy while on a
royal mission on 25 March, 1528.

Vives makes reference in a letter to Cranevelt of 31 December, 1526 (De
Vocht, Ep. 217, p.568) to a French translation of the work that was being
prepared by a certain Clericus, who De Vocht conjectures might be either
Philip de Clerck, Esquire, 'Comoigne meester' of Mechelen, or Charles
de Clerck, a Councillor and chamberlain of Charles V. This may have
circulated in manuscript but no printed copy appeared. The first French
translation is owed to Pierre de Changy and was printed by Jacques Kerver
in Paris, 1542: *Livre de l'institution de la femme chrestienne tant en son enfance que
mariage et viduité. Aussi de l'office du mari.* The translator takes great freedom

---

[18] *The Instruction of a Christen Woman*, ed. Kuschmierz, p.3.

[19] W.A. Jackson, F.S. Ferguson, and Katherine F. Pantzer, *A Short-Title Catalogue of Books
Printed in England, Scotland, and Ireland and of English Books Printed Abroad, 1475–1640*, rev. edn.,
3 vols. (Oxford, 1976–1991), ii, 429, give the date of the first edition as 1529?, with further
editions: 1531?, two in 1541, 1547, two in 1557, 1585 and 1592.

with the text, suppressing many passages, so that it almost constitutes an original work. It was reprinted many times: 1543, 1545, 1549, 1552 and 1579 in Paris, and three times in Lyons by Jean de Tournes, 1545, 1547 and 1549. Of later editions of the 16th century that produced by Christopher Plantin in 1579 is of particular interest. At first he thought of publishing a reprint of the de Changy translation but seeing its poor quality he sponsored a new translation by Antoine Tiron at the instigation of two Antwerp schoolmasters of a girls' finishing school, Sebastiaan Cuypers and Pieter Heyns.

The first German translation dates to 1544, the work of Christoph Bruno, printed by Heinrich Steiner in Augsburg: *Von Vnderweijsung ayner christlichen Frauwen*. It was reprinted together with the *De officio mariti* by C. Egenolffs, Frankfurt-am-Main, 1566.

An Italian translation of the three works appeared in Venice from the presses of Vincenzo Vaugris, 1546, done by Pietro Lauro of Modena, according to the dedication. It was reprinted in Milan by Giovann' Antonio de gli Antonij, 1561.

A Dutch translation based on the French of Changy, *Die Institutie ende leeringe van een Christlijcke Vrowe*, was published by Jan Roelants, Antwerp, 1554.

V.   REVISIONS IN THE 1538 EDITION

Around 1537 an association of printers in Basel, including the Hellenist Joannes Oporinus, Balthasar Lazius, and Thomas Platter, with the financial backing of Robert Winter, launched the publication of numerous works of Vives, some in their original form and others revised by the author.[20] Prominent among these was the *De institutione*, Robert Winter, 1538 and 1540, and Oporinus, undated but probably from the year 1540 or 1542. Vives took this opportunity to submit the work to a thorough revision, stylistic and doctrinal, which constitutes a substantial re-writing of the treatise. One salient characteristic of the new version is the addition of many more citations of ancient authorities, mostly from the Fathers of the Church. Vives announces this intention towards the end of the dedication to the Queen: 'Things that would not accord with generally accepted customs I have supported and sustained with the testimony of great authorities lest they be nullified by the force of public opinion.' He also enlists the classical authors for his cause, as in his insertion of a rather long passage of Tacitus from his

---

[20] According to a close study of the publishing history of Vives' works this printing firm undertook to publish the writings of Vives as the great successor to Erasmus. Cf. Enrique González y González, *Joan Lluís Vives, de la escolástica al humanismo* (Valencia, 1987), pp.43 and 76.

Dialogue on Orators, not a very well known work but one with which Vives would have been familiar because of his interest in oratory and declamation. The Roman historian here eulogizes the pristine virtues of Roman matrons in days gone by, citing the example of Cornelia, mother of the Gracchi, and the mothers of Julius and Augustus Caesar, who were so vigilant in the education of their male children. How much more, reasons Vives, should young girls be guarded from bad example (p.17, §11).

It is in the fourth chapter, on the education of the young woman, that Vives radically revises his previous views on the subject. He prefaces his remarks with a pessimistic paragraph on the proclivity of the human race to vice and the need for instruction in virtue in order to combat the purveyors of evil counsel. This leads up to the refutation of a statement he had made in the first version regarding the dangers inherent in a woman who has been given too much education, the inveterate prejudice against the *femina docta.* He counters this opinion with the assertion that men of evil disposition are just as prone to misuse their intelligence as women. This certainly seems like a reasonable and self-evident statement to the modern mind, but not so in Vives' day. A little further on he elaborates much more fully on the concept that no learned woman was ever found to be unchaste. Ignorance (*inscitia*) alone is to blame. Such a belief seems to accord well with the tenets of Thomas More. To corroborate his contention Vives adds a few more examples of learned women: the poetess Erinna; Saint Barbara, who according to an obscure legend that Vives discovered was supposed to have received instruction from Origen; a woman skilled in rhetoric named Eunomia, who is mentioned by Jerome; Hildegard of Bingen, and a promising young lady of his own city, Angela Zabata. Towards the end of the chapter, disappointingly, there is a reiteration of some of the more uncompromising of Paul's teachings on the place of women, but this is followed by another more lenient counsel of Vives with regard to girls who show less aptitude for learning.

The chapter that received the most radical revisions was Chapter 6 on virginity, as will be clear from the separate apparatus in the appendix. It is obvious that Vives struggled over the proper approach to this subject. In the original version Vives suddenly abandons his more discursive style for a rather personal, and, one might add, paternalistic tête-à-tête with the young girl (*Iam mihi totus sermo erit cum puella*). He takes as his text, explicitly, Augustine's *De sancta virginitate,* which he follows rather closely at the beginning in the comparison of the young girl as the spouse of Christ to the Church as the spouse of Christ in St. Paul to the Corinthians (2 Cor. 11:2). From this image the tone becomes even more mystical in its reference to the one hundred forty-four virgins mentioned in the Apocalypse, who will follow after the Lamb wherever he goes II Cor. 11, 2 (Apoc. 14:4), somewhat inappropriate in the context since the sacred writer speaks of male virgins who have never defiled themselves with women.

After several other Scriptural quotations Vives stages a dialogue between Christ and a young maiden, who is a virgin only physically, but not in mind. Christ remonstrates with her and bids her depart and find other pastures. In a second dialogue that ensues the divine interlocutor is substituted by a human one, presumably the author himself. It takes the form of question and answer, the question relating to what qualities the young girl would desire in her spouse, and the answer given in disparate verses from the Psalms which describe the Divine Spouse. With its mixture of Scriptural quotations and declamatory rhetoric the style is quite strange, in some respects resembling Augustine's own emotional style, but in sentiment diverging quite perceptibly from Augustine's essay on virginity. There the emphasis was on the humility of a virgin, that she not be puffed up by her virtue, whereas Vives seems to glorify this state in almost rhapsodic language.

The revised version is much more sober. In fact, Vives openly states once again, as he did in the preface to the Queen, that he is a teacher, not a panegyrist. He then proceeds to give a formal definition of virginity: 'Integrity of the mind which extends also to the body.' Without acknowledging his source Vives may have had in mind a passage in Ambrose, *De virginitate* 15, which expatiates on this notion. Instead of the Scriptures Vives has recourse to ancient precedent and to the writings of a later interpreter of Augustine, Fulgentius of Ruspe, a rather esoteric authority for the casual reader.

In Chapter 8, on adornments, Vives gives prominence of place to two passages of the princes of the Apostles, Peter and Paul, which he had reserved for the end of the chapter in the first version. He bolsters his argument as usual with further examples from antiquity and from the Fathers, including a very pertinent comment from Tertullian elucidating a passage from the prophet Osee and another from his stern essay on *De virginibus velandis*, decreeing that women should be veiled not only in church but in public. Chrysostom and Fulgentius supply further proofs, whose use Vives defends on the grounds that the subject matter is foreign to him so that he gladly has recourse to the authority of the Fathers.

As the treatise continues, Vives adorns and fortifies it with new material, e.g., the description of the newly instituted custom, as it would seem, of masquerade parties and its attendant evils (§117), a rather long insertion about the scandal of the weak and the leading of others into sin (§130–131), and the selfish actions of parents who choose husbands for their daughters for their own advantage. An edifying story about the wisdom of a certain generation of men in his native Spain makes for a pleasant diversion at §147, and sheds a good light upon women's power of persuasion. A little later a parable from Plato is effectively used, and in general many other additions are made towards the end of the essay.

In addition to these substantive changes to the text there are other innumerable revisions: changes in diction, word order, syntax and a general

redrafting of the essay. The reader may well find in glancing at the *apparatus criticus* that not all of these changes constitute an improvement. In many cases the earlier more spontaneous style that Erasmus criticized seems more effective than the later elaboration. A cursory examination of some revisions introduced into the prefatory letter may afford some insight into this process.

Immediately after the opening *captatio benevolentiae* Vives summons the authority of Aristotle to support his argument about the utility of educating women to virtue, and how virtue is an essential ingredient in any lasting community of life. The added passage seems to reflect a sentiment expressed by Hyrde in his own prefatory address to the Queen: 'For what is more frutefull than the good education and ordre of women, the one halfe of all mankynd, and that halfe also, whose good behavour or evyll tatchis [i.e., taches, 'defects' or 'vices'] gyveth or byreveth the other halfe, almoste all the holle pleasure and commodite of this present lyfe, byside the furtherance or hynderance forther growyng thereupon, concerning the lyfe to come?'[21] Vives then proceeds to cite further authorities, both pagan and Christian, adding to the previous list the two advocates of North African asceticism, Tertullian and Fulgentius. In stylistic changes he modified the tenses of several verbs throughout these first pages, adhering to a more strict sequence of tenses. On page 4, line 16, he corrects a typographical error that he had already registered in his letter to Cranevelt (*videndum* for *vivendum*). The rather inelegant and colloquial *unoculo* is changed to *lusco* (p.4, line 30). Inveighing against writers of scurrilous verse, Vives gives vent to a more forceful expression of his condemnation: '*corruptus animus et veneno tumens inspirare nisi venenum nequit*' becomes the more rhetorical and venomous '*corruptus animus nequitia et veneno putris aspirare nisi venenum nequit*' (p.4, lines 33–34). The second ablative *nequitia* balances *veneno* with its accompanying adjective, now changed into the more graphic *putris*, and the verb *aspirare*, 'to emit,' is more appropriate than the previous one. With the *figura etymologica* '*nequitia ... nequit*' Vives achieves a greater rotundity of diction and rhythm. *Amantes* replaces *amatores*, a subtle nuance of meaning, perhaps with Cicero's distinction in *Tusculan Disputations* 4, 27 in mind. *Otiosi et bene pasti* (p.6, line 25), a comparison of lusty young men to indolent, well-fed stallions is a polite and even humorous mitigation of *salaces*, a more biological word for high sexual arousement in the male animal, which he may have considered too explicit for the Queen. The unclassical *vituperium* is changed to *vituperatio* (p.8, line 9).

In referring to the Queen as a role model in every condition of a woman's life Vives makes a subtle change from *et uxor ... iterum uxor* to *et sponsa ... nunc uxor*, making clear his allegiance in the King's 'great matter.' The

---

[21] Kuschmierz, p.2

Queen together with her fiery duenna, Doña Elvira, had always insisted on the nullity of her marriage to Arthur, which she maintained had never been consummated, although in the complexities of canon law this did not always favour her cause. Vives is less extravagant also in his praise of the royal couple, not wishing implicitly to exalt the King's virtues in this union.

VI. SOURCES AND CULTURAL BACKGROUND

It is curious that although Vives professes in the opening paragraph of his address to the Queen to eschew the merely exhortatory precepts of such writers as Tertullian, Cyprian, Jerome, Ambrose, Augustine and Fulgentius, yet he cites these very authors as the treatise unfolds. The sternest of them, Tertullian and Fulgentius, he adds in the second edition, to strengthen his position. Ambrose was a vehement advocate of virginity, instituting formal rituals for the installation of virgins and exalting this state of life above all others. He was followed in this tendency by Jerome in his letters to various woman followers, which Vives duly cites, especially those to Laeta, Furia and Demetrias, all high-born ladies who had embraced a life of asceticism. But Vives reserves a special place for Jerome's most antifeminist tract, the *Adversus Jovinianum*. Jovinian had taught that all baptized persons, no matter what their station in life—virgin, married or widowed—had equal spiritual merit. In his attack Jerome exalted virginity to the detriment of marriage, which, in this invective at least, he seems to have regarded as only slightly better than fornication. So virulent was his diatribe that his friends in Rome, especially the Christian senator Pammachius, tried to withdraw it from circulation. Jerome obliged his friends by writing a retractation (Epistle 48) but the piece continued to be used by antifeminist writers, thanks especially to the inclusion of an excerpt from a putative work of Theophrastus counselling the wise man not to marry. Cyprian's ascetic views, akin to those of Tertullian, whom he much admired, form part of Vives' arsenal as well as those of the Greek Fathers, Gregory Nazianzen and John Chrysostom (these latter writers were added in the second edition). In addition to the Fathers he quotes liberally and appositely from the Scriptures, both Old and New Testaments.

Of the classical writers Vives makes good use of Quintilian for the early stages of education and shows great familiarity with other Latin writers of Spanish origin: both Senecas, Lucan and Isidore. For antique legends and *exempla* he enlists to his cause Plutarch's *Mulierum virtutes*, Valerius Maximus, Pliny the Elder and Aulus Gellius. He prefers the pseudo-Aristotelian *Economics* to Xenophon's *Oeconomicus*, which is more liberal in its attitude towards women. Even Ovid provides a goodly number of quotable passages, especially from the *Remedia amoris* and the *Fasti*.

Since Vives is writing ostensibly for Catherine of Aragon, daughter of Isabella the Catholic, the position of women in Spanish society must be kept

in mind. Although Isabella herself was brought up in a traditional way in the countryside of Arévalo in the heartland of Castille, she wished her children to be educated in the new humanist learning, especially the knowledge of Latin. Through the instrumentality of Fernando she had two brothers, Antonio and Alessandro Geraldini, come to the court to tutor her children. Alessandro wrote a work on the education of girls, *De eruditione nobilium puellarum*, which unfortunately has not survived. The Castillian Queen would certainly have been seconded in this initiative by her secretary, Beatriz de Galindo, 'la Latina,' as she was called, who had taught at the University of Salamanca. She surrounded herself with learned women and insisted on reforms in education.[22]

At this time in Spain and earlier in the century there was a series of tracts and treatises for and against women, many of which must have been known, at least in name, to Vives.[23] In 1443 the Galician writer, Juan Rodríguez de la Cámara, wrote *El triunfo de las donas*, which attempted to prove not only the equality of women but their superiority by means of specious scholastic argumentation. He dedicated it to Doña Maria, first wife of John II, but was inspired by one of the ladies of her entourage, which may account for its exaggerated claims. Alvaro de Luna, a count also at the court of John II, wrote in praise of women *El libro de las virtuosas y claras mugeres* (1446), in which he parades forth heroines from the Old Testament and Greek and Roman antiquity as well as female saints of the early centuries. Diego de Valera, Alvaro's enemy at court, wrote in the same vein a *Tratado en defensa de virtuosas mujeres*. A book that Vives places on his forbidden list, the *Cárcel de amor* of Diego de San Pedro, published in Seville in 1492, is a covert praise of women under the guise of a tale of unrequited love, and had much success with ladies at court. There was also the *Jardín de las nobles doncellas* of Fray Martín Alonso de Córdoba, written for the Infanta Isabel, the future queen. It is aristocratic in tone, reserving knowledge and learning for queens and princesses.

Less numerous but more influential were the detractors of womankind, chief among whom was Alfonso Martínez de Toledo, Archpriest of Talavera, who entitled his work *Corbacho y reprobación de amor mundano*, after Boccaccio. The second book is a virulent satire against the vices and defects of perverse women. The other misogynist writers are poets: Pere Torroella (whom Vives cites), who wrote *Coplas de maldezir de mugeres* and his imitator, Hernán Mexía, author of *Coplas en que se descubren los defectos de las condiciones de las mugeres*.

---

[22] Cf. María Dolores Gómez Malleda, 'La cultura femenina en la época de Isabel la Católica,' *Revista de archivos, bibliotecas y museos* 61 (1955), pp.137–195.

[23] A good synopsis of all of these is given in León Esteban Mateo, *Hombre-Mujer en Vives: itinerario para la reflexión* (Valencia, 1994) and Jacob Ornstein, 'La misoginía y el profeminismo en la literatura castellana,' *Revista de filología hispánica* 3 (1941), 219–232.

Vives does not participate on one side or the other in this dispute, but steers a middle path. The strong religious and moral impulse that informs his work has more affinity with an earlier Valencian writer. There can be little doubt that Vives was familiar with the writings of the Franciscan friar, Francesc Eiximenis, (c.1340–1409), in particular, his *Llibre de les dones*. Eiximenis reached the peak of his literary career during his years in Valencia, 1382–1408, and his works were well known there, although the first printed edition of his treatise on women did not appear until 1495 in Barcelona. While Vives draws on many other sources that became accessible to the humanists, there are many similarities in the citation of sources by the two writers.[24] Indeed, in some cases Vives repeats passages from Eiximenis that he in turn had taken from a still earlier work, the *De eruditione filiorum nobilium* of Vincent of Beauvais, written for Queen Margarida, the Catalan wife of King Louis IX of France. The long passage from Cyprian's *De habitu virginum* is cited in all three works, as is Jerome's letter to Demetrias and various maxims from Terence and Ovid's *Remedia amoris*. A rather vehement harangue against female adornment from the prophet Isaias is also utilized by both Eiximenis and Vives. Some ideas of Vives on what might be interpreted as universal education for women have a precedent in Eiximenis, as in this excerpt: 'Que tota dona sabés letra, car deys que havia major occasió de esser devota e de occupar si metexa e de informar-se en tot bé.' ('All women should be literate, for in that way they will have more opportunity to be devout and to occupy themselves and inform themselves of all that is good.')[25]

We learn of another source used, undeclared, by Vives through a later imitator of his work. The Venetian printer Gabriel Giolito de' Ferrari entered the *querelle des femmes* on the side of the defenders of the female sex in the mid-sixteenth century. In 1545 he published an Italian translation of Agrippa's treatise, *Della nobilità et eccellenza delle donne*, with a prefatory encomium of womankind by Alessandro Piccolomini. In that same year the Venetian writer and polymath, Lodovico Dolce, entrusted to Giolito his *Dialogo della Institution delle Donne secondo li tre stati che cadono nella vita humana*.[26] Dolce's treatise is a close adaptation, almost a plagiarism of Vives, set in a

---

[24] Parallel passages are listed in David Viera, '¿Influjó el *Llibre de les dones* de Francesc Eiximenis en la *De institutione foeminae Christianae* de Luis Vives?' *Boletín de la Sociedad Castellonense de Cultura* 54 (1978), 145–155.

[25] Francesc Eiximenis, *Lo llibre de les dones*, ed. Frank Naccarato, rev. Curt Wittlin (Barcelona, 1981), p.91. A Spanish adaptation of Eiximenis' treatise was written by an anonymous Franciscan friar at the behest of Pope Adrian VI, published in Valladolid in 1542. It shows a marked influence of Vives in its additions to the original text.

[26] Gioliti produced an edition of *De re uxoria* in 1548 and also of *La nobiltà delle donne* of Lodovico Domenichi in the following year, as well as three different editions of Dolce's work by 1562.

lively dialogue form.[27] It had much more success than the literal translation published in Venice in 1561. Significantly, Dolce omits the epithet *Christianae* of Vives' title and with it many of the references to sacred writings. Under the guise of the male speaker in the dialogue Dolce assumes the role of '*spositor di parole*,' i.e., 'interpreter,' for a female audience of a Latin book that has just arrived from Basel. Only later in the dialogue does the '*spositor*' reveal who the author of the instructional book is. As a modern analogue to the famous story of the faithful wife, Camma, in Plutarch (it occurs in the second book of both Vives and Dolce), Dolce recounts the tale of a Dalmatian woman named Brasilla, first related by Francesco Barbaro in his *De re uxoria* (cf. note to §91) and appropriated without acknowledgement by Vives. The speaker remarks at this point: '*ho letto, dico, in una opera latina del Barbaro, che di sopra io addussi, dalla quale Lodovico Vives non solo ha tolto la maggior parte della sua institution della Donna Christiana, ma alcuni altri ancora di gran nome si sono serviti del principio*' (Dolce *Dialogo* p.45v). Thus Dolce accuses Vives of having taken the greater part of his material from Barbaro, as did some others of great fame, he claims. The accusation is somewhat exaggerated but there are many correspondences of sources in both works. Barbaro had written his treatise for Lorenzo de' Medici at the time of his marriage to Ginevra Cavalcanti in 1416. The work circulated in manuscript for almost one hundred years and was widely known before the first printed edition appeared in Paris in 1513. It is known that there was a manuscript of the work at Valencia, and there can be no doubt that Vives indeed did borrow heavily from it, especially in the citations of *exempla* from Greek and Roman history taken from Plutarch and Valerius Maximus. On the other hand he differs ideologically from Barbaro in many important matters. The Venetian writer used Xenophon's *Oeconomicus* to much greater extent in outlining wifely duties, and concerning the purpose of marriage he followed Augustine's *De bono coniugali*, which Vives cites but once. Dolce's own work contains many new examples from Italian history and literature and scenes from Venetian everyday life, as in an extended analogy between the education of young girls and the art of shipbuilding in Venice's *arsenale*.

Vives surely knew of the writings of other Italian humanists who wrote on education, such as Paolo Vergerio and Francesco Filelfo, whom he mentions in the *De officio mariti* (Majansius IV, p.369). From all of his readings and vast erudition Vives compiled the most systematic treatise on the education of women of all the various essays on the status of women in the Renaissance. His influence on this subject, both in England and Europe, was incalculable.

---

[27] A good account of Dolce's dialogue from a modern feminist point of view is contained in Adriana Chemello, '*L'Institution delle donne* di Lodovico Dolce ossia "l'insegnar virtú et honesti costumi alla Donna",' *Trattati scientifici nel Veneto fra il XV e XVI secolo* (Vicenza, 1985), pp.103–134.

In England Sir Thomas Elyot followed in Vives' tracks with his *Defense of Good Women* (1540). In Italy, to cite but a few examples, there are many reminiscences of Vives in Galeazzo Flavio Capra, *Delle eccellenze e dignità delle donne* (Venice, 1526); Lodovico Domenichi, *La nobiltà delle donne* (Venice, 1549, and Giovanni Michele Bruto, *La instituzione di una fanciulla nata nobilmente* (Antwerp, 1555). In Spain the popular *La perfecta casada* (1583) of Fray Luis de León shows indebtedness to the second book of Vives' work.

A modern reader of the *De institutione* will often be dismayed by the apparent disparity between some of the liberalizing humanist views on the education of women and the traditional depiction of the woman's place in society. This can be attributed to many factors: Vives' upbringing in a Jewish household, his strict adherence to the doctrines of the most conservative of the Fathers of the Church and an almost Manichean distrust and fear of the body. His ideal maiden (*mea virgo*) is an angelic creature, the bride of Christ (a doctrine preached with great fervor by Tertullian), destined for a life of seclusion, subordination and self-sacrifice. Vives quotes freely from both Plato and Aristotle but seems to lean more to the Aristotelian theories about the inferiority of the female sex rather than to the fundamental intellectual equality of both sexes expressed in the fifth book of the *Republic*. Whatever its failings, this treatise of Vives together with his other works on education established him as a foremost authority throughout the sixteenth century.

VII. ABBREVIATIONS USED IN THE INTRODUCTION AND NOTES

1. Ancient Latin authors and works are cited according to the *Thesaurus Linguae Latinae*; for Greek authors the abbreviations of *Der Kleine Pauly* are used.

2. Specific editions of classical and humanist authors:
Erasm. ad. LB II = Erasmus, *Opera omnia*, ed. Clericus, Lugduni Batavorum, P. van der Aa, 1703–1706, vol. II, *Adagia*.
Galenus = *Corpus medicorum graecorum*, ed. Konrad Koch, Leipzig, 1923, vol. 5.4.
Orellius = *Opuscula graecorum veterum sententiosa et moralia*, ed. Io. Conradus Orellius, Leipzig, 1819, vol. I.
PG = *Patrologiae cursus completus. Series graeca*, ed. J.P. Migne, Paris, 1857–1866.
PL = *Patrologiae cursus completus. Series latina*, ed. J.P. Migne, Paris, 1841–1864.
Pseudo-Quintilianus = *Declamationes XIX maiores Quintiliano falso adscriptae*, ed. Hakånso, Stuttgart, 1982.
Suda = *Lexicographi graeci*, ed. A. Adler, Leipzig, 1928–1938, vol. I, i-v.

3. Secondary sources:
Allen = *Opus epistolarum Des. Erasmi Roterodami*, eds. P.S. Allen, H.M. Allen, and H.W. Garrod, Oxford 1906–47, 11 vols.

CWE = Collected Works of Erasmus, Toronto, 1969–

De Vocht = *Litterae virorum eruditorum ad F. Craneveldium,* ed. Henri De Vocht, Louvain, 1929.

OLD = *Oxford Latin Dictionary,* Oxford, 1983.

SIGLA

H   = Vives, *De institutione foeminae Christianae*, Antverpiae, apud Michaelem Hillenium Hoochstratanum, 1524.

W   = Vives, *De institutione foeminae Christianae*, Basileae, per Robertum Winter, 1538.

W²   = Vives, *De officio mariti, De institutione foeminae Christianae, De ingenuorum adolescentum ac puellarum institutione*, Basileae, in officina Roberti Winter, 1540.

B   = Vives, *Opera*, Basileae, in aedibus Nic. Episcopii, 1555.

V   = Vives, *Opera omnia*, cura Gregorii Maiansii edita, Valentiae Edetanorum, 1782–1790.

Γ   = lectiones communes in **WW²BV**.

epist. Cran. = Henri de Vocht, *Litterae virorum eruditorum ad F. Craneveldium*, Lovanii, 1929, Epistola 102, pp.275–276.

J.L. VIVES

DE INSTITUTIONE
FEMINAE CHRISTIANAE

LIBER PRIMUS

IOANNIS LODOVICI VIVIS VALENTINI
IN LIBROS DE INSTITUTIONE FEMINAE CHRISTIANAE

AD SERENISSIMAM DOMINAM CATHARINAM HISPANAM
ANGLIAE REGINAM ETC.
PRAEFATIO

1. Movit me sanctitas morum tuorum et animi tui ardor in sacra studia ut
de Christianae feminae institutione aliquid ad te scriberem, argumento ut
maxime necessario, ita nulli hactenus tractato in tanta ingeniorum scriben-
tiumque varietate ac copia. Quid enim est perinde necessarium atque illarum
animos fingi ad virtutem quae nobis in omni vitae ratione sociae sunt inseparabiles? Benevolentia firma est inter bonos, inter malos autem non diuturna.
Nec immerito Aristoteles eas civitates quae feminarum institutionem parum
habent rectam magna se felicitatis parte ait orbare: videlicet nihil est aeque
molestum ut communionem vitae habere cum improbo; quod ut de civitatibus merito, sic de unaquaque domo iustius dici potest. Porro de re familiari
Xenophon et Aristoteles et de re publica Plato praecepta cum trader-
ent, nonnulla dixerunt quae ad mulieris officium pertinerent. Tertullianus,
Cyprianus, Hieronymus, Ambrosius, Augustinus, Fulgentius de virginibus
ac viduis sic disseruere ut aliquod vitae genus suadeant potius quam forment.
Toti sunt in castitatis laudibus celebrandis magnifico vero opere et illis ingeniis illaque sanctitate digno, sed praecepta formulasque vitae paucissimas
perhibuerunt, satius esse rati adhortari ad optima et manum porrigere ad
altissima quam erudire inferiora. Nos autem exhortationes illis relinquentes
ut aetatis degendae rationem ex auctoritate potius illorum quam ex opinione

10 (line number)
15 (line number)
20 (line number)

1. (Aristoteles) *Aristot. rhet. 1, 5 (1361a); pol. 1, 13 (1260b)*

1 LODOVICI **HWB** LUDOVICI **W²V** / VIVIS VALENTINI **HWW²** VIVIS **BV** ∥
9–15 Quid ... potest **Γ** *deest in* **H** ∥ **15** Porro **Γ** Nam **H** ∥ **17** Tertullianus **Γ** *deest in* **H** ∥
18 Fulgentius **Γ** *deest in* **H**

PREFACE TO THE BOOKS
ON THE INSTRUCTION OF THE CHRISTIAN WOMAN
BY JUAN LUIS VIVES,

ADDRESSED TO HER MOST SERENE MAJESTY,
CATHERINE OF SPAIN, QUEEN OF ENGLAND, ETC.

1. Moved by the holiness of your life and your ardent zeal for sacred studies I have endeavored to write something for Your Majesty on the education of the Christian woman, a subject of paramount importance, yet one that has not been treated by anyone hitherto among all the great multitude and variety of writers and intellects of the past. For what is so necessary as the spiritual formation of those who are our inseparable companions in every condition of life? Feelings of good will are strong among good persons, but not lasting among the wicked. Not without reason does Aristotle say that those states that do not provide for the proper education of women deprive themselves of a great part of their prosperity. Obviously there is nothing so troublesome as sharing one's life with a person of no principles. If this can be said with good cause of states, all the more justly can it be said of the individual household. Moreover, Xenophon and Aristotle, when imparting rules for the management of domestic affairs, and Plato in the *Republic* made observations pertaining to the duty of the woman. Tertullian, Cyprian, Jerome, Ambrose, Augustine and Fulgentius discussed the status of virgins and widows in such a way that they advocate a way of life rather than give instruction about it. They spend all their time singing the praises of chastity, a commendable undertaking in itself and one worthy of those minds and of the sanctity of that virtue, but they gave very few precepts or rules of life, thinking it preferable to exhort their readers to the best conduct and to point the way to the highest examples rather than give instruction about more lowly matters. But I shall leave exhortation to them so that each may choose for herself a way of life based on their authority rather than on

1. zeal for sacred studies: In addition to the usual womanly arts Catherine was tutored in Latin by Antonio and Alessandro Geraldini and was much influenced by Isabella's zeal for religion. Erasmus refers often to her learning in his letters, e.g., in the dedication of his *Paraphrase of Luke* to Henry VIII in 1523, in which he speaks of his 'most noble consort, a unique example in our age of true religion, who ... devotes a good part of her day to holy reading.' (Ep. 976, CWE 6, p.976.)

Republic: Xenophon in chapters VII to X of the *Oeconomicus*; Aristotle in the *Economics*, a work belonging to the *corpus aristotelicum* but whose authenticity has been seriously doubted; Book V, 451d, 457e of the *Republic*.

nostra sibi quisque deligat, ipsa vitae instituta documentis componimus. Itaque, orsi a prima feminae aetate, ipsam usque ad connubia primo libro deducimus; hinc a coniugio ad viduitatem quemadmodum transmittendum illi cum marito tempus bene ac beate censeamus, secundo; postremo, viduitas
5   instituta est.

2. Et quoniam fieri aliter nequiit, multa primo dicta sunt volumine quae ad uxores et viduas pertinent; multa proximo quae ad caelibes; nonnulla tertio quae ad omnes; ne qua vel virgo solum sibi legendum primum librum putet, vel nupta alterum, vel vidua tertium: universos
10   singulis legendos censeo. In quibus breviores forsitan fuimus quam nonnulli voluissent, sed si quis intentius consilii nostri rationem considerarit, non sine causa factum a nobis intelliget. Nam in praecipiendo non in postremis esse debet ratio brevitatis, ne verbositate legentium animos obruas potius quam edoceas; et ea esse praecepta decet quae etiam memoriter quisque
15   facillime comprehensa teneat. Neque enim ignorari oportet leges quibus vivendum est quod Christus, et eum apostoli secuti, Petrus, Paulus, Iacobus, Ioannes, Iudas declararunt; qui pietatis praecepta, ut divina, sic etiam pauca breviaque mundo tradidere. Etenim quis illas servare leges poterit quas ne tenent quidem qui in eis incanuerunt? Ea de causa nec exempla quae attuli
20   plurima extendi nec in communes virtutum aut vitiorum locos egressus sum, amplissimum spatiandi campum et qui se toto subinde opere ostendebat ac velut invitabat, ut modum liber inveniret nec solum legi sine lassitudine, sed relegi quoque posset.

3. Ad hoc, ut virorum institutiones numerosae sint, feminarum certe
25   mores paucissimis formari praeceptis possunt. Quoniam viri et domi et foris et in re privata et in re publica versantur; ideo quae ratio sit tantae diversitatis officiorum non nisi longis voluminibus explicatur. Feminae unica est cura pudicitiae; idcirco cum haec exposita est, abunde illa dimitti videtur instructa. Quo exsecrabilius est illorum scelus qui unicum hoc
30   feminarum bonum corruptum eunt, tamquam si lusco illud quod superest lumen exstinguendum cures. Sunt qui foeda et spurca conscribunt carmina, qui quem, dictu saltem honestum, obtendere consilio suo praetextum possint equidem non video, nisi quod corruptus animus nequitia et veneno putris aspirare nisi venenum nequit, quo interimat vicina. Dicunt se amantes
35   esse. Credo, nam sunt etiam caeci et dementes, quasi tu potiri tua non

---

1 deligat **WBV** deligeret **HW**[2] // **3** deducimus Γ deduximus H // **16** vivendum Γ vi-dendum H *epist. Cran.* // **17** declararunt Γ docuerunt H // **23** posset Γ possit H // **25** formari Γ componi H // **27** explicatur Γ declarari potest H // **30** lusco Γ unoculo H // **31** exstinguendum cures Γ exstinctum properes H // **32** quem Γ quam H / honestum Γ honestam H / praetextum Γ excusationem H // **33** nequitia Γ *deest in* H // **33–34** putris aspirare Γ tumens inspirare H // **34** amantes Γ amatores H

my opinion, and compile practical rules for living. Thus in the first book I begin with the first stage of a woman's life and continue up to the state of matrimony; then, in the second book, I make recommendations on how time is to be passed properly and happily with one's husband from marriage to widowhood, and in the last book instruction is given concerning widowhood.

2. And since it could not be avoided, many things are said in the first book that pertain to wives and widows, many in the following book that pertain to the unwed, and some things in the third book that pertain to all three. I say this so that the unmarried girl will not think that she has to read only the first book or the married woman the second or the widow the third. I think all of the books should be read by each class of women. Perhaps I have been more brief in my treatment than some would have wished, but if anyone will consider carefully the reason for my decision, he will understand that it was not done without good reason. For in giving precepts, brevity should not be among the least considerations, lest through verbosity you overwhelm the minds of the readers rather than instruct them. And the precepts should be such that one can learn them easily and retain them in the memory. For we must not be ignorant of the laws by which we should live. This was revealed to us by Christ and, after him by the Apostles, Peter, Paul, James, John and Jude, who transmitted religious teachings to the world which besides being divine in origin were also few and brief. And indeed, who could observe those laws which are not even kept by those who have grown old in them? For that reason I have not increased the number of examples, of which I have given a good many, nor have I digressed into the common places of virtues and vices, a very extensive topic on which to expatiate and one which often presented itself throughout the work and almost invited elaboration. But I wished my book to stay within limits so that it could be read without fatigue and even be re-read.

3. In addition, although rules of conduct for men are numerous, the moral formation of women can be imparted with very few precepts, since men are occupied both within the home and outside it, in public and in private, and for that reason it requires lengthy volumes to explain the norms to be observed in such varied duties. A woman's only care is chastity; therefore when this has been thoroughly elucidated, she may be considered to have ample instruction. Wherefore, all the more hateful is the crime of those who seek to corrupt this one good that women possess, as if you were set on extinguishing the sight left to a one-eyed person. There are those who write filthy and scurrilous poems, and what pretext, which has even the semblance of respectability, they can adduce for their intent I do not see, save that their minds, corrupted by wickedness and rotted by poison, are capable of emitting only poison, with which they destroy everything around them. They say they are lovers, and I do not doubt it, for they are also blind and insane. It is as if one could not gain mastery over his own loved one without at the

valeas nisi simul cum illa reliquas omnes corrumpas et contamines. Mihi nullus umquam hominum iustius videtur exulasse Ovidio Nasone, si modo propter Artem amandi relegatus est. Ceteri enim cecinerunt lasciva et flagitiosa, hic egregius artifex in formulas (si diis placet) et praecepta nequitiam redegit, magister impudicitiae, publicus corruptor morum civitatis.

4. Non dubito quin aliquibus videbor edere severiora praecepta atque asperiora quam par esset; qui si legerent quam minuta persequuntur sancti scriptores, quam anxii sunt exactores singulorum, quibus verbis, qua gravitate, qua severitate, me utique blandum nimis atque indulgentem iudicarent. Sed ea natura est rerum: bonis apertissima videtur virtutis via et amoenissima; contra, vitiorum angusta et salebrosa; malis nec iucunda via est qua insistunt nec satis lata satisque commoda probitatis. Quod cum ita sit, accedendum potius est bonis et credendum falli citius malos iudicio suo quam consensum bonorum. Pythagoras et eum reliqui in descriptione Y aemulati, superatis primae virtutis difficultatibus, cetera latissime et facillime patere aiunt. Plato ex eiusdem Pythagorae sententia deligendam vitae rationem suadet optimam, quam consuetudo suavissimam reddet. Dominus in Evangelio viam regni Dei arctam appellavit, non quod re vera talis esset, sed quia pauci illam ingrediuntur, nisi quis vanum Illius esse dictum putet: 'Iugum meum suave est et onus meum leve', ac promissum illud: neminem esse qui aliquid propter Ipsum relinquat qui non maiora multo recipiat, etiam in hac vita. Quorsum hoc spectat nisi ad voluptatem et delicias virtutis?

5. Itaque non ignoro quibus haec mea praecepta severa nimis et rigida videbuntur: viris iuvenibus, imperitis, lascivis, perditis; qui ne aspectum quidem probae ferre possunt, qui velut otiosi et bene pasti equas omnes adhinniunt; tum etiam puellis stultis, vanis, insulsis, quae spectari, quae adamari gaudent et approbari sua vitia cuperent multitudine peccantium, ceu conspiratio turbae immutare rerum naturam posset. Novum malis non est odisse bene monentes. Sed in hoc ipso materiae genere Theophrastus, cum de coniugio gravissime multa scripsisset, meretrices in se concitavit; et prosiliit Leontium, Metrodori concubina, quae adversus tantum et facundia et sapientia virum librum sine mente, sine fronte

---

3. (exulasse Ovidio Nasone) *Ov. trist. 2, 207*

4. (Pythagoras) *Diog. Laert. 8, 32; Hes. erg. 289* // (deligendam ... reddet) *Plat. rep. 1, 331A* // (viam ... arctam) *Vulg. Matth. 7, 14* // (Iugum ... leve) *Vulg. Matth. 11, 30* // (neminem ... vita) *Vulg. Marc. 10, 29–30; Vulg. Luc. 18, 25; Vulg. Matth. 19, 29*

5. (Theophrastus) *Hier. adv. Iovin. 1, 47, PL 23, 276–278; Cic. nat. deor. 1, 93* //

1 valeas Γ possis H / et contamines Γ *deest in* H // **5** publicus Γ et publicus H // **6–7** edere ... asperiora Γ severiora praecepta dare et asperiora H // **7–9** quam ... iudicarent Γ *deest in* H // **16** ex eiusdem Pythagorae sententia Γ *deest in* H // **19** vanum Γ falsum H // **22** voluptatem et Γ *deest in* H // **23** severa Γ aspera H // **25** otiosi et bene pasti Γ salaces H // **26** tum etiam Γ et H / insulsis Γ *deest in* H // **32** virum Γ hominem H

same time corrupting and contaminating all other women along with her. To my mind no one was ever more justly exiled than Ovidius Naso, if indeed he was banished because of the *Art of Love*. Others have sung of lewd and disgraceful things but this supreme craftsman reduced depravity to rules and precepts, if you please, a master of unchastity and public corruptor of the morals of the state.

4. I have no doubt that to some I shall seem more harsh and severe than is reasonable, but if they were to read the minute particulars that the sacred writers pursue and see how meticulously they examine every detail, with what severity of language and tone, they would account me to be too mild and indulgent. But such is the nature of things that to the good the path of virtue seems very accessible and pleasant, while that of vice seems narrow and rough. For the wicked neither the path they tread is pleasant nor is the path of uprightness sufficiently wide or accessible. This being the case, we must agree more with the good and believe that the wicked are more easily deceived in their judgment than the generality of good men. Pythagoras and those who imitated him in the description of the letter Y say that after overcoming the difficulties of the first virtue the rest is easy, and Plato, in agreement with Pythagoras, urges us to choose the best way of life, which habit will render most agreeable. Our Lord in the Gospel called the path to the kingdom of God narrow, not because it is so in very fact, but because few enter upon it, unless one were to think that his saying is false: 'My yoke is easy and my burden light,' and the promise that there is no one who leaves anything for his sake who will not have much greater things even in this life. What is meant thereby but the pleasure and delights of virtue?

5. Therefore I know who will find my precepts too severe and rigid—young men, the inexperienced, the lascivious, and the depraved, who cannot bear the sight of a virtuous woman, who like indolent, well-fed horses neigh at every mare. Likewise my precepts will not appeal to stupid, vain and foolish girls, who enjoy being looked at and courted and would like their vices to be approved by the multitudes of sinners, as if a conspiracy of the common crowd could change the nature of things. It is nothing new that the wicked hate those that give good advice. On this same subject Theophrastus gave many stern precepts about marriage and in so doing incited the wrath of the courtesans against him, and Leontion, the concubine of Metrodorus, sprang forward and spewed out a senseless and shameless book against a man of

---

3. Ovidius Naso: Ovid was exiled to the Black Sea in A.D. 8 for having written works subversive of public morals.

4. Pythagoras: The Greek letter Y according to Pythagoras symbolized the two paths of life, virtue and vice.

5. Theophrastus: (c.370–288 B.C.), the successor of Aristotle, most famous for his botanical works. His lost treatise on marriage is referred to in Jerome, *Ad Jovinianum*.

Metrodorus: of Lampsacus (c.331–277 B.C.), the most famous of Epicurus' followers.

evomeret. Quod tam indignum facinus visum est ut tamquam nihil iam superesset bonae spei proverbium natum sit: suspendio arborem eligendam. Sanctus Hieronymus ad Demetriadem de se ad hunc modum scribit: 'Ante annos circiter triginta de virginitate servanda edidi librum, in quo necesse
5 fuit mihi ire contra vitia et propter instructionem virginis quam monebam diaboli insidias patefacere; qui sermo offendit plurimos, dum unusquisque in se intelligens quod dicebatur, non quasi monitorem libenter audivit, sed quasi criminatorem sui operis aversatus est.' Sic ille. En quod hominum genus sancte instituendo offensuri sumus? Quibus placuisse, vituperatione
10 (ut ita dixerim) et culpa non caret.

6. Stabunt a nobis graves et cordati viri, castae virgines, probae matronae, prudentes viduae, omnes denique qui vere et ex animo sunt Christiani, non solo nomine; qui omnes sentiunt ac sciunt nihil fieri posse mitius leniusque praeceptis nostrae pietatis, a quibus numquam sinat Christus mentem ac sen-
15 tentiam nostram vel latum pilum deflectere. Sanctas feminas leviter tantum officii sui admonui; ceteras interdum paulo castigavi acrius, quod viderem documenta sola parum proficere in iis quae ducenti reluctantur et invitae fere trahendae sunt quo oportet. Idcirco apertius quandoque sum locutus, ut foeditatem morum suorum ipsae velut in tabella depictam intuentes,
20 erubescerent et desinerent erubescenda facere. Simul bonae tum se ab illis vitiis procul abesse gauderent, tum darent operam ut longius etiam rece- derent et in sedes virtutis intimas se reciperent; maluique iuxta Hieronymi consilium verecundia parumper quam causa periclitari; sic tamen, ne in pudendum quid prolaberer, quo nihil turpius est praeceptori castitatis. Quo
25 factum est ut intelligenda nonnumquam sint plura quam exprimantur. Quae a receptissimis moribus abhorrerent, ea magnis auctoritatibus suffulcii ac confirmavi, ne dirui possent impetu publici consensus.

7. Hoc opus tibi non secus offero, Regina inclita, quam si pictor faciem tuam artificiosissime expressam daret; siquidem ut in illa imaginem tui
30 corporis depictam cerneres, sic in his libris imaginem videbis animi; quippe quae fuisti et virgo et sponsa et vidua nunc uxor (quod ut diutissime sis

---

5. (suspendio arborem eligendam) *Plin. nat. praef. 29; Erasm. ad. LB II, 373C* // (Ante ... est) *Hier. epist. 130, 19, PL 22, 1122–1123*
6. (verecundia ... periclitari) *Hier. epist. 54, 10, PL 22, 555*

9 vituperatione Γ vituperio H // **10** ut ita dixerim Γ *deest in* H // **16** viderem **HWW²B** viderim **V** // **17** in Γ *deest in* H // **17–18** invitae fere Γ *deest in* H // **18** quo oportet Γ *deest in* H // **22** in sedes ... se reciperent Γ in sedes virtutis intimae penetrarent H // **25** exprimantur Γ dicam H // **25–27** Quae ... consensus Γ *deest in* H // **30** depictam cerneres Γ cerneres pictam H // **31** sponsa Γ uxor H / nunc Γ iterum H

such learning and eloquence. The deed was seen to be so shocking that, as if there were no hope of amendment, it gave rise to the proverb: 'To choose a tree and hang yourself.' St. Jerome writes to Demetrias about something that happened to him in the following manner: 'About thirty years ago I wrote a book on the observance of virginity, in which it was necessary for me to lash out against vices and expose the snares of the devil for the instruction of the young girl whom I was advising. This language gave offense to many since each one, interpreting what I was saying as directed against himself, did not accept my words as a friendly admonition but felt aversion towards me as one who was incriminating his actions.' Thus says Jerome. So, what kind of persons will I offend with my pious admonitions? Those from whom if I were to please I would earn reprehension and blame.

6. On my side I will have men of sobriety and common sense, chaste virgins, virtuous matrons, prudent widows, in a word, all those who are truly Christian at heart and not only in name, all of whom know and recognize that nothing can be more mild and moderate than the precepts of our faith, from which may Christ never allow us to divert our minds and our thoughts one hair's breadth. To holy women I have merely given gentle advice concerning their duties. Others I have chastised a bit severely at times because I saw that precepts alone are of little benefit to those who resist one who guides them and must be dragged along almost against their will to their proper goal. Therefore I have spoken rather plainly on occasion so that seeing the repulsiveness of their conduct depicted in a painting, as it were, they might feel shamed and cease acting in a shameful manner. At the same time good women might have reason to rejoice in being so far removed from these vices and might make all the more effort to distance themselves even further and withdraw into the innermost abodes of virtue. I have preferred, according to the advice of Jerome, to run the risk of offending propriety rather than sacrifice the subject matter, without, however, lapsing into indecency, the worst thing a teacher of chastity could do. As a result sometimes more things are to be understood than are expressed. Things that would not accord with generally accepted customs I have supported and sustained with the testimony of great authorities lest they be nullified by the force of public opinion.

7. I dedicate this work to you, glorious Queen, just as a painter would represent your likeness with utmost skill. As you would see your physical likeness portrayed there, so in these books you will see the image of your mind, since you were both virgin and promised spouse and widow and

---

5. thirty years ago: *Letter 22* to Eustochium, a eulogy of virginity and of the monastic state, written at Rome in 384.

7. promised spouse: It is to be noted that beginning with the Basel edition Vives changed his description of Catherine's marital status with Arthur, prince of Wales, from *uxor* to *sponsa*. (cf. *app. crit. ad loc.*)

Deum precor), et sic in his omnibus vitae generibus cursibusque te gessisti ut exemplum reliquis sit optime vivendi quicquid agas. Sed tu mavis virtutes laudari quam te, etsi nemo commendare muliebres virtutes potest quin te quoque eadem laudatione comprehendat. Parendum tamen erit tibi,
5   modo scias sub excellentibus et egregiis virtutibus alias plerumque tui similes expresso nomine, te semper (etsi tacite) praedicari. Neque enim extolli laudibus virtutes possunt quin pariter et illi commendentur, quamvis innominati, qui plurimum illis ipsis virtutibus praestiterunt. Leget haec monita mea Maria, filia tua, et effinget ea dum se ad domesticum exemplar
10 componit probitatis et sapientiae tuae. Effinget certe, et nisi humanas omnes coniecturas sola fallat, optima et sanctissima ut sit necesse est, te et Henrico Octavo nata, tali et tam laudato coniugum pari. Habebunt igitur feminae omnes, ut per vitam et actiones tuas exemplum, sic per hoc tibi dedicatum opus praecepta et rationem vivendi. Utrumque debebunt probitati tuae, qua
15 et tu sic vixisti, et ego ad scribendum impulsus sum. Vale.
    Brugis, nonis Aprilis 1523

---

1 generibus Γ rationibus H // 2 sit Γ esset H / agas Γ ageres H // 7 extolli Γ celebrari H // 8 ipsis virtutibus Γ *deest in* H // 9 exemplar Γ exemplum H // 12 tali et tam laudato coniugum pari Γ tali pari conjugum ut omnes laudandi rationes, virtutes laudesque vestrae superarint H // 13–14 per hoc … opus Γ per haec tibi dedicata volumina H // 14 et rationem Γ rationesque H // 14–15 qua … sum Γ et quae ipsa egit et quae me ad scribendum adduxit H

now wife (as, I pray God, you may long continue), and since you have so conducted yourself in all these various states of life that whatever you did is a model of an exemplary life to others. But you prefer that virtues be praised rather than yourself. Although no one can praise female virtues without including you in that same praise, I shall nonetheless obey you, provided that you know that under the rubric of excellent and outstanding virtues other women similar to you may be mentioned by name, but it is you always, even if tacitly, who are spoken of. For virtues cannot be extolled with praise without commending those who, though unnamed, excelled in those virtues. Your daughter Mary will read these recommendations and will reproduce them as she models herself on the example of your goodness and wisdom to be found within her own home. She will do this surely and, unless she alone belie all human expectations, must of necessity be virtuous and holy, the offspring of you and Henry VIII, such a noble and honored pair. Therefore all women will have an example to follow in your life and actions, and in this work dedicated to you, precepts and rules for the conduct of their lives. Both of these they will owe to your moral integrity, by which you have lived and through which I have been inspired to write. Farewell.

Bruges, 5 April, 1523.

IOANNIS LODOVICI VIVIS VALENTINI
DE INSTITUTIONE CHRISTIANAE FEMINAE

LIBER PRIMUS
QUI EST DE VIRGINIBUS

CAP. I.   DE EDUCATIONE VIRGINIS INFANTIS

8. Fabius Quintilianus oratorem instituens a cunis ipsis exordiendum censet, nullum tempus debere vacare ratus quod ad finem illum destinatae artis non accommodaretur. Quanto maior cura suscipi debet de virgine Christiana, ut non solum eius incrementa formemus et componamus, sed initia quoque
10 a lacte ipso. Quod velim, fieri si possit, maternum esse: idque consuluerunt Plutarchus, Favorinus et alii maximi philosophi. Sic enim mutua illa inter matrem et filiam caritas fiet maior, cum nihil de matris nomine a matre ipsa in aliam descindetur; nam et nutrices matres appellari sunt solitae. Verius mater filiam existimat suam, quam non solum utero gestavit et peperit, sed
15 etiam infantulam semper in ulnis baiulavit, cui praebuit mammam, quam de sanguine suo aluit, cuius somnos sinu suo fovit, primos arrisus accepit blanda et osculata est, prima balbutiem conantis fari audivit laeta atque adiuvit, et ad pectus infantem pressit, optima precans. Haec vicissim tanta in matrem pietate imbuent filiam ut carior multo sit ipsi mater, cuius amorem rudi
20 adhuc et tenero animo largissime hausit. Quis possit dicere quantam haec in hominibus conciliant augentque caritatem, cum beluae ferae ab omni amoris sensu in alienum genus remotae nutricios atque educatores suos diligant, et quo illos protegant ac propugnent, mortem obire non recusent!
   9. Deinde fit nescio quo pacto ut non amorem modo, verum et pronitatem
25 ad certos aliquos mores sugamus cum lacte. Hoc ipsum est, inquit Favorinus

   8. (Fabius Quintilianus) *Quint. inst. 1, 1, 21* // (Plutarchus) *mor. 3C–D* // (Favorinus) *Gell. 12, 1, 1–23*
   9. (Favorinus) *Gell. 12, 1, 19* //

1 LODOVICI **WB** LUDOVICI **HW²V** / VIVIS VALENTINI **HWW²** VIVIS **BV** //
8 de **Γ** in **H** // **10–11** idque consuluerunt … philosophi **Γ** idque Plutarchus, Favorinus et alii maximi philosophi consuluerunt **H** // **11–12** mutua … maior **Γ** mutua erit inter matrem et filiam caritas maior **H** // **15** praebuit mammam **Γ** mammam praebuit **H** // **16** accepit **Γ** excepit **H** // **17** atque adiuvit **Γ** *deest in* **H** // **19** pietate imbuent filiam **Γ** pietatem indent filiae **H** / carior multo sit **Γ** carior sit **H** // **20** quantam **HWW²** quantum **BV** // **21** augentque **Γ** *deest in* **H** // **22–23** et … recusent **Γ** et mortem obire non recusent, ut illos protegant ac propugnent **H** // **24–25** verum … mores **Γ** verum et mores **H**

JUAN LUIS VIVES
ON THE EDUCATION OF THE CHRISTIAN WOMAN

BOOK ONE
WHICH TREATS OF UNMARRIED YOUNG WOMEN

CHAPTER 1.   ON THE EDUCATION OF THE YOUNG WOMAN AS A CHILD

8. Fabius Quintilian in his book on the instruction of the orator expresses the view that it should begin from the cradle, convinced that no time should be wasted that could be dedicated to the attainment of those skills that we have fixed for ourselves as our objective. How much greater care should be expended in the case of the Christian young woman not only in her early formation and development but beginning with her nurturing at the breast, which, if possible, should be with her mother's milk. This is what Plutarch, Favorinus and other great philosophers counselled. In that way the mutual love between mother and daughter will become greater and the name of mother will not be shared with another, for it is the custom to call wet-nurses mothers also. A mother thinks the daughter to be more truly her own when she has not only borne her in her womb and given birth to her, but carried her continually in her arms as an infant, nursed her, nourished her with her own blood, cradled her in her arms as she slept, listened lovingly to her first happy laughter and kissed her, heard with joy her first stammerings and helped her in her attempt to speak, pressed her to her bosom, praying for every blessing from heaven. These things will in turn engender such filial devotion in the daughter towards her mother that her mother will become much dearer to her since she received such abundant love from her in her tender years. Who can say to what degree this experience will produce and increase love in human beings when wild beasts, which are for the most part alien to any feelings of love for animals of a different species, love those who nourished and raised them and do not hesitate to face death to protect and defend them.

9. Thus it happens, I know not how, that we imbibe with our mother's milk not only love but also a disposition towards certain behavior. This is the reason, says Favorinus in Aulus Gellius, that we are often astonished

---

8. Favorinus: Second-century orator with philosophical interests born in Arles, who obtained his Greek training at Marseille, and rose to high office under Hadrian. His views on maternal breast-feeding were reported by his pupil, Aulus Gellius, from a speech he gave in Greek.

apud Gellium, quod saepenumero miramur quosdam pudicarum mulierum liberos parentum suorum neque corporibus neque animis similes exsistere. Neque vero de nihilo nata est etiam pueris nota fabula illum qui scrofae lacte nutritus esset in caeno se volutavisse. Qua de causa vir acutissimus Chrysippus
5　sapientes optimasque eligi nutrices praecepit, quod nos et sequemur et praecipiemus iis matribus quibus infantes suos proprio lacte non licebit alere. Neque vero tantam curam in quaerenda puero nutrice ponendam volo quantam puellae. Quintilianus satis habuit dicere: 'Videndum ne sit vitiosus sermo nutricibus, propterea quod qui in infante insedit sermonis
10　modus, difficile elueretur.' De moribus non ita fuit sollicitus, quos saepius alibi puer induit quam domi. Et tamen Chrysippi de nutricibus sententiam attulit, velut idem sentiret ipse. At puellam quoniam non perinde doctam volumus ac pudicam et probam, tota est parentum cura illo conferenda, ne quid ei adhaereat vitiosum et turpe, nihil per sensus corporis tale, nihil
15　per nutrimentum irrepat. Nutricem vero primam audiet, primam videbit, et quae rudis discet, haec perita et callida temptabit reddere. Quocirca Divus Hieronymus Laetae filiam instituens nutricem vetat temulentam aut lascivam aut garrulam sumi.

CAP. II.　DE RELIQUA INFANTIA

20　**10.** Ubi iam ablactata fuerit et fari atque ingredi coeperit, lusus omnes sint cum puellis aequalibus, praesente aut matre aut nutrice aut gravioris aetatis proba femina, quae lusiones illas et animi oblectamenta temperet atque ad honestatem virtutemque dirigat. Omnis masculus sexus absit nec assuescat viris delectari. Natura enim in illos diutissime amor noster
25　perseverat cum quibus pueriles horas oblectationesque traduximus. Qui affectus in femina est pertinacior, nempe ingenio ad voluptates propensiore. In illa aetate quae nondum bonum ac malum diiudicat, ne docenda quidem sunt mala, et rudis adhuc animus sanis opinionibus imbuendus. Pestilens opinio eorum qui filios suos volunt et bonum et malum non ignorare:
30　ita demum, aiunt, melius virtutem persecuturos et fugituros vitia. Quanto

---

9. (Chrysippus) *Quint. inst. 1, 1, 4* ∥ (Quintilianus) *Quint. inst. 1, 1, 4* ∥ (De moribus … domi) *Quint. inst. 1, 1, 4–5* ∥ (nutricem … sumi) *Hier. epist. 107, 4, PL 22, 872*

3 Neque vero Γ Nec H ∥ **4** Qua de causa Γ Ea causa H ∥ **5** praecepit Γ praecipiebat H ∥ **13** ac pudicam et probam Γ at bonam H ∥ **16** perita HΓ peritia V / reddere Γ effingere H / Quocirca Γ Idcirco H ∥ **17** nutricem Γ nutricem ipsam H ∥ **18** sumi Γ esse H ∥ **20** et H *om.* Γ ∥ **21** puellis aequalibus Γ paribus puellis H ∥ **22** lusiones illas Γ lusus illos H ∥ **24** viris Γ cum viris H ∥ **24–25** diutissime amor noster perseverat Γ diutissime est amor noster H ∥ **26** pertinacior Γ potentior H ∥ **28** et … imbuendus Γ *deest in* H

when the children of virtuous women do not resemble their parents, either physically or morally. It was not without reason that the fable, known even to children, arose that he who was nurtured with the milk of a sow has rolled in the mire. For which reason the sage philosopher Chrysippus taught that one must select wet-nurses who are wise and of good character, a precept that I too shall follow and recommend to those mothers who cannot nurture their children with their own milk. I do not require that the same care should be taken in providing a nurse for a boy as for a girl. Quintilian put it well when he said: 'One must see to it that the speech of nurses is not defective, because the manner of speech that is instilled in the child is difficult to eliminate.' In the matter of morals he was not so concerned since the boy learns those outside the home more often than in the home. Yet he adopted the opinion of Chrysippus concerning nurses as if he were of the same mind. But since we do not wish the young girl to be as learned as she is chaste and virtuous, care must be taken on the part of the parents that she not be defiled by anything immoral or dishonorable, and that nothing of that nature be acquired through the bodily senses or through her early upbringing. The first person she will hear and the first person she will see is the nurse, and what she will learn as an immature child she will try to reproduce when she is more practised and experienced. In this regard St. Jerome in giving instruction to the daughter of Laeta says that one should not hire a nurse who is given to drink or is of loose morals or talkative.

CHAPTER 2.   ON THE REMAINING YEARS OF CHILDHOOD

10. When she has been weaned and has begun to speak and to walk, all her playtime must be spent with girls of her own age in the presence of her mother or nurse or a good woman of mature years, who will regulate those pastimes and the pleasures of the mind and direct them to goodness and virtue. Anyone of the male sex should be excluded and the girl should not be accustomed to find pleasure in the company of men. For by nature our affection is more lasting towards those with whom we have passed our time in childhood amusements. This attachment is even more persistent in the woman for she is more inclined towards pleasure by her natural disposition. At that age which cannot yet distinguish between good and evil she should not even learn about evil things, and her still immature mind should be imbued with sound opinions. Pernicious is the view of those who wish their children not to be ignorant of both good and evil. In that way, they say, in the end they will better pursue virtue and flee vice. How much more

9. Chrysippus: (c.280–207 B.C.), regarded as the most orthodox of the Stoic philosophers.

rectius et utilius est mala non modo non facere, sed nescire quidem? Quanto
item felicius? Quis non saltem fando audivit illa nos omnes hora miseros
factos, cum primi illi auctores generis humani quid bonum esset quid malum
noverunt? Et profecto patres qui nolunt filios suos malorum imperitos et
inexpertos esse digni sunt quorum liberi ea sciant et, cum malefecisse
paenitebit, recordentur se male facere patribus auctoribus didicisse. Impudica
aut lasciva verba aut gesticulationes parum decoras ne tum quidem discat
cum rerum est rudis, effictura etiam robustior et gnara. Plerisque ita usu
venit ut quae assueverunt, haec crebro insciis et imprudentibus excidant,
interdum reluctantibus ac retinere conantibus elabantur et erumpant invitis;
tanto crebrius, si sint mala, ut est eorum tenacior humanus animus.

11. Caveant parentes ne factum aliquod eius indecens vel risu vel verbis vel
gestu approbent aut, quod turpissimum est, osculis et complexu excipiant. Id
saepe conabitur puella reddere quod gratissimum parentibus putabit. Omnia
sint in primis annis casta et pura, saltem morum gratia, qui ex illa infantili
consuetudine prima velut delineamenta ducunt. Verba aliquot Corn. Taciti
lubet adscribere de indole veterum Romanorum: 'Iam pridem suus cuique
filius ex casta parente natus, non in cella emptae nutricis, sed in gremio ac sinu
matris educabatur, cuius praecipua laus erat tueri domum et inservire liberis.
Eligebatur autem aliqua maior natu propinqua, cuius probatis spectatisque
moribus omnis cuiusdam familiae soboles committeretur, coram qua neque
dicere fas erat quod turpe dictu neque facere quod inhonestum factu
videretur. Ac non studia moresque sed remissiones etiam lususque puerorum
sanctitate quadam ac verecundia temperabat. Sic Corneliam Gracchorum,
sic Aureliam Caesaris, sic Atiam Augusti matrem praefuisse educationibus
ac produxisse principes liberos accepimus. Quae disciplina ac severitas eo
pertinebat ut sincera et integra et in nullis pravitatibus detorta uniuscuiusque
natura toto statim pectore arriperet artes honestas.'

12. Sic ille. Unde apparet qua ratione, quibus artibus antiqui illi in illam
virtutum claritudinem quam ne intueri quidem nunc sustinemus evaserint.
Et narrat haec de viris; quantam erga feminas adhibitam diligentiam existi-
mamus? Ergo ludicris oblectamentis quibus aetas illa indiget absit quicquid
potest rectae institutioni officere, nihil obscenum in animos irrepat, non

---

11. (Iam ... honestas) *Tac. dial. 28, 4–6*

1 rectius Γ certius **H** // **2** item Γ etiam hoc **H** // **5** ea Γ *deest in* **H** // **8–11** Plerisque ...
crebrius Γ Plerisque ita contingit ut quae prius assueverunt, haec ab incautis et imprudentibus
agantur, interdum prorumpant invitis, hoc crebrius **H** // **12** Caveant Γ Videant **H** //
16–p.18,**7** Verba ... addiscit Γ *deest in* **H**

proper and useful is it not only not to do evil but not even to know it! How much more auspicious also! Who has not heard tell that the source of all our misery goes back to that moment when the first parents of the human race learned what was good and what was evil? And of a certainty those fathers who do not wish their sons to be ignorant and inexperienced in evil deserve that their children have knowledge of it, and when their children regret that they have done evil, let them remember that they learned to do evil at their father's instigation. The young girl should not learn obscene or indecent words or unseemly gestures when she is still innocent since she will repeat them when she is grown up and conscious of her actions. It is the experience of many people that they fall into the same behavior to which they have been accustomed without their being aware of it, and although at times they struggle against them and try to control them, they slip out and burst forth against their will. This occurs all the more frequently if they are bad things, so tenacious is the human mind of them.

11. Parents should be careful not to give approval to any unseemly action of hers either by laughing or by word or gesture, or, worst of all, welcome it with kisses and embraces. The girl will often try to repeat what she thinks gives particular pleasure to her parents. In the early years let everything be chaste and pure for the sake of morals, which from childhood habits take on their first features, so to speak. I would like to insert here a passage from Cornelius Tacitus on the character of the ancient Romans:

> In the good old days everyone's son, born of a chaste mother, was brought up not in the chamber of a hired nurse, but in his mother's lap and bosom, and it was her chief glory to watch over the home and devote herself to her children. An elderly kinswoman would be selected, of tried and true character, to whose charge all the offspring of that family were entrusted. In her presence no base word could be uttered nor any disgraceful deed done. With scrupulous piety and modesty she regulated not only the studies and conduct of her charges but also their leisure and recreation. It was in this spirit, we are told, that Cornelia, the mother of the Gracchi, Aurelia, the mother of Caesar, and Atia, the mother of Augustus, presided over their upbringing and raised children who were leaders. The object of this strict discipline was to ensure that the innocent and untainted natural disposition of the child, not yet warped by any vicious tendencies, would immediately seize upon honorable pursuits with whole heart.

12. These are the words of Tacitus, from which it is apparent by what method and practices men of ancient times arrived at such renown for virtue as we cannot even bear to behold these days. And this is what he says about men. How much care do we think was exercised in the case of women? Therefore, in the amusements and diversions needed at that time of life let anything that can harm a proper upbringing be forbidden, let nothing obscene steal into her mind, and do not let her be infected with a proclivity

garrulitatis inficiatur studio. Sed iam tum, ceu per lusus, meditetur quae
postea profutura sunt, castis fabellis ducatur, tollantur pupae, imago quaedam idololatriae et quae comptus ac ornatus cupiditatem docent augentque.
Magis probarim scruta illa quis simulacra totius domesticae suppellectilis
in stanno aut plumbo sunt expressa, cuiusmodi est in hac Belgica magna
copia. Est hoc iucundum infanti ludicrum et interea singulorum nomina
atque usus, aliud agens, addiscit.

CAP. III.   DE PRIMIS EXERCITAMENTIS

13. Aetate qua videbitur iam idonea litteris et cognitioni rerum incipiat ea
discere quae ad cultum animi quaeque ad tuendam regendamque domum
spectant. Tempus nullum diffinio. Alii enim anno septimo exordiendum
putaverunt, ut Aristoteles et Eratosthenes; alii quarto quintove, ut Chrysippus
et Quintilianus. Ego vero totam hac de re deliberationem ad parentum
prudentiam reicio, qui ex qualitate et habitu infantis consilium sument,
modo ne officiat indulgentia qua quidam ita delicatos habent suos liberos,
adeo illis metuunt, ut ab omni arceant labore, ne forte in morbum incidant.
Hi dum eorum vires corpusque putant augere ac confirmare, debilitant et
frangunt. Multum officit filiis parentum indulgentia, quae effrenem illis in
mille vitia licentiam offert atque adeo ingerit, sed feminae in primis. Haec
enim magna ex parte solo cohibetur metu, qui si absit, tum demum habenas
naturae laxat. Si in malum fertur proclivis, eo se praecipitat nec bona evadit,
nisi talis sit suopte ingenio ac natura ipsa, quales nonnullas est invenire. Discet
ergo simul litteras, simul lanam et linum tractare, duas artes iam inde ab
innoxio illo saeculo posteris traditas, utilissimas rei familiari et conservatrices
frugalitatis, cuius convenit in primis studiosas esse feminas. Non descendam
ad minutiora, ne cui humiliora instituto meo persequi videar, sed feminam
nullo modo placet mihi artium quae manibus tractantur imperitam esse, ac
ne principem quidem aut reginam. Quid enim aliud potius aget aut melius,
vacua domesticis negotiis? Confabulabitur scilicet cum viris aut aliis feminis.
Quibus de rebus? Semper loquetur? Numquam conticescet? At cogitabit.
Quae? Celer est cogitatus feminae ac fere inconstans, vagus, peregrinus,
nescio quo lubricitate devolvetur sua.

13. (Eratosthenes ... Quintilianus) *Quint. inst. 1, 1, 16*

9 Aetate ... rerum **Γ** Aetate qua puella rebus discendis videbitur idonea **H** // **17** ac
confirmare debilitant et **Γ** *deest in* **H** // **18–19** quae effrenem ... in primis **Γ** quae illis
in mille vitia licentiam effrenem offert et ingerit, sed in primis feminae **H** // **20** cohibetur
metu **Γ** metu cohibetur **H** // **22** suopte ingenio ac **Γ** *deest in* **H** // **24** utilissimas **Γ** utiles in
primis **H** // **25** convenit ... feminas **Γ** studiosas convenit esse feminas **H** // **29** scilicet **Γ**
deest in **H**

to talkativeness. But even then, in the form of play, let her exercise herself in things that will be of benefit to her later. Let her be edified by chaste tales, and take dolls away from her, which are a kind of image of idolatry and teach girls the desire for adornments and finery. I would be more in favor of those toys made of tin or lead that represent household objects, which are so common here in Belgium. This is a pleasant pastime for the child and in the meantime she learns the names and uses of various things without even being aware of it.

CHAPTER 3. ON HER EARLY TRAINING

13. At the age when the girl seems ready to learn letters and gain some practical knowledge, let her begin by learning things that contribute to the cultivation of the mind and the care and management of the home. I do not prescribe any definite time. Some thought that this should begin at the age of seven, as did Aristotle and Eratosthenes. Others preferred the fourth or fifth year of age, as Chrysippus and Quintilian. I leave all this deliberation to the discretion of the parents, who will be guided by the character and qualities of the child as long as they do not spoil them through indulgence. Some parents treat their children with such gentleness, and are so fearful for them that they keep them from all physical toil lest they fall into some illness. Thinking to increase and solidify their strength, they weaken and enervate them. The indulgence of parents is very harmful to children since it offers them free access to a thousand vices and even thrusts them in their face. But this is especially harmful for the woman, for she is held back to a great degree solely by fear. If that is not present, then all the barriers of nature are let down. If she is drawn to evil by nature, then she plunges into it headlong. She will not turn out well unless she is good of her own nature and character, which may be so in some cases. Therefore she will learn together with reading how to work with wool and flax, two arts passed on to posterity from that former age of innocence, of great usefulness in domestic affairs and contributing to frugality, which should be a matter of prime concern for women. I shall not descend to particulars or I will appear to be searching into matters too humble for my subject. But I should not wish any woman to be ignorant of the skills of working with the hands, not even a princess or a queen. What could she do better than this when free of all the household tasks? She will converse with men, I suppose, or other women. About what? Is she to talk forever? Will she never keep quiet? Perhaps she will think. About what? A woman's thoughts are swift and generally unsettled, roving without direction, and I know not where her instability will lead her.

13. Eratosthenes: (c.275–194 B.C.) The most versatile scholar of his time, royal tutor under Ptolemy Euergetes, succeeded Apollonius of Rhodes as head of the Alexandrian library.

14. At legere optimum est et id in primis consulo; sed iam lectione fessam, otiosam videre non possum. Nec Persicas illas feminas imitabitur, inter eunuchorum agmina cantibus, comessationibus, iugibus et sempiternis voluptatibus immersas, quae ad fastidium vitandum subinde mutabantur et unius finis initium erat sequentis, nec efficere tamen poterant, ut vel haec varietas iucunditate animum expleret. Semper aliquid et in unaquaque desiderabatur et in universis lassitudoque et ipse primus gustus taedium ilico adferebat. Tum repetebant voluptates damnatas; hinc quas maxime placituras existimarant mira anxietate aversabantur. Ita cum nulla satisfaceret, aspernabantur omnes; nimirum non est ille verus animi pastus. Idcirco semper animus quidem ad diversa properabat, tamquam aliena percurrens. At in opere honesto apud probas mentes et actio reficit et quod inde exsistit placet mirifice et bene collocatas horas ducimus quae in hoc consumuntur. Neque aliud requietem suadet quam fatigatio continuae intentionis. Nec mutare vellemus, si per eam liceret.

15. Divus Hieronymus Paulam, nobilissimam feminam ex Scipionum et Gracchorum gente, quae etiam Agamemnonem illum principem regum in stemmate ostendebat, discere vult lanam facere, tenere colum, ponere in gremio calathum, rotare fusum, stamina pollice ducere. Demetriadem quoque pari nobilitate atque opibus habere iubet lanam in manibus et vel staminis pollice fila deducere, vel ad torquenda subtegmina in alveolis fusa vertere aliarumque neta aut in globum colligere aut texenda componere. Fuit enim semper lanificium honestae feminae exercitamentum atque ars. Romanae omnes, cum nuberent, fusum et colum cum lana ad mariti domum afferebant postesque lana attingebant et coronabant, quod illis religiosum fuit. Tum super lanatam pellem sedere nova nupta iubebatur, ut disceret quid factura domi esset. Hinc marito haec dicebat verba: 'Ubi tu Gaius, ego Gaia.' Fuit Gaia Tanaquil Etrusca, summo loco nata, frugalissima mulier ut si qua alia, Tarquinii Prisci regis uxor, quae lanificio

---

15. (lanam ... deducere) *Hier. epist. 107, 10, PL 22, 875* // (Demetriadem) *Hier. epist. 130, 15, PL 22, 1119* // (Romanae ... coronabant) *Plin. nat. 8, 194* // (Ubi ... Gaia) *Plut. mor. 271E* //

2 Nec ... imitabitur **Γ** ut Persicas illas feminas **H** // **5–15** nec efficere ... liceret **Γ** *deest in* **H** // **14** continuae **WW²** continua **BV** // **23–24** exercitamentum atque **Γ** *deest in* **H** // **25** mariti domum **Γ** domum mariti **H** // **29** ut si qua alia **Γ** *deest in* **H** / lanificio **Γ** opificio lanae **H**

14. Reading is the best occupation and I counsel it first of all, but when she is tired of reading I cannot bear seeing her idle. Nor should she imitate those Persian women who sing and banquet amidst bands of eunuchs, immersed in unending, uninterrupted pleasures, which they varied frequently to avoid boredom, so that the end of one was the beginning of another. Yet they were not able to find any solace for their spirit through this alternation of sensual delights. There was always something missing in each one of them taken singly and in all of them together, and the first savouring of pleasure immediately brought weariness and boredom. Then they would seek again the pleasures they had found fault with and turn away in disgust and incredible anguish from the things they thought would give them most pleasure. In the end, since no one diversion satisfied them, they rejected them all. No wonder, for this is not the true nourishment of the soul. Therefore, the soul hurried eagerly after diversity as if pursuing something alien to itself. But in honourable activities engaged in by persons of good conscience the action itself revives the spirit; what results from it gives great satisfaction, and the hours passed in this way to be well spent. Nothing counsels repose so much as the continued exhaustion of one's aim and purpose, which we would not wish to change even it if allowed us to do so.

15. St. Jerome, writing to Paula, a woman of very noble family, who traced her ancestry to the line of the Scipios and the Gracchi and who even displayed in her genealogy the celebrated Agamemnon, king of kings, wishes her to learn to card wool, to hold the distaff, place a wool basket in her lap, turn the spindle, draw the thread with her fingers. Demetrias also, a woman of equal nobility and wealth, he bids to have wool in her hands, and draw the thread from the distaff or turn the spindle in order to twist the yarn in the receptacles or to gather the fibres spun by others into a ball or arrange them for weaving. The working of wool was always the occupation and skill of a good woman. All Roman women, when they married, brought spindle and distaff with wool to the home of their husband and wreathed the door-posts with wool, which constituted a religious rite for them. Then the new bride was enjoined to sit on a skin lined with wool to learn what her household tasks were to be. Next she said these words to her husband 'Whereas thou art Gaius, I am Gaia'. Gaia Tanaquil was an Etruscan, born of high station, a very frugal woman, if ever there was one, the wife of King Tarquinius Priscus. She devoted great toil and care to the making of wool

15. Gaius ... Gaia: This formula went back to the solemn celebration of marriage practised among the patricians called *confarreatio*, at which an offering of spelt bread was made to Jupiter.

Gaia Tanaquil: Wife of Tarquinius Priscus, fifth king of Rome, according to Livy. Vives follows Pliny the Elder in identifying her with Gaia Caecilia, an honest Roman matron who busied herself with weaving. Her spindle and distaff were displayed in the temple of Sancus on the Quirinal.

maximam operam curamque adhibuit. Ideo pro dea culta est eiusque statuae colus addita, pudicitiae et industriae monumentum. Acclamabatur etiam in nuptiis creberrime 'Talassio,' ceu quis dicat quasillum, in quo reponitur lana, ut admoneretur operis sui nupta. Itaque hoc agere argumentum erat prudentis et pudicae feminae. Regii iuvenes, cum orta super uxoribus contentione Romam propere venissent ceterasque regias nurus inter aequales convivantes, Lucretiam vero nocte sera deditam lanae inter lucubrantes ancillas in medio aedium sedentem deprehendissent, pudicitiae laus penes eam omnium consensu mansit.

16. Redacto universo populi Romani imperio in Augusti potestatem, ipse filiam et neptes suas lanificio voluit assuescere. Idem Carolus Magnus fecit. Terentius, cum parcam et pudicam puellam describit, 'Lana,' inquit, 'et tela victum quaeritans.' Salomon in encomio sanctae feminae lanam et linum quaesisse illam dicit et operatam consilio manuum suarum. Nec referre puto lana sit an linum; utrumque ad usus vitae necessarios pertinet et honestissima est feminarum occupatio. Anna, Helcane uxor, Samueli filio suis ipsa manibus tuniculas dicitur annuas confecisse. Castissima Ithacensium regina Penelope viginti annos, quibus Ulysses maritus abfuit, texendo fefellit. Reginae Macedonum et Epiri vestes maritis, fratribus, filiis, parentibus ipsae propriis manibus contexebant et consuebant, e quibus aliquot Alexander Magnus Persicis reginis ostendit, a matre et sororibus confectas. Apud Hispanas veteres praemium fuisse certamini publice propositum tradunt rerum scriptores, quae plurimum nevisset aut texuisset idque statis temporibus iudicabatur, allatis in publicum operibus, honosque erat permagnus ut quaeque multum et industrie laborasset. Manet hodieque idem studium frugalitatis in plerisque et ostentatur diligentia operis, tum apud optimas quasque turpe est otiosam desidere. Regina Isabella, Fernandi coniunx, nere, suere, acu pingere quattuor filias suas doctas esse voluit; ex quibus duae Lusitaniae fuerunt reginae, tertiam videmus Hispaniae, Caroli Caesaris matrem, quartam Britanniae, Henrici octavi coniugem sanctissimam.

15. (Talassio) *Liv. 1, 9, 12; Plut. Rom. 15* // (quasillum ... lana) *Fest. p.351; Paul. Fest p.350* // (Lucretiam) *Liv. 1, 57, 9*
16. (ipse ... assuescere) *Suet. Aug. 64, 2* // (Carolus Magnus) *Einhardus, Vita Carol. 19* // (Lana ... quaeritans) *Ter. Andr. 75* // (Salomon) *Vulg. prov. 31, 13* // (Anna ... confecisse) *Vulg. I reg. 2, 19* // (Alexander) *Curt. 7, 18–22*

3 reponitur Γ servatur **H** // **6** propere Γ *deest in* **H** // **9** mansit Γ fuit **H** // **10** Redacto universo Γ Redacto etiam universo **H** // **11** voluit assuescere Γ assuefecit **H** / Idem Carolus Magnus fecit Γ *deest in* **H** // **12** cum Γ ubi **H** // **16** Helcane uxor Γ *deest in* **H** // **17** tuniculas dicitur annuas confecisse Γ lineum superhumerale confecit **H** // **18** Ulysses Γ *deest in* **H** // **21** confectas Γ factas **H** // **27** desidere Γ agere **H** / Regina Γ Ideo regina **H** // **28** suas doctas esse Γ *deest in* **H** // **30** Henrici octavi Γ Henrici octavi viri optimi **H**

and on that account was worshipped as a goddess, and a distaff was placed on her statue as a tribute to her chastity and industry. The cry 'Talassio' was repeatedly shouted out at weddings, which sounded like the word for the basket in which the wool was deposited, so that the new bride would be reminded of her task. Thus to busy oneself in this occupation was the sign of a prudent and chaste wife. When the king's sons rode hurriedly off to Rome after a dispute concerning their wives had arisen, they found the other daughters-in-law of the king feasting together with their ladies in waiting, but Lucretia they found toiling at her wool late at night with her servants in her own house. The fame of her chastity endured in all people's minds.

16. After all the power and dominion of the Roman people was vested in Augustus, he wished his daughter and nieces to become accustomed to work with wool. Charlemagne did the same. When Terence describes a thrifty and modest maiden, he says: 'With wool and the loom she seeks her livelihood.' Solomon in his encomium of a holy woman says that she sought wool and flax and worked them with the skill of her hands. It makes no difference, I think, whether it be wool or flax; both are essential to the needs of life and both are an honourable occupation of women. Hannah, the wife of Elkanah, is said to have woven a tunic every year for her son Samuel. Penelope, the chaste queen of Ithaca, Penelope, beguiled the twenty years of her husband Ulysses' absence by weaving. The queens of Macedonia and Epirus wove and sewed clothes for their husbands, brothers, sons and relatives with their own hands. Some of these, made by his mother and sisters, Alexander the Great showed to the queens of Persia. Writers of history tell us that among the Spanish women of old a prize was proposed in a public contest for the woman who had spun or woven more than all others and at fixed times an award was conferred and the work exhibited publicly. It was considered a very great honour for the woman to have laboured long and industriously. This same zeal for frugality still persists today in many women, and diligence in work is held up as a desirable quality. In the same way it is dishonourable in the eyes of noble women to remain idle. Queen Isabella, wife of Ferdinand, wished her four daughters to be expert in spinning, sewing and needlepoint. Of these two were queens of Portugal, the third we see is queen of Spain and mother of the Emperor Charles, the fourth is the saintly wife of Henry VIII of England.

---

15. **Talassio:** Vives' explanation is probably based on Plutarch, who connects the word with ταλασία, Greek for 'wool-spinning.' Livy in his account of the rape of the Sabine women traces this wedding-cry back to a certain Talassius, to whose house a gang of men was carrying off one of the fairest of the maidens. More probably the word is of Sabine or Etruscan origin.

16. **four daughters:** Isabella, the eldest, married first Prince Alonso of Portugal, who died a few months later, and then Manuel, sovereign of Portugal. Juana married Philip the Fair of Austria and was the mother of the Emperor Charles V. Maria married Manuel after the death of Isabella, and Catherine married first Arthur, Prince of Wales, and then Henry.

17. Discet ad haec culinariam, non illam popinariam sordidam immodi-
corum ciborum et quae pluribus ministret quam publici coqui tractant, nec
voluptatis nimiae ac gulae, sed sobriam, mundam, temperatam, frugalem,
qua parentibus et fratribus cibos paret virgo, marito vero et liberis nupta. Sic
5   enim et ab illis et ab his non exiguam initura gratiam si non omnia in famulas
reiecerit, sed ipsa suis manibus curarit et concinnarit, quae iucundiora erunt
parentibus, viro, liberis quam a famulabus ministrata, atque eo magis si
aegrotent. Nemini culinae nomen sordeat, necessariae et sine qua nec aegri
convalescimus nec vivimus sani. Quam nec Achilles, rex et regis filius et
10 heroum praestantissimus, fastidivit, ad quem cum Ulysses et Aiax et Phoenix
venissent de reconciliatione cum Agamemnone acturi, ipse paratis mensis
praecinctus culinam ac cibos curavit, optimos carissimosque sibi principes
convivio excepturus suavi et sobrio. Spectat id quoque ad frugalitatem et
munditias, nam praesente domina aut filia familias, omnia fiunt lautius,
15 nitidius, adde etiam accuratius, minore sumptu. Quae ista est tanta manuum
sollicitudo aut tantum culinae fastidium ut ne interesse quidem aut spectare
sustineant quod esurus est carissimus vel parens, vel coniunx, vel etiam
filius? Sciant quae id agunt foedari magis manum si porrigatur alieno viro
quam si intingatur fuligine; turpius esse conspici in chorea quam in culina;
20 vilius taxillos aut lusoria folia scite tractare quam cibos; minus decere probam
gustare in comessatione potum ab alieno viro traditum, quam sorbitiunculam
viro suo tradendam. Hanc ergo artem mea callebit femina, quo magis omni
aetate suos demereatur sibi et quo tum rectius ac purius, tum minoris curatae
dapes ad mensam veniant. Vidi ego et hic et in Hispania et in Francia qui
25 convaluerint cibo ab uxoribus aut filiabus aut nuribus cocto, qui eas postea
multo habuerint quam antea cariores. Vidi contra exosas viris uxores, soceris
nurus, patribus filias, quod se artem negarint tenere instruendi epulas; atque
adeo quod viri in hac Belgica cauponentur saepe ac multum praecipuam

17. (Achilles) *Hom. Il. 9, 209–210*

1 ad haec **Γ** etiam **H** / popinariam **Γ** *deest in* **H** **//** **2** publici **Γ** *deest in* **H** **//** **3** sobriam,
mundam, temperatam, frugalem **Γ** sobriam et castam **H** **//** **4–5** Sic enim … gratiam **Γ** Sic
enim et apud illos et apud hos non parvam inibit gratiam **H** **//** **6** curarit et concinnarit **Γ**
paraverit **H** **//** **7** eo magis **Γ** id magis **H** **//** **8** necessariae et sine qua **Γ** alioqui necessarium
et sine quo **H** **//** **9** vivimus sani **Γ** sani vivimus **H** / Quam nec Achilles, rex et regis filius **Γ**
Quod nec Achilles rex **H** **//** **10** heroum **HWW²** horum **BV** / ad quem cum **Γ** quippe
cum ad eum **H** / Ulysses et Aiax et Phoenix **Γ** Ulysses et Nestor **H** **//** **13** suavi et sobrio **Γ**
sobrio et temperato **H** **//** **14–15** omnia … sumptu **Γ** omnia tractantur accuratius **H** **//**
16 sollicitudo **Γ** cura **H** **//** **20** vilius **Γ** deiectus **H** / lusoria folia **Γ** lusorias chartas **H** **//**
22 Hanc ergo artem mea callebit femina **Γ** Hanc ergo etiam artem mea femina tenebit **H**
// **23** demereatur sibi **Γ** sibi demereatur **H** **//** **23–24** tum rectius … veniant **Γ** rectius
puriusque curati cibi ad mensem exeant **H** **//** **25** cibo … cocto **Γ** cibis … paratis **H** **//**
27 artem … epulas **Γ** culinae administrandae negarint artem nosse **H** **//** **27–p.26,2** atque
… inveniunt **Γ** *deest in* **H**

17. In addition she will learn the art of cooking, not the vulgar kind associated with low class eating-houses that serve up immoderate amounts of food to great numbers, where hired cooks are employed, nor that which caters to self-indulgence and gluttony, but a sensible, refined, temperate and frugal art with which, as an unmarried maiden, she prepares food for her parents and brothers, and as a married woman for her husband. She will win no small favour with the one and the other if she does not leave everything to the servants but attends to things and sets the house in order with her own hands. This will give more pleasure to her parents, husband and children than if these duties were performed by maidservants, and all the more so if they are ill. Let no one hold the name of kitchen in low esteem, for it is an office of great necessity, without which the sick cannot get well and we cannot continue in good health. Achilles, a king and son of a king and pre-eminent of heroes, did not think it beneath him when Ulysses and Ajax and Phoenix came to him to plead for his reconciliation to Agamemnon. He girded himself to prepare the tables, and cooked the food himself to welcome these peerless chieftains with a pleasing and sober repast. This contributes also to frugality and elegance, for when the mistress of the house or her daughters are present, everything is done with more taste and refinement, not to say with more care and less expense. What is this over-concern for their hands or aversion for the kitchen that makes some women unwilling to take part in or even inspect what those dearest to them will eat, whether it be parent, spouse or even son? Let those who act in this way realize that the hand is more soiled if it is extended to a man other than one's husband than if it is blackened with soot, that it is more disgraceful to be seen on the dancing floor than in the kitchen, more debasing to handle dice and playing cards than food, and it is less becoming for an honest woman to taste of a drink offered by another man at a feast than to taste an herbal decoction prepared for her husband. Therefore I would prescribe that a woman be practised in this art so that she may more oblige her dear ones at every stage in her life and so that meals will come to the table prepared more properly and more naturally and at the same time in less quantity. I have personally seen here and in Spain and France those who have recovered from illness through the food cooked by their wives, daughters or daughters-in-law, whom they held much dearer afterwards than before. On the other hand I have seen wives hated by their husbands, daughters-in-law by their fathers-in-law and daughters by their fathers because they said they had no skill in preparing meals. And I have come to the conclusion that the principal reason why men here in Belgium spend so much time in inns and taverns is the negligence and laziness of

esse causam autumo negligentiam et ignaviam feminarum in coquendis cibis, quae cogit viros a domo abhorrere et alibi quaerere quod domi non inveniunt.

CAP. IV.   DE DOCTRINA PUELLARUM

18. In puella instituenda longe plus video adhibendum operae quam vulgus
5   hominum credat. Natura humani corporis protinus ab sua origine proclivis est ad flagitia, in ea nutu suo fertur, sicuti est sacris oraculis proditum. Propellunt eodem tot ubique occursantes mali, qui vel magistri sint vel auctores ad malitiam. Quocumque te verteris, verba se et facta prava ingerunt oculis. Perimus ingenio nostro ad malum vergente, perimus tot exemplis,
10   tanta conspiratione contra bonum, et acerbissimam praeter ceteras infligit plagam diaboli pugna capitalis. Quod si pro bono nihil adsit, non monita, non praecepta sapientiae et recte vivendi, quid reliquum fiet misero homini ad extrema scelerum?
    19. Bene nobiscum ageretur si vel recti notitia a tot malis oppugnantibus
15   nos posset tueri, nedum ut nudi et destituti a bonis consiliis salvi esse possimus. Stulte dixi facere illos patres qui liberos suos bonum et malum scire volunt. Non minus et illi peccant qui eos nec bonum scire patiuntur nec malum. Utinam inter tot malos transigere vitam possemus malitiae ignari. Sed bonum si non tradas, nesciri potest; malum, etiamsi occultes, non potest
20   celari, undique exsistit et se profert nec se in obscuro contineri patitur. Sunt multis suspectae doctae feminae, ceu malitiae naturali accedat adiumentum astutae eruditionis, quasi vero non et viri eadem condicione suspecti esse debeant, si astuta eruditio pravo ingenio addatur. Sed doctrina quam ego toti humano generi velim proponi, sobria est et casta, quae instituat et meliores
25   reddat, non quae ad pravas animi libidines vel armet vel instiget. Cuiusmodi sunt, ut loquar de femina, praecepta vitae et exempla probitatis; quorum si peritia damnosa est, non video quomodo futura sit ignorantia utilis.
    20. Quid ergo? Vis tu filiam tuam malum callere et bonum ignorare? Quae igitur ad scelus adducent tenebit, quae scelere abducent ignorabit? Tam in-
30   ique de scientia bonorum statuis, ut nocituram eam arbitrere, cum non noceat

---

19. (dixi) *inst. fem. Christ. 1, 10*

4–p.28,**6** In puella ... doctrina **Γ** Sunt puellae discendis literis parum idoneae, ut ex viris aliqui; sunt aliae ingeniis vel in id natis vel non repugnantibus. Illae cogendae non sunt, hae sinendae, invitandae etiam atque exhortandae. Video suspectas esse plerisque doctas feminas, ceu malitiae naturae accedat adiumentum astutae eruditionis. Equidem non probarim in acuta et fraudulenta muliere literas quae dolos suppeditent, mores non instituant et probitatem. At praecepta vitae et eorum qui recte vixerunt exempla et sanctitatis peritia, pudoris ac pudicitiae sunt custodes, exemplaria virtutum, et stimuli ad eadem insequenda **H**

their women in cooking meals, which forces men to avoid their own homes and seek elsewhere what they do not find there.

CHAPTER 4. ON THE INSTRUCTION OF YOUNG GIRLS

18. I think we should devote much more care to the instruction of a young girl than is commonly believed. The nature of the human body from its very origins is inclined towards evil and is borne along on that path by its own impulse, as we are told by the prophets. We are driven in that same direction by the multitude of evil people who confront us on every side, who act either as models or as catalysts for the doing of evil. Wherever you turn, evil words and evil deeds assault the eyes. We are doomed by our natural inclination, which is predisposed towards evil; we are doomed by so much bad example, by the universal conspiracy against good, and above all by the cruel wound inflicted on us by the implacable hostility of the devil. But if there is nothing on the side of good, no admonitions, no precepts of wisdom and virtuous living, what will be left to miserable mortals in the face of the most dire ills?

19. It would be to our advantage to have at least a knowledge of good to protect us from the constant onslaught of evil since obviously we cannot be secure if we remain defenceless and destitute of good counsel. I have said that those parents act foolishly who wish that their children know good and evil, but no less in error are those who do not allow them to know either good or evil. Would that it were possible to lead our lives in the midst of so many evil people and remain ignorant of evil. If you do not pass on the knowledge of good, it cannot be known. Whereas evil, even if you conceal it, cannot be hidden; it is ubiquitous and in full view, and does not allow itself to be confined to the darkness. Learned women are suspect to many, as if the acquisition of subtle learning increased their natural wickedness, and as if men should not also be suspect for the same reason if subtle learning is added to a perverse mind. The learning that I should wish to be made available for the whole human race is sober and chaste; it forms character and renders us better. It is not one that equips us or spurs us on to wicked desires of the mind. These are the rules of life and moral principles that I recommend for the education of women. If knowledge of these is harmful, I do not see how ignorance of them will be advantageous.

20. What then? Do you wish your daughter to have knowledge of evil and be ignorant of good? Will she therefore comprehend things that lead to wickedness and be ignorant of things that lead us away from wickedness? Do you have such a prejudiced view of the knowledge of good that you deem it to be harmful while the knowledge of evil is not

scientia pessimorum? Cum ergo a vitio invadetur cui assuevit, quod erit
praesidium ab honestate, quam nullo modo novit? Quod si ista placet
sententia, cur ad sacras contiones adducimus, cur docemus ipsi, castigamus,
admonemus meliorum? Praestabit (credo) rus seponere et ingenium, si quod
5 habent, debilitare ac opprimere, denique beluas efficere ex hominibus, ita
enim longius aberunt a doctrina. Quaerit Aristoteles philosophus cur tibicines
et musici qui festis ac celebritatibus mercede conducti canunt, quos vulgus
Graecorum Dionysiacos vocabat, voluptatibus semper dediti, numquam
ad bonam ullam frugem pervenirent, sed nequiter perditis moribus vitam
10 omnem degerent. Respondet hinc fieri quod cum semper inter delicias et
convivia versentur, nec umquam philosophiae praecepta, quae ad vitam
sancte degendam pertinent, audiant, nec ullum, dum recte vivit, aspiciant,
aliter vivere nesciunt quam quomodo vel audiendo vel videndo vel usu
didicerunt. Nihil porro audierunt, nihil viderunt aut consueverunt nisi
15 voluptuarium et pecuinum, inter voces et clamores absonos, inter saltantes,
osculantes, ridentes, edentes, potantes, vomentes, inter perfusos immodica
laetitia, et omni cura mentis morumque abiecta. Haec eadem moribus et
tota vita ut exprimant necesse est.

21. Mulierem non facile invenias malam nisi quae ignorat aut certe
20 non considerat quantum sit bonum pudicitia, quantum scelus admittat si
eam perdat, quam turpi et levi et momentanea voluptatis imagine quantum bonum commutet, quantum simul malorum agmen introducat, eiecta
castitate. Nec expendit quae sit corporea voluptas, ut inanis et stulta res et
propter quam ni manus quidem esset vertenda, nedum ut illud abiciat quo
25 nihil esse potest in femina pulchrius ac praestabilius; quam leve ac vanum sit
comi anxie, excoli, expoliri, magno ornari; quam perniciosum aliorum in se
oculos et desideria convertere. Nam quae haec et similia vel naturali virtute
ac bono mentis vel ex litteris cogitare didicit, imbuto et munito pectore
sanctis consiliis, numquam ut turpe aliquid admittat animum inducet, aut si
30 inducat, retrahentibus a facinore tot probitatis praeceptis tot sanctis monitis
atque adhortamentis, ex eo coniectura fieri potest qualis esset futura si nihil
de honesto audivisset.

20. (Aristoteles) *Aristot. probl. 30, 10 (956b)*

7–8 vulgus Graecorum Dionysiacos vocabat **Γ** vulgo Graeci Dionysiacos vocabant **H** // **8–9**
numquam ad bonam ullam frugem pervenirent **Γ** bonae ullius sint frugis **H** // **9** nequiter **Γ**
deest in **H** // **9–10** vitam omnem degerent **Γ** vitam transigant **H** // **12** pertinent **Γ** spectant **H**
// **15** pecuinum **Γ** beluinum **H** // **18** ut **Γ** *deest in* **H** // **20** bonum pudicitia **Γ** pudicitia
bonum **H** // **22** eiecta **Γ** exclusa **H** // **24** abiciat **Γ** abiceret **H** // **25** ac praestabilius **Γ**
atque praestantius **H** // **26–27** quam ... convertere **Γ** *deest in* **H** // **27–28** vel ... vel **Γ**
deest in **H** // **29** animum inducet **Γ** indicet animum (*sic!*) **H** // **30–31** tot sanctis ...
adhortamentis **Γ** *deest in* **H** // **32** de honesto **Γ** honesti **H**

harmful? When she is assailed by vice, to which she has grown accustomed, what protection will be afforded by moral rectitude, which she never came to know? If we agree with this opinion, why do we take them to sacred sermons? Why do we teach, correct and admonish them of better things? We might as well relegate them to the country, if you wish my opinion, and weaken and suppress whatever natural ability they may have, in a word, turn human beings into brute beasts, since they will be so far removed from learning. The philosopher Aristotle asks why pipers and musicians hired to play at feasts and celebrations, whom the Greek populace called Dionysiacs, who were dedicated to the pursuit of pleasure, never attained to any virtue, but spent their whole lives wickedly in evil pursuits. He answers that the reason for this is that since they spend their lives amidst sensual pleasures and banqueting and never hear the precepts of philosophy that pertain to leading a holy life and never see models of virtuous living, they do not know any other way to live than that which they have learned by hearing, seeing and experience. Since they have heard nothing, seen nothing and been accustomed to nothing but what is hedonistic and bestial, in the midst of discordant sounds and clamors, surrounded by people dancing, kissing, laughing, eating, drinking, vomiting, vowed to self-indulgence and oblivious of every mental or moral concern, it follows of necessity that they reproduce this same conduct in their morals and way of life.

21. You will not easily find an evil woman save that she be one who is ignorant of or at any rate gives no thought to the importance of the virtue of chastity, and is unaware of the evil she commits if she loses it, not taking into consideration what a blessing she exchanges for a base, empty and momentary illusion of pleasure and what a train of evils she ushers in with the loss of chastity. She does not consider how empty and senseless a thing physical pleasure is and that one should not even lift a finger for its sake, let alone cast away woman's most beautiful and priceless possession, nor does she reflect how trivial and vain it is to be so painstaking about one's hairdo, to be adorned, embellished and richly bedecked; how dangerous it is to attract the glances and desires of others to herself. The woman who has learned to make these and similar reflections either through instinctive virtue or innate intelligence or through her reading will never bring herself to commit any vile act, for her mind will have been strengthened and imbued with holy counsels. And if she were to be so inclined in spite of the many precepts of moral rectitude that would have acted as a restraint and in spite of so many admonishments and exhortations, one can imagine what she would be like if she had never heard anything about honorable conduct.

22. Ac nimirum si revolvere atque explicare superiores aetates libet, nullam fere inveniemus doctam impudicam; immo vero pleraque omnia feminarum huius et superiorum saeculorum vitia (quae sunt sane inter Christianas plura quam umquam in ulla gentilitate aut barbaria fuerunt)
5 ex inscitia sunt profecta, quae egregia illa sanctorum patrum monita de castitate, de solitudine, de silentio, de ornamentis et cultu muliebri neque legerunt neque audierunt. Quae si quo modo cognovissent, fieri non potest ut res esset in insolentiam hanc progressa adeo intolerabilem. Illorum rationes atque auctoritas et erumpentia cohibuissent flagitia et grassantia
10 compressissent. Obiciet fortasse aliquis ex omni memoria gentiles unam aut alteram: Sapphum, poetriam summam, quae non satis caste Phaonem adamarit; et Leontium, Metrodori concubinam, quae adversus Theophrastum scripserit; et Semproniam, Graece et Latine doctam, quam Sallustius parum integre pudicitiam habuisse refert. Ceu vero pro his tribus ad-
15 numerare non ipse sexcentas queam quas ad maximas virtutes evexit eruditio, non modo de nostris, sed de barbaris quoque. Verum antequam id facio, de hisce tribus loquar. Auctores habeo magni nominis qui Sapphum Lesbiam lyricam doctissimam non illam esse putent quae Phaonem deperierit, sed aliam, magna ut eruditione, ita continentia vi-
20 tae. Tum Leontium non venit ad Metrodorum docta, sed illius domi eruditionem percepit et eius generis eruditionem quae ad mores minimum conferret, nempe Epicuream, omnia voluptate metientem, unde illi in Theophrastum rabies, qui voluptatem incesseret. Semproniae doctrina non fuit quam nos probae feminae concedimus rerum moralium et rationis
25 vitae bene agendae, tantum erat sermonis cuiusdam expolitioris cura, in qua non ita multum laboris collocari volumus; idem poterat de Sappho responderi.

23. Iam, si nos doctas acies explicarimus, prodibunt Cornelia Gracchorum mater, quae ipsa pudicitiae exemplar filios suos edocuit; Laelia Mucii, Porcia

---

22. (Auctores ... vitae) *Athen. 13, 596e; Ail. var. 12, 19; Suda, s.v. Sappho.*

2–10 immo ... compressissent Γ *deest in* H // **10–11** Obiciet ... alteram Γ Obicient H // **14** refert Γ tradit H // **15–16** quas ... quoque Γ *deest in* H // **18** Sapphum *sic edd. omnes* (= Sappho) // **20** illius Γ eius H // **22–23** unde ... incesseret Γ *deest in* H // **24** fuit Γ est H // **25** cuiusdam expolitioris Γ politioris H / in **HWW²** *om.* **BV** // **27** responderi Γ dici H // **28** doctas acies explicarimus Γ acies nostras explicemus H // **29** Laelia **V** Laeliae **HWW²B** / Mucii *scr.* Muciae HΓ

22. And, of course, if we wished to go back over past ages, we would not find any learned woman who was unchaste. On the contrary the majority of female vices of this and preceding centuries (and without a doubt they were more numerous among Christians than among any pagan or barbarian nation) sprang from ignorance, because women did not read or hear tell of those splendid exhortations of the Fathers of the Church concerning chastity, solitude, silence and feminine adornment and attire. If they had merely known about them, it is impossible that things would have progressed to this intolerable degree of insolence. The authority of their teachings would have checked this offensive conduct at is inception and would have prevented its getting out of control. Perhaps someone will cite one or two examples from pagan antiquity—Sappho, greatest of female poets, who did not love Phaon chastely enough; Leontion, the concubine of Metrodorus, who wrote against Theophrastus; Sempronia, learned in Greek and Latin, who Sallust says did not hold chastity in proper esteem. As if in place of these three I could not enumerate a thousand women whom learning exalted to the heights of virtue, not only from among women of our nation but from the ranks of the barbarians. But before doing this I shall speak of these three women. There are authors of great renown who maintain that Sappho, the learned poetess of Lesbos, was not the one who died of love for Phaon, but another woman, who combined great learning with sobriety of life. As for Leontion, she was not learned before she met Metrodorus but acquired learning in his household, and it was the kind of learning that contributed very little to good morals, namely, Epicurean, which judges everything in terms of pleasure; hence her hatred for Theophrastus, who criticized pleasure. The learning of Sempronia was not of the kind we attribute to an honorable woman, which has to do with morals and the manner of living a good life. She merely cultivated a polished form of speech, on which I do not think one should expend so much effort. The same thing could be said of Sappho.

23. Now if we extend our learned field of vision, Cornelia, mother of the Gracchi, will appear, who herself a model of chastity, taught it to her own children. There are women like Laelia, the wife of Mucius, and

---

22. Phaon: Ancient tradition knew of him as a ferryman who plied between Lesbos and the mainland. A fable arose about a love-affair between him and Sappho, who because of her unrequited love leapt to her death from Cape Leucas, a promontory on the west coast of Greece.

Sempronia: She is described by Sallust as a woman of great personal accomplishments but of profligate character, the kind of woman Catiline recruited to aid his cause.

23. Cornelia: Daughter of Scipio Africanus, model of the Roman matron, admired for her conduct during her widowhood, when she refused all offers of marriage, devoting herself to the management of her estate and the education of her children.

Laelia: Daughter of Laelius, close friend of Scipio Aemilianus, and skilled orator. She was married to Quintus Mucius Scaevola, famous jurisconsult during the time of the Gracchi.

Bruti, quae de Catonis patris sapientia copiose hausit; Cleobulina Cleobuli
unius ex Septem sapientibus filia, quae tam dedita litteris et sapientiae vixit,
ut Venerem omnem aspernata virgo permanserit. Cuius exemplum secuta
est Pythagorae filia, quae patris scholam eo mortuo rexit virginumque choro
5   praefecta est. Ex eadem secta et disciplina Theano Metaponti nata, insignis
etiam vaticinio, singulari splenduit castitate. Sibyllas decem Hieronymus
virgines fuisse prodit. Cassandram itidem et Chrysein, vates Apollinis ac
Iunonis, virgines legimus; id fere commune feminis vatibus fuit. Pythia
Delphis non aliter quam virgo responsa consulentibus edebat; quarum prima,
10   Phemonoe, heroici carminis inventrix fertur. Sulpiciam Caleni praecepta de
coniugio conscripsisse significat Valerius Martialis, sed quae ipsa prius vita
sua expresserat:

     Omnes (inquit ille) Sulpiciam legant puellae
     Uni quae cupiunt placere viro;
15   Omnes Sulpiciam legant mariti,
     Uni qui cupiunt placere nuptae.
     Castos haec docet et pios amores,
     Lusus, delicias facetiasque.
     Cuius carmina qui bene aestimarit,
20   Nullam dixerit esse sanctiorem.

24. Constat aetate illa nullum maritum Caleno fuisse feliciorem, Sulpicia uxore. Hortensia, Hortensii oratoris filia, patrem ita effinxit dicendo
ut honestissima et venerabilis femina, orationem ad triumviros rei publicae constituendae habuerit pro sexu suo, quam posterior aetas non
25   modo in admirationem et laudem muliebris facundiae, sed ad imitationem
quoque legit, ut Ciceronis scripta vel Demosthenis. Aedesia Alexandrina,

23. (Cleobuli ... filia) *Plut. mor. 148C–E* // (Pythagorae filia) *Hier. adv. Iovin. 1, 42, PL 23,*
273B // (Sibyllas decem) *Hier. adv. Iovin. 1, 41, PL 23, 270C* // (Cassandram ... legimus)
Hier. adv. Iovin. 1, 41, PL 23, 270 // (Phemonoe ... fertur) *Diog. Laert. 1, 40; Paus. 10, 5, 7* //
(Omnes ... sanctiorem) *Mart. epig. 10, 35, 1–4, 8–10, 12*
    24. (Hortensia) *Quint. inst. 1, 1, 6; Val. Max. 8, 3, 3* //

1 copiose Γ *deest in* H // **7** prodit Γ prodidit H / Chrysein *scr.* Crissein H Crissem Γ //
9 aliter quam Γ nisi H // **10–12** Sulpiciam ... expresserat Γ Sulpicia Caleni praecepta
de coniugio sanctissima reliquit, sed quae ipsa prius vita sua expresserat, de qua Martialis
inquit H // **13** inquit ille Γ *deest in* H // **23** et venerabilis Γ *deest in* H

Porcia, the wife of Brutus, who drank in great draughts of wisdom from her father, Cato; Cleobulina, daughter of Cleobulus, one of the seven sages, who spent her life so dedicated to literature and wisdom that she abstained from all carnal pleasure and remained a virgin. Her example was imitated by the daughter of Pythagoras, who directed his school after his death and was in charge of a group of young maidens. From that same sect and school was Theano, born in Metapontum, famous as a prophetess and distinguished for her singular chastity. Jerome records that the Sibyls were ten in number, all virgins. We read that Cassandra and Chryseis, priestesses of Apollo and Juno, were also virgins. This was a prerogative that was common to prophetesses, as a rule. The Pythian priestess at Delphi, who gave answer to those who consulted her, always had to be a virgin. The first of these, Phemonoe, is said to have been the inventor of heroic song. Valerius Martial tells us that Sulpicia, wife of Calenus, wrote rules about married life, but not without having first given the example in her own life:

> Let all young brides read Sulpicia,
> Who would one husband only please;
> Husbands too should read Sulpicia,
> Who would please one bride alone.
> Chaste and holy loves she teaches,
> Amusements, grace and pleasantries.
> He who esteems her verse aright
> Will say that none is holier than she.

24. It is clear that in those days there was no husband more happy than Calenus, having Sulpicia as his wife. Hortensia, daughter of the orator Hortensius, so matched her father in eloquence that as a woman worthy of honor and respect she delivered a speech in behalf of her sex before the Triumvirs, designated to establish the republic, which later ages read not only in admiration and appreciation of her female eloquence but also for imitation, as they would the writings of Cicero or Demosthenes.

---

23. Porcia: Daughter of Cato Uticensis, bitter opponent of Caesar, who took his life at Thapsus in 46 B.C. She shared the political views of her father and her husband.

Theano: Believed to have been the wife of Pythagoras according to some accounts but his daughter according to others. Several apocryphal letters are ascribed to her.

Cassandra and Chryseis: Cassandra was the daughter of Priam and Hecuba, Chryseis the daughter of Chryses, the priest of Apollo at Troy. Both became the concubines of Agamemnon as the spoils of war.

holier than she: Vives omits the next line of Martial, in which he adds that 'none were naughtier than she', referring to a certain risqué element in her verse.

24. Hortensius: One of the greatest of Roman orators, rival of Cicero, who dedicated a treatise to him, now lost. His daughter's speech was given during the time of the Second Triumvirate in 42 B.C.

Syriani philosophi propinqua, ingenti et doctrina et puritate morum, aevo
suo miraculo fuit. Corinna Tanagraea, Archelodori filia, adolescentula
prudentissima, Pindarum vatem carminum certamine quinquies vicit. Teia
Erinna, quae Platonis aetate nondum viginti annos nata fato concessit,
Homerum maiestate heroici carminis fertur aequasse, cum ille Apollini
comparetur. Eunomia, virgo Christiana, sicuti apud Hieronymum legitur,
Nazarii rhetoris filia, in eloquentia patri coaequatur. Paula, Senecae mariti
doctrina instructa, mores quoque aemulata est. Seneca idem Helviam,
matrem suam, sapientum praeceptis mariti iussu imbutam tantum, non
item eruditam dolet. Argentaria Polla, Lucani coniunx, quae marito mortuo
Pharsaliae opus emendavit, etiam adiutasse in scribendo virum dicitur,
insignis genere, opibus, forma, ingenio, pudicitia. De qua sic Calliope apud
Statium Lucano loquitur:

> Nec solum dabo carminum nitorem,
> Sed taedis genialibus dicabo
> Doctam atque ingenio tuo decoram,
> Qualem blanda Venus daretque Iuno
> Forma, simplicitate, comitate,
> Censu, sanguine, gratia, decore.

25. Quinque filias Diodorus dialecticus habuit, illustres artibus et pudicitia, quarum historiam Philo, Carneadis magister, persecutus est. Zenobia,
Palmyraenorum regina, etiam Graece et Latine calluit et historiam composuit, cuius, ut aliarum quarundam, incredibilis continentia proximo a nobis
libro reddetur. Quid Christianas loquar? an Theclam, Pauli discipulam,

---

24. (Corinna ... vicit) *Plut. mor. 347F* // (Teia Erinna ... aequasse) *Anth. Pal. 9, 190* //
(Eunomia) *Euseb. chron. 233, 22* // (Paula) *Tac. ann. 15, 63–64* // (Helviam) *Sen. dial. 12, 17,
5.* // (Nec ... decore) *Stat. silv. 2, 7, 81–86*
   25. (Diodorus) *Hier. adv. Iovin. 1, 42, PL 23, 273B; Clem. Alex. strom. 4, 19*

1 ingenti Γ tanta **H** // **2–3** Corinna ... prudentissima Γ Corinna Theia, mulier casta **H**
// **3–7** Teia Erinna ... coaequatur Γ *deest in* **H** // **8** instructa Γ imbuta **H** / Helviam
scr. Albinam **H**Γ*Nusquam hoc Senecae matris cognomen apud auctores antiquos invenitur.* // **19**
Zenobia **HWW²B** Zenobiam **V** // **20** calluit Γ scivit **H** // **22** reddetur Γ referetur **H** /
discipulam Γ auditricem **H**

Zenobia: Highly praised for her beauty, intelligence and virtue, she seems, however,
to have been a ruthless woman. She was defeated by the Emperor Aurelian in 274 A.D.
and brought back in triumph to Rome, where she lived as a Roman matron. She figures
prominently in Boccaccio's *De claris mulieribus* and Sir Thomas Elyot's *Defense of Good Women*,
in which she is thought to represent Catherine of Aragon.
   Thecla: According to the 2nd c. *Acts of Paul and Thecla* she heard Paul preach in Iconium.
She underwent many torments for the faith.

Edesia of Alexandria, kinswoman of the philosopher Syrianus, was the wonder of her age for her immense learning and purity of life. Corinna of Tanagra, daughter of Archelodorus, a young girl of great intelligence, defeated the poet Pindar five times in poetic contests. Erinna of Teos, contemporary of Plato, who was the victim of fate before reaching the age of twenty, is said to have equalled Homer in the majesty of epic poetry, although he is compared to Apollo. Eunomia, a Christian virgin, as we read in Jerome, the daughter of Nazarius the rhetor, is likened to her father in eloquence. Paula, trained in the teachings of her husband Seneca, imitated him also in her morals. The same Seneca regretted that his mother Helvia in obedience to her husband's command had only an introduction to the precepts of wisdom and was not well instructed in them. Polla Argentaria, the wife of Lucan, who corrected the *Pharsalia* after her husband's death, is said also to have helped him in the writing of it. She was a woman of noble lineage, substance, beauty, talent and virtue, of whom the Muse Calliope speaks to Lucan in these terms in the poem of Statius:

> I give you not only the elegance of song
> But with the marriage torch bestow on you
> A learned woman worthy of your gifts,
> Such as sweet Venus or Juno would award,
> In beauty, purity and gentleness,
> Lineage, riches, decorum and grace.

25. Diodorus the dialectician had five daughters, outstanding in letters and virtue, whose history Philo, the teacher of Carneades, has traced. Zenobia, Queen of Palmyra, was skilled in both Greek and Latin and wrote history, whose extraordinary continence, as well as that of certain other women, will be recounted in the following book. Why speak of Christian women? Need I mention Thecla, the disciple of Paul, a disciple worthy of such a great

24. Edesia: Wife of the Neoplatonic philosopher Hermeias, studied in Athens with her two sons under Proclus, middle of the fifth century A.D. Syrianus was also a Neoplatonic philosopher, the teacher of Proclus.

Corinna of Tanagra: It is difficult to know when she lived. In antiquity there were many stories about her alleged victory over Pindar. In Plutarch's version she found fault with him for neglecting myths, astonishingly enough.

Erinna: A poetess of the Dorian island of Telos (not Teos, as Vives writes) near Rhodes, who probably lived at the end of the 4th c. B.C. She is known for her poem *The Distaff* in 300 hexameters.

25. Diodorus: Diodorus Cronus belonged to the philosophic school of Megara, third c. B.C., which claimed descendancy from Socrates. Philon of Megara, a pupil of Diodorus, wrote a dialogue entitled *Menexenus*, in which he praises the learning and virtue of Diodorus' daughters. Philon, however, could not have been the teacher of Carneades, founder of the New Academy, who lived from 214 to 129 B.C. Jerome, Vives' source here, is doubtless in error.

dignam tanto magistro discipulam? an Barbaram, edoctam ab Origene
Adamantio? an Catharinam Alexandrinam, Costi filiam, quae disputando
maximos et exercitatissimos philosophos superavit? Cognominis eius Catha-
rina Senensis virgo doctissima monumenta ingenii sui reliquit, in quibus
5   puritas illa sanctissimi animi relucet. Nec nos gentilitati suas vates invide-
mus, quippe qui quattuor etiam in eadem habeamus domo virgines vates,
Philippi filias. Hieronymi temporibus sanctae omnes feminae doctissimae
fuerunt. Utinam illis nonnulli aetatis huius senes theologi eruditione pares
essent! Scribit ad Paulam, ad Laetam, ad Eustochium, ad Fabiolam, ad
10   Marcellam, ad Furiam, ad Demetriadem, ad Salvinam, ad Herontiam Hieronymus, ad alias Ambrosius, ad alias Augustinus, ad alias Fulgentius,
suspiciendas omnes ingenio, litteris, vita. Valeria Proba, quae virum unice
dilexit, Vergiliocentones de Christo Domino composuit. Eudociam Theo-
dosii iunioris, rerum scriptores non minus claram peritia rerum et probitate
15   narrant quam imperio, cuius dicitur esse qui circumfertur Homerocenton.
Hildegardis, Germanae virginis, epistolae et eruditi libri sunt in manibus.

　　　26. Aetas nostra quattuor illas Isabellae reginae filias, quas paulo ante
memoravi, eruditas vidit. Non sine laudibus et admiratione refertur mihi
passim in hac terra Ioannam, Philippi coniugem, Caroli huius matrem,
20   ex tempore Latinis orationibus, quae de more apud novos principes opp-
idatim habentur, Latine respondisse. Idem de regina sua, Ioannae sorore,
Britanni praedicant. Idem omnes de duabus aliis, quae in Lusitania fato
concessere. Quibus quattuor sororibus nullae memoria hominum mulieres
sinceriore pudicitia, nullae puriore ac integriore fama, nullae populis suis
25   gratiores atque amabiliores reginae exstiterunt, nullae magis amarunt coniuges suos, nullae obsequentius eis paruerunt, nullae accuratius se ac suos
omnes sine labe conservarunt, nullis magis foeditas aut lascivia displicuit,
nullae absolutius et exactius numeros omnes probae feminae impleverunt.

　　　26. (memoravi) *inst. fem. Christ. 1, 16*

1–2 an Barbaram ... Adamantio **Γ** *deest in* **H** // **2** quae disputando **Γ** quae etiam
disputando **H** // **4** virgo doctissima **Γ** doctissima virgo **H** // **5** relucet **Γ** elucet **H** // **7**
Hieronymi temporibus **Γ** Aetate Hieronymi **H** // **8–9** Utinam ... essent **Γ** Utinam illas
multi huius aetatis viri senes eruditione aequarent **H** // **11** ad alias Fulgentius **Γ** *deest in* **H**
// **15** narrant **Γ** tradunt **H** / dicitur ... Homerocenton **Γ** dicuntur esse qui circumferuntur
Homerocentones **H** // **16** epistolae ... manibus **Γ** epistolas et eruditos legimus libros **H**
// **18** memoravi **Γ** memorabam **H** / refertur **Γ** narrant **H** // **24** puriore ac integriore **Γ**
candidiore **H** // **27** labe **Γ** macula **H** / foeditas **HWW²B** foeditatis **V**

　　　Eudocia: Wrote paraphrases of certain prophetic books of the Old Testament and
completed the Homeric centos begun by a bishop named Patricius.
　　　Hildegard: (1098–1179), abbess of Bingen, visionary mystic, composer, writer of
prophetic treatises, works on medicine and natural history.

master? Or Barbara, who was taught by Origen Adamantius, or Catherine of Alexandria, daughter of Costus, who surpassed the greatest and most experienced philosophers in debate. The most learned virgin of the same name, Catherine of Siena, left fitting monuments of her genius, in which the purity of that saintly intellect is resplendent. We do not envy the pagans their prophetesses since we have four in the same household, the daughters of Philip. In Jerome's time all holy women were very learned. If only some aged theologians of our own day could equal this learning! Jerome writes to Paula, Laeta, Eustochium, Fabiola, Marcella, Furia, Demetrias, Salvina, Herontia. Ambrose, Augustine and Fulgentius write to others, all of them admirable for their talent, literary learning and exemplary life. Valeria Proba, who loved her husband to a singular degree, composed the *Virgiliocentones* about the life of our Lord, Jesus Christ. Chroniclers tell of Eudocia, wife of Emperor Theodosius the Younger, who was no less renowned for her learning and virtuous life than for her rule. The *Homerocenton*, which enjoys wide circulation, is attributed to her. The letters and learned books of the German maiden, Hildegard, are in everyone's hands.

26. Our age has seen the four daughters of Isabel, whom I mentioned a little earlier, each of them well accomplished. People in various parts of the country tell me in words of praise and admiration that Queen Juana, wife of Philip and mother of our Emperor Charles, answered in Latin to the Latin ex tempore speeches that are customarily delivered in every town in the presence of new princes. The English say the same of their queen Catherine, sister of Juana. All say the same of the other two sisters, who met their death in Portugal. There were no women in the memory of man of more pure chastity than these four sisters, none with a more unblemished name, and there have been no queens who were so loved and admired by their subjects. None loved their spouses more, none rendered them more compliant obedience, none preserved themselves and their loved ones more blamelessly and more assiduously, none were so opposed to base behavior and lax morals, none fulfilled to such perfection

25. Barbara: She was shut up in a tower by her father to keep her hidden from men's eyes. According to a Flemish version of the *Golden Legend* of Jacopo da Varagine she sought out the Christian philosopher Origen in Alexandria by means of envoys. He sent a priest named Valentinus to instruct her in the Christian religion. This particular of her legend may well have been known to Vives through this Flemish version, done by Jean de Wackerzeele, published in Cologne in 1495.

Catherine of Alexandria: Martyred at Alexandria c. 310.

Catherine of Siena: Caterina Benincasa (1347–1380). Among her writings are about four hundred letters and a treatise, *Dialogo della divina provvidenza*. She was instrumental in persuading Gregory XI to return to Rome from Avignon.

Valeria Proba: Wife of a Roman prefect, during the years 360 to 370 wrote a cento, or patchwork, of 694 hexameters, made up of passages of Virgil, on Biblical themes. It was very popular in the Middle Ages and was used as a school text.

Crescentem Valentiae meae video Menciam Mendozam, Marchionis Zeneti filiam, quae olim (ut spero) celebrabitur. Si reginae post se de privatis feminis mentionem fieri paterentur, adderem huic numero Angelam Zabatam, civem meam, incredibili ad omnis generis litteras ingenii celeritate ac dexteritate, pudicitia ac prudentia singulari. Tum Thomae Mori filias: Margaritam, Elizabetham, Caeciliam atque earum consanguineam Margaritam Gigiam; quas pater non contentus esse castissimas, etiam doctissimae ut essent curavit, sic fore iudicans ut verius firmiusque essent castae.

27. In quo nec vir ille sapientissimus fallitur nec alii qui idem censent. Res enim est litterarium studium primum quae mentes hominum occupat totas, deinde in cogitationem attollit pulcherrimarum rerum, ut a turpitudinum cogitationibus avocet animos. Et si qua talis cogitatio obrepat, vel eam statim praeceptis ac consiliis bene vivendi munita mens pellit, vel aurem non praebet rei abiectissimae ac spurcissimae, cum alias ipsa purissimasque, solidas et maximi decoris voluptates habeat quibus ducatur. Hinc puto Palladem, ingeniorum atque artium deam, Musasque omnes virgines esse a vetustate existimatas. Nec a libidine solum abhorrebit pectus sapientiae deditum, hoc est, a fuligine res candidissima et a maculis mundissima, sed a levibus quoque et nugacibus oblectamentis, quibus leves puellarum temptantur animi, velut a saltationibus, cantiunculis et lusibus eiuscemodi lascivis ac ineptis. 'Numquam,' inquit Plutarchus, 'saltationibus se mulier recreabit litteris addicta.'

28. 'Sed quaenam sint istae litterae quibus femina formabitur?' quaeret aliquis, 'et quas imbibet?' Initio disputationis huius id attigi: sapientiae studia, quae mores ad virtutem fingant; studia sapientiae, quae rationem doceant optime et sanctissime vivendi. De eloquentia nihil sum sollicitus. Non indiget ea mulier, probitate ac sapientia indiget. Nec turpe est feminam tacere; foedum et abominandum non bene sapere, male vivere. Sed nec protinus

---

27. (Plutarchus) *Plut. mor. 145C*
28. (attigi) *inst. fem. Christ. 1, 10* //

1–2 Crescentem ... celebrabitur Γ *deest in* H // **3–5** Angelam Zabatam ... Tum Γ *deest in* H // **7** doctissimae ut essent curavit Γ doctissimas esse voluit H // **8** essent Γ sint H // **11** cogitationem ... rerum Γ cognitionem rerum pulcherrimarum attollit H // **12** avocet animos Γ animos avocet H // **12–13** eam ... consiliis Γ praeceptis H // **14** abiectissimae Γ vilissimae H // **14–15** purissimasque ... decoris Γ pulcherrimas purissimasque H // **17** existimatas Γ fictas H // **19** quoque et nugacibus oblectamentis Γ etiam H // **20** temptantur Γ tenentur H // **22** recreabit litteris addicta Γ delectabit litteris dedita H // **23** litterae ... formabitur Γ litterae potissimum in quibus femina versabitur H // **24** Initio ... attigi Γ *deest in* H // **24–25** sapientiae ... sapientiae Γ Studia sapientiae dixi, illa inquam, quae mores forment, quae vitam instituant H // **26** vivendi Γ agendi H // **26–27** non indiget ... indiget Γ nec eget ... indiget H // **27** feminam tacere Γ tacere mulierem H // **28** Sed nec Γ Neque H

the ideals expected of the virtuous woman. In my own Valencia I see that Mencia de Mendoza, daughter of the marquis of Zenete, is growing up and it is my hope that one day she will achieve renown. If the majesty of queens would permit that mention be made of ordinary women in the same discourse, I would add to this number Angela Zabata, my compatriot, a young woman of incredible quickness and nimbleness of intellect in all branches of literature and also of singular purity of morals and good sense. Then I shall mention the daughters of Thomas More—Margaret, Elizabeth, Cecily, and their kinswoman, Margaret Giggs—whose father was not content that they be chaste but also took pains that they be very learned, in the belief that in this way they would be more truly and steadfastly chaste.

27. In this that wisest of men is not deceived nor are others who are of the same opinion, for the study of literature has these effects: first, it occupies a person's whole attention; second, it lifts the mind to the contemplation of beautiful things and rids it of lowly thoughts, and if any such thoughts creep in, the mind, fortified by precepts and counsels of good living, either dispels it immediately or does not lend an ear to vile and base things since it has other pure, substantial and noble pleasures to aspire after. For this reason, I think, Pallas Athena, the goddess of poetic inspiration and the arts, and all of the Muses were thought from ancient times to be virgins. Not only does the mind dedicated to wisdom shrink from lust, that is, something innocent and immaculate from filth and defilement, but likewise from trivial and foolish pastimes, by which the fickle minds of girls are tempted, like dancing, singing and frivolous and insipid amusements of that sort. 'Never,' said Plutarch, 'will a woman dedicated to literature distract herself in dancing.'

28. 'But in what kind of literature should a woman be versed?' someone may ask, 'and in what reading will she immerse herself?' I touched on this at the beginning of this discussion: the study of wisdom, which forms morals in the way of virtue, the study of wisdom which teaches the best and holiest way of life. I am not at all concerned with eloquence. A woman has no need of that; she needs rectitude and wisdom. It is not shameful for a woman to be silent; it is disgraceful and abominable for her not to have wisdom

26. Mencia de Mendoza: Marchioness of Zenete, received an excellent education and continued her interest in humanistic studies after her marriage to Henry III, Count of Nassau. She resided later at Breda and gave hospitality to Vives in his later years.

daughters of Thomas More: The last named, Margaret Giggs, was More's adopted daughter, but she received the same education in the 'school' of More, demonstrating great ability in medicine. The most learned of them was Margaret, of whom we have several writings. In Epistle 1402 to John More Erasmus speaks of the letters of More's daughters written in such pure Latin, of their accurate knowledge of the two tongues and their accomplishments in music (CWE 10, p.130).

40 J. L. VIVES

eloquentiam in hoc sexu improbarim, quam Quintilianus et hunc secutus
Divus Hieronymus laudatam in Cornelia Gracchorum matre perhibent, et
in Hortensia, Q. Hortensii filia, et in Eunomia, Nazarii filia. Si feminam
aliquam invenire sit sanctam et doctam quae erudiat, hanc malim. Sin minus,
5 virum deligamus vel grandaevum vel certe optimum et probatissimum, neque
hunc caelibem, sed cui uxor sit et quidem nec deformis et cara; ita demum in
alienas minimum exardescet. Neque haec fuerunt praetermittenda, cum in
educanda femina potissimam ac nescio an solam curam vendicet pudicitia.
   29. Cum docebitur legere, ii libri sumantur in manus qui mores compo-
10 nant; cum scribere, ne sint otiosi versus qui ad imitationem proponuntur nec
lasciva quaepiam aut vana cantiuncula, sed grave aliquod dictum, prudens
et sancta ex litteris Sacris aut philosophorum monumentis sententiola, quam
saepius scriptam tenacius memoria affigat. Et in dicendo quidem nullum ut
viro, sic neque feminae finem statuo, nisi quod virum plurium ac variarum
15 cognitione rerum instructum esse par est, quae et ipsi prosint et rei publicae, tum usu, tum etiam eruditione in alios transfundenda et propaganda.
Mulierem totam esse volo in ea parte philosophiae quae mores sibi formandos
sumpsit ac meliores reddendos. Ad hoc sibi uni discat vel ad summum liberis
pueris adhuc aut sororibus in Domino. Neque enim scholis praefici feminam
20 decet nec inter viros agere aut loqui et verecundiam pudoremque vel totum
vel magna ex parte in publico deterere primum, hinc paulatim excutere,
dum alios docet; quam, si proba sit, domi sedere potius et aliis incognitam
esse convenit. In coetu vero demissis oculis pudibundam tacere, ut videant
quidem eam sane nonnulli, audiat nemo. Apostolus Paulus, vas electionis,
25 ecclesiam Corinthiorum sanctis praeceptis instruens, 'Mulieres', inquit, 'vestrae in ecclesia tacento neque enim permittitur illis loqui, sed subditas esse,
ut lex iubet; si quid vero cupiunt discere, domi viros proprios interrogent.'
Et Timotheo discipulo suo sic scribit: 'Mulier in silentio discat cum omni
subiectione; docere autem mulieri non permitto neque auctoritatem habere
30 in virum, sed esse in silentio. Adam enim fictus est, deinde Eva; et Adam
non est seductus, mulier autem seducta in praevaricatione fuit.' Itaque,
quoniam infirmum animans est femina et iudicio invalido quodque falli

---

28. (Quintilianus) *Quint. inst. 1, 1, 6* // (Hieronymus) *Hier. epist. 107, 4, PL 22, 872*
   29. (Mulieres ... interrogent) *Vulg. I Cor. 14, 34–35* // (Mulier ... fuit) *Vulg. I Tim. 2,*
11–14

1 in hoc sexu Γ *deest in* H // **3** et in Eunomia, Nazarii filia Γ *deest in* H // **3–4** Si feminam
... doctam Γ si femina aliqua inveniatur sancta et docta H // **6** uxor sit Γ sit uxor H / nec
deformis Γ pulchra satis H // **8** potissimam Γ praecipuam H // **10** cum scribere Γ cum
vero scribere H // **11** vana Γ vilis H // **12** sancta Γ casta H / monumentis Γ praeceptis H
// **16** transfundenda Γ diffundenda H // **17** formandos Γ componendos H // **18** Ad hoc Γ
et H / vel Γ *deest in* H // **19–20** feminam decet Γ decet mulierem H // **21** deterere ...
paulatim Γ *deest in* H // **24** sane Γ *deest in* H // **25** instruens Γ formans ac instruens H

and to live a bad life. But I would not necessarily condemn in this sex the eloquence that Quintilian, followed by St. Jerome, considers worthy of praise in Cornelia, mother of the Gracchi, and in Hortensia, daughter of Quintus Hortensius, and in Eunomia, daughter of Nazarius. If it is possible to find a woman who is both pious and learned to teach the young girl, I should prefer her. If not, we should choose a man of advanced years, or at least a good man of proven virtues, not a bachelor, but one who has a wife, who should not be unattractive and who is dear to him. In that way he will be less inclined to conceive a passion for other women. Such considerations should not be passed over lightly, since in the education of a woman the principal and I might almost say the only concern should be the preservation of chastity.

29. When she is taught to read, let her peruse books that impart instruction in morals; when she learns to write, do not have her imitate idle verses or vain and frivolous ditties, but rather some grave saying or a wise and holy sentiment from the Holy Scriptures or the writings of philosophers, which should be copied out many times so that they will remain firmly fixed in the memory. And in the art of speaking I put no limit either on male or female, save that it is reasonable that the man be equipped with the knowledge of many and varied subjects, which will be of profit to himself and to the state, and that he be endowed with experience and learning, which will be diffused and transmitted to others. I wish the woman to be totally given over to that part of philosophy which has assumed as its task the formation and improvement of morals. For this purpose let her learn it for herself alone or at most for her children when they are still small or for her sisters in the Lord for it is not fitting that a woman be in charge of schools or have dealings with or speak to men, and while teaching others, detract from her modesty and decorum either in whole or in great measure, and eventually lose these qualities little by little. If she is a good woman it is best that she stay at home and be unknown to others. In company it is befitting that she be retiring and silent with her eyes cast down, so that some perhaps may see her, but none will hear her. The Apostle Paul, vessel of election, imparting holy precepts to the church of Corinth, said 'Let your wives be silent in church, for it is not permitted them to speak, but to be subject, as the law commands. If they wish to learn anything, let them ask their husbands at home.' And writing to his disciple Timothy, he says 'Let a woman learn in silence with all subjection. I do not permit a woman to teach or to have authority over her husband, but to remain silent. For Adam was created first, then Eve, and Adam was not seduced but the woman was seduced and led astray.' Therefore since woman is a weak creature and of uncertain judgement and is easily deceived

est in proclivi (quod ostendit parens hominum Eva, quam levi argumento
cepit diabolus), idcirco docere illam non oportet, ne cum sibi falsam de re
aliqua opinionem persuaserit, auctoritate docentis in auditores transfundat
et alios quoque in errorem suum facile pertrahat, nempe ultro doctorem
5   sequentibus discipulis. Non excidit mihi quasdam esse de feminis parum
idoneas percipiendis litteris, utique sicut inter viros. Harum non est abicienda
cura; exhibendum sermone quod scripto non potes; et a doctis aliis sui
aequalibus discant, sive dum illae legunt, sive dum ea referunt quae legerunt.

CAP. V.   QUI NON LEGENDI SCRIPTORES QUI LEGENDI

10   **30.** Sanctus Hieronymus ad Laetam de Paula instituenda scribens, sic praecipit: 'Nihil discat audire, nihil loqui, nisi quod ad timorem Dei pertinet.'
Haud dubium quin idem de lectione consulturus. Invaluit consuetudo,
quavis gentilicia peior, ut vulgares libri qui in hoc scribuntur ut ab otiosis tum viris tum feminis legantur, nullam habeant aliam quam de bellis
15   aut amoribus materiam. De quibus libris ne praecipiendum quidem puto,
si modo inter Christianos verba facimus. Quid ego quanta sit ea pestis
dicam, cum igni stipulae et arida subiciuntur ligna? At scribuntur haec
otiosis; ceu vero non satis per se magnum sit vitiorum omnium fomentum
otium, nisi et faces subdantur quibus ignis hic cunctum simul hominem
20   valide corripiat et exurat! Quid puellae cum armis quae ipsi vel nominare dedecus est? Narrant mihi quibusdam in locis morem esse ut puellae
nobiles ludicra armorum avidissime spectent, etiam de armis deque viris
fortibus iudicium ferant; viri vicissim illarum censuram plus revereantur,
pluris faciant quam virorum. Non facile animus est pudicus quem ferri
25   et lacertorum et virilis roboris cogitatio occupavit. Quis inter haec inermi
et imbelli atque imbecillae pudicitiae locus relinquitur? Femina quae illa
meditatur venenum pectore imbibit, cuius haec cura, haec verba apertissima indicia sunt. Letalis est hic morbus; nec detegendus tamen a me,
sed obruendus atque opprimendus, ne alias et odore offendat et contagio

---

30. (Hieronymus ad Laetam) *Hier. epist. 107, 4, PL 22, 871* //

1 est in proclivi Γ non difficile potest **H** / hominum Γ mortalium **H** // **2** idcirco Γ ideo **H**
// **4** pertrahat Γ trahat **H** // **5–8** Non excidit … legerunt Γ *deest in* **H** // **13** gentilicia Γ
gentiliciis **H** // **16** inter … facimus Γ Christianis loquor **H** // **17** subiciuntur ligna Γ
ligna subiciuntur **H** / per se Γ *deest in* **H** // **18** ceu Γ quasi **H** / per se Γ *deest in* **H** // **19** quibus ignis Γ
quibus ardentius ignis **H** // **19–20** simul … exurat Γ hominem corripiat **H** // **20–21** ipsi
vel nominare dedecus est Γ vel nominare dedecus ipsi est **H** // **21–22** morem esse …
spectent Γ nobiles aliquas puellas lusus armorum avidissime spectare **H** // **23–24** viri …
virorum Γ viros vicissim illarum censuram plus metuere, pluris facere quam virorum **H** //
26 relinquitur Γ *deest in* **H** // **29** et odore Γ odore suo **H**

(as Eve, the first parent of mankind demonstrated, whom the devil deluded with such a slight pretext), she should not teach, lest when she has convinced herself of some false opinion she transmit it to her listeners in her role as a teacher and easily drag others into her error, since pupils willingly follow their teacher. I am not unaware that certain women just as certain men are ill-adapted to the learning of literature. The education of such women must not be neglected. You must make known to her by word of mouth what you cannot do through the written word. She may also learn from other learned women of her own age either when they read to her or recount the things they have read.

CHAPTER 5.   WHICH WRITERS ARE TO BE READ
AND WHICH NOT TO BE READ

30. St. Jerome, writing to Laeta about the instruction of Paula, gives this precept: 'Let her not hear anything nor speak anything except what pertains to the fear of God.' Doubtless he would give the same advice with regard to reading. A custom has grown up, worse than any pagan usage, that books in the vernacular, written in that tongue so that they may be read by idle men and women, treat of no other material than love and war. Concerning such books I think nothing more need be said if I am speaking to Christians. How can I describe what a pestilence this is, since it is to place straw and dry kindling wood on the fire? But these books are written for those who have nothing to do, as if idleness itself were not a strong enough aliment of all vices without laying on a torch that will set a person on fire and devour him in its flames. What does a girl have to do with weapons, the very mention of which is unbecoming to her. They tell me that in certain places it is the custom for girls of noble birth to be avid spectators of tournaments of arms and to pass judgement on the bravery of the combatants, and that the men, for their part, respect and make more of their assessment than they do of the men's. But a young woman cannot easily be of chaste mind if her thoughts are occupied with the sword and sinewy muscles and virile strength. What place is there here for defenceless, unwarlike and weak chastity? A woman who contemplates these things drinks poison into her breast, as this interest and these words make clear. This is a deadly disease, which it is not only my duty to expose but to crush and suppress lest it offend others by its odor and infect them with its contagion.

30. Laeta: Daughter-in-law of Paula, a patrician Roman woman, descendant of the Gracchi, close friend and disciple of Jerome.

inquinet. Arma igitur, cum Christianum virum tractare nisi in acerrima atque inevitabili necessitate fas non sit, spectare feminam fas erit, et, si non manibus, certe—quod gravius est—animo et corde versare? Deinde quid mihi amores alienos legis et blanditias et veneni illectamenta sensim
5 hauris ignara et plerumque videns ac prudens, cum nonnullae, in quibus nihil iam superest bonae mentis, ad haec legenda veniant, ut eiusmodi sese amatoriis cogitationibus suavissime pascant? Has non modo praestaret numquam didicisse litteras, sed perdidisse etiam et oculos ne legerent et aures ne audirent. Quanto has satius esset caecas et surdas, ut Dominus in
10 Evangelio dicit, ingredi in vitam quam cum geminis oculis auribusque mitti in gehennam ignis?

31. Haec puella usque adeo Christianis turpis est ut etiam barbaris esset pudenda ac detestanda. Quo magis miror sacros contionatores, cum plerumque res minutas maximis tragoediis exagitent, hoc singulis contio-
15 nibus non clamare. Miror cordatos patres hoc suis filiabus permittere, maritos concedere, mores et instituta populorum dissimulare, ut nequitiae assuescant feminae legendo. Decet humanas leges et magistratus non fora solum et lites spectare, sed mores quoque et publicos et privatos. Itaque conveniret libidinosa carmina et spurca de vulgi ore per leges tolli, ceu vero cani in civitate
20 nihil debeat nisi foedum et quod audire nemo probus queat sine pudore, nemo sapiens sine indignatione, ut videantur qui eiusmodi cantiunculas componunt nihil laborare magis quam ut publicos iuventutis mores corrumpant, non secus ac qui publicos fontes venenis inficiunt? Quis hic est mos ut cantio non existimetur quae vacet turpitudine? Hoc ergo curare leges et magistratus
25 congruit. Tum et de pestiferis libris, cuiusmodi sunt in Hispania Amadisus, Splandianus, Florisandus, Tirantus, Tristanus, quarum ineptiarum nullus est finis. Quotidie prodeunt novae: Celestina lena, nequitiarum parens;

---

30. (ingredi ... ignis?) *Vulg. Matth. 18, 9*

1–2 nisi ... necessitate **Γ** *deest in* **H** // 2 fas non sit **Γ** nescio an fas sit, quomodo **H** // 7 sese amatoriis cogitationibus suavissime pascant **Γ** amatoriis cogitationibus teneantur **H** // 8 didicisse litteras **Γ** litteras didicisse **H** // 9 has **Γ** hoc **H** // 10 cum **Γ** *deest in* **H** // 12 barbaris **Γ** gentilibus **H** // 13 detestanda **Γ** abominanda **H** // 14 minutas **Γ** parvas **H** // 20 probus **Γ** bonus **H** // 23 non secus **Γ** faciunt non secus **H** // 24 vacet turpitudine **Γ** turpitudine vacat **H** / et magistratus **Γ** *deest in* **H** // 26 Splandianus **Γ** *deest in* **H** // Tristanus **Γ** Tristanus Lugdunensis **H** // 26–27 quarum ... novae **Γ** *deest in* **H**

---

a model of worldly wisdom. The *Cárcel de amor* ('Prison of Love'), Seville, 1492, by Diego de San Pedro is the most important Spanish novel of courtly love.

When it is not lawful for a Christian man to handle weapons save in dire and unavoidable necessity, will it be lawful for a woman to be a spectator at such contests? And if she does not hold them with her own hands, she participates in the spectacle with heart and mind, which is surely worse. Then, tell me, why do you read about other people's loves and imperceptibly absorb venomous allurements and enticements little by little, and often with full consciousness of what you are doing? For there are some who have already lost all mental equilibrium who give themselves to this reading in order to find pleasant gratification in amorous reveries of this kind. For such girls it would have been preferable not only that they had never learned literature but that they had lost their eyes so that they could not read, and their ears so that they could not hear. How much better would it be for them to enter into life blind and deaf, as Our Lord says in the Gospel, rather than with both eyes and both ears to be cast into the fire of hell.

31. This kind of girl is such a disgrace not only to Christians that she would be an object of shame and hatred even to the pagans. Wherefore I am all the more astonished that devout preachers, although often inveighing in tragic tones against petty matters, do not decry this practice in their every sermon. I marvel that wise fathers permit this to their daughters, husbands concede it to their wives, and public morals and institutions ignore the fact that women become addicted to vice through reading. It is fitting that human laws and magistrates not only concern themselves with the courts and civil disputes but also oversee public and private morals. It would be expedient that licentious and filthy songs in the mouths of the rabble be forbidden by law. Must it be that nothing be sung in the city but what is bawdy and what no decent person can hear without embarrassment and no intelligent person without indignation? It would seem that those who compose such songs have no other purpose than to corrupt the public morals of youth, just like those who contaminate the public fountains with poison. What manner of custom is this that what is free of filth is not considered a song? This should receive the attention of the laws and the magistrates. They should also concern themselves with pernicious books like those popular in Spain: Amadís, Esplandián, Florisando, Tirant, Tristan, whose absurdities are infinite, and new examples appear every day: Celestina,

---

31. Spain: *Amadís de Gaula* is the best known of the Spanish tales of chivalry, first edition Zaragoza, 1508. *Esplandián* (1510) was a continuation of *Amadís*, in which Esplandián kills his father. *Florisando* was another continuation, published in the same year by Páez de Ribera. *Tirant lo Blanch* was the most famous Catalan chivalric romance, begun by Joanot Martorell and finished by Martí Joan de Galba, first published in Valencia in 1490. Unlike others of its kind the adventures remain more in the realm of the possible. The Celtic legend of Tristan was translated into Spanish as *Tristán de Leonís*, 1501. *La Celestina*, a dialogue novel written by the *converso* Fernando de Rojas, is the most important work written in 15th c. Spain. The earliest surviving edition dates to Burgos, 1499. The procuress and go-between, Celestina, is

Carcer amorum. In Gallia Lancilotus a lacu, Paris et Vienna, Ponthus et Sidonia, Petrus Provincialis et Magalona, Melusina, domina inexorabilis. In hac Belgica Florius et Albus flos, Leonella et Canamorus, Turias et Floreta, Piramus et Thisbe. Sunt in vernaculas linguas transfusi ex Latino quidam, velut infacetissimae Facetiae Poggii, Euryalus et Lucretia, centum fabulae Boccacii. Quos omnes libros conscripserunt homines otiosi, male feriati, imperiti, vitiis ac spurcitiae dediti, in queis miror quid delectet nisi tam nobis flagitia blandirentur. Eruditio non est exspectanda ab hominibus qui ne umbram quidem eruditionis viderant. Iam cum narrant, quae potest esse delectatio in rebus quas tam aperte et stulte confingunt? Hic occidit solus viginti, ille triginta; alius sexcentis vulneribus confossus ac pro mortuo iam derelictus, surgit protinus et postridie sanitati viribusque redditus, singulari certamine duos Gigantes prosternit; tum procedit onustus auro, argento, serico, gemmis, quantum nec oneraria navis posset portare.

32. Quae insania est iis duci aut teneri? Deinde argutum nihil est praeter quaedam verba ex penitissimis Veneris scriniis deprompta, quae in tempore dicuntur ad permovendam concutiendamque quam ames, si forte sit paulo constantior. Si propter haec leguntur, satius erit libros de arte lenonia (sit honos auribus) scribi. Nam in aliis rebus argutae quae possunt proficisci ab scriptore omnis bonae artis experte? Nec ullum audivi affirmantem illos sibi libros placere nisi qui nullos attigisset bonos. Et ipse interdum legi nec ullum repperi vel bonae mentis vel melioris ingenii vestigium. Nam eis qui eiusmodi laudant, quorum ipse quosdam novi, ita demum fidem habebo, si id dixerint postquam Senecam aut Ciceronem aut Hieronymum aut Sacras litteras degustarint, moribus quoque fuerint non omnino corruptissimi. Nam

---

1 Ponthus **HBV** Punthus **WW**[2] // 2 Magalona *scr.* Margalona **HWW**[2] / domina inexorabilis **Γ** *deest in* HMaguelona **BV** // 3 Turias *scr.* Curias **HΓ** // 5 Euryalus et Lucretia **Γ** Aeneae Silvii Euryalus et Lucretia **H** // 5–6 centum fabulae Boccacii **Γ** *deest in* **H** // 10 confingunt **Γ** mentiuntur **H** // 11–12 iam derelictus **Γ** contemptus **H** // 12 protinus **Γ** *deest in* **H** // 13 procedit **Γ** prodit **H** // 15 aut teneri **Γ** *deest in* **H** // 17 paulo **Γ** *deest in* **H** // 20 experte **Γ** experto **H** // 25 moribus ... corruptissimi **Γ** et mores etiam in meliores nonnihil mutarint **H**

---

was originally told by Ovid (*Metamorphoses*, 4, 450–665). There were many versions of it in various languages, beginning with the 12th c. Old French romance *Pyramus et Tisbé*.

   Facetiae : a collection of anecdotes and witty sayings by Poggio Bracciolini first published in 1470, which are, contrary to what Vives says, quite facetious. They were translated into French in 1480 and into Italian in 1483.

   Euryalus and Lucretia: Historia de duobus amantibus was written by Enea Silvio Piccolomini, Pope Pius II, in 1444, a love story in the style of Boccaccio, widely translated. The Spanish translation was published in Salamanca, 1496.

   Decameron: Vives seems to have thought that the *Decameron* was written in Latin. It was translated into Catalan in 1429 and into Spanish c.1450.

the brothel-keeper, begetter of wickedness, the *Cárcel de amor*. In France there are Lancelot du Lac, Paris and Vienna, Ponthus and Sidonia, Pierre of Provence, Maguelonne, and Melusine, the heartless mistress. Here in Flanders there are Flores and Blanchefleur, Leonella and Canamoro, Turias and Floret, Pyramus and Thisbe. There are some translated from Latin into the vernacular languages, like Poggio's unfacetious *Facetiae*, *Euryalus and Lucretia*, the *Decameron* of Boccaccio. All these books were written by idle, unoccupied, ignorant men, the slaves of vice and filth. I wonder what it is that delights us in these books unless it be that we are attracted by indecency. Learning is not to be expected from authors who never saw even a shadow of learning. As for their story-telling, what pleasure is to be derived from the things they invent, full of lies and stupidity? This hero killed twenty single-handed, that one thirty, another with six-hundred gaping wounds and left for dead suddenly rises to his feet and the next day, restored to health and strength, lays two giants low in a single battle; then he proceeds on his way, laden with gold, silver, silks, and jewels in such quantity that even a cargo ship could not carry them.

32. What madness it is to be drawn and fascinated by these tales! There is nothing clever here except for some words taken from the secret archives of Venus, which are spoken at the propitious moment to impress and arouse the one you love if she shows some resistance. If they are read for that reason it would be better to write books on the art of whoring (*sit venia verbi*). For on other subjects what cleverness can come of a writer who is devoid of every good skill? I never heard of anyone who liked these books except one who had never come in contact with good books. I have read some of them myself but never found any trace of a good mind or superior talent. I will lend credence to those who praise such books, some of whom I know personally, if they say this after having had a taste of Cicero or Jerome or the Sacred Scriptures, and if they were not completely depraved themselves. For the most part their

31. France: *Paris et Vienne* (1342) by Pierre de la Céspède tells of the love of the knight Paris and the daughter of the dauphin of Vienna. *Ponthus et la belle Sidoine* (end of the 14th c.) was a kind of composite of all chivalric tales. There are twenty editions of it in all the languages of Europe. *Pierre de Provence et la belle Maguelonne* (anonymous, 1478) was inspired by a local legend of Languedoc; it was translated into Spanish as the *Historia de la linda Magalona y Pierres de Provenza* (1519). *Mélusine* (1387) tells of a fairy of French folklore who turns into a serpent every Saturday.

Flanders: *Floire et Blanchefleur* is an early 13th c. *roman d'aventure* in which the separated lovers are rejoined after many vicissitudes in the emir's seraglio. The story was well known in Flanders from a translation made in the 13th c. by Diederic van Assende, *Floris ende Blancefloer*, and there were twenty printings of the tale by 1517. *Historia del rey Canamoro y de Turián su hijo*, drawn from Breton sources, appeared in 1505. Leonella is Canamoro's wife and Turián his son, whose love for Floreta forms the sequel of the story. *Turias ende Floreta* was published in 1523 in Brussels, but we have only the first few pages of it, enough to show that the story of Canamoro also existed in Flemish. The story of the ill-starred lovers, Pyramus and Thisbe,

plerumque ea sola est laudandi causa, quod in illis ceu in speculo mores suos contemplentur et approbari gaudeant. Postremo, etsi essent acutissima, si iucunda, nolim tamen voluptatem veneno illitam nec exacui feminam meam ad flagitium.

33. Profecto ridenda est maritorum dementia qui permittunt suis uxoribus ut eiusmodi legendis libris astutius sint pravae. Quid de ineptis et imperitis scriptoribus loquar, cum acutissimos iuxta et doctissimos poetas Graecos Latinosque qui amatoria cecinerunt vetet Ovidius attingi ab eo qui mores impudicos fugiat? Quid dici potest Callimacho, Phileta, Anacreonte, Sappho, Tibullo, Propertio, Cornelio Gallo poetis iucundius, dulcius, suavius, argutius, omni eruditionis genere excultius, atque expolitius, quorum ingenium et Musas tota Graecia, tota Italia, totus orbis admiratus est? Et tamen reiciendos castis praecipit, inquiens in secundo libro de Remedio amoris:

> Eloquar invitus: teneros ne tange poetas!
> Summoveo dotes impius ipse meas.
> Callimachum fugito, non est inimicus amori;
> Et cum Callimacho tu quoque, Coe, noces.
> Me certe Sappho meliorem fecit amicae,
> Nec rigidos mores Teia Musa dedit.
> Carmina quis potuit tuto legisse Tibulli?
> Vel tua, cuius opus Cynthia sola fuit?
> Quis potuit lecto durus discedere Gallo?

Ad postremum se quoque vitari iubet:

> Et mea (inquit) nescio quid carmina tale sonant.

Sonant certe, et ea de causa a bono principe in exilium meritissimum ad Getas expulsus es; in quo subit admirari severitatem vel saeculi vel principis illius.

34. Vivimus in civitate Christiana. Quis hodie auctori similium carminum vel leviter succenset? Succenset vero? Quis non amplectitur, non favet? Pellit Plato ex re publica quam instituit bonorum hominum Homerum et Hesiodum poetas. At hi quid turpe habent prae Arte amandi Ovidii, quae a nobis legitur, habetur in manibus, teritur, ediscitur? Sunt magistri

---

33. (Eloquar ... sonant) *Ov. rem. 757–766*
34. (Pellit ... poetas) *Plat. rep. 3, 398A*

2 contemplentur et approbari gaudeant **Γ** cernant **H** / essent acutissima **Γ** acutissima sint **H** // 3 nolim **Γ** nolo **H** // 6 pravae **Γ** sceleratae **H** // 7 iuxta **Γ** pariter **H** // 8 cecinerunt vetet **Γ** scripserunt nolit **H** // 11–12 quorum ingenium et Musas **Γ** quos auctores **H** // 23 vitari **Γ** vitandum **H** // 25 ea de causa a bono **Γ** ideo ab optimo **H** / exilium meritissimum **Γ** meritissimum exilium **H** // 26 es **Γ** *deest in* **H** // 29 Succenset vero ... favet **Γ** *deest in* **H** // 30 Pellit **Γ** Eicit **H** / bonorum hominum **Γ** hominum sapientum **H**

only reason for awarding praise is that they see their own morals reflected in them as in a mirror and are happy to find approval. Finally, even if they were very witty and pleasant, I would not want sensual pleasure that is smeared with poison or that a woman be spurred on to shameful conduct.

33. Surely one can only deride the madness of husbands who allow their wives to read these books so that they may be more clever in their depravity. What shall I say of foolish and ignorant writers when Ovid counsels that the most sagacious and learned Greek and Latin poets who sang of love should be avoided by those who shun immorality? What can be imagined more pleasant, more charming, more delightful, more clever, more cultivated and refined in every kind of learning than the poets Callimachus, Philetas, Anacreon, Sappho, Tibullus, Propertius, Cornelius Gallus, whose talents and inspiration drew the admiration of all of Greece, all of Italy and the whole world? And yet Ovid teaches that they must be repudiated by the chaste, saying in the second book of *The Remedy of Love*:

> Reluctantly I say, eschew the poets of love.
> I cast away my own poetic gift, for shame!
> Beware Callimachus, no enemy of love,
> And the Coan bard can also do you harm,
> Sappho surely made me please my mistress more,
> And the Teian Muse gave no stern morals.
> Who could read Tibullus with impunity
> Or the poet who sang of Cynthia alone?
> Who could depart from Gallus unmoved by love?

and at the end he prohibits the reading of his own poetry:

> And my own poems, too, emit a similar ring.

They have that ring indeed and for that reason you were driven into a most deserved exile among the Getae by a good ruler, an action which solicits our admiration for the strict morals either of the times or of the ruler.

34. We live in a Christian city. Who expresses even slight displeasure with an author of such poems nowadays? Do I say displeasure? Who does not embrace them with enthusiasm and commend them? Plato expels the poets Homer and Hesiod from the republic of good men that he instituted. But what immorality is to be found in them in comparison with Ovid's *Art of Love*, which we read, carry about with us, wear out with use and learn

---

33. Coan bard: The pastoral poet Theocritus (c.300–260 B.C.)

Teian Muse: Anacreon of Teos (born c.570 B.C.), lyric poet, who composed many love poems and convivial poems.

poet who sang of Cynthia: Propertius, elegiac poet of Augustan Rome.

Gallus: Contemporary of Virgil, wrote four books of elegies, of which only a few verses remain.

Getae: A Thracian tribe living by the Danube in the region where Ovid was exiled.

qui suis discipulis praelegant; sunt qui, editis commentariis, nequitiae viam
aperiant. Videlicet Ovidium Augustus relegavit et hos Ovidii interpretes
in civitate retinuisset? Nisi plus esse credimus scripsisse turpia quam explicare et nova adolescentiae pectora tam honestis fecundare seminibus.
5 Exul est qui pondera, qui mensuras fraudavit; exuritur qui adulteravit
nummum, qui falsavit instrumentum; in rebus parvis qui tumultus? Et
honoratus est in civitate atque etiam magister sapientiae corruptor iuventutis? Feminae igitur hi omnes libri non secus quam vipera vel scorpius
aversandi sunt. Si qua est quae sic horum librorum teneatur lectione ut
10 ponere de manibus nolit, huic non modo illi extorquendi sunt, sed si aegre
ac invita meliores evolvit, danda opera vel a parentibus vel ab amicis ut
nullos legendo litteras desuescat, et (si fieri potest) dediscat penitus. Consultius est enim bona re carere quam male uti. Proba femina nec tales
libros in manus sumet nec spurcis cantiunculis os suum contaminabit et
15 quantum praestare poterit efficiet ut aliae similes sui sint bene agendo
simul et bene monendo; adde his etiam iubendo et praecipiendo, si hoc ei
liceat.

35. Porro quinam libri sint legendi (nam hoc quaerat aliquis) de quibusdam nemini non constat, velut de Evangeliis Domini, de Apostolicis tum
20 actis, tum Epistolis, de historicis et moralibus Veteris Instrumenti, de Cypri-
ano, Hieronymo, Augustino, Ambrosio, Chrysostomo, Hilario, Gregorio,
Boethio, Fulgentio, Tertulliano, Platone, Cicerone, Seneca et similibus.
Super quibusdam consulendi sunt docti et cordati viri, ne temere suum
iudicium sequetur femina nec leviter disciplinis et litteris intincta falsa pro
25 veris, perniciosa pro salubribus, inepta et stulta pro gravibus et appro-
batis admittat. Erit omnino sciendi cupida ut rectius vivat, in iudicando
autem meticulosa. Nec de dubiis pronuntiabit, sed tenebit ea quae vel
Ecclesiae auctoritate videbit approbata vel consensu optimorum. Et mem-
inerit semper ac recolet non de nihilo esse quod Paulus docendi aut lo-
30 quendi in ecclesia munere feminis interdixit, sed subdi viris et tacitas quae
opus sit addiscere. Neque vero poetis carebit si capiatur numeris. Aderunt

---

35. (Paulus ... addiscere) *Vulg. I Cor. 14, 34–35*

1–2 nequitiae viam aperiant Γ flagitia declarent H // **4** nova ... seminibus Γ teneros
iuventutis animos illis imbuere H // **6** qui tumultus Γ quanta tragedia H // **9** aversandi
sunt Γ vitandi H // **12** litteras desuescat Γ litteris desuescat H / penitus Γ *deest in* H //
12–13 Consultius Γ melius H // **15–16** sint ... etiam Γ sint simul bene agendo simul bene
monendo, tum etiam H // **17** liceat Γ licet H // **18** nam hoc quaerat aliquis Γ *deest in* H //
19 nemini Γ nullis H // **20** de historicis ... Instrumenti Γ de Vetere Testamento H // **21**
Chrysostomo Γ *deest in* H // **22** Boethio *scr.* Boetho Γ Boetio H / Fulgentio, Tertulliano Γ
deest in H // **23** docti Γ graves H / ne H nec Γ // **26**–p.52,2 Erit ... concedant Γ *deest
in* H

by heart? There are some teachers who give lessons on it to their pupils, others who write commentaries and open up the path to iniquity. Are we to suppose that Augustus, who sent him into exile, would have kept these interpreters of Ovid in the Roman republic? Not unless we think it is worse to write immoral things than to expound them and sow the seeds of such 'ethical' principles in the innocent minds of youth. Exile is the punishment of those who falsify weights and measurements. One who counterfeits money or falsifies a document is burned at the stake. In small matters such ado! And is a corruptor of youth to be given honor in a city and regarded as a master of wisdom? Therefore a woman should avoid these books as she would a viper or a scorpion. And if a woman is so enthralled by the reading of these books that she will not put them down, they should not only be wrested from her hands, but if she shows unwillingness to peruse better books, her parents or friends should see to it that she read no books at all and become disaccustomed to the reading of literature, and if possible, unlearn it altogether. For it is better to be deprived of a good thing rather than make ill use of it. A good woman will not take such books into her hands nor will she defile her mouth with obscene songs, and as far as she can, she will bring it about that others be like her by her good actions and admonitions, and I should add, by direction and instruction, if that is possible.

35. As for what books should be read (for someone will ask me this), there are some on which everyone is agreed, as the Gospels of the Lord, the Acts of the Apostles and the epistles, the historical and moral books of the Old Testament, Cyprian, Jerome, Augustine, Ambrose, Chrysostom, Hilary, Gregory, Boethius, Fulgentius, Tertullian, Plato, Cicero, Seneca and other such authors. But in the case of certain books the advice of learned and sensible men must be sought. A woman must not rashly follow her own judgement lest with her slight initiation into learning and the study of letters she take false for true, harmful for salutary, foolish and senseless for serious and commendable. Her whole motivation for learning should be to live more uprightly and she should be meticulous in her judgement. She will not give her affirmation to dubious statements, but will hold firm to what is approved by the authority of the Church or the unanimous accord of good men. She will always remember and bear in mind that it was not without reason that Saint Paul forbade women the faculty of teaching or speaking in church and that they should be subject to men and silently learn what it behooves her to learn. There need not be any lack of poets if a woman takes delight in the rhythm of poetry. She may read

Prudentius, Arator, Prosper, Iuvencus, Paulinus, qui non multum antiquis concedant. Inveniet profecto in auctoribus lectu dignis omnia acutiora, pleniora, maioris et certioris voluptatis, pastum denique animi iucundissimum, quae omnia tum vitae prosint tum animum mentemque mira delectatione
5 perfundant.

36. Itaque festis diebus assiduo et profestis interdum legenda vel audienda sunt quae mentem in Deum extollant, quae pectus in quietem Christianam componant, quae mores meliores reddant. Optimum erit, antequam ad rem sacram exeas, Evangelium domi et Epistolam eius diei legere, addita, si
10 habes, expositiuncula. Sacris operata ubi domum redieris remque familiarem curaris si qua ad te illius spectat cura, sedato et tranquillo animo aliquid ex illis legere quae diximus, si modo scis legere, sin nescis, audire. Profestis aliquot diebus idem agito, praesertim si aliis operibus domi necessariis non impediris, magis etiam, si libri sint ad manum, maxime cum intervallum
15 est inter festa solito maius. Cave credas ferias esse ab Ecclesia institutas ut ludas, ut otiosa confabuleris cum aequalibus, sed ut tum demum intentius et tranquilliore mente de Deo cogites, de vita hac nostra brevissima deque illa in caelis sempiterna.

CAP. VI.   DE VIRGINITATE

20 **37.** Tanta est virginitas tamque admirabilis ut pauca de illa dici nec possint nec debeant. Nos tamen institutam brevitatem obtinebimus, ut qui recordamur praeceptores esse nos, non praecones. Virginitatem voco integritatem mentis, quae etiam in corpus dimanet; integritatem porro ab omni corruptione ac contagio. Huius generis vita nulla est caelesti similior. Illic enim,
25 abrogata lege carnis, tamquam angeli Dei erimus, nihil iam deinceps a sexu sentientes, ubi nullae nec virorum erunt nec feminarum nuptiae.

---

37. (angeli ... nuptiae) *Vulg. Matth. 22, 30* // (nullae ... nuptiae) *Vulg. Luc. 20, 35* //

4 omnia Γ *deest in* **H** / mentemque Γ *deest in* **H** // **7** pectus Γ animum **H** // **12** sin Γ si **H** // **12–13** Profestis aliquot diebus Γ profestis vero diebus aliquot **H** // **14–15** cum ... maius Γ cum aliquot dierum intervallum est inter festa **H** // **17** brevissima *deest in* **H** // **18** sempiterna Γ futura **H** // **20**–p.54,**28** Tanta ... convertit Γ *deest in* **H** *in quo legitur:* Iam mihi totus sermo erit cum puella, quae in se incomparabile habet bonum, mentis carnisque integritatem. Tot occurrunt dicenda, ut initium non inveniam an illinc praestabit exordiri unde Augustinus de sancta virginitate verba facturus. **H**

Prudentius, Arator, Prosper, Juvencus, Paulinus, who have little to yield to the ancients. She will find without question in authors worth reading more ingenuity, more abundance, greater and surer pleasure, in brief a most pleasant food for the soul, all of which will be of more profit for life and will suffuse the mind and heart with infinite delight.

36. Therefore, on feast days with constant application, and intermittently on ordinary working days they must read and hear things which will elevate their minds to God, compose their feelings in a Christian tranquillity, and improve their morals. It is an excellent practice before going out to hear Mass to read the gospel and epistle of that day at home and a commentary if you have one. After assisting at the holy sacrifice, when you return home and have tended to your domestic cares, if this is part of your duties, read something from the Scriptures with a calm and tranquil spirit, if you know how to read, and if not, listen. On some working days do the same thing, especially if it does not interfere with other domestic chores, and, in particular, if the books are to hand and if there is a longer interval than usual between feast days. Do not think that holy days were instituted by the church for you to amuse yourself and engage in idle conversation with your companions, but that you might turn your thoughts to God more intently and with a calmer spirit, and meditate about the brevity of this life and everlasting life in heaven.

CHAPTER 6. ON VIRGINITY .

37. Virginity is such a great and noble subject that any discussion of it neither can nor should be brief. Nevertheless, I will adhere to my proposed brevity, remembering that I am a teacher, not a panegyrist. I define virginity as integrity of the mind, which extends also to the body, an integrity free of all corruption and contamination. No way of life is more like that led in heaven. For there where the law of the flesh is abrogated we will be as angels, feeling no sexual urges, where no man or woman will be given in marriage.

35. Prudentius-Paulinus: All Christian poets who wrote in the meters and style of the pagan poets. The first of them chronologically is Juvencus, a noble Spaniard who composed an epic poem on the Gospels during the reign of Constantine. Prudentius (348–c.405), also a Spaniard, the greatest of the Christian poets, known especially for his allegorical epic, the *Psychomachia*. Paulinus (335–431) was born of a rich senatorial family in Bordeaux and studied under the poet Ausonius. He married a wealthy Spanish lady named Therasia and removed to Spain for a while. Converted to Christianity he eventually became bishop of Nola in Campania. He wrote hymns and poems in very elegant classical Latin. Prosper of Aquitaine, born at the beginning of the 5th c., composed a series of epigrams on Augustinian maxims, which are more didactic than poetic. Arator, a poet of the 6th c. perhaps born in Milan, wrote a long poem in hexameters, in which he versified the *Acts of the Apostles*.

Quid inter res conditas vel purius est angelicis mentibus vel a sexu et
commistione generationis et corporis servitute liberius? Quid inter homines
magis hoc exprimit quam virginitas? Ceterum puritatis huius ac sinceritatis
praecipua pars ac prope tota in animo est sita, in quo et fons virtutum
omnium. Nam corpus terrenum ac brutum administrum est solum nostrae voluntatis neque illud spectat Deus aut curat, alienissimum a se, sed
mentem, naturam sibi similem et quadamtenus propinquam. Quapropter
quae contaminato animo corpus integrum servant, virginitatis sibi vel nomen
stulte arrogant vel laudem. Huiusmodi Dominus in Evangelio suo virgines
appellat fatuas, quae non aliter virgines sunt quam mortuae vel depictae.
Quid enim fatuum nisi quod saporem naturae non resipit? Virgo fortassis
hominibus fuerit qui oculis carneis carnem intuentur. Deo profecto non
erit qui spiritus spiritu cernit. Quid quod ne hominibus quidem est pro
virgine? Declamator ille de saeculo incestam esse eam pronuntiat, etiam
sine stupro, quae cupit stuprum. Si quae contagium in se hominis admittit,
virginitatis amittit decus et nomen. Quae diabolis prostituta est quomodo
poterit virgo Christi nominari? Quae conventio Christi ad Belial? Quid
purissimo Deo cum animo impuro? Nec immerito discessum a Deo Sacrae
litterae fornicationem appellant, quod animus noster castitatem suam, uni
Deo debitam, adulteris prostituit. Recte Fulgentius: 'Virginitatem,' inquit,
'carnis per hominem nititur diabolus praeripere, cordis vero virginitatem per
se ipsum conatur auferre.'

38. Illuc ergo admovenda sunt validiora praesidia quo maius periculum
incumbit. Mens est diligenter munienda, ne in virgineo sit corpore violata, ut
omnes divitiae, omnis pulchritudo integritatis ibi firma atque inexpugnabilis
perduret. Filia regis, in Psalmo quadragesimo quarto, etiam si ornata aureis
fimbriis et circumamicta varietate, tamen gloriam omnem introrsum convertit. Haec est Ecclesia universa, de qua Augustinus ait quod 'desponsata
est uni viro Christo, sicut Paulus ad Corinthios scribit. Quanto igitur digna
sint honore membra eius quae hoc custodiunt etiam in ipsa carne, quod
tota custodit fide, quae imitantur Matrem viri et Domini sui? Nam Ecclesia
quoque virgo et mater est.' Sic Augustinus. Eiusmodi virgines merito, quod
Fulgentius scribit: 'A virtute nomen accipiunt; istis unigenitus Dei filius,

---

37. (Dominus ... fatuas) *Vulg. Matth. 25, 2* // (incestam ... stuprum) *Sen. contr. 6, 8*
// (Quae ... Belial?) *Vulg. II Cor. 6, 15* // (discessum ... fornicationem) *Vulg. Eph. 5, 5* //
(Virginitatem ... auferre) *Fulg. Rusp. epist. 3, 25, PL 65, 333C*
38. (Filia ... convertit) *Vulg. psalm. 44, 14–15* // (Augustinus) *Aug. virg. 2, PL 40, 397* //
(desponsata ... Christo) *Vulg. II Cor. 11, 2* // (A virtute ... gloriosa) *Fulg. Rusp. epist. 3, 6,*
PL 65, 326C

28 Haec ... desponsata est **Γ** Universa ecclesia virgo est, desponsata **H** // **32**–p.56,**18** Sic
Augustinus ... magistratibus *deest in* **H** *v. appendicem*

What is there in all of creation purer, freer from sex and the carnal relations necessary for procreation, and the slavery of the body than angelic minds? What expresses this more among mankind than virginity? But the essential part of this purity and integrity is situated almost entirely in the mind, which is also the source of all virtues. For the terrestrial and brute body is only the servant of the will, and God does not look to it or have any care for it, a thing totally foreign to him, but attends only to the mind, of a nature similar to his own and to some extent close to it. Consequently those who preserve the body intact but whose mind is defiled foolishly arrogate to themselves the name or the praise proper to virginity. The Lord calls such persons foolish virgins in his gospel, who are no more like virgins than if they were dead or painted. What is meant by foolish but that it does not retain natural taste, that it is insipid? They may perhaps be virgins in the eyes of men, who see with eyes of the flesh. Certainly they will not be so to God, who is a spirit and sees with the spirit. And what of the fact that such a person is not regarded as a virgin even by men? The famous secular orator declared that she is unchaste who even without engaging in an illicit sexual act desires it. If a woman who allows herself to be defiled by a man loses the honor and name of virginity, how will one who has prostituted herself to devils be called a virgin of Christ? What agreement is there between Christ and Belial? What relation between the most pure God and an impure mind? Not without reason do the Sacred Scriptures call fornication a separation from God, because our mind has prostituted its chastity, owed to God alone, to adulterers. Fulgentius said rightly: 'The devil strives to snatch away the virginity of the flesh with the aid of man but virginity of the heart he tries to carry off by himself.'

38. The strongest defenses, therefore, should be moved up where the danger is greatest. The mind must be particularly fortified lest it be defiled in a virgin body, so that all the treasures and beauty of integrity will endure there, firm and unassailable. The daughter of the King in Psalm 44, even if adorned with gold-woven robes and multi-colored brocade, still directs all her glory inward. This is the universal church, which Augustine said 'is espoused to one man, Christ, as Paul writes to the Corinthians. How worthy of honor, therefore, are her members, who preserve in their very flesh what the church preserves with absolute faith, who imitate the mother of their spouse and Lord. For the church is both virgin and mother.' Thus speaks Augustine. Such virgins deservedly, as Fulgentius writes, 'Take their name from virtue. Of these virgins the only begotten son of God and only

unigenitus etiam virginis filius, sponsus est, sanctae virginitatis fructus, decus
et munus, quem corporaliter sancta virginitas peperit, cui spiritualiter sancta
virginitas nubit, a quo sancta virginitas fecundatur ut perseveret intacta, a
quo donatur ut permaneat pulchra, a quo coronatur ut regnet perenniter
5   gloriosa.' Tantum Fulgentius.

39. O felicem vitae condicionem, quae iam nunc in hoc mortali corpore
meditatur quod futuri sumus in aeternitate, quae in Christo patrem habet et
sponsum et filium, ne nihil in illo sit cuius ad virginem ius non pertineat! Sed
tu sponsa es Christi per integritatem mentis. Vide ut maiore sollicitudine ad
10 custodiam huius excubes quam corporis. Ut hanc quidem serves multum
est operae ponendum, sed ut illam multo plurimum sive, ut rectius loquar,
universum. Quantumcumque vales, oculos et aures claude, qua est ingressus
machinis diaboli oppugnantis. Cogitatus rege et habe in tua potestate, ne
arcem animi tui prodant prava aliqua dulcedine illecti ac venditi. Nec exigua
15 res est virginitas corporalis; quam omnes gestant in oculis, vel impudicis
quoque hominibus reverenda, ut non iniuria poetae fabulentur Maiestatem
in terras delapsam ipsis quoque virginibus non aliter assistere quam regibus
et magistratibus. Inter deos ipsos gentilium, alioqui spurcissimos, Cybelen,
quam illi omnes vocabant matrem, virginem fuisse volunt. Diana deis
20 gratiosissima, quod perpetuae se virginitati consecrarit. Minervam tria eximia
suspiciendam reddebant—virginitas, fortitudo, sapientia—et de Iovis cerebro
(quem illi maximum principemque existimabant et patrem deorum ac
hominum) nata fingebatur, unde nefas erat oriri quicquam nisi purum,
castum, sapiens, magnum plane et admirandum. Ita coniunctam putabant
25 sapientiae virginitatem ut eundem septenarium numerum et castitati et
sapientiae dicarint, tum Musas omnes, scientiarum praesides, virgines esse
perhibuerint.

40. In templo Delphici Apollinis sapientissima femina, quae afflatu divino plena consulentibus futura praecinebat, virgo semper fuit, quam vulgo
30 Pythiam cognominabant. Omnes etiam Sibyllas, quas Varro decem numerat,
Hieronymus virgines fuisse perhibet. Romae templum fuit Vestae, cui a virginibus ministrabatur quas Vestales vocabant. Iis assurgebat cunctus Senatus,
his magistratus omnes de via decedebant maximoque in honore fuerunt apud
totum populum Romanum. Semper sacra ac venerabilis res castitas fuit et

---

40. (Varro) *Lact. inst. 1, 6, 8–12* //

18 alioqui Γ *deest in* H // **19** illi Γ *deest in* H / volunt Γ narrant H // **20** consecrarit Γ
sacrarit H // **21** suspiciendam reddebant Γ reddebant admirandam H // **21–23** cerebro
… hominum Γ quem illi maximum principemque exsistimabant deorum cerebro H // **23**
fingebatur **HWW²B** fingebant **V** // **24** magnum plane et admirandum Γ *deest in* H // **25** ut
eundem Γ et H // **27** perhibuerint Γ tradiderunt H // **28** In templo Γ Et in templo H //
29 fuit Γ fuerit H // **33–34** apud totum populum Romanum Γ in toto populo Romano H
// **34** venerabilis Γ *deest in* H // **34**–p.58,1 castitas fuit et potissimum Γ *deest in* H

begotten son of a virgin is spouse, the fruit, glory and reward of holy virginity, whom holy virginity brought forth in the flesh, to whom holy virginity is spiritually wed, by whom holy virginity is made fruitful so that she may persevere intact, by whom she is given the power to remain beautiful, by whom she is crowned so that she will reign forever glorious.' These are the words of Fulgentius.

39. O happy condition of life, that now already in this mortal body practises what we are destined to be in eternity; that has in Christ father, spouse, and son, so that there is nothing in him that does not rightfully belong to the Virgin. But you are a spouse of Christ by virtue of integrity of the mind. See to it that you be vigilant in protecting it with greater solicitude than you would that of the body. To preserve integrity of the body much care must be expended but for the other much more is needed, or to put it more correctly, total vigilance. As far as you can, close your eyes and ears, which give entrance to the machinations the devil makes use of in his assaults upon us. Control your thoughts and hold them in your power lest enticed and corrupted by some perverse attraction they betray the citadel of the mind. Corporal virginity is no small thing, which all carry about in their eyes; it gains the respect even of immoral men, so that the poets are not wrong in imagining that Divine Majesty, descending to earth, lends its assistance to virgins in the same way it does to kings and law-makers. Even among the pagan gods, who were in other respects foul and disgusting, they maintain that Cybele, to whom they gave the title mother, was a virgin. Diana was the darling of the gods because she vowed herself to perpetual virginity. Three distinct qualities gained men's esteem for Minerva: virginity, fortitude and wisdom, and she was imagined as having been born from the brain of Jupiter, whom they considered the greatest and foremost, father of gods and of men. Wherefore it was accounted sacrilege that anything be born of him save that which was pure, chaste and wise, of absolute greatness and nobility. They so linked virginity with wisdom that they dedicated the same number seven to chastity and to wisdom. All of the Muses, the guardians of learning, were reputed to be virgins.

40. In the temple of Apollo at Delphi the very wise woman who was filled with divine inspiration and predicted the future to those who consulted her was always a virgin and was popularly known as the Pythia. All of the Sibyls also, whom Varro puts as ten in number, were virgins according to the testimony of Jerome. At Rome there was a temple to Vesta, served by virgins who were called Vestals. In their presence the entire Senate would rise to its feet, all the magistrates made way for them on the street, and they were held in the greatest honor by the whole Roman people. Chastity was always something sacred and venerable, especially virginity,

58 J. L. VIVES

potissimum virginitas, etiam inter latrones, sacrilegos, facinorosos, nefarios
homines, inter feras quoque bestias tuta et reverenda. 'Thecla,' inquit Divus
Ambrosius, 'naturam bestiarum virginitatis veneratione mutavit.' Tantum
habet virginitas admirationis ut eam vel leones mirentur ipsi. Quanti igitur
5 aestimanda ea res est quae feminas saepenumero ab imperatoribus, a tyrannis, a magnis exercitibus vendicavit ac tutata est? Legimus raptas plerumque
feminas dimissas esse ab insolentissimis militibus, tantum respectu virginalis
nominis, quod videlicet virgines se esse affirmassent. Nefas enim existimabant
propter brevissimam et momentaneam delectationis umbram tantum bonum
10 imminuere malebatque unusquisque tanti facinoris auctorem quemvis potius
esse quam se. O nefariam puellam et vita indignam quae se ultro eo privat
bono, quod rapere milites, omnibus scelerum generibus assuefacti, reformidant, vel amatores ipsi, ardore caeci, furore amentes, cunctantur! Nullus est
enim amans tam perditus, cui si succurrat virginem esse quam deperit, non
15 expergiscatur, non oculos aperiat, non sumat iudicium, non deliberet quid
sit acturus et de mutanda mente consultet. Usque adeo expavent omnes
tanti pretii bonum tollere, quod postea nec retinere ipsi possunt nec reddere,
cum tamen nihil ipsis depereat. Scelerata puella non contremiscit id perdere,
quod perditum semel recuperare in posterum nulla ratione valeat, cum
20 maximum quod habebat bonum ipsi pereat?

41. Et si affectus aliquid valent, ut valere plurimum par est iustos
praesertim et honestos, vertat se quoquo volet puella, amissa pudicitia,
omnia inveniet sua causa tristia, maesta, lamentantia, lugentia, irata sibi et
infesta. Quis dolor consanguineorum cum se omnes dehonestari sentiunt
25 unica puellae illius turpitudine? Quis maeror, quae lacrimae parentum et
nutriciorum? Haec gaudia rependis pro tot sollicitudinibus, tot laboribus?
Estne hoc praemium educationis? Quae detestatio familiarium, qui sermones
vicinorum, amicorum, notorum, exsecrantium sceleratam iuvenem? Quae
irrisio, quae fabulae aemularum virginum, quae aversio amicarum, quae
30 undique fuga et solitudo, cum unaquaeque mater non filias modo, sed etiam
filios a contagio tam pravae atque impurae mentis procul arcet? Quid quod

---

40. (Thecla ... ipsi) *Ambr. virg. 2, 3, 19, PL 16, 211C*

2 tuta et reverenda Γ *deest in* H // 4 vel leones mirentur ipsi Γ etiam leones mirentur H /
Quanti *hic incipit novum capitulum in* H *qui* DE CURA VIRGINITATIS ET PUDICITIAE *inscribitur* // 6
vendicavit ac Γ *deest in* H // 7 respectu Γ una reverentia H // 8 videlicet Γ *deest in* H // 9
umbram Γ imaginem H // 10–11 potius esse Γ potius alium esse H // 11 eo Γ tanto H
// 12 scelerum generibus Γ sceleribus H // 12–13 reformidant Γ exhorrent H // 13 vel
amatores ipsi ... cunctantur Γ etiam amatores ardore caeci cunctantur H // 14 amans tam
perditus Γ tam perditus amator H / succurrat Γ cogitet H / deperit Γ adamat H // 18
contremiscit Γ timet H // 26 nutriciorum HWW² nutritorum BV // 27 qui sermones Γ
quae voces H // 30 et solitudo Γ undique solitudo H // 31 a contagio HW contagio W²BV

even among thieves, men of impiety, criminals and wicked men, and even among wild beasts it was safe and respected. 'Thecla' says St. Ambrose, 'transformed the nature of beasts through the veneration they paid to her virginity.' So much admiration does virginity elicit that lions stand in awe of it. Of how much worth, therefore, is that quality which has so often freed and defended women from emperors, tyrants and mighty armies? We read that very often abducted women were released by arrogant soldiers, solely out of respect for the name of virgin, because, that is, they had declared themselves virgins. For they thought it a great crime to violate such a great good for a brief and momentary semblance of pleasure and each one preferred that anyone but himself should be the perpetrator of such a villainous deed. O wicked girl, unworthy of life, who willingly deprives herself of that boon which soldiers, inured to every kind of crime, shrink from seizing? Even lovers blind with passion and mad with desire hesitate, for there is no lover so desperate who if he reflects that the woman who is the object of his passion is a virgin, does not bestir himself, open his eyes, exercise his judgement, consider on what he is about to do, and think of changing his mind. To such an extent are all in fear of taking away a blessing of such price, which afterwards they can neither retain themselves nor give back, although they are not losing anything themselves.

41. Is a stupid girl not greatly perturbed about losing what, once lost, she cannot in any way recover afterwards, especially since it is she herself who is depriving herself of her greatest good? And if feelings have any power, as it is reasonable that just and honorable feelings should, turn wherever she will, a girl who has lost her chastity will find through her own fault everything sad, unhappy, mournful, hateful and hostile to her. What will be the sorrow of her relatives when they sense that they are all dishonored because of the base conduct of one girl? What will be their grief? What tears will be shed by parents and those who nurtured her? Are these the joys with which you repay them in return for all their anxieties and labors? Is this the reward for your upbringing? What hatred will this arouse in the members of your household! What will be the talk of neighbors, friends and acquaintances in denunciation of this wicked young girl, what derision! What gossip there will be among girls of her own age, what loathing her girl friends will have for her! How she will be avoided wherever she goes! What desolation she will find when mothers keep not only their daughters but their sons far away from the contagion of such a defiled and unclean mind? Even

etiam proci, si quos habebat, discedunt et qui prius amorem simulabant nunc aperte oderunt? Interim etiam detectis verbis exprobrant scelus, ut mirer posse puellae, quae haec videat, non dico vitam iucundam esse, sed omnino ullam esse et non protinus maerore contabescere.

42. Iam quid dicam odia et iras omnium, quibus scimus a multis patribus iugulatas esse filias, a fratribus sorores, a tutoribus pupillas, a consanguineis consanguineas? Hippomenes, Atheniensium princeps, cum filiam vitiatam a quodam deprehendisset, eam cum equo ferocissimo in equili sine cibo conclusit. Equus cum diu inediam tolerasset, naturae etiam truculentia versus in rabiem, puellam dilaniavit ut se pasceret. Pontius Aufedianus Romae, ubi filiam suam Fannio Saturnino a paedagogo proditam comperisset, et servum et filiam interemit. Publius Attilius Filiscus filiam, quod se stupri foeditate contaminaverat, trucidavit. Inventus est in eadem urbe L. Verginius, centurio, qui filiam integram amittere maluerit quam habere vitiatam. Ideo Verginiam suam unicam, carissimam, ne Decemviri libidini servire cogeretur, quando alia nulla re poterat, cultro et oblata morte vendicavit. Patrum memoria in Hispania Tarraconensi duo fratres, quod sororem quam virginem credebant ferre uterum deprehendissent, dolore quousque enixa esset dissimulato et cohibito, simul fetum utero emisit, inspectante obstetrice gladiis in ventrem adactis confecerunt. In eadem Hispaniae parte, me puero, tres virgines sodalem puellam, quam in obsceno facinore deprehenderant, praelargo linteo praefocarunt. Plena est exemplorum historia, plenus vitae communis usus. Nec mirum est haec a patribus et necessariis designari et in tantum odium caritatis affectum subito mutari, cum ipsae, abominando et saevo amore actae, omni prorsus ex pectore eiecta pietate, parentes, fratres, filios etiam oderint, non tantum amicos et familiares. Atque haec non solas puellas velim de se dicta existimare, sed maritas quoque et viduas, omnes in summa feminas.

43. Iam vertat se ad se ipsa femina et suum scelus consideret. Ipsa se formidabit atque exhorrebit nec noctibus nec diebus quiescet, exagitata semper conscientiae flagello et incensa velut facibus ardentibus. A nemine intentius conspicietur quin eum aliquid de suo facinore scire vereatur eique tunc venire in mentem. Nemo summissius loquetur quin de suo scelere

---

42. (Hippomenes) *Ov. Ib., 335* // (Pontius Aufedianus) *Val. Max. 6, 1, 3* // (Publius Attilius Filiscus) *Val. Max. 6, 1, 6* // (Verginius) *Val. Max. 6, 1, 2*

1 habebat **H** habebant **Γ** // 4 contabescere **HV** contabescat **WW²B** // 8 equili **Γ** stabulo **H** // 9 truculentia **Γ** ferocitate **H** // 12–13 se ... trucidavit **Γ** stupri se crimine coinquinaverat, interemit **H** // 17 quod **Γ** cum **H** // 18 deprehendissent **Γ** vidissent **H** // 18–19 dolore ... dissimulato **Γ** dolorem ... dissimularunt **H** // 23 designari **Γ** fieri **H** // 24 mutari **Γ** verti **H** // 27 dicta **Γ** dictum **H** / maritas **W** maritos **W²BV** coniugatas **H** // 30 formidabit **Γ** metuet **H**

her wooers, if she had any, take leave of her, and those who previously simulated love for her now express their scorn openly. In the meantime, giving open expression to their feelings, they reproach her for her misdeed to such a degree that I cannot imagine how a young girl, seeing this, can have any life at all, never mind an enjoyable one, and not be immediately consumed with grief.

42. Need I recount the universal hatred and wrath that caused daughters to be slaughtered by their parents, sisters by their brothers, wards by their guardians, kinsmen by kinsmen? When Hippomenes, leader of the Athenians, discovered that his daughter had been deflowered by a certain individual, he shut her in a stable with a ferocious, starving horse. When the horse had suffered starvation for a long time, driven to a frenzy by its savage nature, it tore the girl to pieces for its food. When Pontius Aufedianius found out that his daughter had been delivered over to Fannius Saturninus by her slave tutor, he killed both slave and daughter. Publius Attilius Filiscus butchered his daughter because she had defiled herself by losing her virginity. In the same city of Rome we encounter the centurion, Lucius Verginius, who preferred to lose his daughter, still inviolate, rather than keep her after she was defiled. Therefore he defended his only beloved daughter Verginia from the lust of the decemvir in the only way he could, offering her as a sacrificial victim by his own hand. In the memory of our fathers it is related that there were brothers in the Tarragon province of Spain, who when they discovered that their sister, whom they believed to be a virgin, was pregnant, concealing and restraining the sorrow until the time she would give birth, as soon as the new-born child emerged from her womb, under the eyes of the midwife, thrust their swords into her belly and dispatched her. In that same part of Spain, when I was a boy, three young girls suffocated a companion of theirs with a large linen cloth when they caught her in an obscene act. History is full of examples, as is the common experience of life. It is not to be marvelled at that such things are done by parents and close friends and that feelings of affection are suddenly changed into the most violent hatred, since these young women themselves, victims of a detestable and savage love, casting away all filial piety from their hearts, have shown hatred for their parents, brothers, even children, not merely friends and relatives. And I should wish that not only young women should consider this as said to them alone, but it applies also to married women and widows, in a word, to all women.

43. Now let the woman turn her attention upon herself and reflect upon her crime. She will fear and be terrified of herself and will find no peace either by day or by night, constantly goaded by her conscience, inflamed as if by burning torches. She will not suffer anyone to gaze at her intently without suspecting that he knows something of her misdeed and that it now occurs to his mind. No one will speak in hushed tones without her thinking that he is

loqui illum putet. Non audiet sermonem de nefariis feminis quin propter se
suspicetur dici. Non audiet nomen corruptoris, etiam in quovis alio, nominari
quin oblique se peti metuat. Nullus strepet occulte domi quin palam factum
scelus suum paveat et se iam iam punitum iri. Serviendum est iis omnibus
quos aliquid suspicetur suspicari; demisse agendum et abiecte, ne si quid
paulo vel liberius dicat vel erectius agat, continuo obiciatur illi dedecus suum.
Semper consternata, semper exanimata vivet, immo non vivet sed privabitur
morte corporis, cum toties animo enecetur.

44. Quae regna velles hoc perpetuo cruciatu empta? Hunc viri con-
scelerati patiuntur, sed feminae longe acerbius, quo foediora sunt omnibus
earum delicta et natura est meticulosior. Ac nimirum si quis expendat accuratius, dignae sunt tum iis malis tum etiam peioribus feminae quae parum
diligenter pudicitiam custodiunt. Nam viro multa sunt necessaria–prudentia,
eloquentia, peritia rei publicae, ingenium, memoria, ars vitae aliqua, iustitia,
liberalitas, magnanimitas et alia, quae omnia longum esset persequi. Horum
aliquid si absit, minus videtur culpandum, si modo adsint nonnulla. At in
muliere nemo vel eloquentiam requirit, vel ingenium, vel prudentiam, vel
artes vitae, vel administrationem rei publicae, vel iustitiam, vel benignitatem,
nemo denique quicquam aliud praeter pudicitiam. Quae sola si desideretur,
perinde est ac si viro desint omnia, quippe in femina pudicitia instar est
omnium. Ignavus et iners custos est qui unicam rem commissam et fidei
suae creditam multisque commendatam verbis et anxie nequit custodire,
praesertim ubi nemo extorturus est invito ac ne nolenti quidem tacturus. Id
unum femina si cogitarit, attentior erit et cautior custos suae pudicitiae. Qua
una ut salva, cetera ipsi omnia in tuto sunt; ita perdita, universa semel cum
ea pereunt. 'Quid enim salvi est mulieri, amissa pudicitia?' inquit Lucretia,
cui tamen animus castus erat in corpore inquinato. Idcirco, 'condito in
viscera sua ferro', ut Quintilianus inquit, 'poenam necessitatis exegit, ut
quamprimum pudicus animus a polluto corpore separaretur.' Non quod
factum imitandum proponam, sed mentem, ut nihil mulieri restare credas,
quae pudicitiam abiecit. Adimas feminae formam, genus, opes, venustatem,
eloquentiam, acumen ingenii, peritiam suarum artium; addas tamen castitatem, omnia cumulatissime dedisti. Contra, largiaris plena manu illa omnia

---

44. (Quid ... pudicitia?) *Liv. 1, 57, 7* // (condito ... separaretur) *Ps. Quint. decl. 3, 11*

4–8 Serviendum ... enecetur Γ *deest in* H // **6** dicat W dicet W²BV // **9** empta? Hunc
viri Γ empta quem multi putant non alium apud inferos futurum. Eundem et viri H // **11**
delicta Γ crimina H / est Γ *deest in* H // **11–12** expendat accuratius Γ accuratius expendat H
// **18** benignitatem Γ liberalitatem H // **22** et anxie Γ *deest in* H // **23** Id Γ Quod H
// **25** ipsi omnia Γ omnia ipsi H // **26** pereunt Γ perduntur H / inquit Γ inquit in
milite Mariano H // **30** mentem Γ animum H / mulieri restare Γ restare mulieri H // **33**
cumulatissime Γ *deest in* H / largiaris plena manu Γ des H

speaking of her misconduct. She will not hear talk of wicked women without suspecting that it may be because of her. She will not hear the name of her seducer even in some other regard without fearing that she is being referred to indirectly. No one will give voice to secret complaints but that she will be afraid that her crime has been discovered and that her punishment is nigh. She must be the slave of those whom she suspects as suspecting. She will have to behave humbly and abjectly for fear that if she says something rather freely or acts a little arrogantly, her disgrace will be immediately thrown in her face. She will live always in a state of confusion, lifeless, or rather she will not live at all, but will be deprived of physical death while undergoing spiritual death many times over.

44. What kingdoms would you wish to purchase at the price of this everlasting torment? Depraved men suffer it but women more acutely since their crimes are more repulsive in the eyes of all and they are more scrupulous by nature. And truly, if one weighs the matter carefully, women who take little care for their chastity are worthy of these calamities and even worse. For many things are required of a man: wisdom, eloquence, knowledge of political affairs, talent, memory, some trade to live by, justice, liberality, magnanimity and other qualities which it would take a long time to rehearse. If some of these are lacking, he seems to have less blame as long as some are present. But in a woman no one requires eloquence or talent or wisdom or skills or administration of the republic or justice or generosity; no one asks anything of her but chastity. If that one thing is missing, it is as if all were lacking to a man. In a woman chastity is the equivalent of all virtues. They are idle and slothful guardians who cannot guard the one thing committed to their care and enjoined upon them with many words and exhortations, especially when no one will take it from them against their will or touch it without their consent. If a woman will reflect on this, she will be a more attentive and cautious guardian of her chastity. If that is safe, all else will be secure; if that is lost, all things perish together with it. 'What can be secure for a woman when her chastity is lost?' said Lucretia; and yet she preserved a chaste mind in a defiled body. Therefore 'burying the sword in her entrails,' as Quintilian said, 'she exacted the penalty imposed by necessity so that a chaste soul would be separated as quickly as possible from a polluted body.' Not that I should propose this act as an example to be imitated, but her mentality, so that you will believe that nothing remains to a woman who has cast away her chastity. You may take away from a woman her beauty, lineage, wealth, charm, eloquence, intelligence, knowledge of the skills suited to a woman, but if you add chastity you have given her everything in full measure. Conversely, you may lavish all those things upon her with all

et dicas impudicam, hoc uno verbo detraxisti omnia; nuda relicta est et
detestanda. Sunt alia tum ex corpore tum etiam ex animo quae ad curam
pudicitiae feminas adiuvent; de quibus nunc loquar.

CAP. VII.   QUOMODO VIRGO CORPUS TRACTABIT

45. Primum omnium illud parentibus consulendum duco quod et Aristoteles
in Historia animalium, ut filias ineunte pubertate maxime custodiant arceant-
que ab omni virorum congressu. Eo tempore proniores esse in libidinem.
Ipsae quoque puellae, cum omni alio tempore, tum hoc in primis, ab omni
occasione seu videndi seu audiendi seu etiam cogitandi turpium debent sese
abducere; in quod per reliquam nihilo minus aetatem dabunt operam. Et
ante connubium crebriora ieiunia proderunt, quae non debilitent quidem
corpus, sed refrenent et comprimant restinguantque iuventutis incendia.
Nam haec demum sunt vera et sancta ieiunia. Victus sit facilis ac parabilis
nec efficacia calidus cogitandumque et primam illam matrem propter cibum
eiectam ex Paradiso et multas iuvenes delicatis cibis assuefactas, cum illos
domi non haberent, foris cum naufragio pudicitiae quaesivisse. Potus erit ille a
natura in commune paratus, liquida et pura aqua. 'Vini usus,' inquit Valerius
Maximus, 'olim Romanis feminis ignotus fuit, ne in aliquod dedecus prolabe-
rentur, quia proximus a Libero patre intemperantiae gradus ad inconcessam
Venerem esse consuevit.' Aquam vero si non feret stomachus, dandum erit
paulum cervisiae aut vini, quantum sat erit ad concoquendum cibum, non
ad corpus inflammandum. Nec id solum ad mores et corporis lasciviam
petulantiamque coercendam iuvat, sed ad firmiorem quoque valetudinem.

46. Apud Hieronymum Furiae scribentem sic legimus: 'Aiunt medici
et qui humanorum corporum scripsere naturas praecipueque Galenus

---

45. (Aristoteles) *Aristot. hist. an. 7, 1 (581b)* // (Vini … consuevit) *Val. Max. 2, 1, 5*
46. (Aiunt … sunt) *Hier. epist. 54, 9–10, PL 22, 554–555* //

1–2 nuda relicta est et detestanda Γ nudam reliquisti ac foedam H // **2** Sunt alia Γ Sunt
et alia H // **4** QUOMODO VIRGO CORPUS TRACTABIT Γ DE CURA CORPORIS IN VIRGINE H //
5 Primum WW²B Quamquam non erat propositi huius de corpore loqui, quia quaedam
tamen in animo sunt ex habitu et ratione corporis interdum si non reguntur, certe inficiuntur,
idcirco de corporis virginei cura nonnulla erunt dicenda. Primum HV / consulendum Γ
praecipiendum H / quod et HWW² quod BV // **7** virorum congressu Γ congressu
virorum H // **9–10** occasione … aetatem Γ occasione turpium seu videndi seu audiendi
seu etiam cogitandi debent se aubmovere in quod reliquo nihilominus tempore H // **11**
connubium Γ coniugium H // **12** restinguantque Γ restringuantque H // **14** efficacia Γ ex
se H / calidus Γ calidus nec aromatis conditus nec exquisitus H // **17** in commune Γ *deest
in* H // **22** mores HWW²B amores V // **25** qui … naturas HWW²B qui de humanorum
corporum scripsere naturis *Hier.* qui humanorum corporum scripsere naturis V

abundance and call her unchaste and with this one word you have removed all. She is left naked and loathsome. There are other things both of body and of mind that help women to care for their chastity, of which I will now speak.

CHAPTER 7.   HOW THE YOUNG WOMAN WILL TREAT HER BODY

45. First of all I should like to recommend to parents the advice that Aristotle gave in the *History of Animals* that they keep special watch over their daughters at the beginning of puberty and keep them away from all contact with men. During that period they are more inclined to lust. The young girls themselves, at this time in particular, should abstain from seeing, hearing or even thinking of unseemly matters, a practice which they will have to maintain for the rest of their lives as well. Before marriage frequent fasts will be beneficial, not those that weaken the body, but that check and control it and extinguish the fires of youth. These are true and holy fasts. Let her nourishment be light, plain and not highly seasoned, and it must be remembered that our first parent was expelled from paradise because of the food she ate and that many young girls who are accustomed to delicacies have sought them outside the home when they no longer had them at home, to the detriment of their chastity. Their drink will be that provided by nature for everyone's consumption, limpid and clear water. 'The use of wine' says Valerius Maximus, 'was unknown to Roman women, so that they would not fall into any disgrace, because it is well known that the next step after Bacchus, father of intemperance, is that which leads to unlawful lust.' If the stomach does not tolerate water, then a little beer or wine shall be given, enough for digestion, but not to inflame the body. Not only is it good for restraining sexual passion, lust and wantonness of the body, but it also promotes more robust health.

46. In Jerome's letter to Furia we read:

> Doctors and those who have written about the nature of the human body, especially Galen in his book *Hygiene*, say that the bodies of young men and women

in libris περὶ ὑγιειῶν puerorum et iuvenum ac perfectae aetatis virorum
mulierumque corpora insito calore fervere, et noxios illis esse cibos aetatibus
qui calorem augeant, sanitatique conducere frigida quaeque in esu et potu
sumere. Sicut e contrario senibus, qui pituita laborant et frigore, calidos
5   cibos et vetera vina prodesse. Unde et Salvator: "Attendite," inquit, "vobis
ne forte graventur corda vestra in crapula et ebrietate et curis huius vitae." Et
Apostolus: "Nolite inebriari vino, in quo est luxuria." Nec mirum hoc figulum
sensisse de vasculo quod ipse fabricatus est, cum etiam comicus, cuius finis
est humanos mores nosse atque describere, dixerit: "Sine Cerere et Libero
10 friget Venus." Primum igitur, si stomachi firmitas patitur, donec puellares
annos transeas, aquam in potu sume quae natura frigidissima est, aut, si
hoc imbecillitas prohibet, audi cum Timotheo: "Vino modico utere propter
stomachum et frequentes tuas infirmitates." Deinde ipsis cibis calida quaeque
devita. Non solum de carnibus loquor, super quibus vas electionis profert
15 sententiam: "Bonum est vinum non bibere et carnem non manducare,"
sed etiam in ipsis leguminibus inflantia quaeque et gravia declinanda sunt.'
Et paulo ante: 'Quid ergo necesse est nos iactare pudicitiam, quae sine
comitibus et appendiciis suis, continentia et parcitate, fidem sui facere non
potest? Apostolus macerat corpus suum et animae subicit imperio, ne quod
20 aliis praecipit ipse non servet. Et adolescentula, fervente cibis corpore,
de castitate secura est? Neque vero haec dicens condemno cibos, quos
Deus creavit ad utendum cum gratiarum actione, sed iuvenibus et puellis
incentiva aufero voluptatum. Non Aetnaei ignes, non Vulcania tellus, non
Vesevus et Olympus tantis ardoribus aestuant, ut iuveniles medullae vino
25 plenae et dapibus inflammatae.' Haec omnia ex Divo Hieronymo. Quae
adduxi ut sciretur quid magister ille continentiae sentiret, qui etiam Salvinae
praecipiens mavult valetudinem corporis quam animi periclitari, dicens:
'Multo melius est stomachum dolere quam mentem, imperare corpori quam
servire, gressu vacillare quam pudicitia.'
30   **47.** Vir sanctissimus Gregorius Nazianzenus, Hieronymi magister, virginem suam pane vult famem placare et sitim aqua. Hilario monachus,
cum in eremo etiam tenuissimo victu vix se sustentans titillari se tamen
nonnumquam a libidine sentiret, ieiuniis corpus suum macerabat, dicens:

46. (puerorum ... sumere) *Gal. san. tuend.*, *5, 3, 5* // (Attendite ... vitae) *Vulg. Luc. 21,
34* // (Nolite ... luxuria) *Vulg. Eph. 5, 18* // (Sine ... Venus) *Ter. Eun. 732* // (Vino ...
infirmitates) *Vulg. I Tim. 5, 23* // (Bonum ... manducare) *Vulg. Rom. 14, 21* // (Quid ...
inflammatae) *Hier. epist. 54, 8–9, PL 22, 553–554* // (Apostolus ... servet) *Vulg. 1 Cor. 9, 27*
// (quos ... actione) *Vulg. I Tim. 4, 4* // (Multo ... pudicitia) *Hier. epist. 79, 10, PL 22, 731*
    47. (Gregorius Nazianzenus) *Greg. Naz. praecepta ad virgines 134, PG 37, 589* //

13 ipsis **Γ** in ipsis **H** *Hier.* // **18** appendiciis **HV** *Hier.* appendicibus **WW²B** // **26** sentiret **Γ**
praeciperet **H** // **26–27** Salvinae praecipiens **Γ** ad Salvinam scribens **H** // **33** a **Γ** *deest
in* **H**

and of mature men and women glow with an innate warmth, and that foods that increase bodily warmth are harmful to them; thus it is conducive to their health to consume cold food and drink. To the contrary, warm food and old wine are beneficial to old men, who suffer from catarrh and cold. Therefore our Saviour said 'Take care that your hearts are not weighed down with dissipation and drunkenness and the cares of this life.' And the Apostle: 'Do not get drunk with wine, in which is debauchery.' And it is not strange that the potter felt this way about the vessel that he fashioned himself, since even the comic writer, whose goal is to know and describe human conduct, said 'Without Ceres and Bacchus, Venus fails.' First of all, then, if the stomach is strong enough to take it, until after the age of puberty drink water, which by nature is very cool. But if weakness prevents this, listen to the advice given to Timothy: 'Partake of a little wine for the sake of your stomach and your frequent ailments.' In solid food avoid things that are too hot. I speak not only of meat, concerning which the vessel of election makes this statement: 'It is good not to drink wine and not to eat meat. But even in the case of leguminous vegetables those that cause flatulence and are heavy should be avoided.' And a little earlier on he says, 'Why, therefore, must we vaunt our chastity, which without its companions and attendants, continence and frugality, carries no conviction?' The Apostle torments his body and subjects it to the dominion of the soul lest what he preaches to others he does not observe himself; and will a young girl, her body glowing with heat and well-nourished, be certain of her chastity? In saying this I do not mean to condemn food, which God has created for our use and for which we should be grateful, but I wish to remove from young men and young women the incentives to pleasure. Neither the fires of Etna nor the island of Vulcan, nor Vesuvius nor Olympus seethe with such fires as the inmost parts of youth filled with wine and inflamed with rich food.

This all comes from St. Jerome. I have introduced it to make known that master's thoughts on continence, who also in his letter to Salvina says that he prefers that the health of the body be at risk rather than that of the soul. He says: 'It is preferable that the stomach be in pain rather than the mind; better to rule the body than be a slave to it, to falter in one's steps rather than in one's chastity.'

47. That very saintly man, Gregory Nazianzen, teacher of Jerome, wishes his ideal virgin to appease hunger with bread and thirst with water. The monk Hilario, though barely sustaining his life in the desert on the most scanty diet, at times felt that his body was being stimulated by lust and would torture his body with fasts, saying 'I will tame you, concupiscence, so that you

'Domabo te, concupiscentia, ut de cibo cogites, non de voluptate.' Et haec quidem dicunt discipuli Christi, socii Pauli, dediti sobriae et castae religioni, quippe qui sciunt sanctorum hominum alimenta, etiam missa divinitus, tenuia et simplicia fuisse, quae satisfacerent naturae citra delicias. Elisaeus se ac filios prophetarum agrestibus alebat oleribus et amarum cibum dulcorari farina iubet, non melle aut saccharo. Idem milites, quibus in Samaria luminum usum ademerat, excipi iubet convivio panis et aquae. Ioannes Baptista, destinatus Christi metator et instantis lucis praeco, locustis et agresti melle in solitudine sustentatur. Abacuch Angeli iussu cibum messorum ad Danielem defert Babylonem. Eliae subcinericius panis et aquae poculum ad refectionem e caelo missum est. Ceu vero non siligineus panis et perdices et capi et phasiani et Martii panes mitti e caelo possent aut coturnices, ut olim filiis Israelis, tam facile quam eiusmodi alimentum. Sed nimirum tali nutrimento sancti egent quod animum contineat in corpore, non submergat.

48. Quid philosophi, quid sapientiae mundi magistri? Modicum cibum et facilem et parabilem commendant omnes, quo sobria sit mens et continens corpus. Socrates, philosophiae parens, tenuitate victus assecutus est ut numquam nec ipse nec eius familia gravi aliquo et periculoso attingeretur morbo. Senecam Stoicum scribit Tacitus in summa opulentia agrestibus pomis et aqua pura naturae satisfecisse. Unde et corpore ad eum modum fuisse extenuato ut apertae Neronis iussu venae sanguinem paene nullum stillarint. Qualem victus rationem putamus in Xenocrate fuisse, cui cum clanculum esset in eius grabatum Phryne formosissimum scortum a discipulis summissum, multum ab ea contrectatus et variis modis sollicitatus ad libidinem commotus tamen non est! Plato in suis Legibus vini usum adolescentibus detrahit. Cicero in Officiis totum victum cultumque corporis ad valetudinem et vires, non ad voluptatem referendum censet: 'Atque etiam,'

47. (Domabo ... voluptate) *Hier. vita Hil. 5, PL 23, 31B* // (Elisaeus ... saccharo) *Vulg. IV reg. 4, 39–41* // (Idem ... aquae) Vulg. IV reg. 6, 22 // (Ioannes ... sustentatur) *Vulg. Matth. 3, 4* // (Abacuch ... Babylonem) *Vulg. Dan. 14, 32–33* // (Eliae ... missum est) *Vulg. III reg. 19, 6*

48. (Socrates) *Plut. mor. 124E, 513D* // (Senecam) *Tac. ann. 15, 45* // (Xenocrate ... est) *Val. Max. 4, 3, 3* // (Plato) *Plat. leg. 2, 666A–B* // (Cicero) *Cic. off. 1, 106* //

4 tenuia **Γ** exigua **H** / citra delicias **Γ** sine voluptate **H** // **6** melle aut **Γ** *deest in* **H** // **7** excipi **Γ** suscipi **H** // **10** Babylonem **Γ** in Babyloniam **H** // **11–12** siligineus panis et **Γ** *deest in* **H** // **12** Martii **HWW²B** mattyae **V** // **12–13** aut ... alimentum **Γ** aeque ac panis facile **H** // **13** Sed **Γ** *deest in* **H** // **14** tali **Γ** hominum omni **H** // **17** commendant omnes quo **Γ** praedicant omnes ut **H** // **19** nec ... familia **Γ** *deest in* **H** / periculoso **Γ** *deest in* **H** // **20** summa opulentia **Γ** summis opibus tamen **H** // **21** pura **Γ** *deest in* **H** / Unde et **Γ** Hinc **H** // **22** Neronis iussu **Γ** *deest in* **H** // **23** stillarint **Γ** stillarent **H** // **24** Phryne **Γ** *deest in* **H** // **25** summissum **Γ** subditum **H** / ea **Γ** eo **H** // **25–26** sollicitatus ad libidinem **Γ** ad libidinem impetitus **H**

will think of food, not pleasure.' This is what the disciples of Christ and the companions of Paul say, dedicated to a sober and chaste religion, since they were aware that the nourishment of holy men, even when divinely sent, was meager and simple, to satisfy nature without gratifying it. Elisha nourished himself and the sons of the prophets with wild herbs and ordered the bitter food to be sweetened with flour, not honey or sugar. The soldiers whose eyes he had put out in Samaria he ordered to be welcomed with a banquet of bread and water. John the Baptist, the predestined precursor of Christ and the herald of the impending dawn, nurtured himself on locusts and wild honey in the desert. Habacuc at the angel's bidding brought the food of the harvesters to Daniel in Babylon. Elias was sent from heaven bread made of ashes and a cup of water to recover his strength. Could not bread made from wheat-flour and partridges and capons and pheasants and marzipan have been as readily sent from heaven, or rock partridges, as formerly was done for the sons of Israel, as easily as that kind of nourishment? But obviously holy men are in need of such nourishment to keep their soul in the body without suffocating it.

48. What of the philosophers and the teachers of worldly wisdom? They all recommend moderate and simple fare, ready to hand, so that the mind will be sober and the body continent. Socrates, the father of philosophy, followed a simple diet with the result that neither he nor his family was ever stricken by any serious or dangerous malady. Seneca the Stoic, writes Tacitus, amidst the greatest wealth satisfied his nature with wild fruit and pure water. His body was so emaciated by living in that way that when he cut open his veins at the command of Nero, hardly any blood issued from them. What must we think the table of Xenocrates was like, for when the beautiful courtesan Phryne was stealthily placed in his cot by his disciples and he was fondled by her and solicited to lust in various ways, he remained unmoved. Plato in his *Laws* denies the use of wine to adolescents. Cicero in the *De officiis* is of the opinion that all food and care of the body should be for the purpose of maintaining health and strength, not pleasure. 'And moreover,'

inquit, 'si considerare volumus quae sit in natura hominis excellentia et
dignitas, intelligemus quam turpe sit diffluere luxuria et delicate ac molliter
vivere quamque honestum continenter, parce, severe, sobrie.' Hoc Cicero.
Ovidius Naso, amoris tradens remedia, eum qui caste victurus sit temperan-
5 tem quoque esse monet eique a cibis illis abstinendum 'qui Veneri corpora
nostra parant' vinumque in primis vitandum, illos autem mensis inferendos
'qui Veneri corpora nostra negant.'

49. Cum de cibis dico vi sua calidis, idem de omni exercitatione volo
intelligi qua viscera inflammantur, quin etiam de unguentis, de aromatis, de
10 confabulationibus ac virorum aspectu. Haec omnia noxia sunt castitati quibus
incendimur flagitioso ardore. Lectus erit non perinde delicatus ac mundus,
ut placide quiescat, non molliter. Quod etiam in vestibus praecipiendum est,
ne sint delicatae aut pretiosae nimium, sed sine sordibus, sine labe. Nescio
quemadmodum mundities animi corporis gaudet munditie; contra, delicatus
15 et enervis et fractus animus sericis ac byssinis vestibus delectatur et omnia nisi
sint talia aspera putat, dura, intolerabilia. Gregorius Nazianzenus aurum,
serica, margaritas virginibus suis aufert. Quam stulti sumus si credimus verba
illa Servatoris Christi: 'Ecce qui mollibus vestiuntur, in domibus regum
sunt,' id significare ut qui in comitatu Christianorum regum aetatem degunt,
20 mollibus induantur. Non novit Christi religio aulas et reges huiusmodi, de
quibus ipse idem dixit: 'Reges gentium dominantur eis et qui potestatem
habent in eas benefici vocantur; vos autem non sic, sed maximus vestrum
fiat ut minimus et ductator velut ministrans.' Si Dominus noster superbiam
ipsis regibus et regnis adimit, quomodo superbiae relinquet instrumenta?
25 Omnino vult Christus suos meminisse Christianos esse se, non mundanos,
quibus dictum est: 'Vos de mundo non estis.' Sancta est et severa Christiana
pietas, cuius ut iugum animabus est facile, dulce, suave et in quo est eis
requies, ita grave ac molestum corporis voluptatibus, cum quibus perpetua

48. (qui ... parant) *Ov. rem. 800* // (qui ... negant) *Ov. rem. 802*
49. (Gregorius Nazianzenus) *Greg. Naz. praecepta ad virgines 85–90, PG 37, 585* // (Ecce
... sunt) *Vulg. Matth. 11, 8* // (Reges ... ministrans) *Vulg. Luc. 22, 25–26* // (Vos ... non
estis) *Vulg. Ioh. 15, 19*

4 Ovidius Naso **Γ** Ovidius **H** / amoris tradens *scr.* amori tradens **Γ** amoris dans **H** // **5**
a cibis illis abstinendum **Γ** cibos illos reiciendos **H** // **6** autem **Γ** *deest in* **H** // **8** dico vi sua **Γ**
dixi **H** // **8–9** exercitatione ... inflammantur **Γ** exercitio intellegendum censeo quo corpus
incalescit **H** // **10–11** quibus incendimur flagitioso ardore **Γ** quippe incendunt ardore turpi
et pernicioso **H** // **11** delicatus ac **Γ** mollis ut **H** // **12** ut ... molliter **Γ** *deest in* **H** //
13 aut pretiosae **Γ** *deest in* **H** // **14** corporis **Γ** etiam corporis **H** // **14–15** delicatus ...
animus **Γ** mollis delicatusque animus **H** // **16** putat, dura **Γ** putat ac dura **H** / intolerabilia
W intolerabiliora **W²BV** *deest in* **H** // **17** margaritas **BV** margarita **HWW²** // **19** aetatem
degunt **Γ** vitam agunt **H** // **20–21** et ... dixit **Γ** neque reges in qua illud audimus **H** // **23**
ut **Γ** sicut **H** // **23–26** Si ... estis **Γ** *deest in* **H** // **27** cuius **Γ** et eius **H** // **28**–p.72,2 cum
... sunt **Γ** *deest in* **H**

he says 'if we wish to consider what is the excellence and dignity of the nature of man, we will understand how base it is to become enervated with luxury and delicate and soft living and how noble it is to live a life of temperance, frugality, severity and sobriety.' Thus speaks Cicero. Ovidius Naso, imparting the remedies of love, teaches that he who would live chastely must also be temperate and must abstain from those foods 'that prepare our bodies for Venus.' Wine, above all, must be avoided and those courses served 'that deny our bodies to Venus.'

49. When I speak of foods that are warm of their own efficacy, I wish this to be understood as well of every physical stimulus that excites our internal organs, such as unguents, perfumes, conversations and the sight of men. These are all harmful to chastity, since they inflame us with shameful desires. A young woman's bed will be clean rather than luxurious so that she may sleep peacefully, not sensuously. The same precepts may be applied to her clothes, which should not be luxurious or too expensive, but neat and spotless. I do not know to what extent cleanliness of mind takes pleasure in cleanliness of the body or conversely, whether a hedonistic, languid and effeminate spirit delights in silks and fine linens and, unless it is bedecked in such finery, regards all else as harsh, coarse and intolerable. Gregory Nazianzen forbids gold, silk and pearls to the young girls he instructed. How stupid we are if we think that those words of our Saviour: 'Behold those who are dressed in soft garments dwell in the houses of kings' mean that those who spend their lives in the retinue of Christian kings should put on soft garments. The religion of Christ is not acquainted with courts and kings of this sort, of whom the Master said: 'The kings of the Gentiles exercise lordship over them and those who have power over them are called benefactors. Not so with you; but let the greatest among you become as the least and the leader as one who serves.' If Our Lord takes pride away from kings themselves and their kingdoms, how will he ignore the accoutrements of pride? Christ wishes that his followers remember they are Christians at every moment and not citizens of the world, for he said to them: 'You are not of this world.' Christian piety is holy and severe and while its yoke is easy, sweet and pleasant to the soul, which finds its rest in it, it is heavy and troublesome to the pleasures of the body, with which it is in continuous

est illi pugna. Hic est mundus qui Christianos odit, quia de mundo non sunt.

50. Somnus sit in virgine non longus, nec minor tamen quam pro valetudine. Cui nos ita prospicimus ut melius valeant quae hanc nostram frugalitatem sequuntur quam quae delicias; quibus deditas marcescere videmus ac pallere. His omnibus addendum est negotium aliquod et occupatio digna virgine, cuiusmodi aliquot recensui. Numquam enim facilius subrepit astus diabolicus quam in otio nec alias promptius exercet artes suas Venus, non in femina modo, sed in fortiore animante ac constantiore, viro. Sunt enim nostri animi ad aliquid agendum nati et appositi, itaque opere pascuntur, roborantur, gaudent; otio vero dissolvuntur, inertia decidunt nec omnino possunt nihil agere ut ad libidinem et flagitia et his graviora etiam facinora prolabantur necesse sit, cum melius aliquid deest quo occupentur. Artifex ille tractandorum amorum Ovidius Aegisthum ea sola causa animum ad Clytaemnestram Agamemnonis coniugem corrumpendam ipsumque Agamemnonem occidendum adiecisse definit, quod desidiosus esset. Hinc inter amoris remedia illud est de praecipuis, ne nos Cupidinis sagitta otiosos ac vacuos deprehendat:

Otia si tollas, inquit, periere Cupidinis arcus
Exstinctaeque iacent et sine luce faces.

51. Adolescit amor et altissimas iacit radices si de eo quod amas multum cogites et crebro. Divus Hieronymus Demetriadi vitandum prorsus otium suadet. Idcirco, ubi perfuncta sit precibus, lanam iubet tractare et parare telam ut hac vicissitudine operum dies longi numquam videantur. Nec ideo non cessandum vult, quod illa egeret quae esset femina inter primarias Romanas locupletissima, sed ut per occasionem operis nihil cogitaret aliud quam quae ad obsequium Domini pertinerent. Quem locum sic claudit: 'Simpliciter loquar: quamvis omnem censum tuum in pauperes distribuas, nihil apud Christum erit pretiosius nisi quod ipsa manibus tuis confeceris, vel in usus proprios, vel in exemplum virginum ceterarum, vel quod aviae matrique offeras.' Sic ille. Profecto ita est: segnis atque ignava, vel etiam (si diis placet) lusibus voluptatibusque aetatem transmittens, indigna est

---

50. (recensui) *inst. fem. Christ. 1, 15–17* // (Aegisthum ... esset) *Ov. rem. 161–162* // (Otia ... faces) *Ov. rem. 139–140*
51. (Simpliciter ... offeras) *Hier. epist. 130, 15, PL 22, 1119–1120* //

9 non in femina **H** nec in femina **Γ** / in ... viro **Γ** in constantiore ac fortiore animante viro **H** // **9–14** Sunt ... occupentur **Γ** *deest in* **H** // **18** ac vacuos **Γ** *deest in* **H** // **21–22** Adolescit ... crebro **Γ** *deest in* **H** // **22** prorsus **Γ** *deest in* **H** // **23–24** parare telam **Γ** telam parare **H** // **25** quae **Γ** cum **H** // **26** cogitaret aliud **Γ** aliud cogitaret **H** // **31** segnis atque ignava **Γ** otiosa **H** // **32** lusibus voluptatibusque **Γ** voluptatibus **H** / transmittens **Γ** transigens **H**

conflict. This is the world which hates Christians because they are not of the world.

50. The sleep of a virgin should not be long, but not less than what is good for her health, to safeguard which we are of the opinion that young girls are healthier if they follow the austerity we recommend rather than sensual delight, which is manifested in its devotees by weakness and pallor. To these instructions must be added some activity and occupation befitting a young girl, several of which I have already mentioned. For the devil's cunning never finds such easy access as in idleness, nor does Venus ply her skills more readily at any other time, not only in women but in the stronger and more stable male. Our minds were born and destined to perform some activity and they thrive, grow strong, and derive enjoyment in work, whereas they are weakened by idleness, lapse into inertia and are incapable of doing anything. Consequently they are bound to lapse into lust and shameful conduct and worse crimes than these since they have nothing better to occupy themselves. That master in the art of love, Ovid, asserts that the only reason that prompted Aegisthus to corrupt Clytemnestra, the wife of Agamemnon, and to kill Agamemnon, was that he had nothing to do. Hence one of the principal remedies against love is that Cupid's arrow does not catch us idle and unoccupied. His words are:

> Take away idleness and Cupid's bow is dead,
> And his torches lie lifeless and unlit.

51. Love grows and sends out deep roots if you think much and often about what you love. Jerome persuades Demetrias to avoid idleness altogether. And to that end he tells her that when she has finished with her prayers, she should take her work in hand and prepare the weaving so that by this alternation of tasks the days will never seem long. He requires this unceasing activity of her not because she had need of it, for she was one of the noblest and wealthiest women of Rome, but that through this constant activity she would think of nothing that did not have to do with the service of God. The passage ends as follows: 'I shall speak simply. Although you distribute all your wealth to the poor, nothing will be more precious in the eyes of Christ than what you do with your own hands, whether for your own use or as an example to other virgins or as an offering to your grandmother and mother.' Thus speaks St. Jerome. And so it is in very fact: a woman who is indolent and slothful or (if you please!) spends her time in amusements and pleasures is unworthy of her sustenance in the Christian church,

alimento suo in Ecclesia Christiana, in qua Paulus, maximus Christi praeco,
clamat ac velut legem pronuntiat: 'Qui non laborat, nec edat.' Communis est illa poena generis humani, a Deo pro prima illa noxia hominum
generi inflicta: 'Per sudorem vultus tui vesceris pane tuo.' Haud dubie
5   istos, qui huic generali poenae subditi non sunt, cum non minus quam alii
peccarint, alia manet vel gravior vel certe non levior. Cum continendos
vel opere vel sanctis et cogitationibus et confabulationibus muliebres animos iusserim ne in flagitia otiosi prolabantur, quonam existimabimus illos
ferri qui foliis aut taxillis lusitant? Quae occupatio in viro cum sit foeda,
10   non poterit non esse in femina detestanda. Quid discere, quid cogitare
poterit femina, aleam ludens? Necesse est solvat animum et in avaritiam
rapiatur suopte nutu illuc propensa; tum in periurium, nummi causa. Hinc
si viri adsint, multa audiat femineis auribus indecora. Quam turpe visu est
feminam pro calatho alveolum tractare, pro fuso talum rotare, pro radio
15   taxillum iacere, pro spathalio aut libro precatorio lusorias chartas evolvere?
Nemo paulo cordatior non eam desidentem malit aspicere quam sic occupatam nec est qui non et illam quae didicit et eum qui illam talia docuit
et eos qui permiserunt cum ingenti animi indignatione grandi convicio
prosequatur.

20   CAP. VIII.   DE ORNAMENTIS

52. Dici non potest quantum inter hunc cultum ornatumque feminarum
intersit et eum quem sancti omnes auctores uno ore praescribunt feminae
baptizatae; nimirum secuti principes Apostolorum et Ecclesiae columina,
Petrum ac Paulum; quorum de ornandis feminis hae sunt breves sane
25   praeceptiunculae, sed quae aliorum longissimas orationes includant. Petrus
sic ait: 'Mulierum ne sit exterior vel capillis complicatis vel circumiectione
auri aut indumentorum amictu ornatus; ceterum mens et conscientia, quae
separata est ab spectantium oculis, si incorrupta sit et placido quodam
agatur spiritu ac tranquillo, ea demum splendida res est apud Dominum
30   et magnifica.' Paulus vero sic: 'Mulieres in habitu ornato, cum verecundia

51. (Qui ... edat) *Vulg. II Thess. 3, 10* // (Per ... tuo) *Vulg. gen. 3, 19*
52. (Mulierum ... magnifica) *Vulg. I Pet. 3, 3–4* // (Mulieres ... opera) *Vulg. I Tim. 2,*
9–10

1 alimento Γ cibo **H** // **8** quonam Γ quo **H** / foliis Γ chartis **H** // **9–10** Quae occupatio ...
detestanda Γ Quod exercitium in viro cum sit foedum in femina detestandum est **H** // **12**
suopte nutu illuc propensa Γ suapte nutu illuc propensum **H** // **15** spathalio (= σπαθαλίῳ)
aut libro precatorio Γ globulis aut libro oratorio **H** // **16** desidentem malit aspicere Γ
otiosam videre malit **H** // **18–19** cum ... prosequatur Γ detestetur **H** // **21**–p.76,5 Dici
... insanias Γ *deest in* **H**

in which Paul, Christ's chief herald, proclaims as if it were a law: 'If anyone will not work then let him not eat.' The penalty inflicted by God upon the human race for that first fault is common to all men: 'By the sweat of your brow will you eat your bread.' Undoubtedly those who are not subject to this general punishment, although they have sinned no less than others, another graver punishment awaits them, or at any rate one not more lacking in severity. Since I recommended that women's minds must be kept under control through work or holy thoughts and conversations so that they will not lapse into shameful conduct in their idleness, to what conceivable actions will those women be driven that divert themselves in games of cards and dice? Since this pastime is disgraceful even for men, it cannot but be loathsome in women. What will a woman be able to learn or think about who gives herself to gambling? It must needs be that her mind will be weakened and she will become the victim of avarice, to which she was already inclined by nature; from there she will fall into perjury for the sake of money. If there are men present at these games of hazard, she will hear many things that are offensive to a woman's ears. What a shameful thing to see a woman not with her basket of wool but at the gaming-board, rolling knuckle-bones instead of the spindle, throwing dice instead of spinning the shuttle, dealing out playing cards instead of battening wool or reading her prayer-book! There is no sensible person who would not prefer that she remain idle rather than occupy herself in this way, as there is no one who would not condemn with great acrimony both the woman who learned these skills, and the one who taught her such vices and those who permitted it.

CHAPTER 8.   ON ADORNMENT

52. It is impossible to say what a difference there is between this adornment and embellishment of women and that which all holy authors unanimously prescribe for the baptized woman. In this, of course, they follow the princes of the Apostles and pillars of the church, Peter and Paul, whose precepts concerning the adornments of women are brief but sum up the long sermons of others. Peter has this to say: 'Let women not cultivate external adornment with braided hair, gold bracelets and fine clothes; rather if her mind and conscience, which are hidden from view, are incorrupt and she is of a gentle and peaceful spirit, that is what is precious in the sight of God.' Paul writes: 'Women should be modest and sensible in their adornment, without braided

et sobrietate ornantes se et non intortis crinibus aut auro vel margaritis vel pretiosa veste, sed, quod decet mulieres pietatem professas, per opera bona.' Haec Apostoli quibus nihil sane opus est pluribus; verum explicatius sunt dicenda nonnulla iis praesertim, quibus multa sunt verba facienda priusquam velint exaudire. Et persequar separatim et configam singulas earum insanias.

53. Principio de fuco; in quo equidem audire pervelim quid spectet virgo, cum cerussa et purpurisso se illinit. Si sic placere sibi, demens est. Quid enim carius aut gratius cuique quam unusquisque per se sibi? Si viris, scelesta. Unicum habes sponsum Christum; ei ut placeas animam orna virtutibus et formosissimus te deosculabitur. At sponsum quaeris virum et ei conciliari studes fuco. Primum docebo quam fatue, deinde quam impie. Perinde mihi videtur esse cupere te fuco pellicere virum aliquem ac persona; quem tantum avertes renudata quantum attraxisti contecta. Misera, si solo fuco ducitur ad te maritus. Quando fucum elueris, quomodo eris grata? nisi forte numquam crustam illam ablatura es, sed sic ibis cubitum incrustata, sic surges, sic in privato versabere, sic in publico. Iam cui tandem potest non esse molestissima fuci cura ut semper sit integer? Quam aliis ad risum expositum est, si quid vel aquae aspergine vel sudore vel aestu de cerussa aut purpurisso liquefactum est et aliquid ostenditur cutis nativae? Nihil potest esse in forma aspectu deformius.

54. Celebrabatur in Graecia convivium multis mulieribus frequens. Inter oblectamenta epulantium, cum alii sunt nonnulli lusus inducti, tum ille ut per vices unusquisque convivarum ceteris omnibus quicquid esset collibitum imperaret. Cum esset ventum ad puellam quandam insigni specie et ingenio non inamoeno eaque animadvertisset adesse complures feminarum cerussa, purpurisso et aliis pigmentis incrustatas, ad pudorem incutiendum 'Rem,' inquit, 'levem iubebo, quam et ipsa obibo prima, ut unaquaeque nostrum madidas manus per os circumducat ac linteo extergat.' Ipsa prima est suum ipsius iussum exsecuta, sed cum nihil gereret fuci, ex lotione illa pulchrior remansit; fucatae vero absurdas in primis et ridiculas facies rettulerunt ludibrioque tunc habitae abstinuerunt deinceps eiusmodi medicamentis et contentae nativa facie, spreverunt empticiam. Ad haec quis umquam pulchras existimet quas sciat pigmentis illitas? Etiam formosae speciei honorem

2 opera bona **W** *Vulg.* bona opera **W²BV** // **6** Principio de fuco **Γ** Videtur ad eundem locum spectare et de ceteris corporum ornamentis disserere. Dicam principio de fuco **H** / in quo **Γ** *deest in* **H** / spectet **Γ** spectat **H** // **7** sic **Γ** *deest in* **H** / demens **Γ** vana **H** // **7–8** Quid ... sibi **Γ** *deest in* **H** // **8** Si viris, scelesta **Γ** Si Christo demens, si viris, scelesta **H** // **9** Christum **Γ** *deest in* **H** // **11** fatue **Γ** stulte **H** // **12** cupere te **Γ** si velis ad te **H** // **13** contecta **Γ** tecta **H** // **14** fucum elueris, quomodo eris grata **Γ** sine fuco eris, quomodo placebis **H** // **15** ablatura **Γ** elutura **H** // **15–16** in privato versabere **Γ** domi eris **H** // **16** Iam cui tandem potest **Γ** Quid quod (ut de te taceam) cui potest **H** // **18** aspergine **Γ** casu **H** // **19–20** aspectu deformius **Γ** visu foedius **H** // **21–32** Celebrabatur ... empticiam **Γ** *deest in* **H** // **32** Ad haec **Γ** Iam quis **H**

hair or gold or jewelry or costly attire; their adornment is to do good works, as befits women who profess to be religious.' These are the words of the Apostle and no more need be said. But some things must be explained more fully especially for those who require many words before they are willing to listen. I will take them up one by one and strike down each of these insanities.

53. First concerning cosmetics. In this regard I should like to know for what reason a young woman smears herself with white lead and purple pigment. If it is to please herself, she is mad. What is dearer or more pleasing to anyone than to be oneself just as we are. If it is to please men, she is stupid. You have one spouse, Christ; to please him adorn your soul with virtues, and he, the most beautiful of men, will kiss you. But if you are looking for a husband and you wish to win him over by painting yourself, I shall first show you how foolish it is and then how impious. It seems to me that wishing to attract a man with make-up is the same as trying to do so with a mask. Just as you attracted him in this disguise so will you drive him away, when you are unmasked. You poor wretch, if you can find a husband only by the use of make-up, when you have taken it off, how will you remain attractive to him? Unless perhaps you never take off that crust, but go to bed with it on, get up with it, and go around both in public and in private made up in this way. How can the constant care to ensure that the make-up remain intact not become an annoying task? And you will become a laughing-stock to others if by some sprinkling of water, perspiration or heat the white lead or the rouge melts and some of the native complexion appears. Nothing can be more hideous in a beautiful woman.

54. There was a banquet celebrated in Greece which many women attended. One of the entertainments provided for the guests among the various games that were presented was that each of the guests in turn would demand whatever he wished from all the others. The lot fell to a certain girl of singular beauty and pleasant wit, who when she noticed that there were several women present encrusted with white lead, rouge and other pigments, to arouse shame in them she said: 'I ask something very simple and I shall be the first to do it, that each person present wet their hands and rub them over their faces and dry it with a napkin.' She was the first to carry out her own command, but since she was wearing no make-up, after washing her face, she remained lovelier than before, whereas those that wore make-up ended up looking absurd and ridiculous, and since they were made the object of derision, they abstained from then on from all such cosmetics and content with their natural appearance had no use for purchased beauty. Moreover, who will ever consider women beautiful when he knows they are besmeared with pigments? Even those who are beautiful lose the honor and praise owed

---

53. white lead: Also known as cerusite, commonly used at this period to produce a white complexion.

laudemque amittunt cum pictae cernuntur. Universus enim decor, omnis gratia attribuitur arti, non naturae. Quid quod et tenella cutis citius rugatur et totus faciei habitus in senilem deformatur modum? Foetet spiritus, scabrescunt dentes, toto denique corpore taeter halitus spiratur, tum ex cerussa et
5   argento vivo, tum vel maxime ex dropacibus, sapunculis et smegmatis quis cutem velut tabellam in postridianam picturam parant, ut iure sint haec ab Ovidio venena dicta. Iuvenalis festive, qui quaerit:

      An quae mutatis inducitur atque fovetur
      Tot medicaminibus coctaeque siliginis offas
10   Accipit et madidae, facies dicetur an ulcus?

      55. Quae omnia possem fusius persequi, in ea natus urbe cuius feminae hac de re apud alias gentes male audiunt, et mea sententia merito. Libet carissimam mihi patriam reprehendere ut quod reprehendendum est pudefacta vitet. Huc accedit quod si aliter nuptura non es nisi dealbata et
15   rubicata, satius est numquam nubere quam offenso Christo nubere et viro dementi nubere, cui plus placitura est cerussa quam tu ipsa. Quid enim de eiusmodi viro sperare potes, cui plus arridet alba crustula quam proba femina? Quis eo insaniae devenit ut, servum vel equum empturus, malit eum mangonizatum sibi ostendi quam rudem et in ea facie quam dedit
20   natura? Hoc facimus in mancipiis et iumentis, non faciemus in uxoribus? Dedit tibi Deus humanam faciem ad imaginem Filii sui nec nudam dedit. Nam inspiravit in eam spiraculum vitae, ut radius quidam vitae illius rerum omnium in ea reluceat. Quid tu eam mihi sordibus obruis et caeno? Si Apostolus Paulus virum velare caput suum prohibet quia imago Dei est,
25   quid eum dicturum censes de imagine Dei in facie mulieris luto illo confoedatam? Hieronymus adversus Helvidium, ne quis putet iocos aut lusus esse, sic scribit: 'Haec ad speculum pingitur et in contumeliam artificis conatur pulchrior esse quam nata est.' Et ad Furiam: 'Quid facit in facie Christiana purpurissus et cerussa? Quorum alterum ruborem genarum labiorumque
30   mentitur, alterum candorem oris et colli, ignis iuvenum, fomenta libidinum, impudicae mentis indicia? Quomodo flere potest pro peccatis suis quae

---

54. (ab ... dicta) *Ov. rem. 351* // (An ... ulcus) *Iuv. 6, 471–473*
55. (virum ... est) *Vulg. I Cor. 11, 7* // (Haec ... est) *Hier. adv. Helv. 20, PL 23, 204A* // (Quid ... agnoscit) *Hier. epist. 54, 7, PL 22, 553*

1 pictae cernuntur **Γ** cernuntur pictae **H** / Universus **Γ** Omnis **H** // 1–2 omnis gratia attribuitur arti, non naturae **Γ** et gratia fuco attribuitur **H** // 2 tenella **Γ** tenera **H** // 3–4 Foetet ... corpore **Γ** Et spiritus foetet et scabrescunt dentes et toto corpore **H** // 5 dropacibus **Γ** *deest in* **H** / smegmatis **HWW²B** smegmatibus **V** // 6 iure **Γ** non sint immerito **H** // 7 festive **Γ** argute **H** // 10 dicetur **HWW²B** dicatur **V** // 14 Huc accedit quod **Γ** Deinde **H** // 14–15 dealbata et rubicata **Γ** fucata **H** // 18–20 Quis ... uxoribus **Γ** *deest in* **H** // 22 radius quidam **Γ** imago **H**

to their beauty when it is seen they are made up. All their comeliness and charm is attributed to art, not to nature. And what is more, young skin becomes wrinkled more quickly, the whole appearance of the face begins to look old, the breath reeks, the teeth become rotten and a foul odor is emitted by the whole body, from the white lead, mercury, and especially from depilatories, soaps and ointments, with which they prepare their face like a wooden tablet for the next day's painting. Ovid rightly called these substances poison, and Juvenal jocosely asks:

> But when she's through with all those medications,
> The mud packs and the moistened poultices,
> What shall we call it? a face, or an ulcer?

55. I could pursue these topics at great length, having been born in a city whose women have a bad reputation in this regard and in my opinion deservedly. I choose to reproach my dear native city so that shamed by my words it may avoid that which is reprehensible. I may add that if you cannot marry except by painting and whitening herself, it would be better never to marry than to marry and give offense to Christ and marry a madman, who likes white lead more than you. What can you hope for from a man who finds more pleasure in a white encrustation than in a good woman? Who has reached that point of madness that when he is going to buy a slave or a horse he prefers that they be shown to him touched up for sale rather than in their natural state? We do this in the purchase of slaves and beasts of burden, will we not do the same with wives? God gave you a human face in the image of his Son, but not just in outward appearance, for he inspired into it the breath of life so that a ray of that life that exists in all things might shine out in it. Why do you cover it with filth and mire? If the Apostle Paul forbids a man to cover his head because it is the image of God, what do you think he would say of the image in a woman's face befouled by that muck? In writing against Helvidius, lest anyone think it was a matter to be laughed at, Jerome says: 'She paints herself before the mirror and in defiance of her maker tries to be more beautiful than she was born.' And to Furia he writes: 'What is rouge and white lead doing on a Christian face, the first counterfeiting the redness of the cheeks and lips, the other the whiteness of the face and neck? They are the fire of youth, the food of lust, the signs of an impure mind. How can she weep for her sins when her tears

---

55. native city: The women of Valencia were known for their extravagance in personal adornment. Vincent Ferrer at the beginning of the 14th c. had excoriated them before Vives and a German traveller named Hieronymus Münzer describes their excesses in his *Itinerarium hispanicum*, 1494: 'Et omnes se fucant in facie et oleis acquisque odoriferis se coinquinant, quod malum est.' *Revue hispanique* 113 (1920), 30.

lacrimis cutem nudat et sulcos ducit in facie? Ornatus iste non Domini est; velamen istud Antichristi est. Qua fiducia erigit ad caelum vultus, quos conditor non agnoscit?' Tantum Hieronymus.

56. Audi nunc sanctissimum martyrem Cyprianum: 'Ornamentorum ac vestium insignia et lenocinia fucorum non nisi prostitutis et impudicis feminis congruunt et nullarum fere pretiosior cultus est quam quarum pudor vilis est. Sic in Scripturis sanctis, quibus nos instrui Dominus voluit et moneri, describitur civitas meretrix, compta pulchrius et ornata et cum ornamentis suis ac propter ipsa potius ornamenta peritura. Nunc quanta ignorantia veri est, quanta animi dementia id velle quod et nocuerit semper et noceat, et putare quod inde ipsa non pereas unde alios periisse cognoscas? Neque enim Deus purpureas aut coccineas oves fecit aut herbarum succis aut conchyliis tingere et colorare lanas docuit, nec distinctis auro lapillis et margaritis contexta serica et numerosa compage digestis monilia instituit, quibus cervicem quam fecit absconderet, ut operiatur illud quod Deus in homine formavit et conspiciatur desuper id quod diabolus adinvenit. An vulnera inferri auribus Deus voluit, quibus innocens adhuc infantia et mali saecularis ignara crucietur, ut postea de aurium cicatricibus et cavernis pretiosa grana dependeant? Et si non suo pondere, mercium quantitate? Quae omnia peccatores et apostatae angeli suis artibus prodiderunt quando ad terrena contagia devoluti, a caelesti vigore recesserunt. Illi et oculos circumducto nigrore fucare et genas mendacio ruboris inficere et mutare adulterinis coloribus crinem et expugnare omnem oris et capitis veritatem corruptelae suae impugnatione docuerunt.

57. Et quidem isto in loco, pro timore quem nobis fides suggerit, pro dilectione quam fraternitas exigit, non virgines tantum aut viduas, sed et nuptas puto et omnes omnino feminas admonendas, quod opus Dei et factura eius et plastica adulterari nullo modo debeat, adhibito flavo colore vel nigro pulvere vel rubore aut quolibet denique lineamenta nativa corrumpente medicamine. Dicit Deus: "Faciamus hominem ad imaginem et similitudinem nostram." Et audet quisquam mutare et convertere quod Deus fecit? Manus Deo inferunt quando illud quod ille formavit reformare et transfigurare contendunt, nescientes quia opus Dei est omne quod nascitur; diaboli quodcumque mutatur.

58. Si quis pingendi artifex vultum alicuius et speciem et corporis qualitatem aemulo colore signasset et signato iam consummatoque simulacro manus alius afferret, ut iam formata, iam picta, quasi peritior reformaret,

---

56–58. (Ornamentorum ... meliore) *Cypr. hab. virg. 12–16, PL 4, 450–456*
56. (civitas meretrix) *Vulg. apoc. 17, 1*
57. (Faciamus ... nostram) *Vulg. gen. 1, 26*

14 serica **HΓ** serie *Cypr.PL.4.462*

lay bare her skin and dig furrows in her face? This is not the adornment of the Lord; it is the veil of the Antichrist. What boldness to raise her face to heaven, which her Creator will not recognize.' Thus speaks Jerome.

56. Hear now the holy martyr Cyprian:

> Outward show in adornments and clothing and the allurements of cosmetics are not fitting in any except prostitutes and shameless women, and in general none spend more money on dress than those whose modesty is cheap. So in the Sacred Scriptures, by which Our Lord wished us to be instructed and admonished, a harlot city is described as beautifully attired and adorned, destined to perish with its adornments or rather because of them. Now what ignorance of the truth and madness of the mind is it to wish for what has always done harm and continues to do so, and to think that you will not perish from things that you know have led to the perdition of others. God did not make sheep scarlet or purple in color, nor did he teach us to dye and color wool with juices from herbs or from shellfish, nor did he make necklaces of precious stones set in gold or silk garments interwoven with pearls arranged in numerous fastenings, in this way hiding the neck, which he made, so that what God fashioned in man is covered and what the devil invented is exposed to view. Did God wish wounds to be inflicted on the ears to torment innocent children still ignorant of the evils of the world, so that later precious stones may hang from these scars and holes? And if they are not heavy of themselves, they are weighted down by the price paid for them. All these things were the invention of the evil arts of sinners and the apostate angels when they fell to the contagion of earth and lost their heavenly power. They also taught how to circle the eyes with black make-up and tinge the cheeks with a counterfeit blush, and to change the color of the hair and to destroy all semblance of truth from the face and the head by an all-out assault of their corrupting influence.

57. And at this point through the fear that faith inspires in me and the love which brotherhood demands I think that not only virgins and widows, but married women also and women in general should be admonished that the work of God, his creation and configuration, should in no way be adulterated by applying yellow coloring or black powder or rouge or any other concoction that will corrupt the native features. God says: 'Let us make man to our image and likeness,' and will anyone dare to change and transform what God has made? They lay hands on God when they try to remake and transform what he has made, not knowing that all that is born is the work of God, and whatever is changed is the work of the devil.

58. If a painter represented the countenance and form and bodily appearance of someone with colors that rivalled those of nature and when his work had been completed and perfected, another applied his hand to it, thinking himself more skilful, and redid what the other had shaped and painted,

gravis prioris artificis iniuria et iusta indignatio videretur. Tu te existimas
impune laturam tam improbae temeritatis audaciam, Dei artificis offensam?
Ut enim impudica circa homines et incesta fucis lenocinantibus non sis,
corruptis violatisque quae Dei sunt, peior adultera detineris. Quod ornari te
5   putas, quod putas comi, impugnatio est ista divini operis, praevaricatio est
veritatis. Dominus tuus dicit: "Non potes facere capillum unum album aut
nigrum," et tu ad vincendam Domini tui vocem vis te esse potiorem? Audaci
conatu et sacrilego contemptu crines tuos inficis, malo praesagio futurorum
capillos iam tibi flammeos auspicaris et peccas (pro nefas!) capite, id est,
10   corporis parte meliore.' Haec Cyprianus.

    59. Pudet post Christianorum praecepta aliquid de barbaris afferre.
Unicum tantum addam hominis prudentissimi, Lycurgi, Lacedaemoniorum
legis latoris, qui cum ex virtutibus spectandas feminas suas, non ex cultu or-
natuque censuisset, fucum omnem muliebrem civitate sua legibus expulit om-
15   nibusque comendi et ornandi corporis artificibus Sparta interdixit, tamquam
corruptoribus virtutis et bonarum artium. Dominus per Osee prophetam
significat mulierem, quae a se ad moechos suos conversa esset, inauribus et
monilibus se ornasse, ut illos sequeretur, non Deum suum. Quae ornamenta
maledicta sunt, ut Tertullianus ait: 'Sine quibus non potuit maledicta et
20   prostituta describi.' Deo si te paras ac bonis hominibus, satis pulchra es cum
bona. Diabolo et malis hominibus non placebis nisi naturali pulchritudini et
proinde virtuti multum detrahas. Quid faciunt auriculae perforatae, quas integra cartilagine natura produxit? Quid ni etiam perforet nares luxuria? Sed
hoc quoque apud barbaras quasdam gentes fit. Quid ni vel digitos vel labia?
25   Nam articulorum singulos radians gemma devincit. Quid prodest tantum
auri pondus, ut etiam congestum videri possit ad vires ostendendas? An melior crederis, an formosior, an prudentior, tanto metallo onerata? Nihil tale.

    60. De bonitate quid attinet loqui? An potest esse bona simulatrix quae
et aliud vult credi quam sit? Quid quod formosiores, mea quidem sententia,
30   illae videntur feminae in quibus pulchritudo faciei elucet in mediocri cultu?
Nam splendor cultus obscurat decus formae. Nihil est enim tantum quin
comparatione maioris minuatur ac velut decrescat. Si tantus est nitor ornatus,
necesse est ut honor speciei appareat minor et quicquid in ea placet femina
cultui attribuatur, non formae. Sapienter Romanus ille qui princeps suae
35   civitatis in humili domuncula habitans: 'Malo', inquit, 'ut domui ego sim

---

58. (Non potes ... nigrum) *Vulg. Matth. 5, 36*
    59. (Lycurgi ... artium) *Plut. mor. 228B–C* // (mulierem ... suum) *Vulg. Os. 2, 13* //
(Sine ... describi) *Tert. cult. fem. 2, 12, PL 1, 1330C*

11 de barbaris **Γ** ex gentibus **H** // **18–20** Quae ... describi **Γ** *deest in* **H** // **21–22** et
proinde virtuti **Γ** *deest in* **H** // **24** quoque **Γ** *deest in* **H** / barbaras quasdam **Γ** quasdam
barbaras **H** // **25** Nam ... devincit **Γ** *deest in* **H** // **28**–p.84,**10** De bonitate ... pertinet
deest in **H**

this would seem to be a grievous injustice to the first painter and he would be justly indignant. Do you think that you can commit such an act of insolence, an offense against the divine craftsman with impunity? Though you may not be immodest and unchaste with men in the allurements of your maquillage, you will be accounted worse than an adulteress in corrupting and violating what belongs to God. What you think is adornment and embellishment is an assault upon the work of God, a prevarication of the truth. Your Lord says: 'You cannot make one hair white or black.' And do you think you can be more powerful by challenging the word of God? With audacious pretension and sacrilegious contempt you dye your hair, and with a bad omen you make it flame-colored and sin—O loathsome thought—with your head, the noblest part of the body.

59. These are the words of Cyprian. It is embarrassing after enumerating Christian principles to relate something from the pagans. I shall merely give the example of Lycurgus, a man of great wisdom, legislator of the Lacedaemonians. Since he thought the women of his country should be esteemed for their virtues and not for their dress and adornments, he forbade by law feminine cosmetics from the state and banned from Sparta all products pertaining to beauty and adornment, as corruptors of virtue and good behavior. The Lord through Osee the prophet teaches us that the woman who turned away from him to her lover adorned herself with earrings and necklaces in order to follow them and not her God. These ornaments are cursed, as Tertullian said, 'Without them she could not be described as cursed and as a prostitute.' If you groom yourself for God and good men you are beautiful enough if you are good. You will not be pleasing to the devil and evil men unless you deprive yourself of much of your natural beauty and therefore of your virtue. What good are perforated ears when nature made them of imperforate cartilage? Why doesn't she perforate her nose as well in her extravagance? This is done in barbarous nations. Why not her fingers and her lips? For a gleaming jewel holds fast every one of her fingers. What is the purpose of all this weight of gold; is it that piled up in this way it is meant to show off your strength? Do you think you are better or more beautiful or wiser, laden down with so much metal? Nothing of the sort.

60. Concerning goodness, what can be said? Can a woman who dissembles, who wishes to be thought of as something other than she is, be a good woman? And for that matter, in my opinion, those women seem more beautiful whose beauty of countenance shines out in moderate personal adornment. Fine attire obscures comeliness of form. There is nothing so grand that it is not lessened and diminished by comparison with something greater. If the adornment is so brilliant, it is inevitable that the lustre of her beauty will appear to be less, and whatever is pleasing in that woman will be attributed to her adornment rather than to her beauty. That famous Roman, who though the leader of his city, dwelt in a humble abode, said

ornamento quam mihi domus nec aliquid volo domi meae visendum praeter
me.' Sic feminae pulchriores censentur in quibus modicus atque honestus
cultus commendat et probum ingenium et amabilem formam; non opprimit
fastuosus ille ac nimis lautus. Decet virum ornatus gravitatis, feminam
5   honestatis. Quid, nullasne olim censetis formosas et fuisse et esse existimatas
et adamatas viris suis apud rude illud saeculum et priscum, cum nondum
malitia tantas vires nacta esset? Ego vero plures autumo et constantius gratas
cum non erat pulchritudo temporaria, sed perpetua, videlicet naturalis,
quam non poneret femina cum veste. Quando igitur nec ad decorem facit
10   cultus ille nec ad virtutem, quorsum pertinet? Dic ipsa. 'Ditior videbor et
ea causa honoratior.' Haeccine cogitatio est, haec vox pectoris Christiani?
Inutili auro collum tuum premitur cum tot circa te esurientibus nummulum
neges? Spolias vicinos ac forsan etiam familiam, liberos, coniugem ipsum, ut
in te auri et gemmarum radii spectantium oculos praestringant? Tam multi
15   exuuntur ut tu una induaris? Haec est caritas Christiana? Hoc in baptismo
conceptis iurasti verbis renuntiare te Satanae ac pompis eius? At quid non
pomparum Satanae tenacius prolixiusque retines quam gentiles ipsae?

61. Totam te specta, Satanae satellitem agnosces. Tu domi exquisitissimis
ad saturitatem utens cibis, ructans capos, perdices, phasianos, delicatas
20   placentulas, pulmenta, condimenta, offulas, omnia magno conquisita et
comparata, inter tot enectos fame? Tu in otio, in lusibus ac voluptatibus,
inter tot sudores et aerumnas vicinorum? Tu in publico, serico et bysso
amicta, inter tot nudos? Tu auro, tu argento, tu gemmis, inter tot mendicos
spectanda? An sic Christi pauperis discipula es et non potius divitis Plutonis?
25   Nolo te squalidam et pannosam conspici, sed nec in vestibus ad ostentationem
et superbiam inventis; imitare cuius merito gaudes nomine cognominari,
Christum; imitare tenuem et frugalem eius Matrem, quam nunc Dominam
homines colunt, inferi tremunt, superi reverentur; cuius ut exterior vestis ex
vulgari et parabili erat panno, sic interior ille vestitus speciosissimo auro et
30   gemmis distinctus atque intertextus. Non potes utrimque esse aurea. Elige
utrum mavis, corpus an animum aureum? Non queo singula argumenti
huius percurrere, quae sunt infinita, nempe vitia.

62. De odoribus tamen dicam. Ut non probat animus recte atque
ad humanitatem institutus immunditiem aut foetorem, moderatos odores

---

10 Dic ipsa **Γ** Quid igitur? Dic ipsa **H** // **10–11** et ea causa honoratior **Γ** *deest in* **H** //
11 Haeccine **Γ** O vanitas animi! Haec **H** // **13** forsan **Γ** forte **H** / coniugem ipsum **Γ**
et coniugem tuum **H** // **14–15** Tam ... induaris **Γ** *deest in* **H** // **17** prolixiusque **Γ**
copiosiusque **H** // **20–21** et comparata **Γ** *deest in* **H** // **24** spectanda **Γ** *deest in* **H** // **25–26**
squalidam ... inventis **Γ** nudam esse, sed nec vestibus tectam in ostentatione et superbia
paratis **H** // **26** merito **Γ** *deest in* **H** // **29** sic **Γ** ita **H** / speciosissimo **Γ** deauratissimo **H**
// **32** percurrere **Γ** persequi **H** / quae ... vitia **Γ** *deest in* **H** // **33–34** Ut ... foetorem **Γ**
Non probat Christianus animus immunditiem, non foetorem **H** // **34**–p.86,**2** moderatos
... affecti **Γ** *deest in* **H**

wisely: 'I prefer to be an ornament to my house rather than the house to me, and I want nothing to be on view in my house except myself.' Similarly those women are accounted more beautiful in whom a modest and respectable adornment commends their good character and attractiveness, not burdened down by excessive and haughty care of the self. Gravity is the adornment of a man, honor of a woman. Do you think, perchance, there were no beautiful women who were considered such and loved by their husbands in olden days, in that pristine, unsophisticated age when vice had not yet attained such power? I think there were more beautiful women at that time and that their beauty was more lasting since it was not merely a temporary beauty, but permanent, that is, natural, which a woman did not put on with her clothing. Since, therefore, this adornment contributes neither to their appearance nor to their virtue, of what use is it? You tell me: 'I shall appear richer and for that reason more honorable.' Is this the thought, are these the words of a Christian heart? Your neck is weighted down with useless gold while you refuse a pittance to so many around you who are suffering from hunger? You despoil your neighbors and perhaps also your family, your children and even your husband so that the rays of gold and jewels will bedazzle the eyes of the onlookers? So many are divested so that you alone may be clothed? Is this Christian charity? Is this what you solemnly swore in baptism, to renounce Satan and his pomps? But do you not hold on to the pomps of Satan with more tenacity and perseverance than the pagans themselves?

61. Look at yourself from head to foot. You will recognize a follower of Satan. Do you consume rich foods at home to the point of satiety, belching up capons, partridges, pheasants, delicate pastries, hors d'oeuvres, sauces, sweetmeats, all sought out and bought at great price, while around you people are dying of hunger? Do you pass your time in idleness, games and entertainments amidst the toils and troubles of your neighbors? Do you go about in public, clad in silk and linen, amidst the naked throngs? Do you preen yourself in gold, silver and jewelry amidst so many beggars? With such behavior are you a disciple of the poor Christ or the rich Pluto? I do not wish to see you in squalor and rags, but neither do I wish to see you in clothes whose purpose is ostentation and conceit. Imitate the one in whose name you rightly glory, Christ; imitate his humble and frugal mother, whom men now worship as their lady, before whom those below stand in trembling and those above in reverential awe. Though her outward garb was made of common and cheap material, her inner vesture is of the most beautiful gold, set and interwoven with precious stones. You cannot be golden in both parts. Which do you wish to be of gold, your body or your soul? I cannot pursue the details of this subject, which are infinite, namely the ramifications of vice.

62. Nevertheless, I shall say something about odors. Just as an upright and cultivated mind does not approve of uncleanliness and stench, and does not

non reicit, quibus spiritus vel reficiuntur defatigati vel excitantur languentes
vel etiam curantur affecti (nam Maria illa unguentum super caput Domini
effudit nardi fidelis pretiosae, quo odore domus tota repleta est; nec id fuit
Christo ingratum), sic odores istos tam immodicos improbat, fomenta istius

5   corporis, cui quo magis indulgetur, eo se in animum erigit insolentius et
universi hominis tyrannidem poscit trahitque ad imas cupiditates omnia,
ubi sedes est suarum deliciarum. Hieronymi dictum est ad Demetriadem
virginem: 'Cincinnatulos pueros et calamistratos et peregrini muris olentes
pelliculas, de quibus illud Arbitri est,

10   Non bene olet qui bene semper olet,

quasi quasdam pestes et venena pudicitiae virgo devitet.' Similis est apud
Martialem versiculus:

      Malo quam bene olere nil olere:

Plautus Mostellaria:

15   Mulier (inquit) recte olet ubi nihil olet.

   63. Respondebit forsan aliqua fastidiosola et quae argutiis ingenii nomen
prudentiae pararit: 'Dandum est aliquid generi, nobilitati, opibus, spectatoribus.' Cedo, cuias es quae ista dicis? Christianane an gentilis? Si gentilis,
tecum non disputo; si Christiana, scito, superbissima femina, non nosse

20   Christum ista discrimina. Arrogantiae sunt haec diabolicae, non modestiae animi Christiani. Inveteravit dictum illud propter veritatem nullum
esse animal ornata femina superbius. Non ornamenta sunt ista corporis
aut naturae, sed fomenta insolentiae tuae. 'Veritati,' inquit Tertullianus,
'nemo praescribere potest, non spatium temporum, non patrocinia per-

25   sonarum, non privilegium regionum; quia Dominus noster Christus, qui
manet in aeternum, veritatem se, non consuetudinem cognominavit.' 'Dandum est,' inquis, 'aliquid receptis moribus, dandum consuetudini.' Quaero,
consuetudini quorum? Si sapientum et bonorum hominum, fateor; si stultorum, cur aliquid concedendum est nisi ab stultis? Quid quod (ut docte

---

62. (Maria ... ingratum) *Vulg. Ioh. 12, 3* // (Cincinnatulos ... devitet) *Hier. epist. 130,*
19, PL 22, 1122 // (Non bene ... olet) *Mart. epig. 2, 12, 4* // (Malo ... olere) *Mart. epig. 6,*
55, 5 // (Mulier ... olet) *Plaut. Most. 273*
   63. (nullum ... superbius) *Iuv. 6, 460* // (Veritati ... cognominavit) *Tert. virg. vel. 1, PL*
2, 889A // (Christus ... veritatem) *Vulg. Ioh. 14, 6*

2 nam Maria **Γ** Nam et Maria **H** // **4** sic **Γ** sed **H** / improbat **Γ** *deest in* **H** // **15** Mulier ...
olet **Γ** Mulierem recte olere ait ubi nihil olet **H** // **17–18** spectatoribus **Γ** *deest in* **H** // **18**
cuias **Γ** quaenam tu **H** // **20** Arrogantiae **Γ** Superbiae **H** // **21** Inveteravit ... veritatem **Γ**
Antiquum dictum est, idem verissimum **H** // **22** femina **Γ** muliere **H** // **22–26** Non ...
cognominavit **Γ** *deest in* **H** // **27** inquis **HWW²** inquit **BV**

reject mild perfumes, by which tired spirits are revived or are roused from their languor or even cured of their ailments (for Mary Magdalen poured upon Our Lord's head ointment made of precious nard, whose fragrance filled the whole house and was not displeasing to Christ), so he condemns excessive odors, fomentations of this body of ours, which the more it is indulged, the more it rebels insolently against the mind, claims tyranny over the whole man and drags everything down to the basest desires, the seat of self-indulgence. This was said by St. Jerome to the virgin Demetrias: 'A virgin should avoid like the plague and as poison to chastity boys elegantly dressed and with their hair curled, wearing skins smelling of some exotic mouse, of whom Martial says:

He who smells good all the time, does not smell good.

There is another similar verse in Martial:

I'd rather have no smell than smell good all the time.

Plautus in the *Mostellaria* says:

A woman smells best when she has no smell at all.

63. Some sophisticated woman who has acquired a reputation for wisdom through cleverness of wit will perhaps respond: 'We must make some concessions to ancestry, nobility, wealth, to lookers-on.' Come now, what is your allegiance if you can say this? Are you Christian or pagan? If you are a pagan, I have no argument with you. If you are a Christian, I must inform you, haughty woman, that Christ does not know of these distinctions. These betray the devil's arrogance, not the modesty of the Christian soul. There is an old proverb that has survived because of its truth: 'There is no living creature more haughty than a richly adorned woman.' These are not adornments of the body or of nature, but incentives to your insolence. Tertullian said: 'No one can put limits on the truth, neither a period of time, nor influence of persons, nor privilege of country, because Christ the Lord, who abides for eternity, called himself truth, not convention.' You say, 'Some concession must be made to received morals, to custom.' I ask 'To whose custom?' If it is that of wise and good men, I grant it. If it is that of stupid men, why should any concession be made, except by the stupid?

Quintilianus ait) consensus bonorum ea sola dici debet consuetudo vitae?
Est inducta mala consuetudo; esto tu princeps eius abolendae et ea penes te
manebit gloria. Sequentur et aliae tuum exemplum ac ut a malis confirmatus
est mos pravus, sic a bonis exstirpabitur atque invehetur bonus. Quod si
5   semper moribus obsecundandum ac indulgendum est, numquam in melius
proficient saecula, semper in peius, cum invehere pessimum licebit morem,
auferre non licebit.

    64. Age, quorum est iste mos quem iactas aut unde acceptus? A gentilibus
feminis. Cur non etiam gentilitatem cum eo more retinemus? Aut si Chris-
10 tianum placet nomen, quin et mores quoque huic nomini congruentes? Illa
gentilis est et ea facit quae Deum non novit nec temperantiam vitae. Tu,
quae Deum nosti et in eo abluta es, quid plus quam illa praestas? Quid est
illud quod renuntiare te Satanae et omnibus eius pompis es professa, si sic
cum gentili certas ut non eam aeques modo pompa, sed superes? Quid dicam
15 aemulari te gentiles? Non illas sanctiores et severiores antiquas, sed iuniores
has, leves, luxu diffluentes, flagitiis et sceleribus delibutas. Non Lacaenas
illas priscas honestissimas, quarum reginae, Lysandri coniugi eiusque filiabus, cum Dionysius Syracusanus rex stolas pretiosissimas misisset, eas illae
spreverunt, hoc dicto: 'Hae dedecori nobis erunt potius quam decori.' Non
20 veteres Romanas, quibus cum Pyrrhus, Epirotarum rex, per legatum Cyneam
aurum, argentum, byssina et serica amicula donaret, nulla inventa est tam
vel cultus studiosa vel avida vel perdita mente et ore perfricto quae acciperet.

    65. Q. Claudia, virgo Vestalis, dubiae pudicitiae fama laboravit, quod
exquisitiore et accuratiore corporis cultu uteretur. Lex fuit Romae Oppia,
25 secundo bello Punico lata, ne qua mulier auri plus semuncia haberet
neu versicolori veste uteretur; quae duravit quoad Asiana luxuria invasit
civitatem. Tunc mulieres tamquam furibundae in publicum se proruerunt,
licentiam sibi cuiusvis ornatus flagitantes. Ne hoc fieret, vir gravissimus

    64. (Non Lacaenas ... decori) *Plut. mor. 190E, 229A, 439D* // (Pyrrhus ... acciperet)
Val. Max. 4, 3, 14
    65. (Q. Claudia ... uteretur) *Ov. fast. 4, 309* // (Lex ... verissimus) *Liv. 34, 1, 3* //

3 manebit gloria Γ gloria erit **H** // **5** obsecundandum ac indulgendum Γ parendum **H** // **6**
invehere Γ invenire **H** // **10** congruentes Γ congrui **H** // **13–14** es professa ... superes Γ
dixisti si non aequas modo pompa gentilem sed superas **H** // **15** aemulari Γ imitari **H** //
16 delibutas Γ obrutas **H** // **18–19** eas ... dicto Γ illae responderunt **H** // **22** et ore
perfricto Γ *deest in* **H** / acciperet Γ accipiet **H** // **24** exquisitiore ... uteretur Γ exquisitius
et accuratius cultu corporis uteretur **H** // **24–25** Romae ... lata Γ secundo bello Punico
Romae Oppia **H** // **26–27** invasit civitatem Γ civitatem invasit **H**

Lex Oppia: This was a war-time sumptuary measure promulgated in 215 B.C., the year
after the disastrous battle of Cannae. It was repealed twenty years later despite the fierce
opposition of Cato.

Quintilian shrewdly said: 'The consensus of good men, that alone should be called the general practice of society.' A bad practice has been introduced. You should be the first to abolish it, and this glory will remain to you. Other women will follow your example and just as a bad custom is established by bad persons, so it will be extirpated by good persons and a good one instilled. But if we must always act in compliance with and condescend to custom, the world will never improve but will grow even worse when it will be possible to introduce bad customs, but never do away with them.

64. Tell me, whose is this custom which you talk about so freely, and where did it originate? From pagan women. Why then do we not retain paganism with that custom? Or if you like the name of Christian, why do you not accept the customs appropriate to that name? She is a pagan woman and she does those things because she does not know God or moderation of life. You, who know God and were baptized in his name, why do you do more than she? What is all this about your profession to renounce Satan and all his pomps, if you are to contend with a pagan woman not merely to equal her in her pomp but outdo her? What do I mean when I say you rival pagan women? Not the matrons of the ancient world known for their piety and severity, but those closer to our own times, frivolous, given to luxury, steeped in sinfulness and crime. Not those upright Spartan women of old, whose queen, the wife of Lysander, and her daughters, when Dionysus, king of Syracuse, sent them precious stoles, refused them with these words, 'These will be more of a disgrace than an honor to us.' Not those women of ancient Rome, of whom when Pyrrhus, king of Epirus, through his ambassador Cineas offered them gifts of gold, silver, and garments of linen and silk, not one was found so ambitious for fine apparel, so greedy, so morally depraved and shameless as to accept them.

65. Quinta Claudia, a vestal virgin, aroused suspicion concerning her chastity because she was too attentive and meticulous in the care of her body. There was a law in Rome called the Lex Oppia, promulgated during the second Punic war, requiring that a woman should not have more than a half ounce of gold, and should not dress in many-colored clothes. This law lasted until Asian luxury invaded the city. Then the women as if in a frenzy burst into public demanding freedom to dress as they wished. To

---

64. Lysander: Spartan general who forced the surrender of Athens in 404 B.C. and established the rule of the Thirty Tyrants.

Dionysius: Dionysius I, tyrant of Syracuse, 404–367 B.C.

Pyrrhus: He inflicted a serious defeat upon the Romans at the battle of Heraclea in 280 B.C. It was after this victory that he attempted this act of bribery.

65. Quinta Claudia: This occurred in 204 B.C. Vives tells only part of the story. Ovid goes on to relate how she vindicated her chastity by taking a rope and moving the vessel conveying the image of Cybele to Rome, a feat that could only be accomplished by a chaste woman according to the soothsayers.

M. Cato consul oratione sapientiae plena dissuasit. Suaserunt duo tribuni plebis, quorum oratio scripta est apud Livium, diluta , sane et auribus stultae multitudinis accommodatior quam sapientum. Pervicerunt tamen importunitate et pervicacia sua mulieres ut superbiae suae freni laxarentur liceretque quantum liberet. Unde quae mala eventura essent praedixit Cato, ut aliis multis suis dictis, ita et hoc vates verissimus. Nam quis explicare queat quanta sit pudicitiae iactura propter hanc cultus contentionem? Dum unamquamque ornatu a socia vinci pudet et ubi compositas se atque instructas intuentur, tunc prodire, tunc ostentare sese et versari cum viris gestiunt. Ibi naufragium pudicitiae. 'Aegyptias mulieres,' inquit Plutarchus, 'calceis uti patrius mos non fuit, ut domi continerentur.' Sic feminae si serica, byssina, aurea, argentea, gemmas, lapillos adimas, facilius domi clausam teneas.

66. Apud eundem auctorem duae sunt, Sophoclis tragici et Cratis philosophi, de ornatu sententiae. Ille de divite cultu inquit: 'Non est hic ornatus, o misera, sed dedecus videbitur et manifestum insaniae tuae argumentum.' Crates ait ornatum esse quod ornat: 'Ornat autem quo mulier honestior fit; talem non reddit aurum aut smaragdus aut purpura, sed quaecumque indicia sunt gravitatis, moderationis, pudoris.' Democrates mulieris ornatum sermonis et ornatus parsimoniam definit, cuius etiam est Sophocles sententiae. Apud Graecos vulgare illud erat et proverbii forma iactatum ornamentum mulieris non aurum esse, sed mores. Aristoteles, philosophus ingeniosissimus, mulieres iubet sumptu, vestitu et apparatu minore etiam uti quam legibus permissum sit, considerare praecipiens non vestimentorum nitorem nec excellentiam formae nec auri copiam tantum valere ad mulieris laudem quantum modestiam in rebus ac studium honeste ac decore vivendi. In hanc eandem sententiam cunctus saecularium sapientium populus vadit. Nullus est in eis qui hanc cultus elegantiam ab stultitiae vanitate profectam non pronuntiet, ut erubescat Christiana femina gentiles sequi, non eos graves et sapientes viros, non probas et honestas matronas, sed stultorum errorem et

---

65. (Aegyptias ... continerentur) *Plut. mor. 142C*
66. (Apud ... sententiae) *Plut. mor. 141E* // (Democrates ... definit) Δημοκράτους φιλοσόφου, γνῶμαι χρυσαί, *ed. Orellius, p.89* // (mulieres ... vivendi) *Aristot. oec. 1, 3 (1344a)*

1 consul ... dissuasit Γ consul dissuasit oratione H // 2 diluta Γ diluta et inepta H // 2–3 sane ... sapientum Γ *deest in* H // 4 pervicacia Γ pertinacia H // 6 vates verissimus Γ verissimus vates H / explicare Γ dicere H // 7 Dum Γ Cum H // 8–9 ubi ... intuentur Γ cum compositae et instructae sunt H // 9 versari cum viris Γ inter viros esse H // 12–13 clausam teneas Γ teneas clausam H // 14 eundem auctorem Γ eundem gravissimum auctorem H // 19 Democrates H Demochares Γ // 21 iactatum Γ *deest in* H // 25 excellentiam formae Γ excellentiae formam H // 26 decore **HWW²B** dedecore **V** // 27–29 In ... pronuntiet Γ *deest in* H // 29 Christiana femina Γ femina Christiana H // 30 matronas Γ feminas H

prevent this the consul Marcus Cato, a man of great dignity, spoke out against it in a speech full of wisdom. Two tribunes of the people also spoke against it, whose speeches are recorded in Livy, but toned down, adapted more to the ears of the stupid populace than to those of wise men. The women won out, however, through their insistence and pertinacity, with the result that all restraints to their vainglory were relaxed and they could do as they pleased. Cato predicted what ills would follow and as in many other of his utterances, so in this instance he proved to be a true prophet. Who could describe what a loss to chastity results from this competition as each is ashamed to be outdone by her peer in personal adornment and when they consider themselves duly groomed and attired, then they long to issue forth into public, put themselves on display and converse with men. That is the shipwreck of chastity. According to Plutarch it was a national custom in Egypt that women did not wear shoes so that they could be confined to the home. So, if you take away from a woman her silks, linens, gold, silver, jewels and precious stones you can more easily keep her in the home.

66. In this same author there are two sayings about adornment, one of Sophocles, the tragedian, and one of Crates, the philosopher. The former said of rich ornamentation: 'This will not be seen as adornment, you poor woman, but as dishonor and a manifest proof of your insanity.' Crates said that adornment is that which adorns, and that which adorns is what makes a woman more virtuous. This does not come about with gold or emeralds or purple but by all that gives proof of dignity, moderation and chastity.' Demochares defined the adornment of women as economy of speech and personal adornment, and this is also the opinion of Sophocles. Among the Greeks there was a popular saying circulated in the form of a proverb that the adornment of a woman is not gold, but good morals. Aristotle, the wisest of philosophers, bids women to make less use of luxuries, clothing and accoutrements than is permitted by law. He urges them to reflect that it is not splendor of attire or preeminence of beauty or abundance of gold that earns praise for a woman, but modesty in her possessions and the desire to lead an honorable and respectable life. This opinion is shared by all the wise men of the secular world. There is not one among them who does not declare that this cult of finery comes from vain stupidity, so that a Christian woman should be ashamed to follow the pagans, not those sage and wise men, nor those virtuous and honorable matrons, but the errors of stupid

insanarum exemplum. Et profiteor me expedire non posse quid, saltem dictu
honestum, ornatui suo mulieres queant obtendere nisi solum ut formosiores
videantur, ut magis illiciant viros.

67. Atqui hoc etiam gentiles puderet confiteri. Loquar cum Christianis.
Ut virorum animas facilius et arctius illaqueent? 'Non de integra conscientia
venit,' inquit Tertullianus, 'studium placendi per decorem, quem naturaliter
invitatorem libidinis scimus.' Chrysostomus non habet in numero virginum
studio comendi ac ornandi sui deditas. Quanto minus si id fecerint ut
libidinem intuentium inflamment? Tu ergo simul superbiae tuae servies et
diaboli retia in tuo corpore ad inspectantium animas capiendas extendes?
O non feminam Christianam, sed diaboli ministram et satellitem! Pronun-
tiabitur tibi indignantis Domini super te atrox comminatio. Per Isaiam enim
sic loquitur Deus: 'Pro eo quod elevatae sunt filiae Sion et ambulaverunt
extento collo et nutibus oculorum ibant et plaudebant et ambulabant et
pedibus suis composito gradu incedebant cum calceolis squamatis, decal-
vabit Dominus verticem filiarum Sion et turpitudinem earum nudabit et
pro ornamento erit ignominia. In die illa auferet Dominus ornamentum
calceamentorum et lunulas et torques et monilia et armillas et mitras et dis-
criminalia et perischelides et murenulas et olfactoriola et inaures et annulos
et gemmas in fronte pendentes et mutatoria et pallia et linteamina et acus et
specula et sindones et vittas et theristra. Et pro suavi odore foetor et pro zona
funiculus et pro crispanti et compto crine calvitium, et pro fascia pectorali
cilicium.' Ista de feminis.

68. De viris quoque propter eas ipsas vilibus et se indignis rebus addictis
et mancipatis: 'Pulcherrimi quoque viri tui gladio cadent et fortes tui in
proelio. Et maerebunt atque lugebunt portae eius et ipsa urbs desolata in
terra sedebit.' Haec Dominus Deus terribilis cum irascitur, cuius sanctus
martyr Cyprianus sic inquit: 'Sed sunt aliquae divites et facultatum ubertate
locupletes quae opes suas praeferant et se bonis suis uti contendant. Sciant
primo illam divitem esse quae in Deo dives est; illam esse locupletem
quae locuples in Christo est; bona illa esse quae sunt spiritalia, divina,

---

67. (Non ... scimus) *Tert. cult. fem. 2, 2, PL 1, 1317B* // (Chrysostomus ... deditas) *Ioh.*
Chrys. in epist. 1 Tim. 2, hom. 8, PG 62, 372, 541–542 // (Pro ... cilicium) *Vulg. Is. 3, 16–24*
68. (Pulcherrimi ... sedebit) *Vulg. Is. 3, 25–26* // (Sed ... ciba) *Cypr. hab. virg. 7; 9–11,*
PL 4, 458–462 //

1–2 quid ... obtendere Γ quem saltem dictu honestum possunt ornatui suo praetextum
mulieres obtendere H // **4** Atqui Γ *deest in* H / confiteri Γ *deest in* H // **5–9** Non ...
inflamment *deest in* H // **9–10** servies ... extendes Γ servis ... extendis H // **15** cum
calceolis squamatis Γ *deest in* H // **16** turpitudinem Γ crinem H // **21** Et pro suavi Γ Et
erit pro suavi H // **22** compto Γ *deest in* H // **23** Ista Γ Haec Dominus H // **24–25** eas
... mancipatis Γ easdem qui vilitate rerum capti sunt H // **29** uti contendant Γ uti debere
contendant H*Cypr.*

men and the examples of foolish women. And I confess that I cannot explain what verbal pretext women can use to excuse their adornment except that they may appear more beautiful and thereby attract men the more.

67. But even pagan women would be ashamed to acknowledge this. I shall speak to Christian women: 'Is it to ensnare the souls of men more easily and more tightly?' 'The desire to please by exterior embellishment does not come from a pure conscience' says Tertullian, 'for we know that to be an invitation to lust.' Chrysostom does not include among the number of virgins those who devote themselves to preening and adorning themselves. How much less would he do so if they have done it to enflame the lust of those that looked at them! Therefore at one and the same time you will be a slave to your vanity and will spread the nets of the devil in your body to capture the souls of those who look upon you. You are no Christian woman but the servant and accomplice of the devil! The dire threat of the wrathful Lord will be uttered against you, for God speaks thus through Isaias: 'Because the daughters of Zion are haughty and walked with outstretched necks and went about with wanton looks, mincing along with measured step, with scaly shoes, the Lord will lay bare the heads of the daughters of Zion and will expose their baseness and in place of adornment there will be ignominy. In that day the Lord will take away the finery of their anklets, their crescents and necklaces and pendants and bracelets and turbans and head-dress and leg-bands and amulets and perfume-boxes and earrings and rings and jewels hanging from their foreheads and capes and mantles and linens and pins and mirrors and muslins and head-bands and summer garments. And instead of a sweet fragrance there will be a stench and instead of a girdle a rope and instead of curly and well-kept hair baldness and instead of rich robes a haircloth.' So he says of women.

68. About men who because of women surrendered themselves like slaves to vile and unworthy things he says: 'Your beautiful men will fall by the sword and your brave men in battle, and her gates will lament and mourn, and the city will sit desolate upon the ground.' These are the words of the Lord God, terrible when he is angered, and his holy martyr Cyprian has this to say:

> But there are some rich women, endowed with an abundance of wealth, who make ostentation of their riches and claim that they are making use of their own resources. Let them know first of all that she is rich who is rich in God; she is wealthy, who is wealthy in Christ; true blessings are those that are spiritual,

caelestia, quae nobiscum apud Deum perpetua possessione permaneant.
Ceterum si tu te sumptuosius comas et per publicum notabiliter incedas,
oculos in te iuventutis illicias, suspiria adolescentium post te trahas, con-
cupiscendi libidinem nutrias, peccandi fomenta succendas, ut si ipsa non
pereas, alios tamen perdas et velut gladium te et venenum videntibus
praebeas, excusari non potes quasi mente casta sis et pudica. Redarguit
te cultus improbus et impudicus ornatus nec computari iam potes inter
puellas et virgines Christi, quae sic vivis ut possis adamari. Locupletem te
dicis et virginem. Sed iactare divitias suas virginem non decet cum dicat
Scriptura divina: "Quid nobis profuit superbia aut quid divitiarum iactura
contulit nobis? Transierunt illa omnia tamquam umbra." Locupletem te
esse dicis et divitem, et utendum putas iis quae possidere te Deus voluit.
Utere, sed ad res salutares; utere, sed ad bonas artes; utere ad illa quae
Deus praecipit, quae Dominus ostendit. Divitem te sentiant pauperes, locupletem te sentiant indigentes, patrimonia tua Deo faenora, Christum ciba.'
Haec martyr.

69. Fulgentius vero explanatius: 'Vestis quoque talis sit sacrae virginis quae
testis exsistat intimae castitatis. Nihil nitoris in habitu exterioris hominis
quaeratur, ne interioris hominis habitus sordidetur. Virgo quae ornatum
corporeae vestis affectat, animam suam virtutum splendore despoliat; nec
habet castitatem veram quae intuentibus parat illecebram; nec fidem servat
Christo quae populo quaerit magis placere quam sponso. Consequenter
autem necesse est ut quae humano conspectui concupiscentiam seminat in
divino conspectu iracundiam metat. Ne dicat igitur puella, cum ornatur:
"Vestis aut monile non malefaciet." Ita est. Sed illac introibit malefactor et
suggestor malae voluntatis.' Hactenus ex Divo Fulgentio. Nam in re tam
aliena a moribus et consuetudine diuturna et confirmata libenter sanctorum
patrum auctoritatem interponimus, quo fides sit apud elegantes istas et
urbanas maior, quae rusticanam et infrunitam esse ducunt, si qua Christiane
vestiatur.

70. Neque vero satis est quod quaedam dicunt: 'Sufficit mihi mea conscientia, quam Deo approbabo.' Sufficit si proximum non laedis, si non es ei
offendiculo in quod impingat. Modestiam nostram Apostolus vult esse notam

---

68. (Quid ... umbra) *Vulg. sap. 5, 8–9*
69. (Vestis ... voluntatis) *Fulg. Rusp. epist. 3, 22, PL 65, 332C*
70. (Modestiam ... hominibus) *Vulg. Phil. 4, 5* //

4 succendas **HWW²B** succendans **V** // 9 virginem **HΓ** *cod. Wurzburgensis VIII-IX saec.*
divitem *PL 4, 458* // 10 iactura Γ iactatio **H** // 17–p.96,24 Fulgentius ... possunt *deest*
in **H**, *in quo legitur*: Quae quanto est satius feminam Christianam et scire et facere quam quae
gentiles, ut has quoque philosophis suis audientes dictis esse par est non facta dementium
imitanda, non stultorum iudiciis sententiisque assentiendum, nisi dementer etiam insaneque
transigere vitam instituimus

divine, heavenly, that remain to us with God as an eternal possession. But if you deck yourself out too elaborately and walk about in public in such a way as to attract attention and draw the glances of young men and have them sighing after you, encourage lustful desires, kindle the fires of sin, so that if you yourself do not perish you cause the perdition of others, and lend yourself as a sword and poison to those who see you, you cannot be excused from blame as if you were chaste and modest in mind. Your shameless apparel and immodest adornment have convicted you. You can no longer be numbered among the young girls and virgins of Christ, since you live in such a way as to be an object of sexual passion. You say that you are rich and a virgin, but it does not become a virgin to boast of her riches since the divine scripture says: 'What has pride profited us, or what has boasting of riches brought us? All those things have passed away like a shadow.' You say you are wealthy and rich, and you think you must use the things that God has wished you to possess. Use them, but for the good of your soul; use them, but for good works; use them for what God has ordained, for what the Lord has taught you. Let the poor feel that you are rich, let the needy know that you are wealthy. Invest your patrimony in God, give nourishment to Christ.

Thus speaks the martyr.

69. Fulgentius elucidates further: 'Let the dress of a sacred virgin be such as to bear witness to her interior chastity. One should not seek magnificence in the dress of the exterior person lest that of the interior person be sullied. The virgin who affects adornment of her bodily clothing despoils her soul of the splendor of virtue. She who rouses allurement in those who behold her does not possess true chastity. She who wishes to please the crowd rather than her spouse does not keep faith with Christ. Of necessity, therefore, one who sows concupiscence in the sight of humans will reap anger in the sight of God. A girl should not say when she is adorning herself: "This dress or necklace will do no harm." That may be. But by that path the evil-doer and the prompter of ill-will will enter.' These are the words of Fulgentius. In a subject-matter so foreign to my way of life and daily habits I willingly resort to the authority of the holy fathers, so that I shall elicit greater belief from those elegant and sophisticated women who regard it as rustic and silly if one dresses in a Christian manner.

70. Nor is it enough to say as some do 'My conscience is sufficient for me, which I will prove to God.' It is enough if you do not hurt your neighbor, if you are not a stumbling-block to him that he will collide against. The Apostle wishes that our modesty be known to all men, not for our glory,

omnibus hominibus, non ad gloriam nostram, sed ut Dominus dicit: 'Quo videant vestra opera bona et glorificent Patrem vestrum, qui in caelis est.' Idem Apostolus ne fratrem offendat carnes se in aeternum non gustaturum profitetur. Tu ne fratrem in laqueum pertrahas, non sustinebis pectus tegere
5　nec alienam faciem tuae imponere? Ubi deinde est caritas proximi, cui praefers, non dico vestem tuam, sed vestis ostentationem? Tertullianus religiose: 'Pudicitiae Christianae satis non est esse, verum et videri.' Tanta enim debet esse plenitudo eius ut emanet ab animo in habitum. An non meministi matrem tuam Evam viro fuisse causam ruinae? Et tu illam
10　in eo aemulari vis? Quanto esset satius ut vos lugubri veste sexus vestri peccatum defleretis quam ut splendido ornatu iuvenum concupiscentiam irritaretis? Quid tu, postquam aliquos diabolo manciparis tuis laqueis, quomodo extricabis cum voles? Quomodo ex diaboli servitute in libertatem Christi vindicabis? Quibus piaculis tam nefarium scelus expiabis? Et ludis in
15　tanto discrimine, secura non magis de alieno corio quam de tuo? At sunt quae obiciant: 'Hoc ipsum scandalum fugimus per cultum, ne aliae cultiores redargui se per mediocritatem nostram interpretentur, cum nec inferiore loco natae simus nec minus possideamus.' Sinite illas, iuxta consilium Redemptoris nostri, quia caecae sunt et duces caecarum, quae malunt
20　offendi quam provocari. Si illae scandalizantur vestris bonis, quin vos potius eorum malis? Illae offenduntur quod ex praescripto Apostolorum ornamini; vos magis offendimini quod illae ex diaboli voluntate ac praeceptis. Egregius esset proximi zelus si te et illum perderes, ne ille offenderetur. O alteras illas delicatas puellas quae ne benefacientes quidem alias ferre possunt!
25　　**71.** 'Quid ergo,' (quaerat aliquis)' sordentes tu et squalidas esse feminas iubes'? Ego vero id nolo, nec tam spurca est mea disciplina, nec mihi umquam immundities cordi fuit. Sed Apostolicam regulam servari velim

---

70. (Quo ... est) *Vulg. Matth. 5, 16* ∥ (ne fratrem ... profitetur) *Vulg. I Cor. 8, 13* ∥ (Pudicitiae ... videri) *Tert. cult. fem. 2, 13, PL 1, 1332A* ∥ (Sinite ... caecarum) *Vulg. Matth. 15, 14*
　71. (Apostolicam regulam) *Vulg. I Tim. 2, 9–10* ∥

25 quaerat **Γ** dicet **H** ∥ **25–26** sordentes ... iubes **Γ** sordidas tu et squalentes iubes esse feminas **H** ∥ **26** id **Γ** tales esse **H** / spurca **Γ** sordida **H** ∥ **27** cordi fuit **Γ** placuit **H** ∥ **27**–p.98,2 Sed ... mulieres **Γ** At quales futuras esse oporteat Petrus et Paulus, ecclesiae columina, duobus brevissimis praeceptis statuunt. Petrus inquit: 'Mulierum ne sit exterior vel capillis complicatis vel circumvectione auri aut indumentorum amictu ornatus.' Ceterum mens et conscientia, quae separata est ab spectantium oculis, si incorrupta sit et placido quodam agatur spiritu ac tranquillo, ea demum splendida res est apud Dominum et magnifica. Paulus sic: 'Mulieres in habitu ornato cum verecundia et sobrietate ornantes se et non intortis crinibus aut auro aut margaritis, vel veste pretiosa, sed (quod decet mulieres) promittentes pietatem per opera bona.' Haec Apostoli cum dicunt non sordidas, non squalentes et obscenas iubent esse mulieres **H**

but as the Lord says: 'So that they may see your good works and glorify Your Father who is in heaven.' The same Apostle says that in order not to offend his brother, he will never eat meat. And will you not consent to cover your breast and refrain from putting another face over your own, so that you will not lead him into a snare? Where then is charity for your neighbor, to whom you prefer, I shall not say your dress, but the ostentation of your dress? Tertullian says sternly: 'It is not enough for Christian modesty that it exist, but also that it be seen.' Its fullness should be such that it should emanate from the soul to the external garb. Or do you not remember that your mother Eve was the cause of man's destruction? Do you wish to rival her in this? How much better it would be if you lamented the sin of your sex in clothes of mourning rather than incite the concupiscence of young men with your splendid attire! After you have enslaved some men to the devil by your snares, how will you extricate them when you want to? How will you rescue them from the servitude of the devil to the freedom of Christ? With what rites of atonement will you expiate such a nefarious deed? Are you gambling in such a critical situation, no more certain of another's skin than of your own? But some may object: 'This is the very scandal we are trying to avoid in our dress, for others better dressed than we will interpret our mediocrity of dress as a reproof to them, since we are no less well-born than they and no less wealthy.' Let them be, according to the advice of our Redeemer, because they are blind, and leaders of the blind, and wish to be offended rather than challenged. If they are scandalized by your good actions, why should you not be by their evil actions? They are offended because you adorn yourselves according to the precept of the Apostles. You are more greatly offended because they follow the will and precepts of the devil. That would be a fine example of zeal for your neighbor if you bring about the damnation of both you and him to avoid giving him offense! How different those fastidious girls who even in doing good cannot tolerate other women.

71. Someone may ask: 'Do you want women to be dirty and squalid?' I certainly do not, and my teaching is not sordid, nor was uncleanliness ever a thing to my liking. I wish that the Apostolic rule that I set out at the beginning

quam initio tractationis huius posui, quae non immundas nec obscenas et
horrentes situ ac squalore iubet esse pias mulieres, non illuvie ac pannis
obtectas; sed ab immodico dehortatur ornatu, simplicemque et parabilem
suadet. Sunt suae frugalitati munditiae, puriores multo quam luxui, ut facilius
est a sordibus exiguum vasculum tueri quam amplam suppellectilem. Non
vestietur serico, at laneo; non byssino, at lineo vulgari; non splendebit vestis,
at nec sordebit; non erit admirationi, sed nec fastidio. Mundus muliebris
nominatur earum ornatus quo mundities significatur, non artificium vel
opulentia auri vel argenti aut margaritarum gemmarumve. Non video rei
tam sumptuosae ad quid valeat usus nisi quorundam lapillorum vires magis
aestimentur quam ostentatio, sicut coralli vel smaragdi, si modo tantillae
rei vires illas natura indidit quas perhibent. Sed quota quaeque propter eas
quidem lapillos quaerit et non potius in vanitatem ut ditior habeatur? Multo
minor est usus sericorum, in quibus quod brevi deterantur, perit expensa, et
sumptus est intolerabilior rei familiari.

72. Ergo mea virgo non fucabit faciem, sed mundabit; non illinet sapun-
culo, sed abluet aqua; non capillos insolabit aut inficiet ut colorem mutet,
sed nec habebit impexos neque furfuribus capitis horrentes; caputque ipsum
et ab sudore et ab squalore tuebitur. Non oblectabitur delicatis odoribus,
minus foetore. Ad speculum sese intuebitur, non ut accurate comat se et
pingat, verum ne quid ridiculum aut dedecens sit in ore et toto capite, quod
cernere non potest nisi per speculum. Tum ibi se componet, ne quid in vultu
sit quod castam et modestam foedet. Postremo, quod Socrates discipulis suis
praecipere solebat putabit et sibi dictum esse, ut se in speculo spectarent:
si formosi essent, curarent ne deformem haberent animum; sin deformes,
pulchritudine animi corporis deformitatem compensarent. Inter haec omnia
pudicae animo semper obversabitur pulchritudinem corporis et plerasque
possidentium in magnam arrogantiam et plerosque spectantium in libidines
taetras atque abominandas, quae utrisque exitio fuerint, impulisse. Quo
factum est ut sanctae complures feminae (quantum poterant) negligendae

71. (posui) *inst. fem. Christ. 1, 52* // (Mundus muliebris ... mundities) *Varro ling. 5, 129*
72. (Socrates ... compensarent) *Plut. mor. 141D*

2 ac pannis Γ pannis et situ **H** // **3** dehortatur Γ dehortantur **H** // **4** suadet Γ malunt **H**
// **5** tueri Γ defendere **H** // **7–9** Mundus ... opulentia Γ *deest in* **H** // **9–10** rei tam
sumptuosae Γ *deest in* **H** // **12** perhibent Γ praedicant **H** / quota quaeque Γ quaenam **H**
// **13–15** Multo ... familiari Γ *deest in* **H** // **16** Ergo mea virgo non fucabit Γ At non
fucabit **H** // **17** insolabit aut Γ *deest in* **H** / mutet **H** mutent Γ // **19** et ab squalore
tuebitur Γ squalore purgabit **H** // **20** comat se **H** comat Γ // **21** ridiculum Γ foedum **H** /
ore et toto Γ *deest in* **H** // **22** componet Γ parabit **H** // **24** praecipere solebat Γ praecipiebat **H** // **26** corporis Γ *deest in* **H** // **27–29** plerasque ... impulisse Γ plerasque possi-
dentes in magnam arrogantiam et plerosque spectantes in libidines adduxisse taetras atque
abominandas **H**

of this chapter be observed. It does not prescribe that women be unclean, or filthy, or unsightly in their squalor and neglect, not covered with dirt and rags, but he discourages them from immoderate adornment and persuades them to dress plainly and simply. Simplicity has its own refinement, purer than that of luxury, as it is easier to protect a small vessel than elaborate furnishings. She will not dress in silk but in wool; not in lace but ordinary linen; her dress will not be resplendent, neither will it be squalid. She will not be an object of admiration, nor one of repugnance. Female cosmetics are named after the word for cleanliness, not artifice or opulence of gold, silver, pearls or precious stones. I do not see the use of this sumptuousness unless it be said that some of these stones are valued more for their power than for mere display, like corals and emeralds, if nature really did give these tiny minerals the powers they are said to possess. But how few there are who seek out these stones for that reason and not rather for the sake of vanity so that they may be thought to be richer? The use of silks is less widespread, because they become frayed in a short time, the investment is lost and the cost is too great for domestic finances.

72. Therefore, my ideal young woman will not paint her face, but clean it; she will not smear it with soap, but wash it with water. She will not bleach her hair in the sun or dye it to change its color, but at the same time she will not leave it unkempt or bristling with dandruff. She will keep her head free of perspiration and dirtiness. She will not delight in delicate perfumes, but will like malodor even less. She will look in the mirror not to preen and adorn herself painstakingly but to make sure nothing in her face and on her head appears ridiculous or repulsive, which she cannot see without looking in the mirror. Then she will groom herself in such a way that there be nothing in her countenance that would defile her chastity and modesty. Finally she will consider the counsel that Socrates used to give his followers as addressed to her, viz., that when beholding themselves in the mirror those who were beautiful should take care that their souls were not ugly, and if they were ugly they should compensate for their physical ugliness by their beauty of soul. In all of this the chaste woman will always bear in mind that physical beauty has often driven those who possess it to great arrogance and those who behold it to foul and abominable acts of lust, which contributed to the perdition of both parties. Wherefore it came about that a good many holy women took pains to neglect their appearance as much as possible

formae dederint operam, ut minus quam erant speciosae apparerent, ne in eas inciderent voragines quas paulo antea indicavi.

73. Haec quae de cultu ex institutis Christi attuli cum feminis congruunt omnibus, tum vel maxime virginibus, quas nescio qua tandem ratione elegantius ornari quorundam mos obtinuit quam coniugatas. Ego vero honestius iudico uxorem aliquando, si ita marito placeat, excultiorem prodire quam virginem in quantocumque genere et opibus. Uxor oculis viri sese ornat, virgo tota Christi est, cui se parat. Nam virum vel poscere vel expetere non est germanae virginitatis, ut suo loco dicam. Ideo Apostolus inquit: 'Mulier innupta et virgo cogitat quae Domini sunt, ut sit sancta corpore et spiritu. Quae autem nupta est cogitat quae sunt mundi, quomodo placeat viro.' Illud vero ne admonendum quidem arbitror feminae virili cultu et vestitu utendum non esse; alioqui evidentissimum fore signum et audaciam virilem et notabilem impudentiam inesse muliebri pectori. Conservatur enim distinctione illa vestitus pudor, parens et nutricius pudicitiae, audiendusque est Dominus his verbis in Deuteronomio vetans: 'Non induetur mulier veste virili nec vir utetur veste feminea. Abominabilis enim est apud Deum qui facit hoc.' Sexuum diversitatem natura insignem fecit in animantium corporibus. Quod si nos corpus tegimus et discrimen illud naturale ab occurrentium oculis avertimus, velamentis uti par est ut indumenta ipsa significationem prae se ferant differentiae; oportet ne nos confundamus quod suis notis natura distinxit. Quocirca qui vestimenta reddit promiscua merito abominandus nuncupatur a Domino, qui rem temptat naturae legibus inimicam, unde multa in hominum coetibus exsisterent pericula. Sed id nulla audet femina nisi quae pudicitiam prius simul cum pudore abiecerit; cui praecepta nostra nec proderunt nec scribuntur.

CAP. IX. DE SOLITUDINE VIRGINIS

74. Tam validum est in hoc inferiore mundo regnum Satanae et ex eo tanta pro malo conspiratio, tam pertinax vitiorum suorum defensor populus ut nemo proferre possit caput in publicum, quin ilico per omnes sensus in animum insiliat quod virtutem et pietatem divexet; ut sapientissime

---

73. (Mulier innupta ... viro) *Vulg. 1 Cor. 7, 34* // (Non induetur ... hoc) *Vulg. deut. 22, 5*

1 apparerent Γ viderentur **H** // **1–11** ne in eas ... viro Γ *deest in* **H** // **12–14** feminae ... pectori Γ mulierem virili veste non amiciendam; alioqui et audaciam virilem et impudentiam femineo in corpore inesse indicabit **H** // **14–15** Conservatur ... pudicitiae Γ *deest in* **H** // **16** vetans Γ loquens **H** // **17–24** Sexuum ... pericula Γ *deest in* **H** // **24** audet Γ temptat **H** / prius Γ *deest in* **H** // **25** abiecerit Γ abiecit et **H** // **28–31** Tam ... divexet Γ *deest in* **H** // **31**–p.102,2 ut ... irrepere Γ Sancti auctores per sensus corporis velut fenestras quasdam mortem aiunt ad animum intrare **H**

in order to seem less beautiful than they were and not fall into that quagmire I mentioned above.

73. These observations I have made concerning personal adornment based on the teachings of Christ are applicable to all women but especially to unmarried women since for some reason or other the custom has been established among certain people that they are more elegantly adorned than married women. In my opinion, however, I think it more reputable that at times a wife appear in public more richly adorned, if it so pleases her husband, than an unmarried woman, whatever her station or lineage. A wife adorns herself for her husband, the virgin belongs entirely to Christ, for whom she bedecks herself. For to ask for or seek out a husband is not a mark of true virginity, as I shall point out in the proper place. For that reason the Apostle said: ' The unmarried young girl thinks about what pertains to the Lord, how to be holy in body and spirit. The married woman is concerned with worldly affairs, how she may please her husband.' I do not think I need to advise a woman against putting on men's clothing and attire. To do so would be a clear sign of a masculine audacity and astonishing impudence in a woman's heart. In the distinction of dress modesty is preserved, which is the parent and guardian of chastity, and we must harken to the Lord's prohibition in these words of Deuteronomy: 'A woman shall not wear a man's clothing nor shall a man put on a woman's clothing, for whoever does this is an abomination to God.' Nature made a sharp distinction of sexes in the bodies of living things. If we cover the body and guard that natural distinction from the gaze of passers-by, it is fitting to use a covering so that our clothes themselves give visible sign of that distinction; we must not obscure what nature has clearly marked. Therefore one who is ambiguous in dress is justly called abominable by the Lord since he is attempting something that is contrary to the laws of nature, which would give rise to many perils in human society. But no woman attempts such a thing unless she has already cast off her chastity together with her sense of modesty. For whom my precepts will be of no use nor are they written for her.

CHAPTER 9.   ON THE SOLITUDE OF THE VIRGIN

74. So powerful is the kingdom of Satan in this world here below, so great is the conspiracy for evil that thrives in it, so obstinately do the common people defend their own vices that no one can venture forth into public without his soul being assailed immediately through all his senses by things pernicious to virtue and piety. It was wisely said by our forefathers that

nostri dixerint per sensusomnes ceu per fenestras quasdam mortem ad animum vel irrumperevel irrepere. Qua de causa vigilandum est perpetuo in custodia animae et reputandum militiam esse hominis vitam in terra, sicut inquit Iobus, ut, quemadmodum Propheta ille fortis luctator, stemus
5   super custodiam nostram et figamus gradum super munitionem. Ianuas has sensuum tanti periculi haud saepe virgo aperiat et cum aperit, adhibendum est praesidium et caute, ne vel impetu se hostis proruat, si vires desint, vel astu sese insinuet, si prudentia. Virgini rarus debet esse egressus in publicum cum neque negotii sit ei quicquam foris et periculum pretiosissimae rei,
10   pudicitiae. Nec solum cum prodibit sit matri comes, verum etiam cum domi sedet, quod et matribus praecipiendum est.

75. Hieronymus Laetae consulit ut itura ad suburbanum filiam in urbana domo ne relinquat: 'Nesciat,' inquit, 'sine te nec possit vivere ac, cum sola fuerit, pertimescat.' Quod sic volo intelligi ut abducat secum filiam mater
15   si aliquamdiu moratura sit. Nam alioqui nihil necesse est semper comitem matri exire filiam quoties domo prodit, praesertim si ipsa vel ad convivia, vel nuptias, vel virorum congressus, vel ad aliquem similem eat locum, sive necessarii officii gratia, sive ut marito gerat morem, quo virginem filiam afferri non convenit. Sed sit domi mulier aliqua proba, pudicitiae custos;
20   quippe nulla est pestis maior neque perniciosior quam quae alitur domi. Hanc quomodo aliter caveas ni expellas prorsum? Quid prodest ab omni externa iniuria lignum defendere, si intus teredine exedatur?

76. Probissimam novi feminam quae, custodiae puellarum commissa, filios cum puellis lascivius lusitantes, quod tenere nimis illos deamaret,
25   reprehendere et arcere ab iniuria castitatis non sustinebat. Quapropter providendum est ne matrona cui puella creditur viros habeat aut filios aut fratres procaciores ac lascivos vel quibus ipsa obsistere non audeat nec commissam rem fortiter propugnare. Sit non casta modo, sed quae se etiam vultu et gravitate tum prudentiae tum morum tum orationis venerabilem et
30   suspiciendam reddat; cuius oculos et supercilium nedum vocem omnes vereantur, et fratres natu maiores. Ipsa in custodia stationis suae nullum vereatur,

74. (militiam ... terra) *Vulg. Iob 7, 1*
75. (Nesciat ... pertimescat) *Hier. epist. 107, 11, PL 22, 876*

2–8 Qua de causa ... prudentia **Γ** Ni prudentia caveris, sollicitantur illiciunturque deliciis mundi, unde capta tenetur et anima. Idcirco **H** // **10** solum cum prodibit **Γ** cum exibit solum **H** // **11** sedet **Γ** manet **H** / et **Γ** *deest in* **H** // **15–16** semper comitem matri **Γ** matri semper comitem **H** // **16** domo **HV** domi **WW²B** // **18** necessarii officii gratia **Γ** quod debet **H** // **19** afferri non convenit. Sed **Γ** ire non decet. Et **H** // **20** est pestis maior **Γ** pestis maior est **H** // **21** prorsum **HWW²B** prorsus **V** // **22** teredine exedatur **Γ** teredinem habet **H** // **27** ac lascivos **Γ** *deest in* **H** // **27–28** nec ... propugnare **Γ** *deest in* **H** // **30–31** vereantur **Γ** timeant **H** // **31** et ... vereatur **Γ** *deest in* **H**

through all the senses as through windows death bursts in upon the soul or stealthily penetrates its defences. For which reason we must keep constant watch over the soul, and man's life on earth must be thought of as a warfare, as Job said. Like that prophet and courageous fighter, let us be on our guard and fix our firm footing on the battlements. The young woman should seldom open these doors of the senses, fraught with danger, and when she does so, every care and precaution must be taken lest the enemy make a sudden attack if she be lacking in strength or infiltrate themselves by cunning if she be lacking in prudence. An unmarried young woman should rarely appear in public since she has no business there and her most precious possession, chastity, is placed in jeopardy. Not only should she be accompanied by her mother when she issues from her house but even when she is staying quietly at home, and this is enjoined upon mothers as well.

75. Jerome advises Laeta that when she has to go to her country home she should not leave her daughter alone in her house in the city. He says: 'She would not know how or be able to live without you, and when she is alone she would be afraid.' I understand this to mean that the mother should take her daughter with her if she is going to be away for some time. Otherwise it is not necessary that the daughter should always accompany her mother every time she leaves the house, especially if she is going to a banquet or a wedding or a meeting at which men are present, or any similar destination where it would not be proper to take a young woman, whether she do this as part of her duty or to comply with her husband's wishes. There should be some upright woman in the home who will be a guardian of her chastity, since there is no greater or more pernicious plague than that which is nurtured at home. How can you be rid of it without expelling it altogether? What good is it to protect wood from every external harm if it is being eaten away from the inside?

76. I know a very virtuous woman who was entrusted with the care of girls and let her sons play with them in a rather free manner, because she was too fond of her children and could not bear reproving them or keeping them from offending the code of chastity. Therefore provision must be made that the matron to whom the girl is confided does not have men, children or brothers in her house who are inclined to licentiousness or unruliness, or persons to whom she does not dare offer resistance for the protection of the charges committed to her. She should not only be chaste but should earn respect and admiration through her facial expression and the austerity of her wisdom, morals and conversation. Her eyes and the sternness of her brow, not to speak of her voice, should inspire esteem in everyone, even her elder brothers. She should fear no one in the fulfilling of her duties of guardian

75. **Laeta:** Daughter-in-law of Jerome's close friend, Paula, a rich Roman patrician woman.

ut sola praesentia sua tuta omnia circum pudicitiam praestet. Illa vero pellenda quam longissime quae exemplo suo ad lasciviam et libidinem invitet; nam quae pretio conducta ab amatore verbis sollicitat et protrudit ad facinus nomine humano caret; nempe res diabolica, quam fugiet puella
5 non secus ac viperam vel aspidem, quam ex civitate sic expulsam oporteret tamquam communem omnium perniciem. Dici non potest quorum sint eiusmodi mulieres malorum causae. Non ferat ergo puella ne aspectum quidem harum, nam basilisci sunt aut catoblepae; oculis praesentissimum venenum inspirant et vel solo intuitu perimunt. Nec putet quis hyperbolice
10 hoc a me dictum. Sunt nonnullae harum tales artifices ut oculis saepe sine verbis capiant; aliae etiam fascinis et incantationibus utuntur, cuius rei utinam rariora essent exempla. Quid quod vel sola salutatione aut arrisu aut etiam obtutu maculam hic serpens aspergit puellae quam aspexerit? Apud illos praesertim qui artem mulieris norunt, ut taceam quanta labes et quam
15 ineluibilis imprimatur domui, in quam aliquoties sit ingressa. Confugiendum ergo ad matrem velut asylum et ei quid nefaria temptarit narrandum aut sic vitanda et aversanda est ut intuentibus significationem praebeas te in ea pestem metuere. Ita et tibi proderis facto et aliis exemplo, cum quid aliis puellis expavendum in ea sit ostendes. E re publica esset in tenues vetulas
20 inquiri, ut censori morum civitatis constaret unde victum parent; qui si desit, certissimae fiunt lenae atque hinc veneficae.

77. Iam de comitibus sic Hieronymus praecipit: 'Nolo de ancillulis suis aliquam plus diligat cuius crebro auribus insusurret. Quicquid uni loquetur, hoc omnes sciant. Placeat ei comes non compta neque formosa atque lasciva
25 quae liquido gutture carmen dulce moduletur, sed gravis, pallens, sordida, subtristis.' Eadem est ad Demetriadem sententia. In puellis sodalibus illud caveri convenit ne qua vel cultu vel verbis vel lusiunculis noceat lascivis. Nihil tibi sit omnino rei cum puellis quae spectari, quae amari gaudent, quae formosum illum aut divitem aut elegantem aut nobilem gloriantur se habere
30 amatorem et ab eo scriptas litterulas circumferunt; interim suis aequalibus

76. (catoblepae) *Plin. nat. 8, 32*

77. (Nolo ... subtristis) *Hier. epist. 107, 9, PL 22, 875* // (Eadem ... sententia) *Hier. epist. 130, 18, PL 22, 1121–1122*

2 pellenda Γ eicienda **H** // **3** pretio Γ *deest in* **H** // **3–4** et protrudit ad facinus Γ et impellit **H** // **5** quam ... oporteret Γ quam omnes ex civitate sic eicere debent **H** // **8** praesentissimum Γ *deest in* **H** // **10** harum Γ *deest in* **H** // **12** utinam rariora essent Γ non sunt rara **H** / aut arrisu Γ *deest in* **H** // **13** obtutu Γ intuitu **H** / aspexerit Γ spectarit **H** // **14–15** et quam ineluibilis Γ *deest in* **H** // **15** Confugiendum Γ Fugiendum **H** // **19** expavendum Γ timendum **H** // **20–21** qui ... veneficae Γ *deest in* **H** // **22** praecipit Γ inquit **H** // **26** Eadem ... sententia Γ Idem Demetriadi praecipit **H** // **26–27** In ... convenit Γ In sociis puellis illud velim **H** // **27** lusiunculis Γ *deest in* **H** // **28** omnino Γ *deest in* **H** // **29** aut elegantem Γ *deest in* **H** / habere **HWW²B** haberet **V**

and her presence alone should ensure that chastity be safeguarded. Anything that would invite to lasciviousness and lust by its example should be kept as far away as possible. The woman in the pay of a lover, who encourages with words and instigates to evil-doing, is not worthy to be called human, for she is something diabolical; the young girl will avoid her as if she were an asp or a viper, and she should be driven out of the city like a public scourge. There are no words to describe the evils that are caused by women such as these. Therefore the young girl should not even tolerate the sight of them, for they are basilisks or *catoblepae*, which transmit a deadly poison from their eyes and annihilate you with a single glance. Let no one think that I am speaking hyperbolically. Some of these women are so skilful that they can often captivate you with their eyes with no words spoken. Others make use of spells and incantations and would to God examples of these black arts were more rare. Why, by a mere greeting or smile or even a look this serpent can defile a girl upon whom it has gazed, especially in the house of those who know the woman's black art, not to mention the ineradicable dishonor that is stamped upon a house they have set foot in. You must flee to your mother as to a sanctuary, and recount to her what the wicked woman attempted to do, or you must avoid and turn away from her in disgust to make clear to the onlookers that you fear her like the plague. In that way you will benefit yourself by your action and others by example, showing other young girls how much she is to be feared. It is in the interest of the state to investigate impoverished old women so that the official charged with public morals may know what is the source of their livelihood. If there is no visible support, they will surely become procuresses and sorceresses.

77. Concerning female companions Jerome has this to say: 'I do not wish a woman to love one servant more than another and continually whisper secrets into her ear. Whatever she says to one must be known to all. She should have a companion who is not elegantly adorned or beautiful and frivolous, who can modulate sweet songs in her clear voice, but one who is grave, pale, shabbily dressed, and somewhat unfriendly.' He gives the same advice to Demetrias. In choosing female companions one must avoid any that may harm us by their personal adornments or by their lascivious words and amusements. Have nothing at all to do with girls who enjoy being looked at and being loved, who boast that they have a handsome or rich or elegant or noble lover and carry around with them letters written by him. From time to time they show them to girls of their own age or recount

---

76. *catoblepae*: Literally 'that looks down'. Like the fabled basilisk it killed whatever it looked at.

ostentant aut facta narrant aut dicta referunt: 'Haec egit, haec dixit; sic me
aggressus, sic me laudavit.' Apage istas, quamlibet tibi sint vicinae, quamlibet
opulentae, necessariae, affines, consanguinae. Quod si sorores sint, id vero
tu nega. Morsae sunt a diabolo, cane rabido, et ipsae in rabiem versae, ubi
nullum est tam carum nomen ut ad commercium pertrahat; quin potius et a
sorore praefocatur soror et a fratre frater et a matre filius.

78. Oblectabit se igitur virgo mea cum delectis virginibus sui similibus,
interim lusibus honestis ac liberalibus, alias sanctis lectionibus aut confabulationibus quas lectio suggeret. Nihil de saltationibus aut convivio aut
voluptatibus referat, ne sociae falsa delectationis specie commoveantur.
Nemo intererit vir. Tum, a sociis relicta sola in cubiculo suo, non prorsus
nihil aget, nam otiosam esse periculosum est, praesertim solam. 'In populo'
(inquit Ovidius de tali) 'tutior esse potes.' Nec cogitationibus animum ut
permittat est tutum, quantumlibet honestis initio et sanctis. Lubricus est
feminae cogitatus nec uno loco facile consistit. A rectis ad prava exiguo
negotio delaberetur. Nec omnino sine causa videtur quibusdam dixisse
Publius Syrus mimographus: 'Mulier cum sola cogitat, male cogitat.'

79. Neque vero Magdalena illa, quae sedens iuxta pedes Domini audiebat
verbum illius, contemplatione tantum rerum caelestium fruebatur. Sed id
faciebat sive dum legit sive dum audit sive dum orat. Idem faciat mea non
virgo solum, sed quaevis femina; nam in multis huius libri locis omnibus in
universum feminis praecipimus. Legat igitur sola vel oret festo die; eadem
agat profesto aut operi manuario intenta sit. Non dubium quin tale aliquid
agentem repperit Mariam Angelus; quae turbata est quod venerandum illud
et perpetuum silentium nec interpellari umquam solitum vox, augustior
quidem, sed virili similis rupisset. Ideoque alma dicitur ab Hebraeis, quod
virginem absconditam sonat. Haec est de qua praedicit Isaias: 'Ecce virgo
abscondita concipiet et pariet Deum et hominem.' Ea demum Virgo concipit
Christum quam nullus praeter Christum novit.

80. Ergo et domum nemo admittetur a virgine nisi quem pater disertis
verbis admitti iusserit. Ipsa matrem domesticis paulatim laboribus incipiet

---

78. (In populo ... potes) *Ov. rem. 580* // (Mulier ... cogitat) *Publil. A. 376*
79. (Magdalena ... Domini) *Vulg. Luc. 7, 38; Vulg. Ioh. 11, 32* // (Ideoque ... sonat)
Hier. adv. Iovin. 1, 32, PL 23, 254C // (Ecce ... hominem) *Vulg. Is. 7, 14*

3 necessariae Γ amicae **H** // **3–4** id vero tu Γ hoc **H** // **4** versae Γ versae sunt **H** // **5**
pertrahat Γ adducat **H** // **12** nihil Γ nulla **H** // **12–13** In ... potes Γ *deest in* **H** // **15**
cogitatus Γ animus **H** / exiguo Γ nullo **H** // **17** Publius *pro* Publilius *edd. omnes* // **19** tantum
rerum caelestium Γ rerum caelestium sola **H** // **20** Idem Γ Sic et **H** // **23** manuario Γ
manuum **H** // **24–26** venerandum ... rupisset Γ viri faciem quam videre eo loci numquam
consueverat tunc videret **H** // **26** virili *scr.* virilis Γ / Ideoque Γ Ideo **H** // **29** quam ...
novit Γ rari norunt praeter Christum **H**

words and episodes. 'He did this, he said this, he accosted me like this, he praised me like this.' Out on these acquaintances, no matter if they be neighbors, wealthy close friends, relatives by blood or by marriage! And even if they are sisters, deny that they are. They have been bitten by the devil, a mad dog, and they have become rabid, in which case no name is so dear that it should lure us into their company. On the contrary, sister is smothered by sister, brother by brother and son by mother.

78. The young woman, therefore, will amuse herself in the company of young women of her own age, sometimes in respectable and ladylike entertainments, sometimes in pious readings or conversations suggested by the reading. She should not recount stories about dancing and banquets and entertainments lest her companions be stirred up by the false appearance of pleasure. No man should be present. Then, when she is alone in her bedroom after her companions have left, she must not remain without doing anything, for it is dangerous for her to be idle, especially when alone. 'She can be safer in a crowd' said Ovid of such a woman. Neither is it safe for them to surrender their mind to thoughts, however honorable and pious they may be at first. A woman's thoughts are inconstant and they do not remain easily fixed in one place. She could descend from good thoughts to bad with very little trouble. Publilius Syrus, the writer of mimes, was right in saying 'When a woman thinks alone, she thinks bad thoughts.'

79. Mary Magdalen, sitting at the feet of the Lord listening to his words, did not enjoy the contemplation of heavenly things only at that moment but while she was reading, listening or praying. Not only should I wish my ideal young woman to do this, but any other woman, for in many passages in this book we give instructions to women in general. Therefore she should read and pray in private on feast days; she shall do the same on ordinary working days, or be intent on manual work. Undoubtedly the angel found Mary occupied in something of that nature when he brought his tidings. She was alarmed when the religious and habitual silence, that was never interrupted, was broken by a voice, which although majestic in tone, was like that of a man. For that reason, she is called *alma* in Hebrew, which means 'hidden virgin.' She it is of whom Isaias speaks when he says: 'Behold a hidden virgin will conceive and will bring forth God and man.' In the end, that virgin conceived Christ, and no one knew her but Christ.

80. Therefore the young woman shall not admit anyone into her house except at her father's explicit command. She will begin little by little to assist

levare, quam et patrem rerum omnium post Deum carissimos habebit.
Hi si iubeant lanae aut lino aut cuicumque opificio filiam intentam esse,
non modeste solum, verum alacriter etiam exsequetur. Hoc diligentius et
sollertius si aliqua victus pars eo labore ad parentes reditura est. Tum
vero felicissima erit et cogitabit se gratiae partem aliquam cui tantam
debet referre et illis alimenta reddere a quibus acceperit. Cum puellae
per negotia domestica soli esse licebit ac orare, primum omnium se totam Deo tradat et dedicet, veneretur Christum eiusque Matrem et veniam
pacemque ab illis petat. Tunc cogitet se esse virginem Christianam, Christi
sponsam, Mariae imitatricem; nihil esse virginitatem corporis nisi pura sit
mens. Haec si adsit, nihil esse mundius, nihil Deo gratius; se sectatricem
sanctissimae Matris Domini, primum omnium debere in se excellentissi-
mam ipsius effingere virtutem, modestiam illam et moderationem animi
quam humilitatem vulgo dicimus. Quae tanta in illa fuit ut cum omnia ipsi contingerint maxima atque amplissima, nihil tamen fuerit quod
illam animo extolleret, quod ei spiritus faceret. Nobilissima puella quae
in stemmate quattuordecim reges tot duces Israelis computabat, ditissimis
orta parentibus, ditata etiam a Magis, formosissima, ingeniosissima, doctissima et sapientissima; at inter haec omnia ut aequabilem gerebat animum
et submissam de se opinionem! Iam conscia caelestis partus et Mater
tanti Filii marito fabro ministrare dedignata non est et consanguineam
invisere eique gravidae assistere ac famulari. Cui se praeposuit? Quam
prae se vel genere vel forma vel ingenio vel dignitate contempsit? Cui se
non posthabuit Virgo angelis quoque praestantior, quorum erat Regina
destinata? Quocirca non probo Divam Virginem in sericis atque aureis
amictibus depictam, gemmis atque unionibus ornatam, ceu his illa delec-
tata esset cum inter mortales ageret. Etiam simulacrum illius quibusdam
in locis synthesin habet et vestes, si Deo placet, mutatorias, cum multi
mortales quotidianis careant. Nihil minus eam refert. Malim simplici illo
cultu quali erat uti solita, quo superbiae nostrae moderatio animi illius
expressius ante oculos proponatur et tacite convicium faciat exsistatque
unde coarguantur ac proinde doceantur divites, unde se pauperes solen-
tur, unde his animus augeatur, illis decrescat, utrisque vero ad iustum

---

80. (marito ... non est) *Vulg. Luc. 1, 39*

1 habebit **Γ** existimabit **H** ∥ 2 cuicumque opificio **Γ** alicui manuum operi **H** ∥ 5 vero **Γ**
demum **H**/ gratiae partem aliquam **Γ** gratiam **H** / tantam **Γ** *deest in* **H** ∥ 7 soli **HWW²V**
solae **B** ∥ 8 dedicet **Γ** dicet **H** ∥ 9 cogitet **Γ** consideret **H** ∥ 14 vulgo **Γ** *deest in* **H** ∥
14–15 tanta ... ipsi **Γ** tanta fuit ut cum omnia illi ipsi **H** ∥ 19 et sapientissima **Γ** *deest in* **H**
/ at **Γ** et **H** ∥ 20 opinionem **Γ** cogitationem **H** ∥ 22 gravidae **Γ** parienti **H** ∥ 27 inter
mortales **Γ** hic **H** ∥ 27–29 Etiam ... careant **Γ** *deest in* **H** ∥ 29–30 illo cultu quali **Γ** cultu
et quali **H** ∥ 30 superbiae nostrae **Γ** nobis **H** ∥ 31 proponatur **Γ** ponatur **H** / et ...
exsistatque **Γ** *deest in* **H** ∥ 32 unde ... divites **Γ** ut sit unde divites doceantur **H**

her mother in domestic duties and will hold her mother and father in deep affection above all else after God himself. If they bid her to occupy herself in the working of wool or flax or some other constructive task, she will set about it not only obediently but with alacrity. She will do it with all the more diligence and skilfullness if the fruits of that labor will return to her parents as part of her daily sustenance. This will make her very happy and she will think she is making requital for part of the great debt she owes her parents and recompensing them for the nurture she received from them. When the young woman has acquitted herself of her household chores and can be alone to pray, let her first consecrate and dedicate herself wholly to God, venerate Christ and his mother and ask pardon and peace from them. Then let her consider that she is a Christian virgin, the spouse of Christ, the imitator of Mary. Virginity of body is nothing if it is not accompanied by purity of mind. If that is present, there is nothing purer, nothing more pleasing to God. As a follower of the most holy mother of God she must first of all reproduce in herself Mary's unrivalled virtue, her modesty and moderation of spirit, which we commonly call humility. This was so preeminent in her that when the greatest and most sublime blessing fell to her lot, nothing would exalt her in spirit and inspire arrogance in her, this noblest of women, who counted in her lineage fourteen kings and as many princes of Israel, born of rich parents, enriched by the gifts of the Magi, most beautiful, most talented, most learned and most wise. But in the midst of all this what equanimity of soul she displayed and lowly opinion of herself! Already conscious that she would give birth to a divine offspring and would be the mother of such a glorious son, she did not disdain to minister to her artisan husband nor to visit her relative and assist her in her pregnancy and converse with her. To whom did she prefer herself? What woman did she look down upon despite her lineage, beauty, talent and dignity? To whom did she not esteem herself inferior, she who surpassed even the angels, of whom she was destined to be queen? For that reason I do not approve that the divine virgin should be depicted in silk and golden garments, adorned with gems and large pearls, as if she had delighted in these things when she dwelt among mortals. In some places her image even has a set of matching articles and clothes to suit the season, if you please, when many mortals lack even everyday vesture. Nothing is of less importance to her. I would prefer that her temperateness of soul be presented more vividly before our eyes in that simple attire to which she was accustomed as a silent refutation of our pride so that the rich will be confuted and at the same time instructed, and the poor consoled. The latter would increase in courage, the former diminish in haughtiness, both brought back to a just

quendam habitum moderationemque reducatur, ut nec etiam desperent locupletes nec nimis confidant egenae, sed sit quaedam inter eas velut exaequatio.

81. Huius ergo tantae Virginis exemplum sequetur mea puella non ficto et simulato, sed vero animo et certo, ne taetrius sit et perniciosius vitium sub facie virtutis latens et venenum sub re salutari ac morbus cute integra et sana contectus eoque se a cura defendens obtentu. Nihil agant feminae fucatum et fictum, ut bonae videantur, nec se rerum naturas aut fallere sperent aut mutare posse. Non idem valent simulata quod vera. Ficta et adumbrata invalida atque imbecilla sunt; ipsa tandem vel se produnt vel deteguntur. Vere igitur sit puella quod prae se ostendit—modesta, humilis, pudica, pudibunda, proba—et esse eam talem convenit et videri. Ita Divae Virgini, quam vere atque expresse vita sua repraesentabit, acceptior facta, tum Christo, qui dignam se sponsam agnoscet. Orabit primum pro se, ut augeatur pietate, proposito sanctae pudicitiae et reliquis virtutibus; tum pro parentibus, hinc pro fratribus, sororibus, consanguineis et ceteris, pro quibus Deum precari eam conveniet. Huius etiam preces gratissimae Deo erunt et efficaces ad quidvis impetrandum, nempe animi purissimi et integerrimi germaneque Christiani. Velim quae orabit ipsam intelligere. Vel loquatur lingua quam norit vel quae latine dicet habeat prius ab aliquo declarata. Nec putet in murmure et agitatione labiorum sitam adorationem, sed in mente et cogitatione cum a rebus istis vilibus ad caelestia divinaque animum erigit. Hoc iubemur in sacris facere quando dicitur: 'Sursum corda;' nos respondemus: 'Habemus ad Dominum.' In quo mentiuntur plane plurimi qui dum id dicunt cor habent in sordida quapiam et ima mundi huius recula detrusum ac defixum; nec attollere eos sinit eadem quae depressit cura. Veros adoratores Christus esse pronuntiat qui spiritu adorant Patrem et hanc illi esse gratissimam adorationem, acceptissimas preces. Videat ergo ne mens, ne animus a verbis dissonent. Idem intus loquatur quod exterius. Immo exterius quantum velit taceat vel loquatur alia, modo intus clamet ad Dominum et possit dicere cum sponsa: 'Ego dormio, at cor meum vigilat.'

---

81. (Veros ... Patrem) *Vulg. Ioh. 4, 23* // (Ego ... vigilat) *Vulg. cant. 5, 2*

1 quendam habitum Γ modum H // **2–3** sed ... exaequatio Γ *deest in* H // **4** tantae Virginis *deest in* H // **6** ac Γ aut H // **7** eoque se a cura Γ et a cura se eo H // **9** posse Γ *deest in* H // **11** prae se Γ *deest in* H // **12** pudica pudibunda Γ pudibunda pudica H / esse ... videri Γ videatur et sit H // **17** etiam Γ enim H // **18** quidvis Γ *deest in* H // **19** germaneque Γ ac vere H / loquatur **HWW²B** loquetur **V** // **25–26** cor ... cura Γ de re aliqua cogitant mundi huius H // **31** possit dicere Γ dicat H

proportion not that the rich will despair or the poor become too confident, but that a certain equality exist between them.

81. My young woman will follow the example of the glorious Virgin not with a feigned and simulated spirit but with true and certain intention lest under the mask of virtue there lurk a more deadly and pernicious vice, a poison under the guise of health and a sickness concealed by a sound and healthy skin and under this cover avoiding cure. Let women do nothing that is counterfeit and feigned so that they may appear good, nor should they hope to change or deceive nature. Things that are simulated do not have the same validity as things that are true. That which is feigned is weak and ineffectual. In the end they give themselves away or they are exposed. Therefore the young woman should be in very fact what she appears to be externally. She must both appear and be humble, chaste, modest and upright. In that way she will become more acceptable to the Blessed Virgin, of whom her life will be the true and exact reproduction, and to Christ as well, who will acknowledge in her a spouse worthy of him. She will pray first for herself that she may grow in piety, in her commitment to holy chastity, and in the other virtues. Next she will pray for her parents, brothers, sisters, relatives and others for whom it is fitting that she pray to God. Her prayers, too, will be most pleasing to God and efficacious in obtaining whatever she asks, since they proceed from a pure, unsullied spirit and one that is genuinely Christian. I wish her to understand what she is saying in her prayers. Whether she prays in a language she knows or in Latin, someone will tell her beforehand what it means. She is not to think that adoration consists in murmuring and movement of the lips, but in the mind and in contemplation, when she raises the soul from vile earthly concerns to the heavenly and divine. This is what we are asked to do in the holy sacrifice of the Mass when it is said: 'Lift up your hearts' and we respond: 'We have lifted them up to the Lord.' A great many of the faithful lie when they say this since their heart is fixed and sunk in some lowly and sordid concern of this world, and that care which has cast them down will not allow them to raise their minds. Christ proclaims that true worshippers are those who worship the Father in spirit; this worship is pleasing to him and these are the prayers most acceptable to him. Be sure, then, that your mind and spirit are not in disaccord with your words. What is said externally must correspond with what is said internally. Or she may be as silent as you please externally or speak of other things, provided that internally she cries out to the Lord and can say with the spouse 'I sleep, but my heart wakes.'

CAP. X.   DE VIRTUTIBUS FEMINAE ET EXEMPLIS QUAE IMITETUR

82. Discet ex libris quos vel leget vel audiet virtutes sui sexus in universum. Decet quidem unamquamque feminam virtutibus omnis generis esse praeditam, sed illi sunt peculiariter necessariae nonnullae, sicuti vitia cum foeda
5 omnia tum vero quaedam abominanda atque exsecranda. Et sunt virtutes aliae coniugatarum, aliae viduarum; de iis tamen quae toti sexui congruunt loquar. Ante omnia sciet castitatem esse principem feminae virtutem et quae una instar sit reliquarum omnium. Si haec adsit, nemo requirit alias; si absit, nemo respicit alias. Et quemadmodum Stoici philosophi in sapientia exis-
10 timabant sita esse bona omnia, in stultitia mala omnia—ut solum sapientem dicerent divitem, liberum, regem, civem, formosum, animosum, beatum; contra vero, stultum, pauperem, servum, exsulem, peregrinum, deformem, ignavum, miserum—sic de pudicitia in feminis iudicandum est pudicam esse formosam, venustam, dotatam, nobilem, fecundam, omnia optima et
15 praestantissima, rursus impudicam mare et thesaurum malorum omnium.

83. Pudicitiae comites individuae sunt pudor et sobrietas; a pudore videtur dicta pudicitia, ut pudica non sit quam non pudet. Hoc est velum quoddam nostrae faciei. Nam cum natura et ratio corruptum corpus et carnem peccati velasset ob pudorem primi dedecoris, faciem autem apertam nudamque
20 involucris istis nostris reliquisset, illi suum amiculum non negavit, pudorem scilicet, quocum humana commendatione operiretur, ut nemo id cerneret, quin magnam aliquam probitatem sub illo tegumento intelligeret latere nullusque esset qui non amaret sic indutum, exutum odisset. 'Erubuit,' inquit ille pater in comoedia de filio, 'salva res est.' Et vir sapiens adolescenti
25 in rubore: 'Confide fili, iste est color virtutis.' Quod si hoc de viris dicitur, quid existimari de feminis par est? Quid de tenellis virginibus? Exsecratur dominus impudicam, dicens: 'Frons mulieris meretricis tibi facta est, depuduit te.' Adeoque faciei nostrae non decoram modo, sed necessariam quoque censuerunt verecundiam, ut os, faciem, frontem pro verecundia et pudore
30 usurparint. Hinc sunt illa iam inde a priscis saeculis deducta proverbia: non habere frontem, durum os, tenerum os et similia, per quae verecundia aut

---

83. (Erubuit ... salva res est) *Ter. Ad. 643* // (Frons ... te) *Vulg. Ier. 3, 3* // (non habere ... tenerum os) *Erasm. ad. LB II, 316B–F*

2 leget Γ leget femina **H** // **4** peculiariter Γ *deest in* **H** / sicuti Γ ut **H** / vitia **HWW²** *om.* **BV** // **6** viduarum Γ viduarum, aliae monasticarum. **H** / tamen Γ *deest in* **H** // **7** Ante omnia Γ Primum **H** // **8** sit Γ est **H** // **9–10** existimabant sita esse bona omnia Γ sita bona omnia existimabant **H** // **14–15** omnia ... praestantissima Γ optima quaeque **H** // **15** rursus Γ contra **H** // **18–21** Nam ... scilicet Γ Nam cum apertam nudamque pannis istis nostris voluisset natura esse faciem humanam, illi suum amiculum addidit pudoris **H** // **23–26** Erubuit ... virginibus Γ *deest in* **H** // **28**–p.114,1 Adeoque ... designantur Γ *deest in* **H**

CHAPTER 10.   ON THE VIRTUES OF A WOMAN
AND THE EXAMPLES SHE SHOULD IMITATE

82. The young woman will learn of the virtues of her sex in general from books she will read or hear read to her. It is fitting, certainly, that every woman should be endowed with virtues of every sort, but some are particularly necessary to her, just as while all vices are ugly, certain vices are abominable and execrable. There are virtues that pertain more to married women and others proper to widows, but I shall speak of those that belong to every condition of women. Above all she should be aware that the principal female virtue is chastity and it is equivalent to all others in moral worth. If this is present, one need not look for others, and if it is absent one should disregard the others. The Stoic philosophers believed that all blessings were contained in wisdom and all misfortunes in stupidity so that they said that only the wise man was rich, free, king, citizen, beautiful, courageous, happy, and that, conversely, the stupid man was poor, a slave, an exile, a stranger, ugly, cowardly and unhappy. So with regard to chastity in women we must consider that the chaste woman is beautiful, charming, gifted, noble, fertile and possessed of every best and outstanding quality while the unchaste woman is a sea and storehouse of all evils.

83. The inseparable companions of chastity are a sense of propriety and modest behaviour. Chastity (*pudicitia*) seems to be derived from shame (*pudor*), so that one who has no sense of shame cannot be chaste. Chastity is a kind of veil placed over our face, for when nature and reason covered the corrupt body and the sinful flesh because of the shame caused by the first sin but left the face open and free of the coverings that we wear, they did not deny it its cloak, namely, shame, with which it could be covered and gain human approval, so that no one could see it without recognizing that great virtue lay under that covering and there was none who did not esteem one so clothed, or hate one who was without it. 'He blushed' said the father of the son in the comedy, 'All's well.' And the wise man to the young man red with blushing: 'Be confident, my son, this is the color of virtue.' If this is said of men, what should be thought of women and young maidens? The Lord curses the unchaste woman, saying: 'Your brow has become that of a prostitute, you have lost all shame.' Not only is shame considered to ennoble our face but it is essential to it, so that the words countenance, face, and brow have become synonymous with shame and modesty. That is the origin of proverbs dating back to early times: 'To have no face,' 'To have a stern face, a tender face,' and the like, which signify shame or lack of shame.

inverecundia designantur. Nascitur ex verecundia modestia et moderatio, sive cogitet quid seu dicat seu agat, ut nihil nec in affectibus nec verbis nec factis exsistat immodicum, arrogans, insolens, lascivum, putidum, petulans, nihil iactabundum aut ambitiosum.

5   **84.** Honores nec se mereri credat nec expetat, immo vero devitet, et si contingant, quasi immerita erubescat. Nulla re insolescet, non forma, non venustate, non genere, non opibus, sciens illa breviter peritura, superbiae vero paratam aeternam poenam. Sobrietas continentiam fovet, ut ebrietas deterit. Nemo ignorat quid crapulam sequi soleat. Additur sobrietati parsi-
10   monia et frugalitas, quas esse in re familiari mulieris partes Plato et Aristoteles non immerito prodiderunt: 'Quaerit vir, custodit et servat femina.' Ideo illi animus additus, huic detractus, quo ille strenue pararet, haec meticulose contineret. Ex hac corporis sobrietate etiam in animum sobrietas derivabitur, ne affectus velut temulenti tumultuentur et turbent tranquillitatem virtutis,
15   sed liceat et bene agere et bene sapere. Pietati dedita sit et modicis contentae praesentia sufficiant. Magnus est quaestus, iuxta Apostolum, pietas cum acquiescentia praesentium; nec absentia aut aliena quaerat, unde oriatur invidia et aemulatio et curiositas alienorum. Decet cum primis femineum sexum devotio rerum sacrarum. Quo foedior est mulier aliena a religione et
20   velut ominosum prodigium aversanda et detestanda.

      85. Cum invidia est illi crebro pugnandum, quae cum sit feminis usque ad ridiculum turpis, nescio tamen quo pacto pertinacissime sexum illum infestat. Sed quae sobria est cuique abunde magna sunt quae naturae necessitatibus satisfaciunt non erit cur alteri velit invidere aut esse alienae domi curiosa.
25   At quae pudibunda est et temperato animo quaeque sobria numquam ira efferetur nec in maledicentiam prorumpet nec in saevitiem aliquam et inhumanitatem rapietur. Cum enim feminarum genus mansuetum natura et benevolum esse conveniat, ut quod imbecillum sit et alieni auxilii vehementer indiguum, quis ferat in muliere impotentem iram et crudelitatem, ut perdere
30   cupiat quae, si sit opus, servare non valeat, et animum iniuriae memorem, quam reponat in occasionem ultionis? Digna est huiusmodi mulier quae tantis afficiatur malis ut numero magnitudineque illorum prostrata et concussa

---

84. (Quaerit ... femina) *Aristot. oec. 1, 3 (1343b)* ∥ (Magnus ... pietas) *Vulg. I Tim. 6, 6*

2 sive ... agat Γ sive quid cogitet sive dicat sive agat **H** ∥ 3 putidum Γ *deest in* **H** ∥ 5 immo vero devitet Γ etiam vitet **H** ∥ 6 quasi Γ tamquam **H** ∥ 9 deterit Γ expellit **H** ∥ 12 detractus Γ ademptus **H** ∥ 13 in animum sobrietas derivabitur Γ animo sobrietas nascetur **H** ∥ 16–17 Magnus ... praesentium Γ *deest in* **H** ∥ 18–19 Decet ... sexum Γ Congruit plurimum femineo sexui **H** ∥ 19 aliena Γ aversa **H** ∥ 20 et detestanda Γ *deest in* **H** ∥ 22 pertinacissime ... infestat Γ pertinacius illas oppugnat **H** ∥ 23 necessitatibus Γ *deest in* **H** ∥ 25 temperato Γ moderato **H** ∥ 26 prorumpet Γ prosiliet **H** ∥ 27 mansuetum Γ amicum **H** ∥ 28 vehementer Γ plurimum **H** ∥ 29 indiguum **WW²B** indigum **H** indignum **V** ∥ 30 memorem Γ retinentem **H**

From the sense of shame come modesty and moderation, whether in thought, words or actions so that in all our conduct there will be nothing that is immoderate, arrogant, insolent, lascivious, offensive, unruly, boastful or pretentious.

84. She should not think that she deserves honors nor should she seek them. On the contrary she shall avoid them, and if they should fall to her lot, she should feel ashamed of them as if they were unmerited. She will not grow proud of anything, neither beauty nor charm nor race nor wealth, knowing they will quickly perish, while eternal punishment is reserved for pride. Sobriety promotes continence as drunkenness impairs it. No one is ignorant of the consequences of excessive drinking. Sobriety also engenders parsimony and frugality. These qualities are the function of the woman in the management of the household, as Plato and Aristotle rightly taught. 'The man acquires, the woman guards and preserves.' Therefore he was given more initiative and it was taken away from her, so that he would strive more energetically and she would hold on to things more carefully. From this sobriety in material concerns will flow a similar moderation of spirit, so feelings will not run riot as if intoxicated and disturb the tranquility of virtue, but rather that she should act well and use good sense. Let her be dedicated to piety and content with little, satisfied with her present situation. 'Piety with acceptance of what one has is a great gain,' according to the Apostle. She will not seek what is absent or what belongs to another, whence arise envy and rivalry and curiosity about things that belong to others. Especially proper to the female sex is devotion to sacred things. There is nothing more repugnant than a woman averse to religion; she should be avoided and detested like an ill-omened apparition.

85. She must frequently do battle with envy, which, shameful as it is for women to the point of absurdity, in some strange way afflicts that sex relentlessly. But one who is possessed of moderation and who is amply satisfied with simple necessities will have no desire to be envious of another or curious about some one else's home. A woman who is chaste and moderate and sober-minded will never be carried away by anger or give vent to abusiveness or be swept away by violence and inhumanity. Since it behooves the female sex to be meek and benevolent by nature in that it is weak and much in need of the help of others, who would tolerate uncontrolled anger and cruelty in a woman, which would make her wish to lose what she cannot preserve if she had need to? And who would suffer a mind that does not forget an injury, waiting for the occasion to avenge it? A woman of this kind is worthy of being visited with so many evils that overwhelmed and shaken by their number and magnitude she would admit

victam se fateatur ac de ira et ultione ceterisque insaniis desinat cogitare,
de salute sollicita; quod multis saepenumero videmus accidere, iusto iudicio
Dei, nec sine approbatione eorum quibus nota erat ferocia illius ac saevitia.
Plane cum immanibus beluis—superbia, ira, atque invidia—propositum est
incautae feminae certamen, quod levibus earum et teneris animis offensio
omnis gravissima atque intolerabilis videtur et atrociter vindicanda; nimirum
res exiles ac minutissimae, tamquam ingentes se ac solidissimas imperitis
ac vitiosis offerunt oculis, tanto magis offusa nebula vel fumo. Itaque nisi
tam immanes hostes vel arte vitarit vel superarit strenuitate, periculum
est ne ipsa ab eis conficiatur, habitura sempiternum et in hac vita et
in altera cruciatum.

86. Credo perspicuum esse pudicitiam velut reginam esse in virtutibus
feminae; hanc sequi inseparabiles comites duas, ex pudore sobrietatem gigni,
ex queis duabus reliquum muliebrium virtutum chorum mundumque componi ac fabricari—modestiam, moderationem, frugalitatem, parsimoniam,
domesticam diligentiam, religionis curam, mansuetudinem. Quas omnes
virtutes, cum ipse aliis locis aliquanto fusius explicabo, tum uberius a sanctis
sapientibusque viris tractatas passim inveniet. Delineatam intuemini honestatis imaginem, quae tanta specie tamque praestanti forma est ut, si corporis
oculis cerni posset, quemadmodum est a Platone scriptum in Phaedro,
mirabiles amores excitaret sui. Neque sic pulchritudo ulla oculos nostros
capit et tenet, ut arriperet duceretque secum honestas aperta nobis atque
ostensa.

87. Tum colliget virgo vel audiendo vel legendo sancta exempla virginum, quae sibi proponat imitanda quarumque se similem esse et cupiat
et operam navet non segnem ut efficiat. Primum omnium, ut dixi, principis illius ac decoris virginitatis, Mariae, Christi hominis ac Dei Parentis,
cuius vitam non solae virgines habent tamquam exemplar propositum ad
quod se componant effingantque, sed nuptae etiam ac viduae. Omnibus
enim omnia facta est ut omnes ad suae castitatis maximarumque virtutum exemplum provocaret et adduceret; virginibus modestissima virgo,
nuptis castissima est nupta, viduis religiosissima vidua. Prima insuetam

---

86. ⟨tanta ... sui⟩ *Plat. Phaidr. 250D*

1 ceterisque insaniis **Γ** et de ceteris insaniis **H** // **2–3** de ... saevitia **Γ** *deest in* **H** // **6–8**
nimirum ... offerunt **Γ** et res exiles ac minutissimas tamquam ingentes ac solidissimas se
imperitis offerunt **H** // **8** oculis ... fumo **Γ** *deest in* **H** // **9** immanes **Γ** saevos **H** // **10** ipsa
ab eis conficiatur **Γ** absumatur **H** // **14** muliebrium **Γ** femineatum **H** // **14–15** componi
ac fabricari **Γ** *deest in* **H** // **17** cum ... tum **Γ** et ... et **H** // **18** passim **Γ** *deest in* **H** //
22–23 aperta nobis atque ostensa **Γ** aperta atque ostensa nobis **H** // **25–26** et cupiat ...
efficiat **Γ** *deest in* **H** // **26** Primum omnium **Γ** Et in primis **H** / principis **Γ** praestantissimae **H**
// **30–31** maximarumque virtutum **Γ** *deest in* **H**

defeat and cease to think of anger and revenge and other insanities, and be anxious only for her salvation. We see this occur often to many by the just judgement of God and not without the approval of those to whom her violence and cruelty were well known. The incautious woman has to face a struggle with savage beasts—pride, anger and envy—because to their inconstant and weak minds every offense seems grave and intolerable and deserving of fierce revenge. Indeed, slight and minute matters present themselves to their inexperienced and defective eyes as huge and insuperable, all the more so because they are obscured by a cloud or by smoke. And so if she does not avoid these terrible enemies by her ingenuity or conquer them by sheer endurance there is danger that she will be undone by them and will suffer unending torment both in this life and in the next.

86. I think it is abundantly clear that chastity is, so to speak, the queen of female virtues. Two inseparable companions follow: modesty and sobriety, which it engenders, and from these two the whole chorus and firmament of female virtues is composed and fashioned—modesty, moderation, frugality, parsimony, diligence in household duties, the observance of religious obligations, meekness. Although I will expound all these virtues in greater detail in other parts of the work, the young woman will find more copious treatments of the subject in the writings of wise and holy men. Contemplate the image of moral rectitude as it is delineated, a thing of such beauty and preeminence of form that if it could be seen by bodily eyes, as Plato wrote in the *Phaedrus*, it would arouse extraordinary love for itself in us. No other beauty so captures and entrances us as moral integrity, which, if it were revealed and shown to us, would sweep us away and carry us off with it.

87. Then the young woman will collect examples of virgins from what she hears and reads, which she will hold up to herself for imitation, desire to be like them and make every effort to bring this about. The first model to place before herself, as I have said, is the queen and glory of virginity, Mary, the mother of Christ, God and man, whose life should be the exemplar not only for virgins to follow but for married women and widows as well. She became all things to all so that she might inspire and lead all women to the example of her chastity and of all lofty virtues. To virgins she was a most humble virgin, to married women a most chaste spouse, to widows a most pious widow. She was

118 J. L. VIVES

hanc omnibus retro saeculis virginitatis rationem ac viam magno animo et
pientissimo proposito est ingressa. Prima in coniugio vixit supra humanum
morem nullo carnis usu angelica vita, ut custodem suae pudicitiae sumpserit,
non virum. Quae quoniam miracula erant, ideo maiore miraculo stupente
5 natura Filium mundo edidit. Vidua vero iam facta, quoniam tota eius vita ex
spiritu pendebat et in corpore vivens supra corporis se condicionem extulerat,
in uno Deo et obsequentissimum nacta est Filium et castissimum sponsum
et indulgentissimum Patrem, ut quae propter Deum cuncta contempserat in
Deo cuncta inveniret.

10   **88.** Sed quid ago, Diva, quid incepto? An de tuis infinitis laudibus
dicere? Atqui hoc nec huius est vel torpedinis vel infantiae vel angusti loci.
Opus est latissimo otio, opus facundia exercitatissima, opus ingenio summo
ac eruditissimo. Vos hanc, virgines, imitamini quotquot integram servare
castitatem vultis. Vos hanc sequimini, coniugatae, quibus curae est maritis
15 placere et praestare quod iurastis. Vos hanc semper spectate, viduae, ex
qua et solacium amissi coniugis et consilium tuendae prolis et exemplum
reliquae degendae vitae fructuosissimum percipietis. Secutae sunt huius
institutum maxima nostrarum milium agmina, sicut Psalmista praenuntiarat:
'Adducentur Regi virgines post eam.' Quarum acta non modo in praesens,
20 verum et omni posteritati proderunt ad aemulationem. Nec gentiles virgines
tacent historiae nobilitatas sola pudicitia; quarum catalogum ex Graecis
historiis Hieronymus contra Iovinianum disputans recensere gravatus non
est, quod videret in eiusmodi rebus non parum homines exemplis moveri
neque enim factu difficile videtur quod factum aliquando sit. Adduxit multas
25 quae vitae quoque maluerint iacturam facere quam pudicitiae. Equidem
gravissimo iuxta et sanctissimo viro non hanc contumeliam faciam, ut quae
ille collegit vel tamquam supervacanea praeteream vel aliis ponam verbis,
quasi melius ipse dicturus, quin ut ab eo posita sunt adscribam. Sic ergo
inquit:
30   **89.** 'Triginta Atheniensium tyranni cum Phaedonem in convivio
necassent, filias eius virgines ad se venire iusserunt et scortorum more
nudari ac super pavimenta patris sanguine cruentata impudicis gestibus
ludere. Quae paulisper dissimulato doloris habitu, cum temulentos convivas
cernerent, quasi ad requisita naturae egredientes, invicem se complexae

88. (Adducentur ... eam) *Vulg. psalm. 44, 15*
89–90. (Triginta ... existeret) *Hier. adv. Iovin. 1, 41, PL 23, 271–273*

1 hanc ... viam **Γ** hanc ante virginitatis viam **H** // **2** vixit **Γ** fuit **H** // **5** mundo **HWW²B**
modo **V** // **13** virgines **H** virginem **Γ** // **14** quibus **Γ** quotquot **H** // **15** praestare quod
iurastis **Γ** quod iurastis praestare **H** // **17** huius **Γ** huius virginis **H** // **27** ille collegit **Γ**
ipse narravit **H** / ponam **Γ** recenseam **H** // **28** quasi ... dicturus *deest in* **H** quin **Γ** quin
potius **H**

the first to enter upon this road of virginity, unknown to previous centuries, with great courage and pious determination. She was the first who lived in marriage a life above that of ordinary mortals, without carnal relations, an angelic life, taking not a husband, but a guardian of her chastity. Since these were miraculous things, so by a greater miracle, to the astonishment of nature, she brought forth a Son to the world. When she had become a widow, since her whole life was based on the spirit and though living in the body she had raised herself above the condition of the body, she found in God alone a most obedient Son, a most chaste spouse and a most indulgent father, so that she who had despised all things for the sake of God found all things in God.

88. But, what am I about, virgin divine? What am I undertaking? To tell of your infinite praise? But this is a task beyond my dull wit, lack of eloquence and narrow limits of this work. It would require a great amount of leisure time, a very practised eloquence, a superior and very learned intelligence. Imitate her, virgins, all you who wish to preserve your chastity intact. Imitate her, you married women, whose concern it is to please your husbands and to fulfil the oath you made. Look to her at all times, you widows, and you will receive from her solace for your departed spouse, counsel for watching over your offspring and a most useful example for passing the rest of your lives. Thousands from among our ranks have followed her mode of life, as the Psalmist had foretold: 'Virgins shall be led to the king in her train.' Their works are not only beneficial for the present moment but will be a model for all generations. History is not silent about virgins in pagan times, ennobled by chastity alone. Jerome does not hesitate to include a catalogue of them taken from Greek history in his polemic against Jovinian, because he saw that in matters of this sort people are forcefully moved by example, since it does not seem difficult to do things that were once done. He introduced the examples of many women who preferred to sacrifice their lives rather than their chastity. I will not insult this revered and holy man by passing over what he compiled as if it were superfluous, or putting it into other words as if I could say it better. Rather I shall transcribe just what he put down, which is as follows:

89. When the Thirty Tyrants of Athens had slain Pheidon at a banquet, they ordered his daughters to be brought to them and to be stripped like harlots and to cavort with unseemly gestures on the floor stained with their father's blood. They concealed their feelings of sorrow for a while, and then when they saw that the guests were drunk, they left the banquet hall as if to answer the needs of nature, embraced one another and plunged into a well to preserve their virginity

88. Jovinian: He denied the superiority of virginity over matrimony, affirming that baptismal grace was given to all equally. Jerome wrote his *Adversus Jovinianum* in 393. It drew much criticism for its exaggeration and polemical tone, which Jerome answered in three letters, 48–50.

89. Pheidon: Killed at the instigation of his enemy Critias, one of the Thirty.

praecipitaverunt in puteum, ut virginitatem morte servarent. Demotionis
Areopagitarum principis virgo filia, audito sponsi Leosthenis interitu, qui
bellum Lamiacum concitarat, se interfecit, asserens quamquam intacta esset
corpore, tamen si alterum accipere cogeretur, quasi secundum acciperet,
cum priori mente nupsisset. Spartiatae et Messenii diu inter se habuere
amicitias, in tantum ut ob quaedam sacra etiam virgines ad se mutuo mitte-
rent. Quodam igitur tempore, cum quinquaginta virgines Lacedaemoniorum
Messenii violare temptassent, de tanto numero ad stuprum nulla consensit,
sed omnes libentissime pro pudicitia occubuerunt. Quamobrem grave bellum
et longissimum concitatum est et post multum temporis Mamertia subversa
est. Aristoclides Orchomeni tyrannus adamavit virginem Stymphalidem,
quae, cum patre occiso ad templum Dianae confugisset et simulacrum eius
teneret nec vi posset avelli, in eodem loco confossa est. Ob cuius necem tanto
omnis Arcadia dolore commota est ut bellum publice sumeret et necem
virginis ulcisceretur. Aristomenes Messenius, vir iustissimus, victis Lacedaemoniis et quodam tempore nocturna sacra celebrantibus quae vocabantur
Hyacinthina, rapuit de choris ludentium virgines quindecim et tota nocte
gradu concito fugiens, excessit de finibus Spartanorum. Cumque eas comites
vellent violare, monuit quantum potuit ne hoc facerent et ad extremum
quosdam non parentes interfecit, ceteris metu coercitis. Redemptae postea
a cognatis puellae, cum Aristomenem viderent caedis reum fieri, tamdiu ad
patriam non sunt reversae quamdiu iudicum advolutae genibus defensorem
pudicitiae suae cernerent absolutum.

90. Quo ore laudandae sunt Scedasi filiae in Leuctris Boeotiae, quas traditum est absente patre duos iuvenes praetereuntes iure hospitii suscepisse, qui
multum indulgentes vino vim per noctem intulere virginibus? Quae amissa
pudicitia nolentes supervivere, mutuis conciderunt vulneribus. Iustum est et
Locridas virgines non tacere, quae cum Ilium mitterentur ex more per annos
circiter mille, nulla obsceni rumoris et pollutae virginitatis fabulam dedit.
Quis valeat silentio praeterire septem Milesias virgines, quae Gallorum impetu cuncta vastante ne quid indecens ab hostibus sustinerent, turpitudinem
morte fugerunt, exemplum sui cunctis virginibus relinquentes honestis mentibus magis pudicitiam curae esse quam vitam? Nicanor, victis Thebis atque

---

89. (Demotionis ... filia) *Diod. 11, 60* // (Orchomeni tyrannus) *Paus. 8, 5, 11* //
(Aristomenes) *Paus. 4, 19, 4*

4 acciperet **H** *Hier.* accipere **Γ** // **16** nocturna **HBV** nocturno **WW²** // **17** Hiacynthina
HΓ *edd. vet. Hier.* (= Hyacynthia)

---

90. Nicanor: A general of Alexander the Great involved in the destruction of Thebes in
335 B.C.

by their death. The virgin daughter of Demotion, leader of the Areopagites, hearing of the death of her promised spouse Leosthenes, who had stirred up the Lamian war, killed herself. She declared that although still unsullied, if she were forced to take another man, it would be the equivalent of having a second husband since in her heart she was married to the first. The Spartans and the Messenians had a long friendship with each other, to such an extent that they even exchanged virgins for certain sacred rites. On one occasion when the Messenians tried to violate fifty virgins sent by the Lacedaemonians, of that great number none consented to their debauchery, but all willingly died for their chastity. Whence there arose a grave and prolonged war and after a long time the Mamertines were defeated. Aristoclides, tyrant of Orchomenus, fell in love with a young girl of Stymphalus, who after her father was killed, took refuge at the shrine of Diana and, embracing her statue, could not be dragged away by force. She was run through on that very spot. All of Arcadia was so moved with sorrow at her death that war was declared officially and the virgin's murder was avenged. Aristomenes of Messene, a man of highest integrity, after the defeat of the Lacedaemonians, while they were celebrating nocturnal rites called the Hyacinthia, carried off fifteen virgins from the chorus of dancers and fleeing through the night at a swift pace, left the borders of the Spartans behind him. When his companions wished to violate them, he warned them as sternly as he could not to do so and finally had to kill some who did not obey, which deterred the others. Afterwards the young girls were ransomed by their relatives, and seeing that Aristomenes was accused of murder, they would not return to their native country until, prostrate at the feet of the judges, they saw the defender of their chastity acquitted.

90. What words of praise should be reserved for the daughters of Scedasus in Leuctra in Boeotia? It is related that in the absence of their father they showed hospitality to two young men passing through the city, who, having indulged too much in wine, ravished the virgins in the course of the night. Not wishing to go on living after the loss of their virginity, they killed each other. Nor would it be right to omit mention of the virgins of Locris, who were sent to Ilium according to a custom which had lasted for nearly a thousand years, and yet not one of them gave rise to slanderous talk concerning her reputation or the defilement of her virginity. Who could pass over in silence the seven virgins of Miletus, who, when the Gauls were sacking the city, escaped disgrace by taking their lives rather than suffer any indignity from the enemy, leaving an example to all virgins that for noble souls chastity is a matter of greater concern than life? After the conquest and subjection of Thebes Nicanor was

89. Leosthenes: Athenian commander who defeated Antipater, Alexander's general, but then was killed by a stone while besieging the town of Lamia in 322 B.C.

Mamertines: Mercenary troops from Campania who had made themselves masters of the town of Messene.

Aristoclides: Jerome or the textual tradition is in error here; the tyrant's name was Aristocrates. The story is told in Pausanias, *Guide to Greece*, 8,5,11.

Aristomenes: Legendary hero of Messenia who resisted the incursions of neighboring Sparta.

Hyacinthia: Festival in honor of Hyacinth, beloved of Apollo, celebrated in Amyclae in Lacedaemonia in mid-July.

subversis, unius virginis captivae amore superatus est; cuius coniugium expetens et voluntarios amplexus quod scilicet captiva optare debuerat, sensit pudicis mentibus plus virginitatem esse quam regnum et interfectam propria manu flens et lugens amator tenuit. Narrant scriptores Graeci et aliam
5   Thebanam virginem quam hostis Macedo corruperat, dissimulasse paulisper dolorem et violatorem virginitatis suae iugulasse postea dormientem seque interfecisse gladio, ut nec vivere voluerit post perditam castitatem nec ante mori quam sui ultrix exsisteret.'

91. Haec omnia Hieronymus, ut si quis est pudor, erubescant Christianae
10   feminae quae parum castae integritatem sub castissimo Christo castissimae Matris Filio in castissima Ecclesia servant, cum gentiles feminae spurcissimum Iovem et impudicissimam Venerem colentes pudicitiam carissimis universis rebus praetulerint. Quid? Ego huc exempla sanctarum Virginum afferam ad eas commovendas quas non pudet vel castas gentiles nomi-
15   nari? Quam potissimum proponam imitandam, cum se per millia nobis offerant? Theclamne? an Agnetem? an Catharinam? an Luciam? an Caeciliam? an Agatham? an Barbaram? an Margaritam? an Dorotheam? an potius exercitum undecim milium virginum, quae omnes, dictu mirabile, mortem obire maluerunt quam libidini hostium sua corpora praebere? At
20   hunc consensum tam sancti propositi vix in duobus viris invenias quod in undecim tenellarum virginum milibus tam ratum fixumque permansit. Quis numerus capiat eas quae iugulari se, quae caedi, truncari, suffocari, mergi, secari, exuri facile sunt passae, ac libenter, dum pudicitiam tuentur? Quae mortem cum nollent sibi afferre, arte quaesierunt in discrimen castitatis
25   adductae: ut Brasilla, Dyrrachina primaria virgo, quae cum imminentem suae pudicitiae crudelem victorem cerneret, pacta est, si salvam integritatem reliquisset, herbam daturam se cuius succo illitus nullis telis violari posset. Condicionem accepit miles. Illa ex proximis hortis vulsa herba quae prima ad manum fuit, iubet in se vim eius experiri, infectoque iugulo: 'Hoc,' inquit,
30   'feri ad faciendum periculum, nam res est comperta.' Feriit et virginem

---

7 gladio **BV** *Hier. PL 41, 271* gaudio **HWW²** *et plerique MSS.* // 8 exsisteret **HWW²B** exsistere **V** // 23 ac libenter **Γ** *deest in* **H** // 24–25 in discrimen castitatis adductae **Γ** in discrimine castitatis sitae **H** // 26 crudelem victorem cerneret **Γ** saevum victorem videret **H** // 27 telis **Γ** armis **H** // 29 experiri **Γ** periclitari **H** // 30 feri ... comperta. Feriit **Γ** caede ut experiaris. Cecidit ille **H**

---

eleven thousand virgins: Saint Ursula and her companions, said to have suffered martyrdom at the hands of the Huns in Cologne in defense of their chastity.

Brasilla: Vives got this story from Francesco Barbaro, *De re uxoria*, who in turn took it from the *Memorandarum rerum liber* of Giovanni Conversini of Ravenna. The Slavic pirate chieftain was named Čerič. The Venetians were familiar with these stories since they had long waged wars with the Dalmatian pirates.

overwhelmed with love for a young maiden he had taken captive. He sought to marry her and wished to receive her willing embraces, which one might expect a captive maiden would desire. But he realized that virginity was dearer to chaste minds than kingly power when with tears of mourning he held her in his arms slain by her own hand. Greek writers tell of another virgin, also of Thebes, whom a Macedonian soldier had defiled. For a little while she concealed her sorrow but later while her ravisher was asleep, she cut his throat and then killed herself with the same sword, for she neither wished to continue to live after the loss of her chastity nor die without having avenged herself.

91. Jerome relates all these stories so that, if there is any shame at all, Christian women may be ashamed, who, too little chaste, preserve their virtue under the most chaste Christ, son of the most chaste Mary, within the most chaste church, while pagan women, worshippers of foul Jupiter and immoral Venus, have preferred chastity to the most priceless things of this world. Why should I bring forward examples of holy virgins to move those who are not ashamed to hear tell of the chastity of pagan women? Whom shall I propose for their imitation of the thousands that present themselves to us? Shall I mention Thecla or Agnes or Catherine or Lucia or Caecilia or Agatha or Barbara or Margaret or Dorothea? Or rather the army of eleven thousand virgins, all of whom, marvelous to relate, preferred to face death rather than offer their bodies to the lust of the enemy? You could hardly find among two men this unanimity in a holy cause that remained so firm and fixed in eleven thousand tender virgins. What number can be devised for those women who readily and willingly allowed themselves to have their throats cut, be slain, dismembered, suffocated, drowned, cut to pieces, burned alive, as long as they could preserve their chastity? Not wishing to take their own lives, they sought death by clever stratagems when their chastity was at stake, like Brasilla, a virgin of noble birth from Dyracchium, who, seeing that the cruel conqueror had designs on her chastity, made a pact with him that if he respected her virginity, she would give him an herb whose juice smeared over his body would make him invulnerable to all weapons. The soldier accepted the condition. She pulled up the first herb that came to hand in a nearby garden and invited him to test its efficacy on her. Smearing it on her throat she said: 'Strike here to make proof of it, for there can be no doubt of its

91. Agnes: Roman maiden martyred under Diocletian at the age of 12 or 13. She became the patroness of chastity.

Lucia: Little is known of the life of this saint. She is said to have been martyred in Syracuse, where her tomb still exists in the catacomb named after her.

Caecilia: One of the most famous of Roman martyrs, patroness of music.

Agatha: Born in Catania, mentioned in all the martyrologies.

Margaret: Eastern saint born in Antioch, denounced by her father as a Christian, and decapitated, perhaps during the reign of Diocletian.

Dorothea: Legendary martyr of Caesarea in Cappodocia.

interemit. Quid quod occidere se feminam ut castitatem tueatur nec Hieronymus videtur damnare? Et Ambrosius libro de Virginibus tertio huic quaestioni martyris Pelagiae opponit exemplum: 'Nihil assertione opus,' dicens, 'ubi factum sit martyris virginis annorum quindecim, quae cum matre
5 et sororibus in flumen se praecipitavit.' Sophroniam, nobilem feminam, Eusebius in Ecclesiastica historia tradit, cum videret maritum suum urbis praefectum in defendenda sua pudicitia a libidine Maximini cunctari ac nutare, abditam in cubiculum ferro pectus aperuisse, quam tamen Ecclesiae consensus martyrum numero adscripsit.

10   **92.** Haec omnia castitatis exempla in ecclesia leguntur et audet impudica mulier eo venire? Nec exhorret in coetum virginum lupanar inferre suoque vultu sanctissimos inquinare oculos, suis vocibus tenerrimos auditus polluere? Nefaria mulier, tu vel Catharinam vel Agnetem vel Barbaram sonare audes et sacra nomina impurissimo ore contaminare?
15 Tu te aliquo ex illis nominibus insignis? Et similis videri vis nomine cuius es moribus inimica? Nec tibi cum vocaris occurrit qualis illa fuerit cuius gestas nomen? Cumque illam purissimam, castissimam, optimam, te, contra, impuram, impudicam, scelestam cogitas, non te furiae exagitant noctes et dies? Non te exterrent? Non te ardentibus facibus perse-
20 quuntur? O confidentissima feminarum! Et natalem sanctae Virginis tu audes celebrare, indigna quae nascerere osque tuum impudicum pudicissimis oculis ostendere? Et vis eam te aspicere vel audire, sceleribus obrutam, quae viros, nec bonos quidem, dum in corpore viveret, vel viderit vel audierit? Quanto satius esset te numquam in earum conspec-
25 tum venire, ne in te ulciscerentur iniuriam sexus nec eius nomine vocari, ne de te poenas sumerent nominis sui violati! Ego vero id serio dico, neque enim hic est iocandi locus, edicto publico deberet caveri ne qua manifesto impudica mulier Maria nominaretur. Cur nos ei nomini, cui merito assurgimus, cui poplitem flectimus, non tantum hon-
30 oris habeamus quantum quibusdam suis gentiles? Athenis, quod Harmodius et Aristogiton tyrannos civitate exegissent, decreto sancitum est ne servis aut iis qui artem parum liberalem exercerent illorum nomina inderentur.

---

91. (Nihil ... praecipitavit) *Ambr. virg. 3, 7, 33–37, PL 16, 229* // (Sophroniam ... aperuisse) *Rufin. hist. 8, 14, 17*
    92. (Harmodius ... inderentur) *Gell. 9, 2, 10*

2 videtur damnare Γ damnare videtur H // **3** opponit exemplum Γ exemplum opponit H // **9** adscripsit Γ adiecit H // **11–12** inferre Γ inducere H // **12** inquinare oculos Γ oculos inquinare H // **15** insignis Γ nominas H // **16** inimica Γ tam dissimilis et capitalis hostis H // **27** deberet caveri Γ caveri deberet H // **28** manifesto Γ aperte H // **31** tyrannos Γ tyrannum H

power.' He struck and killed the virgin. And what am I to say if even Jerome does not seem to condemn a woman who kills herself to preserve her chastity? And Ambrose on this question adduces the example of the martyr Pelagia in the third book of his *De virginibus* saying: 'There is no need of further justification when it is the deed of a fifteen-year old martyr, who threw herself into a river with her mother and sisters.' Eusebius in his *Ecclesiastical History* relates that when the noblewoman Sophronia saw her husband, prefect of the city, hesitating and indecisive in defending her chastity from the lust of Maximinus, she secluded herself in her bedroom and plunged a sword into her breast. By the consensus of the church she was admitted into the list of martyrs.

92. All these examples of chastity are read in church, and will an unchaste woman dare enter therein? Does she not shudder to introduce a brothel into the company of virgins, to defile their pure eyes with her face, to pollute their delicate hearing with her words? Wicked woman, do you dare pronounce the names of Catherine or Agnes or Barbara, and contaminate their sacred names with your impure mouth? Do you adorn yourself with any of these names and wish to be known by a name to which your morals are inimical? Does it not occur to you when you are called by this name what kind of person she was whose name you bear? When you reflect how pure, chaste and virtuous she was whereas you are impure, unchaste and wicked, do not the Furies hound you night and day? Do they not terrify you and pursue you with flaming torches? O most presumptuous of women, do you dare to celebrate the birthday of the Blessed Virgin, when you did not deserve to be born, and to show your shameless face to her most pure eyes? And do you wish her to look upon you or listen to you, buried in vice, when she, while she dwelt on earth, neither saw nor heard men, not even good men! It would have been better that you never came into their sight so that they would not take vengeance on you for the harm done to their sex, nor be called by one of their names, so that they would not exact punishment of you for the outrage done to that name! I say in all seriousness, for this is no time for pleasantries, that it should be forbidden by public decree that any overtly unchaste woman should be called Mary. Why should we not render the same homage to that name, at which we rise to our feet and bend the knee, that pagans give to certain names of theirs? In Athens, from the time that Harmodius and Aristogiton had driven the tyrants from the city, it was ordained by public decree that those names would not be given to slaves or anyone who did not exercise a liberal occupation.

CAP. XI.   QUOMODO FORIS AGET

93. Prodeundum erit aliquando, sed quam fieri poterit rarissime propter multa. Principio, quod quoties in publicum exit virgo, toties de sua et forma et modestia et prudentia et pudentia et probitate iudicium subit paene
5   capitale, quoniam nihil est fama et existimatione feminarum tenerius aut magis iniuriae obnoxium, ut non immerito videri possit de filo araneae pendere. Idque quoniam illa quae dixi exacta desiderantur in femina, nostra vero iudicia morosa et suspiciosa sunt, ac (quemadmodum Ovidius inquit):

10   Nos in vitium credula turba sumus.

Porro 'Maledicto' (ut Cicero ait) 'nihil est magis volucre, nihil facilius emittitur, nihil citius excipitur, nihil latius dissipatur.' Quod si semel haesit in puella ex hominum existimationibus nota aliqua, sempiterna fere perdurat nec eluitur nisi maximis pudicitiae et sapientiae ostensis argumentis.
15   Loqueris pauca in publico? rudis crederis; multa? levis; indocte? hebes; docte? malitiosa. Non facile respondes? superba, male educata; respondes? non magno impulsu casura. Sedes composito vultu? dissimulatrix; gesticularis? natura stulta; spectas? eo ferri animum; rides cum quis ridet, etsi alio intenta? arisisse actum esse; audis virum? placere tibi quae dicit nec
20   difficilis expugnatu. Quid dicam? Quanta undique flagitiorum et scelerum in publico materia? Egressa est Dina, filia Iacob, ut videret mulieres civitatis. Ibi statim repperit a quo probro ac dedecore afficeretur et violata. Causa fuit cur masculi omnes Salem cum rege et eius filio a Simeon et Levi contrucidarentur; ut non iniuria videatur tragicus dixisse: 'Virgines in turba
25   conspici nefas.' Quanto praestaret manere domi quam has tam varias, tam iniquas adire censuras, tam praesentia pericula! Nec est ubi magis valeat illa Graeca sententia: 'Vive ignotus.' Idcirco Thucydides illam demum optimam esse mulierem censuit de cuius vel laude vel vituperatione minimus est sermo.

30   **94.** Latere debet mulier nec multis esse nota. Indicium est non integrae seu castitatis seu famae noscitari a plerisque. Quid vero per civitatem cantari vel aliqua nota insignive designari, ut alba, clauda, straba, sima, vara, lusciosa,

---

93. (Nos … sumus) *Ov. fast. 4, 312* // (Maledicto … dissipatur) *Cic. Planc. 57* // (Egressa … contrucidarentur) *Vulg. gen. 34, 1–27* // (tragicus) *Eur. El. 343* // (Vive ignotus) *Epik. fg. 551* // (illam … sermo) *Thuk. 2, 45*

---

5 quoniam nihil est **Γ** cum nihil sit **H** // **7** desiderantur in femina **Γ** in femina desiderantur **H** // **11** volucre **HWW²V** volvere **B** // **13–14** perdurat **Γ** est **H** // **21–24** Egressa … contrucidarentur **Γ** *deest in* **H** // **26–27** illa Graeca sententia **Γ** illud Graecum praeceptum **H** // **28** censuit **Γ** dixit **H** / est **Γ** esset **H** // **31** Quid vero **Γ** Et vel **H** // **32** sima **Γ** *deest in* **H**

CHAPTER 11.   HOW SHE WILL BEHAVE IN PUBLIC

93. She will appear in public on occasion, but as rarely as possible, for many reasons. First, because every time she issues forth into public she undergoes what we might almost call a fatal judgment of her beauty, modesty, prudence, propriety and integrity, since there is nothing more fragile or more vulnerable than the reputation and good name of women, so that it may well seem to hang by a cobweb. That is because those qualities I mentioned are expected in a woman and our judgments are exacting and suspicious, and, as Ovid said: 'The masses are prone to detect vice.' Moreover, to quote Cicero, 'There is nothing more volatile than slander, nothing is uttered more easily, nothing is accepted so quickly, nothing is spread abroad so widely.' If some slur has attached to a girl's reputation from men's opinion of her, it usually remains forever and is not erased except by clear proofs of her chastity and wisdom. If you speak little in public you are thought to be uneducated; if you speak a lot, you are light-headed; unlearnedly, you are accounted ignorant; learnedly, you are malicious; if you are slow in responding, you are haughty and ill-mannered; ready with an answer, a little push will make you stumble; if you sit with composed mien, then you are a dissembler; if you gesticulate, you are stupid by nature; if you look at something, that means your mind is drawn there; if you laugh when someone else laughs, even if your attention was directed elsewhere, your smile has betrayed you; if you listen to a man, it means you approve of what he says and you will be an easy conquest. What more can I say? How many occasions there are for corruption and misconduct when one is in public? Dina, the daughter of Jacob, went out to see the women of the city. Immediately she found there one by whom she was reduced to shame and dishonor and was violated, which was the reason why all the male population of Shechem together with their king and his son were slaughtered by Simeon and Levi. The tragedian is right to have said: 'It is wrong for young women to be seen in public.' How much more profitable would it be for them to remain at home than to incur such manifold and unjust criticisms and such imminent dangers! Nowhere is the truth of the Greek proverb more apparent: 'Live a hidden life.' For that reason Thucydides expressed the opinion that in the end the best woman was the one of whom there was least talk, whether in praise or blame.

94. A woman should live in seclusion and not be known to many. It is a sign of imperfect chastity and of uncertain reputation to be known by a great number of people. What good is it to be talked about all through the city or to be referred to by some mark or characteristic, as light-skinned, lame, cross-eyed, flat-nosed, bow-legged, suffering from night-blindness, two-faced,

93. Shechem: Vives writes Salem.

vatia, parva, magna, pinguis, manca, balba? Ignorata haec vulgo oportuit
in proba femina. Numquamne ergo ferendus extra privatum pes? Grande
scilicet nefas. Semper delitescendum domi, hoc est, (sicut quaedam interpre-
tantur vanae et ut vel spectent vel spectentur cupidae) in carcere, in ergastulo?
5   Prodeundum vero aliquando, si res poscet aut iubeat parens. Prius tamen
quam pedem ianua efferat, non secus quam pugnatura paret animum. Cogitet quae visura, quae auditura sit, quae dictura. Reputet apud se undique
aliquid occursurum quod pudicitiam et bonam mentem sollicitet et concutiat.
Adversus haec diaboli undecumque ingruentia iacula clipeum sumat pectoris
10   bonis praeceptis ac exemplis muniti, propositum firmum pudicitiae, animum
in Christum intentissimum ac defixum. Nec ignoret se ad vanitatem et diaboli praestigias atque illusus ire, quis ne capiatur maximopere providendum
est. Nec aliud existimandum est id quod foris videbit quam spectaculum
quoddam vitae humanae, ex cuius vitiis ante oculos positis ipsa non modo
15   contagio non corrumpatur, sed etiam emendet sua. Et quo momento a Deo
in homines sese convertet ut, sive probet eos sive ab eis probetur, a Christo
in adulterium discedit. Si bona viderit, sequetur propter Christum; sin mala,
vitet propter Christum. Avertat ne sic se componat, sic incedat, sic agat aut
loquatur ut pedica diaboli sit viris. Non solum ipsa peccare non debet, sed,
20   quantum potest, praestare ne causa sit aliis et incitamentum peccati, alioqui
membrum erit eius diaboli cuius est et instrumentum, non Christi. Divam
Virginem ea modestia ac moderatione gestus atque universi corporis fuisse
ferunt ut, si qui lasciviores oculi in eam incidissent, velut si ardens pruna
in aquam cecidisset, turpe illud incendium protinus exstingueretur et ceu
25   vis quaedam intrinsecus emanans continentiae ac temperationis pravas illas
intuentium cupidines coercebat animosque convertebat in sui naturam.
      95. His atque eiusmodi cogitationibus armata, domo exeat cum matre, si
habet et si licet; sin minus, cum gravi aliqua femina vidua aut coniugata aut
etiam virgine probatae vitae, casti et sobrii sermonis, sanctae verecundiae.
30   Homerus pudicam Penelopem in consessum procorum descendisse canit,

---

94. (spectent ... spectentur) *Ov. ars 1, 99* // (clipeum ... pectoris) *Vulg. Eph. 6, 16*
95. (Homerus ... ancillis) *Hom. Od. 1, 331* //

1 vatia **Γ** *deest in* **H** // 4 vel spectent vel spectentur **HWW²B** vel spectentur **V** / in ergastulo **Γ**
deest in **H** // 5 iubeat **Γ** si iubebit **H** // 11 ac defixum **Γ** *deest in* **H** // 11–12 et diaboli
... ire **Γ** *deest in* **H** // 12 quis ne capiatur **Γ** qua ne rapiatur **H** // 15 corrumpatur **Γ**
tangatur **H** // 16 sese convertet **Γ** se vertet **H** // 16–17 a Christo in adulterium discedit **Γ**
discedit et ex sponsa Christi sit subito adultera **H** // 17 sequetur **Γ** amet **H** // 18 incedat **Γ**
ineat **H** // 20 et incitamentum **Γ** *deest in* **H** // 22 gestus ... corporis *deest in* **H** // 23–24
pruna in aquam cecidisset turpe **Γ** in aquam cecidisset titio foedum **H** // 24–26 et ceu ...
naturam **Γ** *deest in* **H** // 27 His ... armata **Γ** His et similibus cogitationibus instructa **H**
// 29 casti et sobrii **Γ** moderati **H** // 30 consessum **HWW²** consessu **BV** / canit **Γ**
ait **H**

small, big, fat, crippled, stuttering? These things should not be commonly known in a good woman. Should she never set foot outside her own house? Evidently that would be a great crime. Must she always hide herself at home, which certain vain women, anxious to see or be seen, interpret to mean in prison for a life sentence? She should go out at times, if circumstances demand it or a parent orders it. But before she steps over the threshold let her prepare her mind as if she were entering a combat. Let her think about what she will see, what she will hear, what she will say. Let her reflect within herself that she will be confronted on all sides by things that will perturb and upset her chastity and her good conscience. Against these shafts of the devil hurled from every side let her take up the shield of a mind fortified with good precepts and examples, a firm commitment to chastity, a mind intent and fixed on Christ. She must not forget that she is pitted against vanity and the tricks and illusions of the devil and she must take care she is not ensnared. She must be persuaded that all she sees around her is nothing but a spectacle of human life and not only must she not be corrupted by the contagion of the vices laid before her eyes but must emend her own. And the moment she turns away from God towards men, whether to approve them or be approved by them, she departs from Christ into adultery. If she sees good things, let her follow them for the sake of Christ; if she sees bad things, let her avoid them for the sake of Christ. Let her be on her guard that she does not comport herself, walk, act or speak in such a way that she becomes a snare of the devil for men. Not only must she not sin herself but she must, as far as possible, be responsible for seeing that she is not a cause or incitement to sin for others. Otherwise she will be a member of the devil, whose instrument she already is, not of Christ. They say that the Blessed Virgin was of such modesty and composure in her actions and in her whole body that if any lascivious look were directed at her, that loathsome fire would immediately be extinguished like a live coal that has fallen into the water, or as if some radiating force of continence and temperance held in check those perverse desires of those who looked at her and converted their feelings to her own nature.

95. Armed with these and similar reflections, let her leave her house with her mother, if she has one and if it is possible; if not, with a women of austere morals, a widow, a married woman or even a young woman of proven virtue, chaste and sober speech, and seemly behavior. Homer sings that the chaste Penelope went down to the assembly of the suitors not alone but

sed non solam, verum duabus comitatam probis ancillis, cum tamen domi
suae esset et Telemachus filius inter procos sederet, iam tum adolescens.
Divus Paulus nullo pacto vult feminam caput nudare. De reliquo autem
corpore Hieronymus iubet ut procedens in publicum non pectus et colla
5   denudet nec pallio revoluto cervicem aperiat, sed celet faciem et vix uno
oculo qui viae necessarius est patente, ingrediatur, nec spectare cupiat nec
spectari, nec oculos mobiles huc atque illuc iactet, nec curet quaerere quis
illic aut illic habitet quae vix vicinos suos debet nosse. Tecta vult esse omnia in
virgine praeter oculos, viae duces. Nec video quid possit esse honesti et pudici
10 in ostentatione colli (sed hoc tolerabile), pectoris etiam et papillarum, tum
interscapilii, ita ut aliquae humeros ipsos renudent. Id vero quam foedum sit
caeci (quod aiunt) vident, cum ex intuentibus alii rem taetram abominentur;
lasciviores, insolita corporis parte conspecta, ceu igne subiecto accendantur.
Quorsum pertinere credimus inventas manicas praelongas et chirothecas?
15 Numquid ut manus foverentur molliter ac odorate? Non erat tam ingeniosa
in luxum et delicias vetustas; certe ut necessitati consuleretur et manus nisi
in opere laterent; ne quid cerneretur ex corpore, mancipio vilissimo ac
nequissimo, nec in facie exsisteret aliud quam probitas et verecundia.

96. Milesias virgines eo correptas olim animi furore legimus ut se passim
20 suspenderent, neque huic malo remedium inveniebatur ullum. Edicebatur
horribilibus poenis ne fieret, contemnebantur poenae. Quae enim morte
atrocior quam ipsae ultro appetebant? Custodiebantur; inter custodum
manus exitum inveniebat spiritus. Edictum est tandem ut quae se occidisset
nuda per medium forum media luce traheretur. Hac sola poena deterritae
25 sunt ne nudae cernerentur, licet exanimes. O pudorem incredibilem et
praedicandum! Quae mortem, malorum ultimum, comtemnebant pudorem
etiam in mortuo corpore curabant. Ita furor ille compressus ac sedatus est.
Quid quod provida rerum natura mater verecundiae feminarum consuluit?
Dictu mirabile! Virorum corpora proiecta in mare Plinius in Historia rerum

---

95. (Divus Paulus ... nudare) *Vulg. I Cor. 11, 5–6* // (iubet ... ingrediatur) *Hier. epist.
130, 18, PL 22, 1122* // (caeci ... vident) *Erasm. ad. LB II, 332B*
96. (Milesias ... exanimes) *Plut. mor. 249B–D* // (Virorum ... prona) *Plin. nat. 7, 17*

1 verum **Γ** ceterum **H** / probis **Γ** castis **H** // 2 Telemachus ... procos **Γ** filius suus
Telemachus inter illos **H** // 2–4 iam ... corpore **Γ** *deest in* **H** // 4 Hieronymus iubet
ut **Γ** Tum quod Hieronymus iubet **H** // 11 aliquae humeros ipsos **Γ** nonullae humeros **H**
// 13 conspecta **Γ** visa **H** / accendantur **Γ** accenduntur **H** // 14 manicas praelongas
et **Γ** *deest in* **H** // 15 Numquid ut manus **Γ** nisi ut etiam manus **H** // 15–16 foverentur
... manus **Γ** *deest in* **H** // 17–18 ne quid ... verecundia *deest in* **H** // 23 inveniebat
spiritus **Γ** spiritus inveniebat **H** // 24 sola **Γ** *om.* **B** // 25 cernerentur licet exanimes **Γ** etiam
exanimes conspicerentur **H** // 26 malorum ultimum **Γ** ultimum malorum **H** // 27 etiam
... curabant **Γ** reverebantur et in mortuo corpore **H** / ac sedatus est **Γ** quievit **H** // 29
Dictu mirabile **Γ** Mirabile dictu **H**

accompanied by two virtuous handmaids, but when he was at home her son Telemachus, already a young man, also took his place among the suitors. St. Paul insists that a woman should not have her head uncovered. As for the rest of her body, Jerome recommends that when she appears in public she should not expose her breast or neck, or by rolling back her pallium show the back of her neck, but she should conceal her face, leaving only one eye uncovered as she walks, to see her way. She should not desire to see or be seen, or cast her glance this way and that, or be anxious to know who lives here or there when she should barely know who her neighbors are. He wishes that a young woman be completely covered except for her eyes, which guide her way. I do not see how there can be any modesty or virtue in showing off one's neck (although this can be tolerated) but also the breast and the nipples, and the part between the shoulder-blades, indeed some even expose the shoulders themselves. As the saying goes, even the blind can see how shameful that is, although of those who witness this exposure some loathe it as abominable, while the more wanton, seeing a part of the body not usually exposed to view, are enflamed as if they had caught fire. For what purpose were long sleeves and gloves invented? Was it to keep the hands snug in soft and fragrant wrappings? Antiquity was not so ingenious in luxury and self-indulgence. Certainly they were invented out of necessity and so that except when engaged in work the hands would be hidden and that no part of the body, vile and useless servant, would be seen. The countenance, too, should reveal nothing but uprightness and modesty.

96. We read that the young women of Miletus were seized with such frenzy that they hanged themselves throughout the city. No remedy could be found for this plague. Edicts were passed forbidding this practice and threatening dire punishment but these measures were ignored. What more horrible death could be devised than the one they meted out to themselves? They were kept under guard but in the hands of their guardians their spirit found a way out. Finally it was decreed that whoever killed herself would be dragged naked through the middle of the forum in broad daylight. This penalty alone deterred them, for they did not wish to be seen naked even in death. What incredible and laudable modesty! Those who despised death, the last of all evils, had concern for modesty even in their dead body. Thus that madness was restrained and laid to rest. What could I add save that the providence of mother nature herself took thought for the modesty of women? Astonishing to relate, men's bodies float face up when they are thrown into the sea, Pliny tells us in his *Natural History*, while

tradit supina ferri, feminarum prona. Naturae ergo pudor earum curae est, ipsae suum negligunt?

97. In ingressu nec celeritates suscipiat femina nec tarditates notabiles. Iam ubi in hominum conventu considebit, magna et vultus et totum cor-
5 pus convestiendum ornandumque erit modestia, quae non ex ostentatione nascatur, sed ex miti et vere Christiano pectore. Haec demum solida et durata est modestia gratiamque spectantium bona fide conciliat. Tum pudorem addendum pudicitiae, ceterarum quoque virtutum mundum atque ornamentum. Oculos contineat demissos nec attollat nisi raro et modice et
10 verecunde; neminem intente ac inconiventer aspiciat. Si viri seorsum sedeant et in puellas spectent ac inter se colloquantur, ne credat virgo se spectari, de se illos loqui. Fit enim ut puellae quaedam, quae pulchritudinis aut venustatis opinionem ipsae sibi confinxerunt, in se unas coniectos omnium oculos autument, omnium sermones in se dirigi. Ita si quis eas aspiciat
15 vir, etiam aliud agens et cogitans, suam spectari formam ratae subrident et ne hoc ipsum ridere videantur, frigidum aliqua de re sermonem iniciunt quem ipsae putent ad risum movendum esse aptum. Cernere est interdum viginti pariter considentes, quas si quis intueatur, rideant omnes, obtendentes se vel verbum vel factum aliquod cuiusquam earum ridere, minime tamen
20 ridiculum cum unaquaeque se solam inusitata et prodigiosa forma spectaculo atque admirationi esse sibi persuadeat, in quo levitatem suam et dementiam apertissime declarant.

98. Mea virgo et negliget formam nec se esse pulchram putabit nec dictis insulsis aut frivolis arridebit nec gaudebit se intentius conspici ac
25 velut scopum esse se confabulationum iuventutis; cum hoc magis sit ei lacrimandum, excellentissimum bonorum suorum a tot hostibus, tot machinis impeti atque oppugnari, quibus an obsistere omnibus possit ignorat; suam faciem velut facem quandam iuvenum animos ad inconcessas turpesque libidines inflammare. Et quoniam de risu agimus, qui maxime levis solutique
30 animi est index, caveat ne effusius riserit, ut corpus totum cachinno videatur concuti aut compressum non valeat spiritum recipere, neve frigidis aut insulsis de causis, ut quod aliquis sit calvus aut varus aut vacia aut balbus aut blaesus aut verbum protulerit inversum, neu levibus, ut quod interpolatum

---

1 Naturae ... curae est Γ Natura ergo pudorem earum curat **H** ∥ **4–5** considebit ... modestia Γ fuerit, magnam et vultu et toto corpore praeferat modestiam **H** ∥ **6** miti ... pectore Γ modesto et vere Christiano animo **H** ∥ **6–7** Haec ... conciliat Γ *deest in* **H** ∥ **7–8** pudorem ... ornamentum Γ pudorem pudicitiae ac ceterarum virtutum decus et ornamentum **H** ∥ **9–10** Oculos ... sedeant Γ nec intueatur viros nec se intueri putet. Si separati sint **H** ∥ **14** autument Γ existiment **H** ∥ **17** ad risum movendum esse aptum Γ risum movere **H** ∥ **18** pariter Γ una **H** / quis intueatur Γ inspexerit quis **H** ∥ **21** esse Γ *deest in* **H** ∥ **24** frivolis arridebit Γ ineptis ridebit **H** ∥ **25** iuventutis Γ iuvenum **H** / magis Γ citius **H** ∥ **27** impeti atque Γ *deest in* **H** ∥ **30** caveat Γ videat **H** ∥ **30**–p.134,**10** ut corpus ... Dei Γ *deest in* **H**

women's bodies lie face down. Therefore when nature looks after their modesty, will they themselves neglect it?

97. In her walk a woman should not be too hurried nor deliberately slow. When she is present at a meeting in the company of men, her countenance and her whole body should exhibit great modesty of attire and adornment, born not of ostentation but of true Christian gentleness and humility of spirit. This, after all, is real and lasting modesty, which by its sincerity wins the favor of those who look at her. A sense of propriety, the adornment and embellishment of all the other virtues, must be joined to her modesty. She will keep her eyes cast down, and will raise them but rarely and with modesty and decorum. She will not stare at anyone intently or in an unbecoming manner. If the men are seated apart and look at the young women and talk among themselves, she should not think that she is being looked at or that they are talking about her. For it happens that some young women, who have devised a false opinion of their beauty and comeliness, think that the eyes of all are fixed upon them and that they are the subject of every conversation. So if a man turns his glance towards them, even if he is occupied with something else and his thoughts are directed elsewhere, they think their beauty is being admired and they smile complacently. Then to avoid giving the impression that this has occasioned their smile they inject some vapid comment into the conversation which they think will make them laugh. Sometimes one can see twenty damsels sitting together, and if anyone looks at them, they all break out into laughter, pretending that they are laughing at some witticism or action that is not at all funny, since each of them is convinced that she is the object of looks of admiration for her extraordinary and miraculous beauty, and in doing so gives clear proof of her shallowness and folly.

98. The young woman, as I envisage her, will have no regard for beauty and will not think herself beautiful; she will not laugh at insipid and frivolous remarks, nor will she find pleasure in being stared at as if she were the subject of young men's conversations. Rather she should weep the more that this most prized of her possessions is assailed and attacked by so many enemies and engines of war which she is not certain she can resist, and that her face like a firebrand ignites the minds of young men to illicit and foul lusts. And since we were speaking of laughter, which is the surest index of a light and frivolous mind, let her take care that she does not laugh too freely so that her whole body seems so convulsed with boisterous laughter that she cannot regain her breath. Neither should she laugh for silly or stupid reasons such as if someone is bald, or bow-legged, or knock-kneed, or lisps or stammers, or inverts a word, nor for trivial reasons, e.g., because someone wears his hat

gestet pilleum aut praepostere vel dissutum calceum vel fractam zonulam aut quod in nasum cuiusquam musca involarit aut quod transilierit scamnum felis.

99. Sed potissimum cavendum ne ex cuiuspiam calamitate risus sumatur, seu derisus verius, cum sint humani casus omnibus communes et causae ignorentur cur eveniant. Signum est animi atrocis atque immanis in calamitatibus humanis lascivire aut insolescere nec reverentis aut reputantis incognita quidem illa. Ceterum admiranda atque adoranda consilia divinae mentis, quae alios facit in hac aevi brevitate miseros, alios felices, prout visum est aequissimae illi sapientiae aeterni ac omnia moderantis Dei. Illud ne admonenda quidem est ne iuveni ridenti arrideat, quod plane non fit nisi vel ab impudica vel ab amenti. Ne sinat se vellicari vel lascivius tangi. Mutet locum et abeat si vitare aliter non possit. Nihil viro det, nihil a viro accipiat. 'Beneficium accipere' (inquit prudens vir) 'libertatem vendere est.' Nec immerito illud apud Hispanos et Gallos usitatum est: 'Femina quae accipit se vendit; femina quae dat se dedit.' Itaque honesta nec dabit nec accipiet.

100. Garrulam nolim esse nec inter puellas. Nam inter viros miror esse quosdam tam impudentes qui probent. Consuetudo illa accepta et iussa est, quantum arbitror, suffragiis infernis, ut laudi vertatur feminas scite ac facunde cum viris confabulari idque in multas horas. Quaeso vos, quid loquetur imperita puella cum iuvene imperito bonarum rerum, peritissimo malarum? Quid ignis cum stuppa? (Puto de Christo aut Diva Virgine aut de animo componendo). Quae poterit esse materia confabulationis tam longae? An non uterque mutuo ardore incensus, de igne quo ardebit, velit nolit, cogetur loqui? Has vocant feminas palatinas sive aulicas; quaero, a palando an a balando? Nam aulicas esse satis apparet ex plerisque aulis temporum nostrorum, parentibus flagitiorum omnium et sedibus Satanae, quas non tantum Christianus aversetur, sed et gentilis qui pauxillum habeat mentis melioris. Atqui ex illis non sunt omnes impudicae, aiunt isti. Primum nescio; deinde etiam si sunt corpore pudicae, certe animo impudicissimo

---

99. (Beneficium ... est) *Publil. A. 89*

10 Illud Γ Nam illud **H** // **12** amenti Γ stulta **H** // **13** vitare ... possit Γ sit opus **H** // **19** probent Γ non improbent **H** / accepta et iussa Γ approbata **H** // **23** Quid ignis cum stuppa **HWW²B** *hic om.* **V**; *v.l.* **24–25** // **23–24** aut de animo componendo Γ *deest in* **H** // **24–25** tam longae **HWW²B** tam longae. Quid ignis cum stuppa? **V** // **26** palatinas sive Γ *deest in* **H** / quaero Γ credo **H** // **26–27** a palando ... apparet Γ *deest in* **H** // **27** plerisque Γ *deest in* **H** // **28** flagitiorum omnium Γ scelerum enormium **H** // **29** qui Γ modo **H** // **30** illis Γ istis **H** // **31** etiam *deest in* **H**

backwards or in an unusual way or if his shoes are untied or his belt broken or because a fly lands on someone's nose or a cat walks across the bench.

99. But especially to be avoided is that laughter or, I should say, derision be caused by someone's misfortune, since human calamities are common to us all, and their causes are unknown. It is the sign of a cruel and inhuman spirit to make light of human tragedies or make them the butt of insolence without any regard or consideration for these unexplained happenings. Whereas the designs of the divine mind should be admired and worshipped, which makes some unhappy in this brief life and others happy in accordance with the will of that most equitable wisdom of the eternal God, who is the moderator of all things. I need not even admonish the young woman not to return the smile of a young man, which only a woman with no modesty or sense would do. She must not allow herself to be pinched or touched in a lewd manner. Let her change her place and leave if she cannot avoid it any other way. She should not give anything to a man or receive anything from him. 'To accept a kindness' a wise man said 'is to sell one's liberty.' And with good reason the French and the Spaniards repeat the saying: 'A woman who accepts sells herself; a woman who gives has given herself.' Therefore the virtuous woman will neither give nor receive.

100. I do not wish that a young woman be talkative, not even among her girl companions. I am amazed that there are some men impudent enough to approve of this. The custom to give praise to a woman for her ability to converse wittily and eloquently with men for hours on end is something that is welcomed and prescribed by ordinances of hell, in my opinion. I ask you, what will an inexperienced girl talk about with a young man who is ignorant of good things, but expert in evil? What is fire doing together with flax? I suppose they will be talking about Christ or the Blessed Virgin or the subordination of the spirit? What could be the subject of such a long conversation? Will not both of them, burning with the same ardor, be forced to speak about the fire that consumes them, whether they will it or not? Are these the women they call ladies of the court or of the palace? Tell me, what is the derivation of the word? Is it from *palor*, 'to stray abroad' or perhaps *balo*, 'to bleat'? Courtly dames they are indeed, judging from the courts of our day, begetters of every vice, the abode of Satan, which not only the Christian will avoid but even the pagan who has a modicum of good sense. But not all of them are immodest, some will say. I really do not know, but even if they are pure in body they are certainly most impure in mind and

99. the French and the Spaniards: 'Femme qui prend, elle se vend. / Femme qui donne, s'abandonne.' 'La mujer que prende, su cuerpo vende.'
100. fire with flax: Cf. the Spanish proverb 'La estopa de junto al fuego quitala luego,' and the English proverb: 'Put not fire to flax.'
palor: The true derivation of the word *palatium* is *Mons Palatinus*, where the imperial palaces were built, beginning with that of Augustus.

sunt, et si non corpore, at animo viris prostitutae. Nec istis quicquam defuit
ad impudicitiam praeter occasionem, quod prope semper in oculis multorum
et frequentia versantur. Inquit Ovidius:

> Quae quia non licuit non dedit, illa dedit.

5   Sapienter Divus Aurelius Augustinus: 'Nos per aurem conscientiam conve-
nimus, occultorum nobis iudicium non usurpamus.' Si tu non aliter loqueris
quam meretrix, qua fronte uti te pudicam esse credam postulas?

101. 'Non vidisti,' inquis, 'me cubantem cum viro.' Nec meretricem vidi.
Sed quod argumentum in omni natura usurpamus non vis in te valere, ut
10 de internis per externa iudicemus? Postulas ut aquam contineri credam in
dolio ex quo video vinum profluere? Sed quid nos cum istis disputamus?
Quis probatus vir haec probat? Qui laudant nisi qui nec umbram quidem
norunt castitatis, qui vellent omnes mulieres (fieri si posset) impudicas esse,
quo promptius invenirent ubi infinitam suam libidinem explerent, qui ipsi ad
15 ambas aures flagitiis, facinoribus, sceleribus immersi, nec intueri sua vitia iam
possunt nec aliena? Exuant prius istas scelerum tenebras quibus opprimuntur,
tunc credemus eis de virtute iudicantibus. Antiquis Romanis feminis in schola
illa castitatis comitatem parum probatam fuisse auctor est Cornelius Tacitus.
Postumiam, Vestae sacerdotem, incestus accusatam Plutarchus tradit tantum
20 ob solutiorem risum et liberiora cum viris colloquia, sed absolutam Pont.
Max. Spurius Minucius admonuit ne sermonibus uteretur inculpatae vitae
indecentibus.

102. Puellam et virum in loco aliquo solos diutine confabulari ne si
sint quidem fratres sinendum est. Multa possunt adduci et vetera et nova
25 exempla foedorum facinorum quid fratres etiam ipsi sint ausi, nacti solitudinis
occasionem. Sic Amon, Davidis regis filius, Thamar sororem suam violavit;
sic Caunus sororem Byblim. Numquam Augustinus cum sorore sua habitare
sustinuit. Malum dicebat feminam videre, peius alloqui, pessimum tangere.
Pionis Abbatis aegrotabat soror. Rogatus ut eam antequam fato defungeretur

---

100. (Quae ... dedit) *Ov. am. 3, 4, 4* // (Nos ... usurpamus) *Aug. civ. 1, 26*

101. (comitatem ... probatam) *Tac. dial. 28, 4–6* // (Postumiam ... indecentibus) *Plut. mor. 89F*

102. (Amon ... violavit) *Vulg. II reg. 13, 10–14* // (Caunus sororem Byblim) *Ov. met. 9, 450–665* // (Malum ... tangere) *Aug. serm. 349, 4, PL 39, 1531*

3–11 Inquit ... profluere **Γ** *deest in* **H** // **6** iudicium **BV** *Aug.* indicium **WW²** // **11** istis **Γ**
istis hominibus **H** // **14** quo promptius ... explerent **Γ** quo facilius ubi infinitam suam
libidinem explerent invenirent **H** // **15–16** intueri sua vitia iam possunt **Γ** videre sua
vitia possunt **H** // **17–22** Antiquis ... indecentibus **Γ** *deest in* **H** // **23–24** Puellam ...
sinendum est **Γ** Colloqui puellam et virum in loco aliquo solos ne si sint quidem fratres
patiendum est **H** // **24–26** nova exempla ... occasionem **Γ** nova foeditas exempla quid
inter fratres actum nactos solitudinis occasionem **H** // **29–p.138,1** eam ... conveniret **Γ** ei
ante fatum loqueretur **H**

have prostituted themselves to men in mind if not in body. The only thing lacking to their impurity has been the opportunity, since they are constantly in view and engaged with many people. Ovid said 'The woman who did not yield because she did not have the opportunity, has already yielded.' Saint Augustine wisely said: 'We are privy to the secrets of conscience through what we hear; we do not usurp judgment on things hidden from us.' If you speak no differently than a prostitute, with what effrontery do you demand that I believe you are chaste?'

101. You say, 'You did not see me lying with a man'. I did not see you plying the trade of a prostitute either. But do you wish to exempt yourself from the criterion we use in all of nature, that we judge the interior from the exterior? Do you want me to believe that a cask contains water when I see wine flowing out of it? But why dispute with such people? What man of worth approves such things? Who praises them save those who do not even know the semblance of chastity, who would wish, if it were possible, that all women were unchaste so that they could more readily find an outlet for their boundless lust. Immersed up to their ears in shameless acts, crimes, and wrongdoing they are unable to see their own vices or those of others. Let them first throw off this veil of depravity that envelops them and then we will believe them when they give their opinions on virtue. Among Roman women of old, trained in that strict school of chastity, Tacitus tells us that affability was not looked upon with approval. Plutarch reports that Postumia, the priestess of Vesta, was accused of incest solely because of her unrestrained laughter and her too free discussions with men. She was acquitted by the pontifex maximus, Spurius Minucius, with the warning that she should not engage in conversations that were unbecoming to a blameless life.

102. It is not to be permitted that a young woman and a man should converse alone anywhere for any length of time, not even if they are brother and sister. Many examples, both old and new, can be adduced of horrible crimes that even brothers and sisters dared to commit when the opportunity of seclusion offered itself. So it was that Amon, son of King David, violated his sister Thamar, and Caunus his sister Byblis. Augustine never consented to live with his sister. 'It is evil,' he said, 'to see a woman, worse to talk to her, and worst of all to touch her.' When the sister of the Abbot Pion was sick, he was asked to visit her before she died, but he came to her room reluctantly,

conveniret, alieno ductu et clausis oculis ad cubiculum aegrae venit. Paucis
allocutus eundem in modum e vestigio revertit. Nec fratres cum sororibus
aut propinquos cum propinquis puellis, quamlibet casti sint et spectatae
continentiae, lusitare, non eas osculari, palpare, vellicare patiar. Quid hoc
aliud est quam puellam impudentioribus coqui et maturare, ut si quid
petulantiores illi rogent, istae excalfactae aliquid haud conveniens pudicitiae
suae cogitent?

103. Nec in frequenti atrio vel cubiculo velim in angulum secedere. Quid
dicturi sunt soli quod reliqui audire non possint si casta modo et pura
locuturi sunt? Colloquia de rebus bonis secretum non petunt. Ibi secretum
desideratur ubi conscius timetur et pudorem adfert si ad alios dimanet sermo.
Nec multos inter iuvenes, virum et puellam, sermones seri convenit etiam
arbitris aliis, nisi tam aperte honesta et pura sint omnia ut nulla possit
incidere suspicio obscenitatis. Sunt enim quidam in nequitia usque adeo
ingeniosi, qui sic verbis ambiguis obliquisque quae sentiunt involvunt, ut quo
tendant non difficile intelligatur ab ea cui dicuntur. Ambiguitas tamen faciat
ut negare possint se hoc sensisse et tamquam malignos interpretes incessere
qui ad turpitudinem rapiant quae ipsi sincero dixerint animo ac simplici.
Et acutuli sibi videntur, si his artibus valeant, omnium bonarum expertes,
potentes prudentesque ut faciant malum. Quae res non arguit ingenium,
sed malarum rerum pravam industriam, quae, ut Seneca inquit, 'Somno
et languore turpior est.' Nec ingenium fraudibus censendum est et fallaciis,
nisi diabolos sanctis angelis de ingenio praeferimus, cum unus beatorum
angelorum diabolis universis acutior et sapientior sit.

104. In summa, praestat semper quam minimum cum viris intercedere
commercii. Paucissima cum eis sunt verba commutanda atque ea modestiae,
pudicitiae, prudentiae plena. Non existimaberis filia infantior, sed sapientior.
Quod si sententia de moribus tuis pronuntianda est, malo videaris malis
parum docta quam bonis parum proba. Cedo, quam multa legis Mariae
verba in tota quattuor Evangeliorum historia? Intrat ad eam Angelus et paucis
verbis tanti mysterii nuntium absolvit iisque sapientissimis et sanctissimis.

---

103. (Somno ... est) *Sen. contr. 1, 8, 2*
104. (Intrat ... sanctissimis) *Vulg. Luc. 2, 19* //

---

1 venit **Γ** profectus est. **H** // **1–2** Paucis ... revertit **Γ** Sic allocutus rediit **H** // **4–6** Quid
... rogent **Γ** quid illi obsceni petant **H** // **6** haud **Γ** harum **H** *epist Cran.* // **8** Nec ...
velim **Γ** Nec in aula frequenti velim **H** // **9** modo **Γ** *deest in* **H** // **10–11** Colloquia ...
sermo **Γ** *deest in* **H** // **12–13** Nec multos ... aliis **Γ** Nec multa velim intercurrere inter
iuvenes, virum et puellam, verba, etiam arbitris aliis consciis **H** // **13** pura sint omnia **Γ**
sancta sint **H** // **19** omnium bonarum **Γ** omnibus bonis **H** // **21** pravam **Γ** *deest in* **H** // **23**
de ingenio praeferimus **Γ** ingeniosiores putamus **H** // **24** acutior et **Γ** *deest in* **H** // **25–26**
quam minimum ... commercii **Γ** quam minimum habere cum viris commercii **H** // **26**
sunt *deest in* **H** // **31** tanti mysterii nuntium **Γ** rem **H**

led by another with his eyes closed, and after addressing a few words to her he departed in the same way in which he came. I would not allow brothers and sisters or close relatives, no matter how chaste they are and of proven virtue, to play together, kiss each other, touch or tickle each other. What else is this but to enflame the young girl and weaken her defences for more shameless acts so that if more aggressive advances are made upon her, in her aroused state, she may conceive of things not conducive to her chastity?

103. Nor would I have them retreat into a corner of a crowded hall or room. What will they say to each other in solitude that others cannot hear if their conversation is to be pure and chaste? Conversations about good things do not require secrecy. That is necessary only when there is fear of a witness and when embarrassment will result from the divulging of their words to others. It is not becoming that many words be exchanged between young people of opposite sex even if there are others present unless the whole tenor of the conversation is so clearly pure and virtuous that no suspicion of indecency could arise. There are some who are so clever in their wickedness, who disguise their feelings in such ambiguous and indirect language that their intentions are not difficult to divine by the woman to whom they address their words. Yet their ambiguity may enable them to deny that these were their sentiments and to reproach their hearers as malicious for turning to evil purpose what they said in a pure and simple spirit. And they think themselves quite clever if they are good at these wiles, devoid of all good qualities, but expert and cunning in the devising of evil. This is no proof of cleverness but rather of a perverse assiduity, which, as Seneca said, is worse than sleep and idleness. Talent is not to be measured by fraud and deceit, unless we give preference to devils over the blessed angels in the matter of genius, for a single blessed angel is more keen-witted and wise than all the devils put together.

104. To sum up, it is best to have as little contact with men as possible, few words are to be exchanged with them and those should be instinct with modesty, propriety and discretion. You will not be accounted a more inarticulate young woman but rather a wiser one. If judgment is to be pronounced on your character, I prefer that you appear deficient in learning to the wicked rather than lacking in virtue to the good. Tell me, how many words of Mary do you find in the whole story of the four Gospels? The angel comes to her and in a few words she accepts the message of so great a mystery, words of great wisdom and holiness. She goes to visit Elizabeth

Visit Elizabetham, loquitur ut Deum laudet. Parit Filium Deum, celebratur
ab angelis, adoratur a pastoribus et tacet, conservans omnia quae ab illis
dicebantur, conferens in corde suo. Adoratur a Magis qui procul eo venerant;
quid ipsam legis locutam? Alia forsan de illa regione fuisset percontata, de
opibus, de sapientia illorum, de astro; ipsa, quod teneram decebat virginem,
muta semper. Offert Filium templo et vaticinantem de illo Simeonem rogasset alia aut quaedam aut eorum quae dixerat rationem et modum. Vertit
sermonem ad Virginem senex de Filio: 'Ecce positus est hic in ruinam
et resurrectionem multorum in Israel et in signum cui contradicetur. Et
tuam ipsius animam dissecabit gladius, ut aperiantur multorum cordium
cogitationes.' Alia mulier quando, quomodo, ubi futurum esset sciscitata;
ipsa nihil legitur dixisse. Amittit carissimum Filium Hierosolymis; quae-
situm tribus diebus, tandem inventum: quot verbis compellat? 'Fili, quid
fecisti nobis sic? Ecce pater tuus et ego maesti quaerebamus te.' Natu
iam grandior in nuptiis illud tantum admonet: 'Fili, vinum non habent.'
Ad crucem omnino elinguis nihil ex Filio quaerit, cui se relinquat, quid
moriturus mandet quod in publico loqui non didicerat. Hanc, virgines,
hanc, feminae omnes, imitamini pauciloquam quidem, sed ad miraculum
sapientem.

105. Theano Metapontinae vati et virgini doctissimae magnum feminae
ornamentum silentium esse placuit; idem et Sophocli, quippe silentio castitas
et prudentia suavissime condiuntur. Illa demum erit mihi femina facundis-
sima cui, cum verba erunt ad viros facienda, rubor toto ore suffundetur,
turbabitur animus et verba non suppetent. O eloquentiam hanc singularem
et efficacissimam! Non es patrona, o filia, nec in foro agis, ut causam vel
tuam vel clientis affligas, nisi loquaris. Tace tu tam audacter quam alii
loquuntur in foro. Sic enim melius pudicitiae tuae causam defenderis, quae
apud aequos iudices superior videtur silentio tuo quam sermone. Puerum
quendam tradunt rerum scriptores productum in rostra populi Romani
super causa pudicitiae, defixis in terram oculis et pertinacissimo silentio pudicitiam suam vehementius populo commendasse quam longis et accuratis
orationibus disertissimi oratores.

104. (Visit ... laudet) *Vulg. Luc. 1, 46–55* // (adoratur ... suo) *Vulg. Luc. 2, 8–19* //
(Ecce ... cogitationes) *Vulg. Luc. 2, 34–35* // (Fili ... te) *Vulg. Luc. 2, 48* // (Fili ... habent)
Vulg. Ioh. 2, 3
105. (Theano ... silentium) *Porph. Pythag. 19* // (quippe ... condiuntur) *Soph. Ai. 293*
// (Puerum ... oratores) *Val. Max. 6, 1, 7*

6 muta semper Γ tacet H // **10** dissecabit Γ caedet H // **12** Hierosolymis Γ Hierosolymae H
// **14** maesti Γ dolentes H // **15** admonet Γ dicit H // **16** elinguis Γ muta H // **22–25**
Illa ... efficacissimam Γ *deest in* H // **27** defenderis Γ defendes H // **28** tuo *deest in* H //
32 disertissimi Γ *deest in* H

and she opens her mouth only to praise God. She brings forth her divine son, she is extolled by the angels, adored by the shepherds, and she remains silent, treasuring all that was said to her and pondering it in her heart. She receives the homage of the Magi, who had come there from afar. What do you read that she said? Another woman might have asked them perhaps about their country, about its riches, about their wisdom, about the star, but as befitted a young maiden, she uttered not a word. She offers her Son in the temple. When Simeon made prophesies about him, another woman would have put various questions to him or asked the meaning and substance of what he said. The old man addressed her with these words: 'Behold this child is set for the fall and the rise of many in Israel and he will be a sign that will be contradicted. And your own soul a sword shall pierce so that the thoughts of many hearts may be revealed.' Another woman would have inquired when, how and where this would take place. She is reported as having said nothing. She loses her beloved Son in Jerusalem. After seeking him for three days and finally finding him, how many words does she speak to him? 'My Son, why have you treated us in this way? Behold, your father and I have been looking for you anxiously.' When he was a grown man, she makes this simple observation: 'My son, they have no wine.' At the cross she was entirely speechless; she asked nothing of her son, to whom he would leave her, what were his dying wishes, because she had learned not to speak in public. Imitate her, virgins and all women, imitate this woman of few words, but of remarkable wisdom.

105. Theano of Metapontum, a most learned young woman and a prophetess, was of the opinion that silence was the greatest adornment of a woman. Sophocles was of the same opinion, and indeed silence is a sweet seasoning for chastity and prudence. In conclusion, the most eloquent woman for me is the one who when required to speak to men will become flushed in her whole countenance, perturbed in spirit and at a loss for words. O extraordinary and effective eloquence! You are not an advocate, my child, nor are you pleading a case in the forum, where your silence would do harm to your cause or that of your client. Show as much courage by your silence as others do in speaking in the forum. In that way you will better defend your cause of chastity, which in the eyes of fair judges will be made stronger by your silence than by your speaking. Writers of history relate that a boy was brought forward to the rostrum of Rome on a charge involving chastity, and with his eyes fixed on the ground and with unwavering silence he commended his chastity more strongly to the people than the most eloquent orators could have done in long, elaborate speeches.

142   J. L. VIVES

106. Sed ut de feminis loquar, Sancta Susanna de flagitii crimine pertinaci silentio se purgavit, non meditata oratione. Divum Ambrosium audiamus: 'Susanna mulier tacuit et inimicos suos vicit. Non enim apud Danielem iudicem verborum se ratione defendit, non patrocinii sermone tutata est, sed in sancta femina, tacente lingua, pro ea castitas loquebatur.' Idem libro de Virginibus tertio, sic inquit: 'Deesse sermonem virgini quam superesse malo. Nam si mulieres etiam de rebus divinis in ecclesia iubentur tacere, domi viros suos interrogare, de virginibus quid cautum putamus, in quibus pudor ornat aetatem, taciturnitas commendat pudorem?' Sic ille. Nec solum sic inter viros se geret, sed inter feminas quoque modestus decebit sermo et parcior, non sonorus, non arrogans aut virilis animi indicium, nullo admisto iure iurando, quod cum in viris deforme sit, non poterit non esse in femina flagitiosissimum. Feminam iurare tam alienum videtur mihi a natura quam armis indui. Sed neque sit vox fracta et delicata nec vultus in atrocitatem et saevitiem compositus nec in severitatem quidem aut tristitiam aut fastidium neque varius aut prae se delicias ostendens vel contemptum; non renidens, non mobilis, non vagus et solutus, similis animi index certissimus.

107. Sunt quaedam corde tam fluxo et pertuso ut inter pares omnia, et aliena et sua, loquacissime effutiant nihilque pensi habeant quid loquantur. Quicquid in buccam venerit profundunt. Hinc studium mentiendi cum vera desunt et fabulae de illis ortae, quae ex uno corvo fecerunt centum et ex uno homine occiso mille et ex cane mediocri maiorem elephanto Indico, ut iam nemo quibus verbis rem usque adeo praeposteram et ridiculam apte insectetur inveniat. Naso et irrisionibus omnes excipiunt, quod ad summam reprehensionem sufficiat narrasse. Aliae hoc agunt, quod ineducatae sibi videntur futurae, si quando taceant, vel parum amicae, nisi secretissima quaeque et maxime tacenda in sinum alterius effuderint, etiam cum periculo. Sunt quae non arbitrentur se in hoc peccare. Aliae, quoniam in eis sermo cogitationem praecurrit, ante effutierunt quod erat tacendum quam vel cogitarent quid dicturae essent vel expenderent an dici conveniret, omnino prius quam sentirent se eloqui prolocutae sunt.

106. (Susanna ... loquebatur) *Max. Taur. hom. 46, PL 57, 333A, quondam Ambrosio adscripta* // (Deesse ... pudorem) *Ambr. virg. 3, 3, 9, PL 16, 222*
107. (Quicquid ... venerit) *Cic. Att. 12, 1, 2*

1 pertinaci Γ *deest in* H // 2 meditata Γ *deest in* H // 9 Sic ille Γ *deest in* H // 13–14 Feminam ... indui Γ *deest in* H // 16 vel contemptum Γ *deest in* H // 17 index certissimus Γ argumentum H // 18 corde Γ animo H / et pertuso Γ *deest in* H // 20 profundunt Γ *deest in* H // 23–24 ut iam nemo ... inveniat Γ ut iam nemo quibus verbis rem eam praeposteram et turpem insectetur sciat H // 25–26 quod ineducatae ... taceant Γ quod inciviliores sibi futurae videntur si taceant H // 26 quando Γ *deest in* H // 28 etiam Γ *deest in* H // 28–144,3 Sunt ... alienis Γ *deest in* H

106. But to return to women, Saint Susannah acquitted herself of the accusation of adultery by her resolute silence, not by a prepared speech. Let us listen to the words of St. Ambrose: 'Susannah kept silence and defeated her enemies. Before the judge Daniel she did not defend herself by verbal argumentation nor did she protect herself with the language of the law court, but in this holy woman, though her tongue was silent, chastity spoke in its place.' The same author in the third book of his *De virginibus* said: 'I prefer that speech be lacking to a virgin rather than that it be copious. For if women are bidden to be silent even concerning divine things in church, and to ask questions of their husbands at home, what precautions should be taken in the case of virgins, in whom modesty is their greatest adornment and silence the greatest commendation of their modesty?' These are the words of St. Ambrose. She will not only comport herself in this manner before men but among women too; modest and restrained speech will become her, not loud or arrogant or typical of a man's spirit, or interspersed with oaths, which while unseemly in men cannot but be a very grave fault in women. For a woman to swear seems as unnatural to me as for her to bear arms. Her voice should not be affected or delicate and her countenance should not have a cruel or fierce expression or one that denotes severity or sadness or disgust, nor should it be changeable or display an air of superiority or disdain, not grinning, shifting, wayward and uninhibited, since this is a sure indicator of a similar mind.

107. There are some women of such inconstant and unsound mind that among their peers they blurt out everything loquaciously, their own and others' affairs, giving no thought to what they say. Whatever comes to their mind they make public knowledge of it. From this comes their inclination to tell lies, when they don't know the truth. They invent fantastic tales—of a single crow, they invent a hundred, one slain man becomes a thousand, and a dog of average size they magnify into one bigger than an Indian elephant—to such an extent that it is impossible to find words to reprehend something so preposterous and ridiculous. Everyone takes these stories with a grain of salt and mockery. Their very recounting of such tales is reproof enough. Some do this for fear that they may appear impolite if they keep silence or unfriendly if they do not pour out into some one else's bosom things that should be kept secret, even when this involves some risk. There are some who think they do nothing wrong in this. Others who speak before they think blurt out things that should have remained unspoken before they think of what they are going to say or consider whether it is suitable to be said. They give utterance to their thoughts without even being aware that

Multae laborant ea vanitate, aperiunt secretissima solum ut tales existimentur
quibus res tantae facile soleant concredi. Misera, quis committet tibi sua, qui
experimentum de te sumpserit in alienis? Hinc multis arrepta ansa praeci-
piendi: 'Arcanum feminae numquam credendum, non sorori, non matri,
5   non uxori.'

108. Sed hoc vitium quarundam esse, non sexus, ostenderunt constantissi-
mae aliquot, quae ne tortae quidem quae scirent prodiderunt, ut Pythagorea
illa, quae dentibus suam sibi evulsam linguam in faciem torquentis tyranni
conspuit, ne eloqui ulla necessitate cogeretur. Praetereo Milesias, quae con-
10   silium maritorum multis diebus, quamdiu videlicet opus fuit, constanter et
prudenter Massiliae celaverunt. Epicharim scribit Tacitus consciam Piso-
nianae coniurationis, iussam tormentis dilacerari ut indicaret, primo die
non verberibus, non ignibus, non ira eo acrius torquentium ne a femina
spernerentur commotam ut aliquid se scire confiteretur; postero die, cum ad
15   eosdem cruciatus retraheretur gestamine sellae (nam dissolutis membris insis-
tere nequibat), vinculo fasciae, quam pectori detraxerat in modum laquei ad
arcum sellae restricto, indidit cervicem et corporis pondere conixa, tenuem
iam spiritum expressit. Aristogitonis, qui Pisistrati filios expulit, amicam
Leaenam nomine Athenienses memoriae mandarunt, tortam a tyrannis
20   ut amicum proderet in silentio tormenta omnia perpessam esse. Si haec
impudicae, quid pudicae?

109. Fugienda etiam alienae domi curiositas, ne omnia rimari et scrutari
cupias nec plus velis seu capere seu scire quam ultro concedatur. Con-
tendendum et rixandum in publico non est, non dico leviculis de rebus,
25   sed nec si de magna aliqua possessione ageretur. Praestat fortunarum pati
detrimentum quam nominis et frontis et rerum iure carissimarum. De festis et
celebritatibus et conviviis nescio quid praecipiam Christianis in tam receptis
moribus plus quam gentiliciis, ut demens putetur qui non simul cum orbis
consensu ultro se rapiendum permittat, sed unus potius aut cum paucis tanto
30   se et tam incitato populorum torrenti opponat.

---

108. (Pythagorea ... cogeretur) *Plut. mor. 506A* // (Epicharim ... expressit) *Tac. ann.*
15, 57 // (Aristogitonis ... esse) *Plut. mor. 506A; Paus. 1, 23, 1; Plin. nat. 7, 87*

3 Hinc Γ Unde **H** // **11** consciam Γ conscientia **H** // **23** velis **HWW²B** velit **V** // **24** non
est **HWW²V** *om.* **B** // **25** ageretur Γ agatur **H** // **29** se rapiendum permittat Γ rapiendum
se et tradendum permittat **H** / potius Γ *deest in* **H** // **30** et tam incitato Γ *deest in* **H**

they are speaking. Many are under the vain illusion that by revealing secrets they will be thought to be worthy of having important things confided to them. Poor fool! Who is going to confide her own affairs to you after seeing how you treat the secrets of others? This is what gave rise to the precept: 'A secret should never be confided to a woman, not to your sister, nor your mother, nor your wife.'

108. But that this is the vice only of certain women, and not of their entire sex, is proven by some examples of women of great constancy, who even under torture did not reveal what they knew, like that disciple of Pythagoras who bit off her own tongue and spat it in the face of the tyrant, who was torturing her, so that she could not be forced to speak. I shall not mention the women of Miletus who for many days, as long as was necessary, guarded with fidelity and prudence the plans of their husbands in Marseilles. Tacitus tells us how Epicharis, who knew of the Piso conspiracy, was condemned to be torn to pieces with the most cruel torment to make her reveal her secret. On the first day neither beatings nor fire nor the wrath of her tormentors, who did not wish to be scorned by a woman, could move her to confess to what she knew. On the next day, when she was being delivered to the same torture seated on a saddle (since she could no longer stand up on her weakened limbs), she took a band that was tied around her breasts, fastened it in the form of a loop to the pommel of the saddle, then tied it around her neck and let her body fall under its own weight and breathed forth the little life she had left in her. The Athenians commemorated the memory of Leaena, the friend of Aristogiton, who drove out the sons of Pisistratus, because she suffered every torment in silence rather than betray her friend. If unchaste women could do this, what of chaste women?

109. Curiosity about another household should be avoided. Do not be eager to pry into and investigate everything or desire to understand and know more than is allowed. You must not dispute or quarrel in public, neither concerning trivial matters, nor even if some great possessions were at stake. It is better to suffer loss of fortune rather than of name, reputation and things rightly most dear to us. Concerning feast days, celebrations and banquets I do not know what instruction to give to Christians with respect to these worse than pagan customs which have become so firmly established, that anyone who would not let himself be carried away by them with everyone else would be regarded as mad to resist the popular frenzy and stand alone or in the company of very few in his opposition.

108. disciple of Pythagoras: The woman in question was Leaena, mistress of Aristogiton, who together with Harmodius had conspired against the tyrants, Hippias and Hipparchus in 514 B.C. The plot failed and they were put to death, but Leaena refused to reveal the names of others involved in the conspiracy.

Leaena: The Athenians erected a monument of a tongueless lioness (the meaning of her name) to Leaena to commemorate her heroism.

110. Auscultent ergo gentiles quae Christianum nolunt. Ovidius flagitiosa illa tradens amandi praecepta de publicis spectaculis dicit:

> Spectatum veniunt, veniunt spectentur ut ipsae;
> Ille locus casti damna pudoris habet.

5   Iuvenalis in Satira negat in theatris, in choreis, in celebritatibus inveniri illas quae gravi et honesto viro placere ac satisfacere coniuges possint. Convivia Veneris et Cupidinis esse arma testatur idem Ovidius. Et profecto, quae potest esse pudicitiae custodia dum tot oculis expetitur puella, tot vultus eam intuentur, tot ipsa conspicit? Necesse est urat et vicissim, nisi saxea sit, suo et

10   ipsa quoque igne incalescat. Accedit ardenti igni maximus ex convivio fomes cibi, potus, confabulationum, arrisionum blandarum et illicium aspectuum, tactionum, vellicationum et aliorum, quorum magnam praebet Liber ille Bacchus licentiam. Quis inter haec animus purus et integer libidinosa nulla cogitatione temeratus? Amentissimus populus non aliter putat puellas

15   peccare nisi cum viris cubent. Tu ergo, qui baptizatus es per Evangelium Christi, quomodo vel legis vel audis illa Christi in Evangelio verba: 'De omni verbo otioso reddendam rationem in die iudicii'? At inter iuvenes et puellas in conventibus et compotationibus quot volitant non modo otiosa verba, sed quae corruptissimi nostri mores etiam laudabilia faciunt exitiosa iacula?

20   **111.** Tum et illud eiusdem Dei: 'Quisquis viderit alienam mulierem ad concupiscendum eam iam adulteratus est eam in corde suo.' An non etiam de muliere virum intuente putas dictum? In saeculo dixit quidam: 'Incesta est etiam sine stupro quae cupit stuprum.' Et Menander ait colloquiis pravis corrumpi mores probos, quem versiculum consecravit Paulus, epistolae

25   cuidam suae inserens. Postremo, non Christianus es et spiritalis, sed carnalis gentilis, immo vero pecus, si non virtutum et vitiorum fontem intus esse in animo intelligis nec referre qualis quisque sit corpore, sed mente. Ausim dicere post pubertatis annos paucas ex conviviis et celebritatibus virorum redire animo virgines ut ierant. Aliae forma capiuntur et quasi tenentur

---

110. (Spectatum ... habet) *Ov. ars 1, 99–100* // (Iuvenalis ... possint) *Iuv. 6, 60–62* // (Convivia ... arma) *Ov. ars 1, 229* // (De ... iudicii) *Vulg. Matth. 12, 36*
       111. (Quisquis ... suo) *Vulg. Matth. 5, 28* // (Incesta ... stuprum) *Sen. controv 6, 8* // (colloquiis ... probos) *Men. Sent. 803 (ed. Jaekel, p. 79)* // (quem ... inserens) *Vulg. I Cor. 15, 33*

1 Auscultent **Γ** Audiant **H** / gentiles **Γ** gentilem **H** / Ovidius **Γ** Ovidium qui **H** // **2** dicit **Γ** loquens ait **H** // **9** conspicit **HWW²B** conspici **V** / et vicissim **Γ** et ipsa vicissim **H** // **9–10** suo ... incalescat **Γ** suo tangatur igne **H** // **11** arrisionum ... aspectuum **Γ** *deest in* **H** // **14** temeratus **Γ** maculatus **H** // **19** quae ... faciunt **Γ** *deest in* **H** / exitiosa **Γ** perniciosa **H** // **20** eiusdem Dei **Γ** *deest in* **H** // **22–25** In saeculo ... inserens **Γ** *deest in* **H** // **26** immo vero pecus **Γ** *deest in* **H** / virtutum et **Γ** *deest in* **H** / vitiorum **Γ** scelerum **H** // **27** intelligis **Γ** credis **H**

110. Those who do not wish to listen to a Christian may heed what the pagans have to say. In his scandalous manual on the art of love Ovid says this about public spectacles:

They come to see and also to be seen.
That place bodes ill for purity of life.

Juvenal in his famous satire says that in theatres, dances, and crowded places women who would make obedient and complacent wives for a dignified and honorable man are not to be found. Banquets are the weapons of Venus and Cupid, Ovid testifies. And, in fact, what safeguard is there for chastity when a girl is the center of so much attraction, when so many glances are fixed on her, and she herself gazes at so many men? She cannot but be enflamed with desire in turn, and unless she is made of stone, grow hot with her own fire. Much fuel is added to the fire at a banquet: food, drink, conversations, cajoling smiles, enticing looks, touches, pinching and other such things, to which Bacchus gives free rein. What mind can remain pure and unblemished, undefiled by any lustful thought amid all this? The foolish crowd thinks that girls cannot sin except by lying with a man. You who were baptized in the Gospel of Christ, how do you read or hear those words of Christ in the Gospel: 'For every idle word an account must be rendered on the day of judgment.' But in gatherings and drinking parties among young men and women how many words fly about that are not only idle but are deadly shafts, which our corrupted morals consider praiseworthy?

111. Then there is this precept of the Lord: 'Whoever will look upon another woman with desire for her has already committed adultery with her in his heart.' Do you not think that this saying also applies to a woman looking at a man? A secular writer has said: 'A woman who desires illicit intercourse is unchaste even without engaging in intercourse.' And Menander wrote: 'Bad company corrupts good morals.' Paul consecrated this verse by including it in one of his Epistles. Finally, you are not a Christian and a spiritual person, but a sensual pagan, I should say a brute beast, if you do not understand that the source of virtues and vices is inside us, in the mind, and it is not the body that matters, but the mind. I would venture to say that after the age of puberty few girls return from these banquets and celebrations among men with the same virginal spirit they had when they went. Some are captivated

irretitae, aliae ingenio, aliae divitiis, aliae facundia, aliae agilitate. In coetu virorum haec omnia puella invenit extenta velut plagas. Difficile videtur non illis saltem capi ad quas propensior fertur.

112. Quam praestat non amare periculum, ne iuxta consilium Sapientis pereas in eo! Mea sententia est, immo Christi (ut opinor) debere contineri virgines domi, abstinere publico, nisi sacri gratia et bene tectas, a conspectu virorum separatas, quod Divus Chrysostomus solitum aetate sua fieri scribit, ne laqueum vel praebeant vel reperiant. Cum nuptiis, cum virorum conventibus et conviviis nullum debet esse aut quam rarissimum Christianae virgini commercium. Sexcentis conventibus et conviviis intersit femina: in nullo eorum vel audiet vel videbit unde redeat domum melior, in omnibus plurima unde peior. Sunt non parum multi quibus sola haec est ars, eiusmodi celebritates petere ac inibi aliquid vel dicere vel facere quod probitati detrimentum adferat. Quid de puellis sentiam hinc intelligi potest quod et pueros adhiberi conviviis nolim, tum quod inimicum hoc est viribus et valetudini crescentis aetatis, tum quod convivium omne, ut nunc sunt mores, seminarium est multorum vitiorum, quantumvis sobrium et temperatum. Multa spectat ibi puer turpia, multa discit flagitiosa, etiam inter senes graves. Quid inter feminas et viros dicam, ubi accensis qua intrinsecus qua extrinsecus in libidinem animis, quantumlibet pudoris comprimantur frenis, erumpunt tamen et efferunt se immodice ac turpiter nec habenas audiunt et secum rapiunt vectorem? Quid porro si ultro stimulentur calcaribus? Ibi vero nec modus nec modestia est ulla nec pudoris respectus.

CAP. XII.   DE SALTATIONIBUS

113. Dicamus et de illo nonnulla quo nihil agunt pleraeque feminarum libentius quodque magna cura etiam a parentibus docentur, ut docte saltent. Nolo

112. (periculum ... eo) *Vulg. Sirach 3, 27* // (a conspectu ... separatas) *Ioh. Chrys. in Matth. hom. 73, PG 58, 677*

1 coetu Γ multitudine **H** // **4** iuxta consilium Sapientis Γ sicut ait Sapiens **H** // **5** opinor Γ autumo **H** // **6** abstinere publico Γ non in publico esse **H** // **6–7** a conspectu ... scribit Γ *deest in* **H** // **6** conspectu **WW²** conspectis **BV** // **9** nullum **H** nihil Γ / aut quam rarissimum Γ *deest in* **H** // **10–14** Sexcentis ... adferat Γ *deest in* **H** // **14** intelligi Γ sciri **H** // **14–15** et ... nolim Γ nec pueros ad convivia ducendos velim **H** // **15** inimicum Γ adversum **H** // **16–17** tum quod convivium ... vitiorum Γ tum quod seminarium est convivium multorum vitiorum **H** // **17** temperatum Γ modestum **H** // **18** spectat Γ videt **H** / graves Γ quamlibet sapientes **H** // **19** qua ... qua Γ et ... et **H** // **20–22** quantumlibet ... vectorem Γ quantumvis pudoris contineantur frenis, efferunt tamen se immodice ac turpiter, nec habenas audiunt et vectorem secum rapiunt **H** // **22** porro Γ dicam **H** / stimulentur calcaribus Γ calcaribus stimulent **H** // **23** modestia ... respectus Γ modestia nec ullus pudoris respectus est **H** // **25** pleraeque feminarum Γ puellae quaedam **H**

by beauty and are caught in the net, so to speak; others are swayed by talent, others by riches, others by eloquence, others by quickness of intellect. In the assembly of men a girl finds all these things laid out as in a trap. It seems difficult that she should not be captured by things to which she is naturally drawn.

112. How much better not to love danger lest, according to the advice of the wise man, you perish in it! My opinion is, or I should say Christ's opinion, that young women should be kept at home, should stay out of public, except for attendance at sacred offices, and be well covered, separated from the view of men, which St. John Chrysostom writes was the custom of his time, so that they will neither provide a snare nor discover one. A Christian young woman should have nothing or as little as possible to do with weddings, male gatherings or banquets. A woman may be present at a hundred meetings and banquets. In none of these will she hear or see anything by which she will return home better, but in all of them she will see things that will make her return home worse. There is no small number of persons whose sole occupation it is to seek out these festivities and say or do things there that will detract from their good name. My feelings concerning young women can be deduced from the fact that I am contrary to young men participating in banquets, both because it is harmful to their strength and health in their adolescent years and because all banquets in the present moral atmosphere are the seedbed of numerous vices, no matter how moderate and temperate they may be. The young man sees many shameful things there; he learns many disgraceful habits even among old men of good morals. What shall I say of meetings where both men and women are present, where souls are so enkindled to lust by internal and external factors, despite the constraints of modesty, that they burst forth and are transported in a wild and base manner, and oblivious of the reins, drag the rider along with them. What if, in addition, they are goaded on with spurs? Then there will be neither measure, nor moderation, nor respect for decency.

CHAPTER 12. ON DANCING

113. Let us say a few words also about an activity in which many women find great delight and which they are taught with great diligence even by their parents, namely the art of dancing skilfully. I do not wish here to discuss

hic disputare de chironomia et palaestra vetere, quam Plato et Stoicorum plurimi utilem dixerunt liberis pueris, Cicero et Quintilianus necessariam oratori, quae aliud nihil erat quam formatio quaedam gestus totius ac motus, ut decora et essent omnia et moverentur; quae ars prorsus (ut aliae
5 permultae) ex usu abiit. Ad istam venio saltationem, sic enim appello, non tripudium modo, verum etiam palaestram horum temporum, quae molli peragitur incessu. Nam in utraque simile est flagitium seu idem verius. Quin palaestra vel chironomia, etsi exiguis interdum et fractis nec se multum attollentibus, sine salticulis tamen nequaquam exercetur. Saltationem ergo
10 cum a Romana gravitate, tum etiam a Graecis ipsis paulo cordatioribus ac frugalioribus repudiatam videmus. Demosthenes orator comitatum Philippi Macedonum regis apud cunctum populum Atheniensem incessens, nihil potuit gravius in eos iacere quam esse illos qui nihil dubitarent ebrii saltare, prudentes vero et probos qui saltationes non ferrent a se reppulisse. Nec ulla
15 ex castis illis Romanis matronis saltasse legitur. Sallustius Semproniam scribit doctius cantasse et saltasse quam necesse esset probae. Cicero Murenam defendens refert obiectum esse illi a Catone quod in Asia saltasset; hoc crimen tantum erat ut defendere recte factum non sit ausus, sed constanter pernegarit. 'Nemo' (inquit) 'fere saltat sobrius, nisi forte insanit, neque in
20 solitudine neque in convivio moderato atque honesto; intempestivi convivii, amoeni loci, multarum deliciarum comes est extrema saltatio.' Ita saltationem necesse est omnium vitiorum esse quasi cumulum.

114. At nos in civitatibus Christianis scholas saltandi habemus, sed in eisdem in quibus etiam publica lupanaria, tantum gravitate morum a
25 gentilibus vincimur. Neque vero illi hoc nostrum norant novum saltandi genus immoderatum, iactabundum, accensionem libidinis, plenum impudicis contrectationibus et basiis. Quid sibi volunt tot basia? Credo, ut columbas effingamus aves Veneris, ut veteres putabant. Olim solis consanguineis ferre osculum licebat, nunc passim in Gallia, in Britannia fertur
30 quibuslibet; scilicet hoc facit baptismus ut omnes, si Deo placet, fratres esse

---

113. (chironomia) *Plat. leg. 7, 795D* // (palaestra) *Plat. rep. 3, 403C; Aristot. pol. 8, 4 (1339a); Cic. Tusc. 2, 36; Quint. inst. 1, 11, 17; 1, 2, 16* // (Semproniam ... probae) *Sall. Catil. 25, 2* // (Nemo ... saltatio) *Cic. Mur. 13*
114. (aves Veneris) *Verg. Aen. 6, 190*

1 chironomia et **Γ** *deest in* **H** // **5–11** sic enim ... videmus **Γ** quae hodie est apud nos frequens, quam nonnulli Graecorum probarunt ut alias plerasque res partim ineptas, partim etiam foedas, quae a Romana gravitate repudiatae sunt **H** // **11–14** Demosthenes ... reppulisse **Γ** *deest in* **H** // **17** refert **Γ** scribit **H** // **22** quasi cumulum **Γ** postremum **H** // **24** publica **Γ** *deest in* **H** // **25** Neque vero **Γ** At nec **H** // **28** columbas effingamus aves Veneris **WW²** columbas effingamus Veneris aves **H** columbas aves effingamus Veneris **BV** / ut veteres putabant **Γ** *deest in* **H** // **29–30** fertur quibuslibet **Γ** omnibus fertur **H** // **30** scilicet **Γ** si **H** / si Deo placet **Γ** *deest in* **H**

the rules of gesticulation and the ancient palestra, which Plato and most of the Stoics said were profitable for free-born children and which Cicero and Quintilian considered essential for the orator. This consisted of a specific training in every gesture and movement, which ensured a graceful bearing, an art which like many others fell into complete disuse. I refer to the type of dancing—to call it that—not only the *tripudium* but also the palestra of these times, that is performed with a languid step. For in both the offense to decency is similar, or, I should say, the same. Both the palestra and the art of gesticulation cannot be executed without some little dance steps, even if it merely consists of short, jerky movements that do not rise too far off the ground. We see that dancing was repudiated not only by the severe Romans, but also by those Greeks who were a little more sensible and sober-minded. When the orator Demosthenes was denouncing the followers of Philip, King of Macedon, before the Athenian people, he could make no more grave accusation than to say that they indulged in drunken dancing and that men of good sense and integrity who did not abide dancing shunned their company. We do not read that any of those Roman matrons of old, famed for their chastity, ever danced. Sallust writes that Sempronia sang and danced with more skill than befitted a woman of good morals. In his defense of Murena Cicero mentions that the defendant was accused by Cato of having danced in public while in Asia Minor. This was such a serious charge that Cicero did not attempt to defend this action but consistently denied it. He said: 'Hardly anyone dances when he is sober unless he is out of his mind, whether he be alone or at a respectable banquet. Dancing is the final escort of dinner parties starting at an early hour, in attractive surroundings and amidst all sorts of sensuous delights.' Thus it must be considered, as it were, the culmination of all vices.

114. But we have dance schools in Christian cities, side by side with public brothels. To such a level have we sunk in seriousness of conduct compared to the pagans. And they were not familiar with this new type of dancing that we have, uncontrolled, audacious, arousing the passions, full of unchaste touches and kisses. What is the meaning of all these kisses? I suppose, to imitate doves, the birds of Venus, as the ancients thought. At one time kissing was allowed only among relatives, now kisses are bestowed indiscriminately on anyone in France and in England. I suppose this is because baptism makes us all brothers, if you please!

113. *tripudium*: A ritual dance in triple time performed by priests in honor of Mars, in which the dancers leaped, hence their name, *Salii*.

114. England: Erasmus writes exaggeratedly about this custom in England to his friend, Fausto Andrelini, in 1499: 'When you arrive anywhere, you are received with kisses on all sides, and when you take your leave they speed you on your way with kisses.' (Ep 103, CWE 1, p.193).

videantur. Equidem scire velim quo pertineat toties osculari? Ceu aliter con-
stare non posset vel amicitia vel caritas cum feminis. Initium illud est turpi-
tudinis, quam nolo explicare. Plane mos mihi foedus videtur ac barbaricus.

115. Sed pergo de saltationibus dicere. Quorsum tot saltus puellarum,
subiectis a viris cubitis quo altius se attollant? Quid usque in medias noctes
sine satietate aut lassitudine agitari eas, quae si iubeantur proximum templum
petere, ire se negent posse nisi equo vectas aut raeda? An non plane clamant
se intemperiis exagitari? Audisse memini me quosdam procul in nostrum
orbem ab extrema illa Asia deductos cum saltantes vidissent mulieres territos
fugisse, quod illas dicerent novo et inusitato sibi furoris genere concitari. Ac
profecto quis non mulieres credat furere cum saltent, si saltantes numquam
antea conspexerit? Quis non mente captas cum sic ad aliquem membranae
vel chordae sonitum, manus, caput, totum corpus in gesticulatione movent?
Iam in illis celebritatibus iuvat contemplari quam compositae aliae sedeant
spectantes, quo gestu aliae, quo incessu, quanta moderatione, quanto fastu
saltent aut incedant! In quo earum dementiam cognoscas licet, quod rem
tam stultam prudentissime conantur agere; videlicet universa illarum mens
a capite in extremos pedes desiliit. Ibi est nimirum magis necessaria cum
saltatur quam in cerebro vel corde. Quae umquam legitur saltasse sanctarum
feminarum? Quota quaeque est ex istis gravioribus et prudentiam rerum usu
nactis quae vel non dissimulet se artem illam scire vel rogata ut prodeat non
recuset omnino et contumeliae loco ducat? Nimirum non ignorant stultum
illud esse, alioqui ultro facturae. Quid quod eiusmodi nec frequentes adsunt
ubi saltatur nisi necessarii officii gratia ibique sic agunt ut invitae videantur
retineri, vultu et gestu toto illa aspernantes tamquam non probent. Quo
loco quae potest custodia esse pudicitiae, spectatis tot virorum corporibus
et sollicitatis animis per oculorum ostia, artibus subtilissimi atque astutissimi
hostis nostri?

1 Equidem scire velim **Γ** Laudo mentem sin quid secus? Non video **H** // **2–3** feminis. Initium
... explicare **Γ** feminis, nisi forte in frigidis regionibus illis velut stimulis iacentem excitare
libidinem instituerunt alioqui perituram **H** // **5** attollant **Γ** tollant **H** // **6** aut lassitudine
Γ *deest in* **H** // **7** se negent posse **Γ** non possunt **H** / vectas **Γ** vectae **H** // **8** intemperiis
exagitari **Γ** furore correptas insanire? Quid dixi insanire? **H** // **9** ab extrema illa Asia **Γ** *deest
in* **H** / deductos **Γ** allatos **H** // **10** novo et inusitato **Γ** insolito **H** // **11** saltent **Γ** saltant **H**
// **12** conspexerit **Γ** conspectarit **H** // **12–13** Quis ... movent **Γ** *deest in* **H** // **14** Iam
... contemplari **Γ** Iam videre est **H** // **15** quanto fastu **Γ** *deest in* **H** // **16** aut incedant
Γ *deest in* **H** / dementiam **Γ** stultitiam **H** // **17** tam **Γ** *deest in* **H** // **17–19** videlicet ...
corde **Γ** *deest in* **H** *in quo autem legitur* nec intelligunt quid sit, quid agant rem sine mente aliqua
et, ut recte dixit Cicero, multorum magnorumque vitiorum comitem // **21** artem illam **Γ**
artem illam saltatoriam **H** / prodeat **Γ** saltet **H** // **22** omnino ... ducat **Γ** *deest in* **H** // **23**
eiusmodi ... adsunt **Γ** nec eunt facile **H** // **24–25** nisi ... probent **Γ** *deest in* **H** // **27** ostia
Γ fenestras **H** / subtilissimi atque astutissimi **WW²** subtilissimi **HBV** // **28** hostis nostri **Γ**
artificis diaboli **H**

I for one would like to know what is the point of all this kissing, as if there were no other way of demonstrating friendship and affection to women. It is the beginning of shameful actions which I prefer not to mention. As far as I am concerned it is an utterly vile and barbaric custom.

115. I return to the subject of dancing. What is the purpose of these dances in which the girls are lifted higher into the air in the arms of their male companions? How can they move in this frenzied way until the middle of the night without having enough or becoming tired? But if they are asked to pay a visit to a nearby church, they say that they cannot go unless on horseback or in a carriage. Do they not make it clear that they are carried away by their excesses? I remember being told once that certain men had been brought to our part of the world from far-off Asia and when they saw women dancing they fled in terror because they thought they were victims of some strange and unfamiliar type of madness. In fact, who would not believe women are mad when they are dancing if he had never seen women dancing before? Who would not believe they were not mentally deranged when to the sound of a membrane or a string they move their hands, their heads, and their whole body in wild gesticulations? It is interesting to see how they behave in these crowded gatherings, how some of the female spectators sit there composed while others dance or strut about with such movements, such a bearing, such control and such arrogance. You can recognize their madness from the fact that they try to make such a stupid thing appear sensible. All their mental concentration has leaped down from their head to their feet, where, evidently, it is more necessary when one dances than it is in the brain or the heart. Do we read that holy women ever danced? How few of those respected matrons who have learned wisdom through experience would admit to knowing this art, or if asked to participate, would not refuse and consider it an insult to be asked! Obviously they regard it as something absurd, otherwise they would willingly learn it themselves. Such women do not frequent places where there is dancing unless obliged to do so through some duty, and they conduct themselves in such a way as to give the impression that they do not wish to be there, and in their facial expression and attitude indicate their aversion and disapproval. In these places what safeguard can there be for chastity, when so many men's bodies are visible and the soul is attacked through the portals of the eyes by the wiles of our most subtle and astute enemy?

116. De opere ipso sanctus vir pronuntiavit malle se arare festis diebus et
fodere quam saltare. Divus Ambrosius sorori suae scribens inquit: 'Debet igitur bonae conscientiae mentis esse laetitia, non inconditis commessationibus,
non nuptialibus excitata symphoniis. Ibi enim intuta verecundia illecebra
suspecta est ubi comes deliciarum est extrema saltatio. Ab hac virgines Dei
procul esse desidero. Nemo enim (ut dixit quidam saecularium doctor) saltat
sobrius nisi qui insanit. Quod si iuxta sapientiam saecularem saltationis aut
temulentia auctor est aut dementia, quid divinarum Scripturarum cautum
putamus exemplis, cum Ioannes, praenuntius Christi, saltatricis optione
iugulatus, exemplo sit plus nocuisse saltationis illecebram quam sacrilegi
furoris amentiam? Exstruitur regifico luxu ferale convivium et explorato
quando maior solito turba convenerit, filia intimis mandata secretis in con-
spectum virorum saltatura producitur. Quid enim potuit filia de adultera
matre discere nisi damnum pudoris? An quicquam est tam pronum ad
libidines quam inconditis motibus ea quae vel natura abscondit vel disciplina
velavit membrorum operta nudare, ludere oculis, rotare cervicem, comam
spargere? Merito inde in iniuriam divinitatis proceditur. Quid enim ibi verecundiae potest esse ubi saltatur, strepitur, concrepatur? Tunc rex (inquit)
delectatus dixit puellae ut peteret de rege quid vellet.' Hactenus Ambrosii
verba.

117. Inventus est mos non ita pridem ut viri et feminae personati urbem
totam circumcursitent, saltantes per celebres domos, quales sunt procerum,
divitum aut in quibus aliqui convivantur seu potant verius. Atque huic
ludicro ita sunt quidam dediti ut nihil affirment esse paris oblectamenti
quam eum in modum capite obvoluto domos circumire. Vident ipsi et
noscunt omnes, a nemine cogniti, ut infantes pueruli, qui magnam capiunt
voluptatem cum admotis ori manibus putant se ab aliis non cerni et
audiunt se ab aliis requiri. Sed sub larva eiusmodi multa delitescunt flagitia.
Primum curiositas immodica mulierum, quae scire quid ubique agatur
vehementer avent, qui conviventur, quo ordine, quomodo ornati, quam
splendido apparatu. Unde nascitur invidentia, loquacitas, detrac<ta>tio,
infamatio. Amicum credit se quis recipere, tecta facie: hostis est et quidem
capitalis, qui exploratum ingreditur qua noceat; et inimicum retectum licet
excludere, hunc opertum non licet. Tum habenae laxantur impudentiae
muliebri. Quae enim aliquo proficisci et saltare erubescere cognita non
veretur, id facere larvata; eoque nullus est illic respectus aetatis, dignitatis,
fortunae, existimationis. Nec solum audiunt obscena et se indigna, sed dicunt

---

116. (Debet ... vellet) *Ambr. virg. 3, 5, 25, PL 16, 227C*

1 sanctus vir pronuntiavit Γ sancti viri sententia est **H** // **9** optione Γ opinione **H** // **16**
velavit **HWW²B** *Ambr.* velabit **V** / nudare **H** *Ambr.* velare Γ // **18** strepitur **H** *Ambr.* strepitu
Γ // **21**–p.156,**12** Inventus ... castigasse Γ *deest in* **H** // **31** detractatio *scr.* detractio Γ

116. Concerning the art of dancing a holy man declared that he preferred to plough and dig on feast days rather than dance. Saint Ambrose writing to his sister said:

> Happiness of mind must be found in a good conscience, not in wild banqueting or nuptial music. For where dancing is the last escort of self-indulgence, modesty is threatened and sensual enticements are everywhere present. From this I wish the virgins of God to be far removed. No one, as a certain learned man of the world wrote, dances when he is sober, unless he is out of his mind. If according to the wisdom of the world drunkenness or madness instigate us to dance, what precautions do the Holy Scriptures set before us by example, as in the slaying of John, the precursor of Christ, at the wish of a dancing girl? It proves that the incitement of the dance was more harmful than the madness of sacrilegious frenzy. The funeral banquet is prepared with regal luxury and at the moment when a great crowd of people had gathered, the daughter of the tyrant under secret instructions is brought forth to dance before the male onlookers. What could the daughter of an adulterous mother learn but the loss of all decency? Is there anything more conducive to carnal lust than to reveal with crude movements those hidden regions of the body which either nature or moral discipline has concealed, to cavort with the eyes, to roll the head around, to toss back the hair? As a natural consequence this will lead to an offense against the divinity. What sense of shame can exist where there is dancing, loud confusion and noise? Then the king, delighted with the spectacle, told the girl she could ask of him what she wished.'

117. There is a custom of recent institution for men and women to run about the city wearing masks, dancing in famous houses, as those of leading citizens, the rich, or where there is banqueting, or, I should say, a drinking party going on. There are some so dedicated to this pastime that they claim there is nothing equally enjoyable as to go the round of people's houses with their heads covered in this manner. They see and know everyone but are not recognized by anyone, like little children who take great pleasure in covering their face with their hands and thinking that they are not seen by anyone and hearing people calling them by name. But under that mask many shameful things are concealed. The first of them is the uncontrolled curiosity of women, who are dying to know what is happening everywhere—who is out banqueting, at whose invitation, how they are dressed, with what splendid apparel. From this arise envy, talkativeness, detraction and defamation. You may think you are receiving a friend into your house with his face covered, but it is an enemy, a deadly enemy who enters, in order to find out how he may harm you. You can exclude an enemy who is visible but not one whose identity is hidden. Then female shamelessness is given free rein. A woman who would be ashamed to go out and dance if she were known is not afraid to do so when she is masked, and consequently there is no respect for age, social status, fortune or reputation in those circumstances. Not only do they hear obscenities and things unworthy of them, but they say fearlessly

intrepide quae ne cogitare quidem auderent si noscerentur. Verum omnia exaequat oculis spectantium larva velut tenebrae quaedam obiecta. Ita assuescunt paulatim impudentiae ut detrimentum, quod sub persona accepit verecundia, citra personam proferat et ostendat. Et in Gallia, Germania,
5 Britannia, ubi populi simplicius vivunt minusque inter se homines astute versantur, flagitia haec sequuntur non negligenda. In Hispania, Italia et aliis regionibus, in quibus propter ingeniorum acumen plus est calliditatis et vafriciei, verendum est ne magnorum scelerum occasionem praebeant eiusmodi ludicra, quae hactenus pauca quidem contigerunt, etsi nonnulla
10 nimirum re adhuc non admodum vetere neque usitata. Sed ea mala satius fuerit cogitationi uniuscuiusque relinquere quam dicendo explicare, ne admonuisse magis videamur quam castigasse.

CAP. XIII.   DE AMORIBUS

118. Ex congressibus colloquiisque cum viris amores nascuntur. Inter volup-
15 tates enim, convivia, saltationes, risus, delicias, regnum exercent Venus et Veneris puer Cupido. Istis illiciuntur et illaqueantur humani animi, sed in primis feminei, in quos impotentissime voluptas dominatur. O miseram puellam si capta ex coetu illo discedis! Quanto praestitisset mansisse domi aut fregisse crus corporis quam crus mentis! Conabor tamen praesidium
20 adferre, si nondum sis capta, ne capiaris, et si capta sis, subsidium ut elabaris. Primum, omitto quae a philosophis, quae etiam a sanctis viris, quae denique a cunctis sapientibus contra cupidineum amorem dicuntur. Illa quoque taceo quae etiam ab iis scribuntur qui amorem ex professo videntur voluisse laudare. Quanta illi faciunt convicia! Tyrannum illum nominant, durum,
25 asperum, taetrum, crudelem, foedum, scelestum, exsecrandum, impium, auctorem atque impulsorem pessimorum facinorum. Ex Aristotele, Seneca et Plutarcho Divus Hieronymus sic inquit: 'Amor formae rationis oblivio est et insaniae proximus, foedum minimeque conveniens animo sospiti vitium. Turbat consilia, altos et generosos spiritus frangit, a magnis cogitationibus
30 ad humillimas detrahit; querulos, iracundos, temerarios, dure imperiosos, serviliter blandos, omnibus inutiles, ipsi novissime amori facit. Nam cum fruendi cupiditate insatiabilis flagrat, plura tempora suspicionibus, lacrimis,

---

118. (Amor ... odio est) *Hier. adv. Iovin. 1, 49, PL 23, 280C*

15 exercent ... Cupido Γ est Veneris et Cupidinis H // 17 voluptas dominatur Γ dominatur voluptas H // 19 praesidium Γ remedium H // 20 subsidium Γ *deest in* H // 24–26 Tyrannum illum ... facinorum Γ illum tyrannum, illum taetrum, illum durum, asperum, crudelem, foedum, scelestum, exsecrandum, impium, auctorem pessimorum facinorum nominantes H

what they would not dare to think if they were recognized. But a mask levels everything in the eyes of the beholder as if darkness were cast around them. Thus little by little they become used to shamelessness so that the harm that modesty suffered under the mask is now flaunted and displayed without the mask. Even in France, Germany and England, where people live more simply and social relations are less sophisticated, these shameful customs are pursued quite prevalently. In Spain, Italy, and other regions, where through greater acuteness of intellect there is more cleverness and ingenuity, it is to be feared that these amusements may be the occasion of great misconduct. Up to now there have been few instances of this, but there have been some, even though the custom has been introduced quite recently. But it is preferable to leave these evils to everyone's imagination than to explain them in words lest I seem more to rebuke than to correct.

CHAPTER 13.   ON LOVE AFFAIRS

118. From meetings and conversations with men love affairs arise. In the midst of pleasures, banquets, dances, laughter, self-indulgence, Venus and Cupid, her son, reign supreme. Such things attract and ensnare human minds, but especially those of women over which pleasure exercises an uncontrolled tyranny. Poor young girl, if you emerge from these encounters a captive prey! How much better it would have been to remain at home or to have broken a leg of the body rather than of the mind! I shall try to be of help, if you have not yet been captured, so that you will not be captured, and if you are already caught, so that you may escape. First of all, I shall omit all that has been said by philosophers, holy men and all men of wisdom against passionate love. I shall also refrain from mentioning things that have been written by those who seem overtly to have sung the praises of love. What censures those first mentioned heap upon it! They call it tyrannical, stern, harsh, vile, cruel, ugly, wicked, accursed, impious, the author and instigator of the worst crimes. Taking his cue from Aristotle, Seneca and Plutarch, St. Jerome writes: 'Love of beauty is the oblivion of reason and close to madness, an ugly vice that ill befits a sound mind. It bewilders judgement, breaks lofty and noble spirits and drags them down from great thoughts to lowly ones. It makes them querulous, irascible, temerarious, harshly imperious, servilely flattering, useless for everything, in the end even for love. For when it burns with insatiable desire for pleasure; it loses much in suspicions, tears

conquestionibus perdit, odium sui facit et ipse novissime sibi odio est.' Sic
Hieronymus.

119. Quis consequi dicendo possit quot periuria, quot fraudes, quot
caedes, quas strages, quas eversiones urbium, gentium, regionum hic amor
5 dederit? Quid ego hic Troiam deletam narrem propter Helenam, tot ibi ex-
ercitus caesos, tantum bellum inter Lacedaemonios et Messenios propter raptas virgines? Ipsum quoque Lacedaemoniorum imperium ab Epaminonda
Thebano ad Leuctras Boeotias concussum vindicante (ut Plutarchus ait)
Scedasi genio filias a Lacedaemoniis iuvenibus stupratas et patris queri-
10 moniam a magistratibus contemptam? Florentes Hispanias Rodericus rex,
concubitu Cavae, Iuliani comitis filiae, perdidit lacerandasque et concul-
candas Mauris reliquit. Genus hominum prostravit et afflixit Adam propter
amorem Evae.

120. Exclamat ille: 'Quid non cogit aurum?' Immo vero, quid non cogit
15 saevus amor? Mitissimum Davidem impulit ut innocentem Uriam praesen-
tibus periculis obiceret, quo potiretur libere Bethsabee. Salomonem, sapien-
tissimum regem, dementavit usque ad idololatriam. Samsonem debilitavit.
Medeam adegit fratrem lacerare, filios occidere. Catilinam filium proprium
interimere, ut in vacuam domum Orestillam duceret. Oderunt parentes et
20 consanguineos puellae, quod suo amori obsistant. Sunt quae matres ipsae
suas, ex quibus erant natae ac educatae, veneno sustulerint ut cum amatoribus fugerent. Messalina, Claudii imperatoris uxor, illo vivo et Hostiam
ad sextum decimum ab Urbe lapidem profecto, ipsa, nulla divortii mentione
facta, publice, media luce, Romae Gaio Silio nubere ausa est. Praetereo
25 quod privata fiebat ex Augusta. Certe, id conflabat periculum, sub quo et
ipsam et Silium et omnes tam nefarii connubii conscios perire erat necesse,
sicut evenit. Haec facerent Orestes ulli aut Aiaces aut illorum quisquam
quos exagitatos a furiis accepimus? Nec in ullis tigribus, leonibus, lupis, ursis
talis annotari potest furor. Nimirum eo protrudit conscientia sceleris oestro
30 percita, quod vecordia ne cogitare quidem secura possit. Denique hunc tam

119. (Ipsum ... contemptam?) *Plut. mor. 773C–774D*
120. (Quid ... aurum?) *Verg. Aen. 3, 56* // (Davidem ... Uriam) *Vulg. II reg. 11, 14–15*
// (Salomonem ... idolatriam) *Vulg. III reg. 11, 4–5* // (Catilinam ... duceret) *Sall. Catil.*
15, 2 // (Messalina ... ausa est) *Tac. ann. 11, 26*

12 Mauris **Γ** Agarenis **H** // **15** saevus **Γ** *deest in* **H** // **20** obsistant **Γ** obsisterent **H** //
20–21 Sunt ... sustulerint **Γ** Veneno multae matres sustulerunt **H** // **22–30** Messalina ...
Denique **Γ** *deest in* **H** // **22** Hostiam **Γ** = Ostiam

and complaints, it makes itself hateful and in the end becomes hateful even to itself.' So writes St. Jerome.

119. Who can rehearse in words how many perjuries, deceptions, murders, catastrophes, destruction of cities, people and regions this love has brought about? Shall I recount here how Troy fell for the sake of Helen and how so many armies were slaughtered? Shall I tell of the great war between the Spartans and the Messenians because of the abduction of young girls? Or of the breaking of the power of the Spartans by the Theban Epaminondas at Leuctra in Boeotia when, as Plutarch tells us, the spirit of Scedasus revenged the rape of his daughters by Spartan youths and a father's plaint ignored by the magistrates? King Rodrigo by lying with Cava, daughter of Don Julián, caused the ruin of the flourishing country of Spain and left it to be ravished and crushed by the Moors. Adam caused the downfall and affliction of the human race through his love for Eve.

120. The poet cries out: 'To what excesses does gold not drive us?' With more truth he could have said the same of savage love. It drove mild-mannered David to expose the innocent Uriah to imminent danger so that he could freely possess Bathsheba. It drove Solomon, wisest of kings, to madness, to the point of idolatry. It weakened Samson, it forced Medea to rend her brother limb from limb and kill her children. It led Catiline to slay his own son so that he could bring Orestilla into an empty house. Girls hate their parents and relatives because they stand in the way of their love. There are those who have poisoned their own mothers, from whom they were born and by whom they were brought up, so that they could fly away with their lovers. Messalina, wife of the emperor Claudius, while he was still alive and had left for Ostia, sixteen miles from Rome, with no mention of divorce, publicly, in broad daylight, dared to marry Gaius Silius in Rome. I shall pass over the fact that from an empress she became an ordinary citizen. In reality, this augmented the danger of death that hung over her and Silius and all those who were accomplices of the wicked marriage, as indeed came to pass. Would an Orestes or an Ajax or any of those who we learn were hounded by the Furies do such things? Such frenzy is not observed in tigers, lions, wolves or bears. The consciousness of the crime, roused by passion, pushed them to such extremes that not even the most deranged mind could conceive of

119. Leuctra: The battle of Leuctra in 371 B.C. took place near the tomb of the young girls who had been slaughtered by the Spartans some years previously. The spirit of Scedasus appeared to a general of the Theban army, requesting sacrifice of a white colt at the girls' tomb.

Don Julián: The daughter of the Spanish nobleman, Don Julián, who governed Ceuta in North Africa, was raped by King Rodrigo. In retaliation he assisted the Arabs to cross the straits and invade Spain. The story is told by Alfonso el Sábio, *Primera crónica general* and in the Spanish version of the Latin *Historia Gotica* by Rodrigo Jiménez de Rada, Archbishop of Toledo.

immanem affectum et atrocem si quis oculis corporis posset cernere, non
secus terreretur ac cohorresceret quam si subito truculentissima occurreret
belua et quam longissime se territus abriperet.

121. Si non es ergo huius scorpii veneno icta, reputare animo tuo
versiculum illum mimi debes:

　　　Amor animi arbitrio sumitur, non ponitur,

esse in tua manu amorem admittere; et postquam admiseris, iam te tui
iuris non esse, sed illius; non licere tibi illum extrudere cum libeat; illi
vero et licebit et libebit domicilio te tuo deturbare. Itaque nisi hospitem
eiusmodi venientem ad te arceas, ipsa a te arcebere. Faciendum est quod
deinceps pati erit necesse nisi feceris. Quippe amor, quo ipse immoderatius ac
profusius in animo nostro dominetur et omnia pro libito conturbet, sursum
ac deorsum involvat ac misceat, mentem primum omnium vel excaecat
vel eicit, ut cum nihil cernat aut procul absit, cognoscere nec possit quid
domi suae agatur, sed cunctam se amoris arbitrio tractandam et versandam
permittat. Atrox venenum quod luminibus nos orbat et excaecatos per mille
abrupta, per totidem praecipitia trahit raptatque et plerumque in exitiabilem
voraginem devolvit! Nullum adeo est vel inhumanum et immane facinus
vel sic inusitatum atque inauditum quod non suscipiamus, si in hoc amori
parendum aut gratificandum sit. Fraudare amicos, occidere consanguineos,
parentes iugulare, trucidare quos pepereris levia sunt in gratiam amoris; nec
illa gravia: a stirpe patriam regionem genus humanum exscindere.

122. Quae inter haec memoria sancti, pii, aequi? Deus et religio et bona
mens nugae omnia suimetipsius iam oblito. Qui sanus est et haec reputans
non dat operam quo in hanc mentis phrenitidem caecitatemque ad omnia
numquam incidat, nimirum dignus is est qui perpetuo illa teneatur nec
inveniat suorum malorum finem aut modum, sed agitetur diebus ac noctibus
face illa Cupidinis. Nec cibum sumat nec dormiat nec videat nec quiescat;
et cum sit homo, nullo tamen humano munere fungatur. Affectus hic,
cum animos mortalium omnium impotentissime rapit, tum vero feminarum,

---

121. (Amor ... ponitur) *Publil. A. 47*

2 ac cohorresceret Γ *deest in* H / truculentissima occurreret Γ ferissima offerretur H **// 4**
icta, reputare Γ tacta, tractare H / tuo Γ *deest in* H **// 8–16** non licere ... permittat Γ
non licere illum eicere cum libebit. Quis talem hospitem libens excipiat? Quis domo suo non
arceat? Amor enim primum omnium, quo ipse immoderatius in animo nostro dominetur et
omnia pro libito conturbet, sursum ac deorsum involvat ac misceat, mentem ipsam excaecat,
ut cum nihil cernat, cognoscere nec possit quid domi suae agatur, sed totum se arbitrio amoris
tractandum et agitandum permittat H **// 17** et Γ vel H **// 19** inusitatum atque Γ *deest*
in H / suscipiamus Γ subeamus H **// 20** aut gratificandum Γ *deest in* H **// 21** in gratiam
amoris Γ propter amorem H **// 24** suimetipsius Γ propriae salutis H **// 25** phrenitidem Γ
insaniam phrenesimque H / caecitatemque ad omnia Γ *deest in* H

without anxiety. If one could see this monstrous and dreadful passion with bodily eyes, he would be as terrified and horrified as if a ferocious beast were to cross his path and would flee in terror as far as he could.

121. If you have not yet been stricken by the poison of this scorpion, you should meditate on this verse of the Mime: 'Love is entered into at our own free choice, but not laid aside in the same manner.' It is in your power to let love in, but once you have let it in you no longer belong to yourself, but to it. You cannot drive it out at your pleasure, but it will be able and will take pleasure in ousting you from your own house. So if you do not drive this guest away upon arrival, you will be driven away by him. You must do what would later be done to you if you do not do it. You must understand that in order to gain more unlimited and extensive dominion over our mind and wilfully throw everything into confusion, engulf and muddle everything from top to bottom, love first of all blinds the mind or banishes it so that when it sees nothing or is far removed it cannot know what is happening in its own dwelling and lets itself be managed and directed entirely according to the whims of love. It is a deadly poison that deprives us of our sight and drags us in our blindness over a thousand ravines and precipices and often plunges us to our death in an abyss! There is no deed so inhuman, so monstrous, strange and unheard of that we would not undertake if we have to give heed to love or gratify its wishes—to defraud friends, kill relatives, cut the throats of parents, slaughter those to whom you gave birth are trifling matters in order to satisfy love. It is of no great consequence to destroy utterly one's native land or the human race from the very base.

122. In all this turmoil can there be any remembrance of what is holy, pious and just? God and religion and a good conscience are mere trifles to one who has forgotten himself. Anyone of sane mind who would reflect on these things and not take care in every respect that he never become a victim of this madness and total blindness deserves to be its prisoner forever and find no end or limit to his woes, but be tormented night and day by Cupid's torch. May he not take food, nor sleep, nor see, nor rest, and though he be a human being, let him not perform any human function. While this passion violently sweeps away all human hearts, it does so all the more with women's feelings,

quanto teneriores sunt quam viriles. Quo circumspectius cavere illis expedit
ne sensim illum hauriant insciae. Illabitur enim quandoque improvisus iis qui
in discrimina adducti et in occasionibus positi, securi sunt quo motu animi
invadantur amoremque, ubi primum irrepsit, tamquam blandum suavemque
5   amplectuntur et fovent, ignarae quam capitalem ac formidandam pestem
sub illa frontis blanditie occultam.

123. Ergo primis quibusque occasionibus fortiter obsistendum, quod et
magister amorum Ovidius consulit. Neu sine adolescere parvulos Babylonis,
sed iuxta Psalmistae monita, 'Allide illos ad petram,' et comminue in
10 firmamento religionis Christo Iesu, qui in Canticis virgines admonet inquiens:
'Capite nobis vulpes parvulas, quae demoliuntur vineas.' Et eo suadet
accuratius capiendas si vinea bonorum fructuum iam flores ostendit. Accipit
amor vires ex mora ut aliae res permultae:

Vidi ego quod fuerat (inquit Ovidius) primo sanabile vulnus
15 Dilatum longae damna tulisse morae.

Non magis audiendus amans quam incantator aut veneficus. Aggreditur
hic suavis ac blandus et primum omnium puellam laudat, captum se dicit
eius forma, postremo perire prae amore immodico. Videlicet non ignorat
multarum vanos animos quae unice laudibus suis delectantur. Sic volucrem
20 auceps fallit visco et fistula. Vocat te formosam, venustam, ingeniosam,
facundam, nobilem; et forsan nihil horum es, sed tu illa mendacia libenter
audis. Stulta, putas te videri talem cum non sis? Sed fac esse. Num etiam
prudentem adiecit, num pudicam? Si praetermisit haec, nihil dixit; sin
adiecit, quid a te sperat? Si sperat, mentitum esse apparet. Quomodo igitur
25 oravit? Captum se ait istis tuis dotibus. Quid inde? Periturum nisi potiatur.
Hinc illae lacrimae.

124. Vide iam tu ne et ipsa illius verbis capiare ac pariter et una pereatis.
Moriturum se deierat atque etiam (si diis placet) iam iam mori. Credis tu hoc?
Demens, proferat tibi ille, quot amore interierint ex tot amatorum milibus.

---

123. (primis ... obsistendum) *Ov. rem. 91* ∥ (Allide ... petram) *Vulg. psalm. 137, 9* ∥
(Capite ... vineas) *Vulg. cant. 2, 15* ∥ (Vidi ... morae) *Ov. rem. 101–102* ∥ (Hinc illae
lacrimae) *Ter. And. 99; Erasm. ad. LB II, 138F*

---

1 quanto ... viriles Γ *deest in* H ∥ **2** hauriant insciae Γ insciae admittant H ∥ **3** securi sunt
Γ non laborant H / motu animi Γ affectu H ∥ **4** suavemque Γ et suavem H ∥ **5** ignarae
Γ ignari H ∥ **5–6** quam capitalem ... occultam Γ quod venenum quam perniciosum et
horrendum sub illa frontis blanditie occultum H ∥ **7** Ergo Γ Itaque H ∥ **9** Psalmistae
monita Γ praeceptum Psalmistae H ∥ **16** Non magis audiendus amans Γ audiendus amator
non magis H ∥ **17** suavis Γ dulcis H / omnium Γ *deest in* H ∥ **18** immodico Γ *deest in* H
∥ **20** visco et fistula Γ *deest in* H ∥ **23** praetermisit Γ non adiecit H ∥ **24** mentitum esse
apparet Γ mentitus est H ∥ **28** deierat Γ dicit H ∥ **29** interierint Γ perierint H

which are more tender than men's. Wherefore it behooves them to be all the more cautious that they do not slowly imbibe it without knowing it. For it will steal upon them without warning when they are in critical situations or in the right circumstances, thinking themselves free of any assault upon their emotions. When once love has crept into their hearts they embrace and cherish it as something sweet and pleasant, unaware that a deadly and terrible pestilence is hidden beneath those external blandishments.

123. Therefore a strong resistance must be made to the first stirrings, which even Ovid, the preceptor of love, counsels. Do not allow the children of Babylon to grow up but according to the advise of the Psalmist: 'Dash them against the rock' and crush them on the groundwork of the religion of Christ Jesus, who admonishes the virgins in the Canticle: 'Capture for us the little foxes that destroy the vineyards.' And he admonishes this all the more carefully if the vineyard already shows the blossoms of good fruit. Love gathers strength with time as do many other things. As Ovid says:

> I saw a wound at first susceptible of cure,
> But neglected, suffered the bane of long delay.

A lover should be given no more attention than one who casts spells or a poisoner. He approaches smoothly and persuasively and first of all praises the girl, says that he has been captured by her beauty and ends by saying that he is perishing of his uncontrollable love. He is well aware of the vain minds of many women, who take singular pleasure in being praised. In this way the fowler deceives the bird with bird-lime and the decoy's cry. He calls you beautiful, charming, clever, eloquent, noble, and perhaps you are none of these things but you like to hear those lies. Stupid girl, do you think you appear such, when you are not? But suppose you are. He did not mention that you were prudent or that you were chaste, did he? If he omitted these, he said nothing, but if he did add them, what does he hope for from you? If he does hope, it is evident that he lied. How did he plead his case? Did he say that he was captivated by your good qualities? Then what? That he would die unless he had you? Now we know the reason for those tears.

124. Make sure you are not captured by his words for then the two of you will perish together. He swears he will die and even (may the gods forgive me) that he is already dying. Do you believe this? You fool, let him demonstrate how many have died of love out of so many thousands of lovers.

Excruciat quandoque amor, numquam perimit. Quod si perit, quanto consultius est tibi perire illum quam te, aut etiam unum perire quam duos? Quid attinet explicare ut promptum et commune sit id carmen amatoribus, ut omnes memoriter teneant, cum saepenumero ne gutta quidem amoris aspersi sint? Solum id occinunt ut fallant. Puella quaedam Gallica, ex iis quae Margaritam Valesiam comitatae sunt in Hispaniam, visentem Franciscum, Franciae regem, fratrem suum Caroli Caesaris captivum, cum a iuvenibus Hispanis subinde audiret: 'Amore enecor,' 'Morere iam tandem,' inquit, 'ut amatorem aliquem mori videam ex tot moriturientibus.' Quod si te amator tui fruatur ad satietatem, ibi ostendet quantum amarit. Si amasset ille te, hoc est, animum tuum, numquam eum, quamdiu vixisses, fastidium aut satietas tenuisset tui, sed quia corpus tantummodo deperibat et brevem ex te voluptatem, ideo flaccescente corpore deferbuit ille ardor expletusque voluptate fastidivit copiam.

125. Non sunt rara exempla nec vetera necesse est advocare. Nullus est tam rerum imperitus qui non audierit, qui non viderit sexcenta virorum milia, ubi puellis essent abusi, abiecisse illas plerumque in fornicem aliquem cum eas numquam dilexissent; alios qui adamarunt ex ardentissimo amore in capitale odium versos caecidisse aut iugulasse amicas. Nulla est civitas in qua non quotidie haec audiantur, ut magis puellarum furorem demirer, quae se in tantum malorum mare non invitae immergant. Unde, quaeso, tam frequentia lupanaria? Praefandus est honos, sed haec non sunt tacenda, quorum similia non dubitavit Hieronymus eloqui. Unde tot prostibulae, etiam honesto natae genere? Unde tot in ptochotrophiis et valetudinariis ulcerosae etiam adolescentulae speciosissimae? Unde tot stipem poscentes, pallidae, aegrae, taeterrimis morbis contabefactae nisi ex istis exemplis? Si nullus te virtutis, nullus probitatis, pudicitiae, religionis respectus movet, si nulla sanctarum virginum revocant acta et exempla, hi saltem miserarum puellarum casus flectant, qui te indubii manent si eandem quam illae viam insistas.

126. Fallet te amator vel quia solitus fallere vel quia hoc est praemium obsceni amoris vel quia id suadet voluptatis satietas. Proderunt etiam multa

---

125. (lupanaria ... eloqui) *Hier. adv. Iovin. 1, 12, PL 23, 239*

1 perimit Γ necat H // 1–2 consultius Γ melius H // 3 promptum et commune Γ cognitum et vulgare H // 4 aspersi Γ attincti H *epist. Cran.* // 5–9 Puella ... moriturientibus Γ *deest in* H // 9–10 Quod si ... amarit Γ quod si te fruantur ad satietatem, ibi ostendent quantum amarint H // 10 ille Γ *deest in* H // 12 tantummodo deperibat Γ tantum amabat H / ex te Γ *deest in* H // 13 deferbuit ille ardor Γ evanuit amor H // 17 dilexissent Γ amassent H // 19 puellarum furorem demirer Γ mirer amentiam puellarum H // 20 non invitae immergant Γ ultro demergunt H // 21 Praefandus est honos Γ *deest in* H // 24 speciosissimae Γ *deest in* H / pallidae, aegrae Γ pallidae ac aegrae H // 25 taeterrimis morbis contabefactae Γ *deest in* H // 27 et exempla Γ *deest in* H // 28 insistas Γ ingrediaris H // 29 Fallet te Γ Fallet enim te H // 30 voluptatis satietas Γ fastidita iam ex copia voluptas H

Love torments us at times, but it does not kill us. But if he dies, how much better it is for you that he die and not you, or that one die instead of two? What is the use of explaining that this is the ready and common refrain of all lovers, who know it by heart, although often they have not been touched by a drop of love. They sing this song only to deceive. There was a certain French girl among the retinue of those who accompanied Marguerite of Valois to Spain to see her brother Francis I, king of France, who was held captive by the Emperor Charles. When she heard young Spaniards constantly crying out 'I am dying of love,' she said, 'Well, die and be done with it so that I can see one of these lovers die of all those who say they are going to die?' But if a lover enjoys you until he is tired of you, then he will show how much he loved you. If he had loved you, that is to say, your soul, he would have never become bored or sated with you. But since he died only for your body and the brief pleasure he could get from you, when the body became droopy his ardor waned, and after satisfying his pleasure he grew tired of the ready abundance.

125. Examples are not rare and it is not necessary to invoke the past. No one is so inexperienced that he has not heard or seen a hundred thousand men who take advantage of girls and then consign them to a brothel, since they had never loved them. There are others who fell in love, and their burning love turning to deadly hatred, they killed or strangled their mistresses. There is no city in which these things are not heard daily, which makes me wonder all the more at the madness of young girls, who willingly immerse themselves in such a sea of evils. Whence come so many whorehouses, I ask you? I must beg your indulgence, but these things should not be kept silent, for St. Jerome did not hesitate to use similar language. Why are there so many prostitutes, and some of them of good family? Why are there so many beautiful young women with festering ulcers in poorhouses and hospitals? Why are there so many begging for alms, pale and sick, consumed with ugly sores, except that they were of this number? If you cannot be moved by virtue, honor, chastity or respect for religion, if the deeds and examples of holy virgins do not dissuade you, then let the fate of these miserable young women, at least, influence you, which undoubtedly awaits you if you enter upon that same path.

126. Your lover will deceive either because he is used to deceiving or because this is the reward of an illicit love or because satiety of plea-sure will persuade him to do so. Many of the things I said about the

---

124. Emperor Charles: In 1525 after the battle of Pavia Francis I was taken prisoner by the troops of Charles V and imprisoned in Madrid, but quickly freed. In a letter of 12 March 1525 addressed to Henry VIII Vives pleaded for leniency for the French king and the French nation. It was probably not a politically wise move.

ex iis quae in custodia pudicitiae diximus, ut amorem nec victus ratio gignat aut alat, nec otium nec conversatio cum viris. Apud Lucianum Sophistam quaerit ex Cupidine mater Venus cur cum Iovem, Neptunum, Apollinem, Iunonem, se etiam matrem denique deos omnes iaculis suis configat, Minervae et Musis et Dianae manum non admoliatur? 'Minerva' inquit ille 'mihi venienti comminatur, haec occasionibus it obviam et resistit. Musae vero reverendae sunt et semper honestis exercitiis occupatae; hae maiestate sua et negotii intentione ab amore se vindicant. Diana in silvis et solitudinibus errat; haec amorem non haurit consuetudine. Multum enim amoris per sensum se insinuat, quod postea teneris cogitationibus alitur et excrescit.' At capta est puella; remedium quaerendum est plagae antequam cogat id perpetrare quod paenitentiam aeternam afferat. Primum hoc dolendum, quod in eam te voraginem videns prudensque conieceris. Nec audiendi sunt qui fuisse in manu sua negent amorem non admittere. Vox ea est hominum praetexentium crimini suo excusationem necessitatis tamquam inviti fecerint et ignorantium amoris naturam ac vim. Cogitandus est igitur aeque versiculus Mimi:

> Amor extorqueri non potest, elabi potest;

qui aperte indicat non amorem vi irrupisse nec vi expellendum, sed ut illapsus est, ita sensim a nobis exprimendum. Non sines vagari animum tuum, nam eo sponte sua revolvetur.

127. Sunt cordatiores aliquot quae amatorias cogitationes aliis diversi generis extrudunt veluti clavum clavo. Itaque vehementi studio alicui se exercitamento cunctas dedunt, in quo universa animi intentio occupata alias curas meditationesque excludat. Ergo vel telam magna compendii spe ordiuntur vel avidissime discunt acu pingere, vel legere vel scribere litteras latinas, quod sive praesentis commodi illecebra sive spe venturi animum in se vertat ac detineat. Porro cum paulum amoris conquiescent stimuli et pondere ac violentia illius relaxata vacabit mente aliquid cernere, revolves ac reputabis cum animo tuo quam multa per amorem egeris stulta, caeca, sine mente, sine sensu; quomodo tantum boni temporis in eo triveris inutilibus et stultis curis, in quo amiseris occasiones

---

126. (Minerva ... excrescit) *Lukian. 8, 19, 1* // (Amor ... potest) *Publil. A. 39*
127. (clavum clavo) *Erasm. ad. LB II, 70B*

1–2 ut amorem ... alat Γ ut nec victus ratio alat amorem H // **4–5** iaculis suis configat Γ iaculo feriat H // **7** occupatae Γ laboriosae H // **7–8** hae maiestate ... intentione Γ hae otio H // **11** capta est Γ capta est forsan H // **13** dolendum **HWW²** docendum **BV** // **19** qui Γ quod H / expellendum Γ pellendum H // **21** revolvetur **WW²** revolveretur **BV** revolvetur si non cohibeatur H // **22–30** Sunt cordatiores ... aliquid cernere Γ *deest in* H // **22** quae **V** qui **WW²B** // **30–31** revolves ... sine sensu Γ Interdum tamen considerabis quam multis egeris stulta, caeca, sine mente, sine sensu per amorem H

safeguarding of chastity will be profitable to you, so that love will not be engendered or nurtured by your diet or through leisure time or dealings with men. In the dialogues of the Sophist Lucian, Venus asks of her child Cupid why he transfixes with his arrows Jupiter, Neptune, Apollo, Juno, and even herself, his mother, and in general all the gods, but does not lay a hand on Minerva, the Muses and Diana. He answered 'Minerva threatens me when I approach her, she takes counter-measures and puts up a resistance. The Muses are to be respected and are always occupied in honorable activities, they defend themselves from love by their majestic presence and their attention to their task. Diana wanders in the woods and solitudes, her way of life makes her immune to love.' A great part of love is instilled through the senses, and it is then nourished and increased by tender thoughts. But the girl has been captured. We must find a remedy for this plague before it forces her to perpetuate that which will bring eternal punishment. The first thing to regret is that you threw yourself into this abyss knowingly and wittingly. We cannot give ear to those who say that it was not in their power to turn love away. Those are the words of persons who cloak their misdeed with the excuse of necessity as if they acted unwillingly and were ignorant of the nature of the force of love. You should meditate on the verse of the Mime: 'Love cannot be removed forcibly but it can be escaped.' This clearly indicates that love does not break in by force nor can it be expelled by force, but as it slipped in little by little, so can it be ejected. Do not allow your mind to wander because it will always return to thoughts of love of its own accord.

127. There are some judicious women who expel amatory thoughts by other thoughts of a different nature, like driving out a nail with a nail. For example, they give themselves over entirely with great zeal to some activity, in which all their attention is absorbed and which excludes all other cares and concerns. So they prepare a job of weaving with hope of remuneration, or they eagerly learn how to embroider or read or write, or study Latin, which either by the prospect of present advantage or hope of it in the future diverts the mind and recalls it to itself. Then when the stimulants of love are quieted and the soul is relieved of its violent constraints, you will have leisure to see things with your mind and reflect within yourself on how many stupid, blind things you did, thoughtlessly and senselessly. You will see how much valuable time you spent on useless and inane cares and lost so many

rerum optimarum; qua face arseris; quam multa cogitaris, dixeris, feceris, partim inepta, partim insana, partim etiam impia; in quantum malorum seminarium te praecipitabas caeca. Quantum est beneficium oculos tibi esse restitutos ac ad meliorem redire mentem velle! Haud mediocre Dei munus hoc esse nec parvam ei ob illud deberi gratiam. Tum redi ad opus aliquod. Cura ne rem amatam aspicias, ne de illa audias. Si cogitationi occurrit, animum alio retorque vel lectione vel oratione vel sermone aliquo vel etiam cantiuncula honesta vel cogitatione rei iucundae, modo purae et castae.

128. Hinc si quid is quem amas vitii habet, si quid deformitatis, id fac potius menti obversetur quam si quid boni et pulchri. Nullus est mortalium in quo non insit quod improbes; id occurrat primum de illo cogitanti. Iam reputa latere ingentia sub virtutis specie mala, multa sub honesti facie perniciosa. Superbos et fastidiosos reddit forma, nobilitas insolentes, divitiae temerarios, robur corporis feros ac immanes. Revoca in memoriam non si quid dixit quod placuerit, sed si quid quod displicuerit. Fieri aliter non potest quin ipsa illum recorderis aliquid egisse aut dixisse ineptum, frivolum, stultum, foedum, taetrum, abominandum, nequiter, flagitiose, dementer, nefarie. Ex hoc quod prodiit fac coniecturam qualia sint alia quae intus maxima cura occultentur. Nam nemo quantum potest vitia sua non celat; nemo non ostentat virtutes. Ita fit ut et hae sint semper minores quam videantur, vitia vero maiora quam appareant. Adde quod affinitatibus vitiorum et virtutum fallimur quoniam quisque melior quam sit videri affectat nosque imperite et ad vulgarem trutinam virtutes examinamus. Igitur liberalem vocamus qui sit profusus, fortem qui temerarius, eloquentem qui loquax, ingeniosum qui levis. Istis saepe capiuntur puellae cum nec ipsae satis iudicare sciant et de homine iudicent ex eo quod extrinsecus apertum omnibus obviumque circumgeritur, praesertim cum nemo ad amicam accedat qui non se in habitum componat et optimi viri et fortunatissimi, ne quid ei credatur deesse quod in aliquo mortali ad amorem conciliandum optari posse videatur.

---

1 rerum optimarum Γ optimarum rerum **H** // **3–4** beneficium ... restitutos Γ beneficium te oculos recepisse **H** // **7** retorque Γ verte **H** // **10** Hinc Γ Tu **H** // **11** menti obversetur Γ cogites **H** // **12** insit Γ sit **H** / Iam Γ Tum **H** // **14** reddit forma Γ forma facit **H** / temerarios Γ intolerabiles **H** // **15** feros ac Γ *deest in* **H** / Revoca in memoriam Γ Volve animo **H** / dixit Γ dixerit **H** // **16–17** Fieri ... recorderis Γ *deest in* **H** // **17** egisse aut dixisse Γ vel egit vel dixit **H** / frivolum Γ *deest in* **H** // **20** sua Γ *deest in* **H** // **21** ostentat virtutes Γ virtutes ostentat **H** / hae **HWW²B** haec **V** // **22** Adde quod Γ Hinc etiam **H** // **23** quoniam Γ cum **H** / videri affectat Γ studiat videri **H** / nosque Γ et nos etiam **H** // **26** iudicare Γ vindicare **H** // **27** iudicent **H** iudicant Γ // **27–28** apertum ... circumgeritur Γ omnes vident **H** // **29** optimi viri et fortunatissimi Γ optimi et fortunatissimi viri **H** // **30–31** ad ... posse Γ expetendum **H**

excellent opportunities; with what passion you were consumed, how many silly, insane and even impious things you thought, said, and did; into what a hotbed of wickedness you blindly hurled yourself. What a blessing that your vision has been restored to you and that you are willing to return to a better state of mind. This is no small favor of God and no small gratitude is owed to him for it. Then return to your task. Be sure not to see the beloved object or hear anything about it. If it comes to mind, divert your attention elsewhere, either by reading or prayer or conversation or even an uplifting song or the thought of something pleasant, provided it be pure and chaste.

128. Next, if the one you love has some defect or some deformity, concentrate on that rather than on something good and beautiful. There is no mortal in whom there is not something to criticize. Let that occur to you first when you are thinking of him. Consider that beneath the appearance of virtue there lurk great evils and many pernicious things under the guise of integrity. Beauty renders men proud and haughty, nobility makes them insolent, riches make them presumptuous, strength of body makes them fierce and cruel. Recall to mind not things he said that pleased you, but those that displeased you. You cannot help but remember that he did or said something fatuous, silly, stupid, base, offensive, abominable, wicked, criminal, mad, nefarious. From what has emerged you can conjecture what other defects are kept carefully hidden. There is no one who does not conceal his vices, as far as possible, no one who does not show off his virtues. It thus happens that the latter are always less than they seem and the former greater. Add to this that we are deceived by the similarities between vice and virtue, since everyone strives to appear better than he is and we in our ignorance measure virtues according to a popular scale of values. Therefore we call liberal one who is extravagant, courageous one who is foolhardy, eloquent one who is loquacious, clever one who is light-headed. Girls are often captivated by these qualities, since they are not capable of making judgement and they judge a man from externals that are obvious to all observers. This is especially true since no one approaches a girl without putting on the airs of an excellent and fortunate gentleman lest he be thought to be lacking in anything that could be desired in any mortal for the winning over of love.

129. Hunc in modum improvidis puellis imponunt cum tenuissima boni
specie detestandas malorum voragines contegunt, ut aucupes viscum cibo
et hamum piscatores esca. Haec omnia reputare puella debet antequam
sera teneatur paenitentia et incipiat sapere cum nihil iam prodest. Quod si
5   amorem prorsus exueris, tum velut sanitati restituta et receptis luminibus
intelliges ut cum aliorum complurium, tum vel huius beneficii nomine,
numquam Deo sis solvendo, qui te ex numero dementium exemptam inter
sapientes reposuerit. Quae enim sancta femina Christiana quae habita
inter gentiles vel mediocriter prudens et proba adamavit umquam nisi
10   maritum? Nec cupies hoc amoris genere te amari neu improbis artibus ignes
viri accendas perventuro et ad te facile incendio proximo. Gloriantur se
quaedam habere amatores quos dedita urant opera. Sed istae quae venatum
a diabolo ducuntur expansione formae, cultus, sermonis, sibi ipsae non
minus tendunt rete quam viris durioremque sibi reddunt custodiam suae
15   pudicitiae quam tot expetant atque impetant.

130. Aegre retinetur quod tam multi laborant extorquere. Ita contingit
eis merito quod Iesus ait, filius Sirach: 'Qui in altum mittit lapidem super
caput eius cadet, et plaga dolosa dolosi dividet vulnera. Et qui foveam
fodit incidet in eam, et qui statuit lapidem proximo suo offendet in eo; qui
20   laqueum alii ponit peribit in illo.' Scelerata, non vides te hunc in casses
diaboli tuis fraudibus impellere, eodem et tu cum illo casura, ut ministerii
tui mercedem accipias? Et ille ardebit quia victus diabolo et tu quia diabolo
victrix? Uterque stipendia meret peccati ampla. 'Stipendium autem peccati,'
quemadmodum testificatur Apostolus, 'mors.' Lex Christi, quae formula
25   est dilectionis mutuae, non vestitum modo et universa fortuita, sed corpus
quoque ipsum et sanguinem et vitam cuiusque nostrum animae proximi
postponit. Omnes enim intenti atque expediti in profectionem incumbimus
ad destinatam immortalitatis felicitatem. Quam convenit nos gaudere cum
exemplo vel monitis vel incitatione nostra fratri ad virtutem profuimus, tam
30   dolere cum ille nostra causa fit peior. Si detestatur illum Dominus per quem
scandalum venit, quid illi fiet qui sciens et prudens offendiculum obicit
pedibus ambulantis proximi in quod ille cum gravi casu impingat?

---

130. (Qui ... illo) *Vulg. Sirach 27, 28–29* // (Stipendium ... mors) *Vulg. Rom. 6, 23* //
(per quem ... venit) *Vulg. Matth. 18, 7*

---

1 improvidis Γ stultis **H** // **2** detestandas ... voragines Γ horrendas facies **H** // **4** prodest
Γ proderit **H** // **5** receptis Γ redditis **H** // **6–7** intelliges ut cum ... sis solvendo Γ intelliges
quantum vel hoc beneficio Deo debeas **H** // **8** reposuerit Γ collocarit **H** // **10** maritum Γ
maritum suum **H** / improbis Γ *deest in* **H** // **11** accendas *scr.* accendes improba **H** accendens
Γ // **12–20** Sed ... illo Γ *deest in* **H** // **20** casses Γ ditionem **H** // **21** cum illo casura Γ
itura cum illo **H** // **22** ardebit Γ ardeat **H** // **23** meret **W²BV** meretur **HW** / peccati Γ
deest in **H** / autem Γ vero **H** // **24** quemadmodum testificatur Γ inquit **H** // **24**–p.172,22
Lex ... fugavit Γ *deest in* **H** // **29** nostra **WW²** nostri **BV**

129. In this way they deceive unwary girls, covering over the yawning chasms of evil with their veneer of goodness, as the fowler hides the bird-lime under food and the fisherman places bait on the hook. A girl should reflect on these things before she is seized by repentance when it is too late and begins to have some sense when all is of no avail. But if you expel love altogether, then as if restored to health and regaining your eyesight, you will understand that as with innumerable other blessings you will be forever indebted to God for this favor of having delivered you from the ranks of the foolish and placed you among the wise. What holy Christian or pagan woman who had any reputation for wisdom and decency ever fell in love with anyone except her husband? You would not wish to be loved by this kind of love nor would you kindle passion in a man by devious arts, knowing that the fire will easily spread to you because of its proximity. Some women boast that they have lovers whom they enflame of set purpose. These women are led by the devil on this hunt and through the lavishing of their beauty, adornment and conversation they spread the net no less for themselves than for their quarry and they make the safeguarding of their chastity all the more difficult, as it is the target and object of so many men's assaults.

130. It is difficult to hold on to what so many are intent to wrest away from you. They justly merit the fate predicted by Jesus, son of Sirach: 'If one throws a stone into the air, it will fall on his own head and a treacherous blow will wound the one who perpetrated it. He who digs a ditch will fall into it and he who places a stone in his neighbor's path will stumble upon it himself. He who lays a snare for another will perish in it.' Foolish girl, don't you see that by driving him into the devil's snare by your deception you will fall into it together with him and so receive the reward for your service? He will burn because he was defeated by the devil and you because you were victorious thanks to the devil. Each of you will merit ample reward for your sin. 'The wages of sin is death' as the Apostle testifies. The law of Christ, which is the standard of mutual love, places the soul of one's neighbor not only above external raiment and all incidental things, but above the body itself and blood and life of each of us. All of us set out on our journey intent and unencumbered, pressing on to our destined goal of eternal happiness. As it befits us to rejoice when by example, precept or encouragement we have been of profit to our brother in his striving after virtue, so we should be sad when he becomes worse because of us. If the Lord detests those through whom scandal comes, what will become of him who knowingly and wittingly casts obstacles in the path of his neighbor, which he will run into with grave consequences?

131. Nec secus maerebit proba femina se alicui occasionem aut ansam fuisse flagitii quam si a se esset occisus. Quanto scilicet levius est cervicem iugulare quam animam et a trunco separare caput quam animam a Deo. Sine anima morietur corpus, vivet nihilo setius anima; sine Deo nec corpus nec anima. Quocirca studebit femina diligenti opera ut eum revocet ad mentem quem ipsa dementarit. Primum, quantum poterit verbis et bene admonendo, quae si parum proficiant, aversione sui et reiectione illius. Rarius cum illo colloquetur, rarius se illi aspiciendam offeret, minuet ea quibus ille est captus, formam, venustatem, cultum, sermonem. Cogitabit illis non ornari se quae ruinam fratri praebent, sed diaboli se exhibere administram ad offensam Dei. Non potest Christianus appellari qui vel cum impendio proprii corporis salutem fraternae animae non procurat. In historiis nationum legimus adolescentem eximiae formae, cum in se videret puellas aliquot exardescere, cultello faciem suam deformasse. O exemplum omnium feminarum! O adolescentem illustri memoria dignum! Id fecit et vir et gentilis. Christiana virgo aut mulier pilum unum de cultu, de verbis, de colloquiis non detrahet quibus et perimit fratrem et maiestatem violat Christi? Nec feminis in suo sexu desunt exempla si imitari meliora est animus. Fuit Barcini quae ut amatorem suum perditum ad mentem revocaret brassicas putres sub axillis aliquamdiu tenuit. Edit item brassicas crudas et propius ad amatorem accedens tamquam secretum colloquium expetens taeterrimo illo foetore in perpetuum ab se illum absterruit ac fugavit.

CAP. XIV.   DE AMORE VIRGINIS

132. Et quando hominum mentes aptae atque appositae sunt ad amandum, ostendam tibi puros et sanctos amores, qui amorem hunc pravum atque adulterinum extrudant. Habes primum quem ames, Patrem Deum, sponsum Christum. Habes Matrem eius et sororem tuam, Divam Virginem. Habes tui similem, Dei Ecclesiam. Habes tot virgines sanctissimas quarum animae in caelis agunt beatae, nomina in terris sacrata sunt. Habes parentes qui te genuerunt, qui tibi sunt Dei vice, qui te tanto labore aluerunt, tanta educarunt caritate ac cura, quos et ames et quantum opis erit tuae iuves, eorum iussa semper habeas sacrosancta modesteque illis obtemperes; nec in animo sit nec vultu aut gestu aliquam prae te feras contumaciam putesque

---

11 administram **W** ministram **W²BV** ∥ 24–26 Et ... extrudant **Γ** At ne omnino amoribus puella careat. Nam videtur hominum genus ad amorem esse appositum et concinnatum ut inter se caritate quadam copuletur, sed non Cupidine isto, nec Venere terrestri carnea, spurca, caeterum caelesti, (ut inquit Plato) spiritali, quae sanctos amores immittit. **H** ∥ 28 tui similem **Γ** *deest in* **H** / Dei Ecclesiam **Γ** Ecclesiam Dei **H** ∥ 31 caritate ac **Γ** *deest in* **H** ∥ 32 obtemperes **Γ** pareas **H** ∥ 33 prae te feras **Γ** ostendas **H**

131. An upright woman will feel the same grief for having been the occasion of sin to a person as she would if she had killed him. How much less serious, obviously, is it to cut a man's throat than to annihilate his soul or to sever his head from his body rather than his soul from God. The body will die without the soul, but the soul will live on. But without God neither the body nor the soul will live. Therefore a woman will strive with strenuous effort to bring back to his right senses a man whom she has driven mad. She will do this first by words and admonitions, as much as she can, and if these are of no profit, by keeping away from him herself and by rejecting him. She will speak to him more rarely and see him more rarely. She will de-emphasize the things that ensnared him—beauty, charm, adornment, conversation. She will resolve not to adorn herself with those things that bring about the destruction of her brother and make of her a minister of the devil and cause offense to God. One cannot be called a Christian who does not even at the risk of his own body procure the salvation of his brother's soul. In pagan chronicles we read that a young man of exceptional beauty, seeing that some young girls were passionately in love with him, disfigured his face with a knife. What an example for all women! O noble young man worthy of illustrious memory! This was done by a man, and a pagan. Will a Christian girl or woman not sacrifice one tiny bit of her adornment, her words and conversations, by which she both destroys her brother and violates the majesty of Christ? There is no lack of examples for women from their own sex if they have a mind to imitate what is better. There was a woman of Barcelona who in order to bring her desperate lover back to his senses kept rotten cabbages under her armpits for a period of time. She also ate raw cabbage and drawing close to her lover as if to initiate a conversation she frightened him off with the foul odor and chased him away forever.

CHAPTER 14.   ON THE LOVE BEFITTING A VIRGIN

132. And since human minds have a tendency and aptitude for loving, I shall point out to you pure and holy loves that will drive away this depraved and adulterated love. You have first of all one whom you can love, God the father, and your spouse, Christ. You have his mother and your sister, the Blessed Virgin. You have one like yourself, the Church of God. You have so many holy virgins, whose souls lead a blessed existence in heaven, and whose names are sanctified on earth. You have your parents, who gave birth to you, who take the place of God, who nourished you with such care, brought you up with such love and solicitude, whom you can love, and when there is need of it, help. You must hold their commands as sacrosanct and obey them with all humility. Do not show in mind, countenance or gesture any defiance towards them and think of them as a true and solid image of God,

illos imaginem quandam solidam et veram tibi referre illius rerum omnium parentis Dei. Habes animum tuum tibi vel naturae voce commendatum. Habes in aliis virtutes et animos Christo deditos. Habes eos qui te cupiunt salvam atque incorruptam, denique aeternam laetitiam summamque illam et numquam finiendam felicitatem. Hi demum sunt veri ac recti amores. Nam ille corporum fictus est verique amoris perversus simulator quae libido potius quam amor debet nuncupari. Illa omnia si bona fide amas, nec Deo praepones hominem nec sponso Christo iuvenem scortatorem nec Divae Virgini lenam nec Ecclesiae Dei lupanar nec consortio sanctarum virginum coetum impudicatum nec parentibus extraneos, immo hostes, nec animo tuo corpus nec alienis virtutibus vitia nec animis Christi cultoribus animos diaboli ministros nec eis qui te servatam atque integram esse volunt eos qui perditam et corruptam nec brevissimam et momentaneam delectatiunculam aeternae laetitiae nec inferorum miseriam beatitudini suis omnibus numeris absolutae.

133. Ita magis apud te valebunt Dei iussa quam hominis suasus dolosi et males Christo fidem habere quam verbis impurissimi nebulonis et sequeris potius quo te ducet Diva Virgo quam quo libido et cariorem habebis quem illa tibi conciliarit quam quem lena et Ecclesiae leges non violabis ut serves fornicis et males aggregari inter Catharinas, Agnetes, Claras, Margaritas, Barbaras, Theclas, Agathas quam inter impudicas, quarum ut vita Deo ita et nomina hominibus ignota sunt, utraque sunt diabolo cognita et perscripta. Nec deseres parentes ut amatores sequaris nec aeternam relinques eis animi aegritudinem ut exiguam des fraudulento amatori de te voluptatulam nec males corpori tuo bene esse quam animo et gaudere corpus, tristi mente, nec auscultabis potius quid ex scelere quis dicat quam quid ex virtute nec credes citius satelliti diaboli quam ministro Christi nec committes te ei qui vult perimere, sed qui vult servare, et eliges citius perfecta et aeterna in caelis perfrui laetitia quam hic falsa imagine gaudii attingi, eadem ut fugacissima sic et maerori adeo permista ut maior merito pars maeror dici atque existimari debeat. Tum horrebis magis illam sine fine ullo miseriam quam captabis voluptatem hanc mundi, si modo sit hoc nomine censenda volvesque animo illud sancti viri: 'Momentaneum est quod delectat, aeternum quod cruciat.'

3–4 cupiunt salvam atque incorruptam **Γ** volunt servare **H** ∥ **5–7** Hi … nuncupari **Γ** *deest in* **H** ∥ **7** Illa omnia **Γ** Quae omnia vere **H** / bona fide **Γ** *deest in* **H** ∥ **10** immo hostes **Γ** *deest in* **H** ∥ **11–12** nec alienis … eos **V** nec alienas virtutes vitiis, nec animos Christi cultores animis diaboli ministris, nec eos qui te servatam volunt, iis **HWW²B** ∥ **13** et corruptam **Γ** *deest in* **H** ∥ **17** impurissimi **Γ** incesti **H** ∥ **20** aggregari **Γ** numerari **H** ∥ **20–21** Margaritas, Barbaras **Γ** *deest in* **H** ∥ **22** ignota **Γ** ignorata **H** / et perscripta **Γ** atque explorata **H** ∥ **24** aegritudinem **Γ** maerorem **H** / exiguam **Γ** exiguum **H** / voluptatulam **Γ** gaudium **H** ∥ **28** perimere **Γ** perdere **H** / citius **Γ** potius **H** ∥ **30** atque existimari **Γ** *deest in* **H** ∥ **31** ullo **Γ** *deest in* **H**

creator of all things. You have your own soul to love, commended to you by the voice of nature. You have in others virtues and minds dedicated to Christ. You have those who wish you to be safe and uncorrupted; finally you have eternal joy and that highest and never-ending happiness. These are in the end true and right loves. For physical love is feigned and a perverse imitator of true love. It should more justly be called lust rather than love. If you love all those things in good faith, you will neither prefer man to God nor a young libertine to your spouse, Christ, nor a procuress to the Blessed Virgin, nor a brothel to the Church of God, nor immoral companions to the company of holy virgins, nor outsiders or even enemies to your parents, nor your body to your soul, nor vices to other people's virtues, nor souls subservient to the devil to souls dedicated to Christ, nor those who wish to ruin and corrupt you to those who desire your salvation and integrity, nor a brief and ephemeral pleasure to eternal happiness, nor the misery of the damned to perfect beatitude.

133. Therefore the ordinances of God will have more efficacy for you than the deceitful persuasions of men and you will prefer to place your trust in Christ rather than in the words of a vile scoundrel, and you will follow where the Blessed Virgin leads you and not the promptings of lust, and you will hold dear him whom she commends to you rather than the man procured for you by a brothel-keeper. You will not violate the laws of the Church in order to keep those of the brothel and you will prefer to be numbered among the flock of Catherine, Agnes, Clara, Margaret, Barbara, Thecla, and Agatha rather than among unchaste women, whose names are as unknown to men as their lives are to God, but both their names and their lives are known and recorded by the devil. Do not desert your parents to follow after lovers nor cause them unending anguish of heart in order to give your fraudulent lover some short-lived pleasure; do not prefer the well-being of your body to that of your soul and physical pleasure to sadness of soul. You will not listen to what someone says out of wickedness in preference to what someone says with virtuous intent, nor will you put more credence in a henchman of the devil than in a servant of Christ. Confide not in one who wishes to destroy you but in one who wishes to save you, and choose to enjoy perfect and eternal happiness in heaven rather than to be touched by the false image of joy here on earth, which is not only fleeting, but so mixed with sadness that it might more rightly be called and thought of as sadness. Then you will shun more that unhappiness without end than aspire after the pleasure of this world, if indeed it deserves this name, and you will meditate on that saying of a holy man: 'Present delights are momentary, torment is eternal.'

In te ergo, tot ac tantis amoribus stipata ac freta Dei, Christi, Mariae, Ecclesiae, virginum, parentum, tui ipsius, beatitudinis divinae, quis patebit obscenitati aditus? Non erit tam impudens et temerarius Cupido ut impetere locum non reformidet tam venerandis custodibus munitum ac saeptum, qui
5 Musas studiorum causa reveretur. Quod si ausit, in illum certe suum sibi telum retorquebitur, nam ubi haereat in eiusmodi puella non inveniet.

CAP. XV.   DE QUAERENDO SPONSO

134. Humanum genus, mortale in singulis, suffectione sobolis fit perpetuum et ut soboles sancta sit ac pura Deus coniugium instituit, quo auctore
10 servire possumus naturae sine peccato. Ideo Paulus ait: 'Qui virginem suam viro collocet non malefacere, tantum in Domino.' Et quandoquidem vir quaeritur feminae socius fortunarum omnium publice ac privatim comesque individuus ac inseparabilis, ut sola alterutrius mors possit illos seiungere, maior est et gravior haec deliberatio quam pro hominum opinione, cum
15 ex iis sit in quibus, sicut dici solet, non est bis peccare. Si semel peccatum sit, ferendum est deinceps quicquid acciderit, velis nolis. Quocirca maximo opere providendum est ne aberretur. Vera virginitas coniunctionem sexus nec novit nec appetit ac ne cogitat quidem, ab omni illius sensu beneficio caelesti vindicata et libera. Itaque virgo, dum parentes de ipsius condicione
20 consultant, totam eiusmodi curam ad illos releget qui et ei non minus bene cupiunt quam ipsamet sibi, face a natura in illorum pectoribus accensa et per aetatem atque usum rerum longius prospiciunt. Quomodo enim poterit puella domi clausa virorum nosse mores atque ingenia ut sibi ex illis deligat, vel ignara rerum, quid expediat videre?
25   **135.** Apud Homerum autem, cum Nausicaa per quietem esset a Minerva submonita uti vestes ablueret, breviter futura sponsa, illa currum ab Alcinoo patre petiit ut in flumine vestes lavaret, aliam tamen praetendens causam; nam eam vel coniugii meminisse puduit. Quod imitatus Vergilius in duodecimo Aeneidos, cum Latinum et Amatam coniuges colloquentes fecisset cum

134. (Qui ... Domino) *Vulg. I Cor. 7, 38–39*
135. (Nausicaa ... puduit) *Hom. Od. 6, 66* // (Latinum ... deliberant) *Verg. Aen. 12, 64–66* //

1 In te **Γ** Tibi **H** / stipata ac freta **Γ** occupatae **H** // **2–3** patebit obscenitati aditus **Γ** vacabit obscenitati locus **H** // **3–4** ut ... reformidet **Γ** ut feriendum sibi eum locum putet **H** // **4–5** qui Musas **Γ** qui etiam Musas **H** // **5** studiorum causa **Γ** *deest in* **H** // **5** Quod si **Γ** Et si **H** // **6** eiusmodi **Γ** *deest in* **H** // **8–28** Humanum ... imitatus **Γ** *deest in* **H** // **27** flumine **BV** flumen **WW²** // **28–29** Vergilius in duodecimo Aeneidos **Γ** Sapiens poeta libro duodecimo Aeneidos **H** // **29–p.178,1** coniuges colloquentes ... destinabatur **Γ** coniuges cum Turno colloquentes fecisset; Laviniae, cui Turnus maritus destinabatur **H**

When you are surrounded and protected by so many great loves, love of God, of Christ, of Mary, of the Church, of virgins, of parents, of yourself, of divine beatitude, what approach will lie open to obscene behavior? Cupid will not be so rash and impudent as not to dread attacking a place fortified and hedged in by such respected sentinels, since he is one who reveres the Muses for their studious pursuits. But if he should hazard an attack, his shaft will be turned back upon himself, for in a girl of this sort the arrow will not find a vulnerable spot.

CHAPTER 15.   ON SEEKING A SPOUSE

134. The human race, mortal in each of its members taken singly, becomes eternal through the supply of offspring, and so that this offspring would be holy and pure God instituted marriage, by whose sanction we may serve nature without sin. Therefore Paul said; 'He who gives his daughter to a man in marriage does not act wrongly, as long as it is done in the Lord.' And since a man is sought for a woman to share all her fortunes publicly and privately, as her indivisible and inseparable companion so that only the death of either party can separate them, this decision is greater and more serious than people think, being one of those in which, as it is said, you cannot err twice. If an error has been made once, whatever happens afterwards must be suffered, whether you like it or not. Therefore the greatest care must be taken not to make a mistake. True virginity knows nothing of sexual union nor seeks after it and indeed does not even think of it, being protected and free of all such feelings through a heavenly gift. Therefore when her parents are deliberating about her marriage, the young woman will leave all of that concern to those who wish her well as much as she does herself through the love enkindled in their hearts by nature, and who by their years and experience see further ahead. For how can a girl who has been confined within the walls of her house know the character and morals of men so that she can choose among them, or in her complete inexperience know what she should observe?

135. In Homer when Nausicaa was instructed in her sleep by Minerva to wash her clothes, since she was soon to be married, she asked her father Alcinous for the chariot so that she might wash her clothes in the river, but gave another excuse, for she was ashamed even to mention her marriage. Imitating this passage in the twelfth book of the *Aeneid*, in which he has Latinus and his wife Amata talking to Turnus, the future spouse of their

Turno; Laviniae illorum filiae, cui Turnus destinabatur, lacrimas tantum dedit et ruborem, non verba, significans virginem non decere interloqui ubi mater et pater de connubio ipsius deliberant. Romanus olim mos fuit inter matronas illas, exemplaria pudicitiae, ut nupta, quo primum die ad mariti aedes deducebatur, ipsa per se non ingrederetur mariti limen, sed intro ferretur sublata; ceu vi quadam reluctans et invita in eum veniret locum ubi virgineum decus esset amissura. Quomodo id potest virgo simulare quae ultro nuptias expetiit et postulavit?

136. De Rebecca sic loquitur Divus Ambrosius: 'Non est virginalis pudoris eligere maritum, sed iam desponsata viro, de profectionis consulitur die. Nec immerito dilationem non attulit. Iure etenim properare debuit ad maritum. Unde illud Euripideum quod mirantur plerique unde translatum sit, manifestum est. Ait enim in persona mulieris quae tamen maritum volebat relinquere et ad alias petebatur nuptias: "Sponsalium quidem meorum pater meus curam subibit, hoc enim non est meum;" ergo, quod et ipsi philosophi mirati sunt, servate virgines.' Tantum Ambrosius, qui ne viduis quidem permittit ut ipsae sibi condicionem quaerant. In oratione Sarae, filiae Raguelis, haec sunt verba: 'Tu scis, Domine Deus, quod numquam concupivi virum et mundam servavi animam meam ab omni concupiscentia. Numquam cum ludentibus miscui me neque cum iis qui in levitate ambulant participem me praebui.' Quemadmodum vero ait viros sibi a parentibus traditos suscepisse audiamus: 'Virum' inquit 'cum timore tuo, non cum libidine mea consensi suscipere.'

137. Puella igitur, dum illa cogitatio parentes occupat, votis ac compreca-tionibus negotium adiuvet. Poscat purissimo affectu a Christo ut is contingat sponsus qui a pietate non deterreat, non avertat aut impediat, sed invitet, ad-hortetur, adiuvet et iuxta vaticinium Apostoli: 'Sanctificetur mulier infidelis

135. (Romanus olim mos) *Plut. mor. 271D*
136. (Non est ... virgines) *Ambr. Abr. 1, 91, PL 14, 153C* // (Sponsalium ... meum) *Eur. Andr. 987–988* // (Tu ... praebui) *Vulg. Tob. 3, 16–17* // (Virum ... suscipere) *Vulg. Tob. 3, 18*
137. (Sanctificetur ... fidelem) *Vulg. I Cor. 7, 14*

2 interloqui Γ loqui **H** // **3** de connubio ipsius deliberant Γ et coniugio ipsius verba faciunt, sed totam curam parentibus mandare, a quibus non diligitur minus quam a se, nec minus sibi consulturos parentes existimet quam sibi ipsam. Primum usu rerum et prudentia maiore, deinde caritate non minore. Adde quod decorum non est virginem vel optare nuptias vel certe hoc declarare. **H** / olim Γ *deest in* **H** // **5** aedes Γ domum **H** / mariti Γ viri **H** // **6–7** ceu vi quadam ... amissura Γ ceu vi quod indicaret, eam non ultro ad eum locum venire, ubi amissura virginitatem esset **H** // **7–23** Quomodo ... suscipere Γ *deest in* **H** // **24** Puella igitur Γ Ipsa ergo **H** // **24–25** ac comprecationibus Γ *deest in* **H** // **25** Christo Γ Christo eiusque matre **H** // **26** qui pietate non ... impediat Γ qui non deterreat aut impediat a cultu pietatis **H** // **27**–p.180,**33** et iuxta ... admonere Γ *deest in* **H**

daughter, Lavinia, Virgil merely makes reference to her tears and maidenly modesty, but does not have her speak a word. By this he wished to signify that it does not befit a young woman to speak when her mother and father are discussing her marriage. It was an ancient Roman custom among those famous matrons, examples of modesty, that on the day when the bride was escorted to her husband's house, she did not cross the threshold herself but was carried in as if she unwillingly and forcibly entered that place where she would lose the honor of her virginity. How can a young woman pretend to do this when she has sought and asked for the marriage of her own will?

136. St. Ambrose says this of Rebecca: 'It is not becoming to virginal modesty to choose a husband, but once a girl is betrothed to a man she is consulted about the day of the procession. And with good reason she did not interpose any delay. It was fitting that she hasten to her husband. Hence the clarity of that saying of Euripides, which made many people wonder where it came from. He said in the person of a woman who wished to leave her husband and was sought after for another marriage: 'My father will attend to my marriage, for that is not mine to decide.' Therefore, young women, observe this modesty, which even the philosophers marvelled at.' So says Ambrose, who does not even permit widows to look after their marital situation. In the prayer of Sarah, daughter of Raguel, we find these words: 'You know, Lord God, that I never desired a man, and I kept my soul free of all concupiscence. I never joined in with those who play nor did I share the company of those who walk in fickleness.' Let us hear how she says she received the men who were given to her by her parents: 'I have consented to take a man out of respect for you, not because of my desire.'

137. Therefore, when her parents are engaged in these considerations the young girl should help them by her prayers and supplications. Let her ask of Christ with purest intention that she be given a spouse who will not discourage, distract or impede her from the practice of piety, but will invite, exhort and assist her, and according to the prediction of the Apostle: 'Let the unbelieving wife be sanctified by the believing husband.' In making this

per virum fidelem.' Parentes ipsi non modo in consilio eiusce rei capiendo caritatem patrum in liberos obtineant et praestent, sed affectum quoque induant puellae, ut ita eligant quemadmodum si ipsi essent nupturi. Multi enim vel imprudentes patres vel mali peccant in deliberando quod quem sibi ipsi commodum generum putant eundem credunt bonum fore maritum filiae. Ita saepe numero divitias solas vel sanguinem vel opes ac potentiam spectant generi, quae sibi utilia rentur fore, non ea quae expedient filiae, domi cum illo intra eosdem parietes habitanti. Eiusmodi homines hostes sunt, non parentes, seu, ut aptius dicam, negotiatores filiarum, qui illas impendunt ut sibi sit bene.

138. Non est nodus qui possit dissolvi. Si quo sis filium missurus coenatum, diligenter prius inquiris qui sint convivae; si quo peregre, qui sint futuri viae comites; si asseclam, si famulum admittis, qui sit, cuias, quibus propinquis, quibus moribus, qua fide. Haec omnia quanta sedulitate scrutaris cum illae tamen adiunctiones brevissimi sint temporis? Tenellae tuae virgini, rerum omnium ignarae ac rudi, quae tibi fidit uni, in cuius manibus spes omnes suas et vota collocat, non alium habitura quam quem ipse dederis socium, non aliam fortunam et sortem, non dubitas adiungere qualem non velis habere servum, tam accommodum societati quam vel ursum vel lupum vel suem. Haud iniuria proverbium usurpant illud Galli: 'Non esse feliciter natum qui non sit feliciter maritatus,' ut infortunatum coniugium nobilitati, formae, valetudini, opibus ac potentiae, ad miseriam praegravet. Quod si iure de viro id dicunt, quanto causatius de femina, cui tanto est accuratius providendum ut probus contingat vir quam contra viro ut proba femina, quanto videlicet levius est imperare malo quam parere.

139. In coniugio duo sunt spectanda, convictus et soboles. In priore sunt victus, hinc usus familiaris et consuetudo quotidiana. Prima cura debet esse victus, sed ea levissima, secunda corporis mariti, tertia sobolis, quarta et potissima morum atque ingenii, de quibus praecipiemus singillatim. Sed in his omnibus in universum est curandum ut aequalitas sit quaedam vel similitudo verius inter virum et puellam qua nihil tenacius animos et copulat et continet. Artissimum est enim amoris vinculum similitudo idque videtur admonere Pittacus Mytilenaeus, qui fuit unus ex septem illis

---

139. (Pittacus ... congruat) *Diog. Laert. 1, 80; Plut. mor. 13F* //

29 singillatim *scr.* sigillatim Γ // **33**–p.184,**22** Pittacus Mytilenaeus ... quam bonum herum Γ Patres dictum ilud in mentem revocent Themistoclis Graeciae principis, qui consultus a quadam utri collocaret filiam, diviti malo an pauperi bono, 'Malim' (inquit) 'virum sine pecunia quam pecuniam sine viro.' Tum etiam factum Pittaci Mytilenaei, quem cum rogasset iuvenis quem duae appetebant, altera opulentissima et genere magno, altera ipsi aequalis et genere et opibus, utram duceret, sapiens illum ad pueros ludentes remisit qui ex ludi legibus subinde clamitabant: 'Tu tibi sume parem,' admonens hoc esse faciendum. Magna

decision parents should not only have and exhibit the affection of parents towards their children, but they should also assume the feelings of their daughter so they make a choice that they would make if they themselves were to marry. It often happens that many parents, whether unknowingly or through deliberate malice, act wrongly in this decision because they think that the son-in-law whom they deem desirable for themselves would also be a good husband for their daughter. Often they look only to riches, noble lineage, wealth and power in their son-in-law, things that will be to their own advantage, not what is best for their daughter, who must live with him within the same walls. These are enemies, not parents, or to put it more aptly, vendors of their own daughters, whom they sell for their own advantage.

138. Marriage is a knot that cannot be untied. If you are going to let your son go out to dinner, you will first carefully inquire who the invited guests are. If he is to undertake a journey, you will find out who will accompany him. If you admit a dependent or servant into your house, you will inquire who he is, from what country he hales, who are his relatives, what are his morals, and what is his trustworthiness. With what scrupulosity you will investigate all these matters, although they are associations of brief duration. For your tender young daughter, innocent and inexperienced in worldly affairs, who puts all her trust in you, and places all her hopes and aspirations in your hands, who will have no other partner in life but the one you give her and no other future or destiny, will you have no qualms about coupling her with a person whom you would not wish for a servant, who is as ill-adapted to human fellowship as a bear, a wolf, or a pig? The French proverb is to the point: 'He who is not happily married was not happily born.' So much does unhappy marriage outweigh nobility, beauty, health, wealth and power and lead to complete misery. If this can be said of a man, how much more truly can it be said of a woman, for whom greater diligence must be exercised in procuring a good husband than a good woman for a man, since it is easier to rule over an evil person than to obey one.

139. Two things should be considered in marriage: living together and offspring. The first includes the necessities of life, hence family life and daily habit. First, care must be given to material sustenance, although that is of little consequence; second the physical well-being of the husband; third the offspring; and fourth and most important, character and morals, all of which I shall discuss one by one. In all of this one thing must be heeded, that there be a certain equality, or better, similarity between man and wife, which unites their souls and holds them together more tenaciously than anything else. Likeness is the tightest bond of love, which was what Pittacus of Mytilene, the most famous of the Seven Sages of ancient Greece, taught.

138. French proverb: A proverb from Auvergne illustrates this: 'Un homme mal marié, il vaudrait mieux qu'il fût noyé.'

Graeciae sapientibus celebratissimus. Hunc enim cum adolescens, quem duae appetebant, altera genere et opibus superior altera par, utram duceret rogasset, sapiens illum ad lusitantes pueros remisit, qui subinde clamitabant, λάβε καθ' ἑαυτόν, 'Sume quae tibi congruat,' innuens hoc esse faciundum.

5 Minima est quidem ac, si pretium recte aestimetur, infima tuendi corporis cogitatio, sed inevitabilis necessitas effecit ut esset, si non maxima, certe prima. Si filiae tantum es pecuniae collaturus in dotem, quantum satis sit familiae sustinendae, totam tuam curam ad generi ipsius considerationem transfer, quo sit corpore, quo animo. Si illum aliquid necesse est conferre,

10 intuendum non quam magnas possidet divitias, sed quam artem vel parandi quae non habet vel conservandi parta. Nullae sunt tantae opes quae si tueri ac retinere nescias, non brevi exhauriantur tempore. Themistoclis Graeciae principis consilium fuit de condicione quaerenda malle se virum sine pecunia quam pecuniam sine viro. Qui nec artem callet bonae frugis aliquam nec

15 pecuniam possidet, hunc servituti aptiorem deputo quam connubio.

140. Matrimonium esse non debet sine patrimonio, ut alterum videatur adferre femina, nempe matronae virtutes et facultatem pariendi filios, alterum vir, quod ad vitam sustentandam pertinet. Et in artibus vitae sunt quaedam fugiendae omnino ut flagitiosae: velut ea quae rem facit

20 pecunia faenori data. Crudeles item atque inhumanae, quales sunt carnificum, piratarum, militum mercenariorum, qui exigui quaestus gratia manus suas accommodant iugulandis hominibus, depopulandis agris, exurendis aedificiis, quo nihil dici potest immanius. Sunt aliae probrosae, ut ubique cauponum, interpolatorum, mediastinorum; ad quos non descendemus nisi

25 vel desperata condicione alia quacumque vel si de eadem et nos simus nota. Immodicae opes et nostris longe superiores insolentes reddunt maritos et uxorum despectiores, quibus non tamquam legitime coniunctis, sed ut ancillis abutuntur, eoque magis si opulentiae accedat potentia vel generis claritudo.

30 **141.** In corpore contemplamur formam, aetatem, valetudinem; exiguum bonum et momentaneum est forma, nec deformitas impedire coniugium debet si adsint reliqua, modo ne omnino foedissma sit et portentosa. Aetas magis est spectanda, ne sit vel minor quam exigat auctoritas patrisfamilias, qui uxorem, liberos et familiam possit regere, neu maior quam ut suppetant

---

139. (Themistoclis . . . viro) *Val. Max. 7, 2, 9*

cura est deligere filiae maritum nec leviter est suscipiendum. Non est nodus qui facile solvatur: sola illum mors rumpit. Aut in perpetuam felicitatem adducunt parentes filias, si bonis dant viris, aut in miseriam totius vitae, si malis. Hic multum cogitandum, versandum animo, consulendum, deliberandum antequam statuas. Multa sunt in coniugio fastidiia, multa toleranda molestissima. Unica res potest feminae facere coniugium leve: si bonus et prudens contingat vir. **H**

When asked by a young man whom he should marry of two women who sought him in marriage, one superior to him in family and wealth, the other equal to him, the wise man directed him to a group of boys who were playing and shouting out: 'Take what belongs to your sphere.' By this he intimated what the young man should do. Of very little concern, and, if its right value be esteemed, of least importance, is thought for the sustenance of the body. But unavoidable necessity has dictated that if not the greatest concern, it is at any rate the first. If you have to collect enough money for the bride as a dowry to provide for the maintenance of the family, concentrate all your attention on the son-in-law, on his physical and moral qualities. If he must contribute something, you must consider not what riches he possesses but how he will acquire what he does not have and how he will hold on to what he has acquired. There are no resources so great that if you do not know how to protect and maintain them they are exhausted in a short time. The advice of the Greek leader Themistocles concerning the choosing of a marriage partner was that he preferred a man without money to money without a man. One who is not adept at being thrifty and does not possess any money I esteem more worthy of slavery than of marriage.

140. A marriage should not be without patrimony. The woman brings one thing, namely womanly virtues and the ability to bring forth children, and the man's contribution is to provide sustenance. Of life's occupations some should be avoided altogether as dishonorable, such as that which accumulates wealth by lending out money at interest. Others are cruel and inhuman, such as the occupations of executioners, pirates and mercenary soldiers who for the sake of small gain lend their efforts to the slaughter of human beings, the devastation of lands and the burning of buildings, acts of the most savage brutality. There are other disreputable livelihoods, such as those of innkeepers and go-betweens, to which we will not descend unless our circumstances are even more desperate or we are branded with the same stigma. Immoderate wealth, far superior to our own, makes husbands insolent and disdainful of their wives, whom they regard not so much as legitimate spouses as servants, all the more so if joined to wealth are power or illustrious ancestry.

141. In the body we consider beauty, age and health. Beauty is a slight and short-lived blessing, and ugliness should not be an impediment to marriage if the other qualities are not missing, unless it is truly horrendous and abominable. Age is a more important factor, which should not be less than what is required to exercise paternal authority and to govern wife, children and servants, nor too advanced to possess the strength necessary for domestic

139. 'Take what belongs to your sphere.': Refers to a game in which children spun tops.

vires ad munia domestica, neve prima statim inter initia coniugii filiis
adhuc infantibus concedat naturae uxoremque ac liberos praesidio suo
orbatos destituat. Valetudinis maior est habenda ratio, tum propter domus
ac familiae munia, quae sanum rectorem crebro postulant, tum propter
5   uxorem et liberos, quos morbo suo inficit si sit contagiosus, idque tanto est
cavendum accuratius si taeter sit morbus atque abominabilis et ex iis quos
medici hereditarios nominant. Quid dicam si sit insaniae aut dementiae genus
quod multis exemplis deprehendimus ad posteros transferri? Illuc potissimum
dixi curam et cogitationem universam debere conferri ut ingenium ac mores
10 contemplemur. Haec est una hominis censura, hinc homo est aestimandus:
nihil vel in corpore est vel in fortunis unde iudicium fieri possit certum
de homine: non divitiae, non possessiones, non genus, non potentia, non
gratia, non dignitas, non clientelae, non forma, valetudo, aetas, integritas,
proceritas, non horum adversa; nihil denique praeter ingenium, in quo sunt
15 acumen, eruditio virtutes; vel contra hebetudo, ruditas vitia.

142. Multa in connubii cursu molesta intercurrunt, multa sunt devoranda
fastidiosa et gravia. Praedicebat hoc Paulus de coniugibus: 'Infirmitates
carnis habebunt hi.' Multae res exacerbare possunt hoc vitae genus, unica
vero condire ac levare, si bonus et prudens contingit vir. Proba mulier
20 peculiare est donum Dei viro (ut inquit Sapiens), quod illi pro benefactis
confertur. Quid mulieri probus vir, nisi forte iucundius ac felicius censemus
bonum habere famulum quam bonum herum? O stultos parentes! O insanas
et vecordes puellas, quae vel formosos vel locupletes vel nobiles bonis
praefertis! Augetis vobis curas, anxietates, molestias quas per se se adfert
25 ipsum connubium. Calamitosa sunt coniugia quae sola conciliat vel pecunia
vel voluptas, ut Helenae et Paridis; quorum illa opes Asianas concupivit, hic
vero voluptatem egregiae formae. E diverso placidum ac felix fuit Ulyssis ac
Penelopis consortium: quippe vir erat sobrius et sapiens, uxor moderata et
casta.
30 **143.** Si quis esset de numero aliquo electurus viae comitem, an non
furiosum eum omnes iudicarent si divitem libentius sumeret aut bene
vestitum aut speciosum quam hilarem et facundum, qui est in itinere pro
vehiculo, sicut habet vetus sententia, aut prudentem ac providum, a quo
et taedium levari posset itineris et in periculis adiuvari? Quod si nihil est
35 vita aliud quam via, quanta vecordia est eam quae ex se est undique
tot incommodorum referta pluribus adhuc augere discordia coniugum!

---

142. (Infirmitates ... hi) *Vulg. Rom. 6, 9* // (Proba ... confertur) *Vulg. prov. 12, 4; 18, 22*
143. (pro vehiculo) *Publil. A. 17* //

22–23 insanas et vecordes **Γ** stultas **H** // 23 locupletes **Γ** divites **H** // 23–24 bonis
praefertis **Γ** praefertis bonis, habiturae perpetuum cruciatum **H** // 24–36 Augetis ...
coniugum **Γ** *deest in* **H** // 27 Ulissis **Γ** = Ulixis

obligations nor such that at the very beginning of the marriage, while the children are still infants, he should pay his debt to nature and leave wife and children bereft of his support. Much attention should be given to good health both for the sake of household duties, which often demand a healthy person at the helm, and for wife and children, whom he will afflict with his illness if it is contagious. This is to be guarded against all the more carefully if it is a foul and horrible disease, one of those that doctors call hereditary. And what should be said of insanity or some form of mental illness which is proven by many examples to be transmitted to posterity? The greatest care and consideration, as I said previously, must be given to the future husband's character and morals. This is the one criterion we should use. On this we must base our judgement. There is nothing in physical attributes or material well-being that can provide us with a sure estimation of a man, not riches, possessions, race, power, influence, dignity, entourage, beauty, health, age, soundness of body, stature, nor their opposites, nothing, in a word, but native ability, in which are to be found intelligence, learning, virtues, or their opposites, dullness, ignorance and vice.

142. Many unpleasant things occur during the course of a marriage, many distasteful and painful things must be swallowed. Paul made this prediction of spouses: 'They will have infirmities of the flesh.' Many things can irritate this way of life. Only one thing can make it palatable and alleviate it, the good fortune of having a good and wise husband. An upright woman is a singular gift of God to a man, as the wise man said, which is conferred upon him for his good deeds. What is a good man to a woman? Surely we do not think it more pleasant and profitable to have a good servant rather than a good master. O stupid parents! O senseless and foolish girls who prefer handsome, rich or noble spouses to good ones. You increase your cares, anxieties, and troubles, which a marriage brings with it of itself. Marriages based on money or sensual pleasure are disastrous, like that of Helen and Paris, she desirous of the riches of Asia and he lusting after exceptional physical beauty. In contrast, the union between Ulysses and Penelope was happy and peaceful since he was a sober-minded and wise husband, she a temperate and chaste wife.

143. If one were to choose a companion for a journey out of a fixed number of men, would she not be accounted mad by everyone if she should prefer a rich or well-dressed or handsome man over one who was cheerful and eloquent, who is like a vehicle upon the journey, as the ancient proverb has it, or wise and provident, who can mitigate the tedium of the journey and be a helper in danger? If life is nothing but a journey, what madness it is to increase the host of difficulties with which it is encumbered

Nubis formoso, hunc species fastuosum reddet. Nubis diviti, hunc divitiae fastidiosum. Nubis nobili, hunc genus insolentem. Denique superbia, quae ex fortuitis donis nascitur, non sinet inter vos concordiam bona fide coalescere. Si pulchro formae causa nubis, in quo nec mens est nec probitas nec salis mica, ut est in veteri dicto (quemadmodum usu solet deprehendi, ut in istis elegantibus hospitiis sit hospes turpissimus), eodem consilio nuptias expetieris tabulae aut signi marmorei pulchre delineati ac decolorati. Vis opulentum stolidum propter opes; quin potius auream statuam? Clarum genere, spurcum, intemperantem, propter sanguinem; cur non eadem mente simulacrum Scipionis aut Caesaris? Et quanto esset satius cum signis, tabulis et statuis vitam degere quam cum homine improbo atque intolerabili! Itaque parum apposite mutis rebus assimilavi homines malos; rectius asinis, suibus, ursis, lupis contulissem.

144. Equidem fabulam esse rebar Pasiphaen concubuisse cum tauro. Nunc factum est mihi verisimilius postquam eas vidi quae ab illis non abhorrerent quorum ingenium peius beluino, spurcis videlicet, ebriis, iracundis, stupidis, imprudentissimis, fatuis, immanibus, sanguinariis, qui minus habent hominis quam quaevis ferae. A sapientibus, a moderatis viris fugiunt et abhorrent; ut huiusmodi feminas quidam nostrati carmine iure incessierit, dicens

---

143. (salis mica) *Erasm. ad. LB II, 505F*

1 species fastuosum reddet Γ forma superbum facit **H** // 2–3 Denique ... coalescere Γ *deest in* **H** // 4 Si ... nubis Γ Si formoso iungeris propter formam **H** // 4–5 salis mica Γ mica salis **H** // 5 ut ... dicto Γ *deest in* **H** // 6 elegantibus Γ pulchris **H** / hospes turpissimus Γ turpis hospes **H** // 6–13 eodem consilio ... contulissem Γ Sicut dixit Sapiens ille Graeciae, eadem mente posses, vel signo, aut tabulae nubere. Vis uxor esse stulti opulenti propter opes? Sic velles statuae aureae. Vis nobilis, spurci et intemperantis propter sanguinem, cur non potius statuam Scipionis eligis aut Caesaris? Et quanto esset satius nubere signis, tabulis et statuis quam malis, stultis et insanis viris? Itaque non bene illis improbos et dementes comparavi, melius vel asinis, vel suibus vel leonibus et lupis contulissem **H** // 14 rebar Γ credebam **H** // 14–p.188,14 cum tauro ... recedant Γ cum tauro et alias mulieres taetriora perpetrasse. Nunc mihi factum est verisimilius, postquam feminas vidi libenter cum spurcis et ebriis et iracundis, et stolidis et stupidis et immanibus ac sanguinariis volutari. Quid inter istos et asinos, sues, tauros, apros, ursos interest? Quae malum dementia est eiusmodi hominum generibus delectari (sicut Plutarchus inquit) a sapientibus, ut quaedam faciunt, et modestis viris, non secus atque a venenatis animalibus abhorrere ac fugere? Ut non absurde dixerit quidam nostrati carmine luparum naturae feminas esse in deligendo, quae ex multis masculis, qui sectantur, vilissimum ac putidissimum sumit. Unde et ab eo ingenio translatum est ad mulieres luparum nomen. Atqui viri non capiuntur femina, nisi dos aliqua, vel fortunae, vel corporis, vel ingenii in ea eluceat. Mulieres quaedam saepe amant quosdam, tantum quod nihil amore dignum habent, quo apertius se nulla duci ratione ostendant. Quod dictum est de plerisque, quibus nihil est commercii cum animo, totae corporibus innixae atque commistae, in quas paulo acrius sum invectus, quod hae multos bonos iuvenes dementant et spurcitiae ac stoliditati tradunt, cum studentes feminis placere, vident se aliter illis gratos esse non posse, nisi ab humano ingenio quam longissime recedant **H** // 16 peius **WW²BV** peius est **W**

by adding marital discord. If you marry a handsome man, his beauty will make him conceited; a rich man, his riches will make him contemptuous. Marry a nobleman and his noble birth will make him insolent. Finally pride, which is born of fortuitous gifts, will not allow concord founded on good faith to exist between you. If you marry a handsome man for the sake of his beauty, in whom there is no sense, or honesty, or a grain of salt, as the saying goes, (just as it is usually the case that in the most elegant dwelling places there dwells the most foul of hosts) you might just as well seek to marry a painting or a marble statue that is beautifully carved or painted. Do you wish an insipid rich man for the sake of his riches? Why not marry a golden statue? Do you want someone of illustrious family, but who is filthy and licentious, merely because of his blood? Why not settle for a statue of Scipio or Caesar? How much better it would be to lead your life with images, paintings and statues than with an unprincipled and intolerable man! And yet my comparison of wicked men with mute objects was not altogether apposite. It would have been more accurate to compare them to asses, swine, bears and wolves.

144. I used to think that the mating of Pasiphae with a bull was a fairy tale. Now it has become more plausible, since I have seen women who do not recoil from men whose nature is worse than that of brute beasts—dirty, drunk, wrathful, stupid, imprudent, fatuous, cruel and bloodthirsty, who have less in common with men than with wild beasts, who flee and avoid the company of wise and temperate men. This conduct inspired one of our own writers, in a poem written in the vernacular, to attack them, saying

luparum eas esse naturae in deligendo quae ex multis lupis masculis qui
eam sectantur vilissimum dicitur ac putidissimum sumere, a quo ingenio
translatum est ad mulieres luparum nomen. Atqui viri non tam facile
capiuntur femina, in qua non aliqua sive fortunae sive corporis sive ingenii
5   dos eluceat. Mulieres aliquae saepe amant quosdam, tantum quod amore
nihil penitus dignum habeant, quo apertius declarent se iudicium, rationem,
consilium, mentem flocci non facere, numquam istis duci, quicquid agant,
semper animi morbo impelli rationis experte, immo vero inimico.

145. Dici non potest quantam nobis iuventutis partem eiusmodi cor-
10   rumpant mulieresne appellem an olida morticina? Neque enim tantae
iacturae meminisse possum sine stomacho. Affectant scilicet imperiti iuvenes
et rectioris consilii ignari approbari se puellis quas adamant, quas concu-
piscunt. Vident non posse aliter nisi ab omni honesta arte, a cultu ingenii
ac morum quam longissime recedant. Omnia postponunt amoris imperiis.
15   Itaque amores eiusmodi feminarum simillimi sunt pharmacis veneficae illius
Circes quibus illam homines in beluas mutasse perhibent. Nam quemadmodum pueri lusibus dediti, qui nihil per aetatem altius aut melius sapiunt,
eos admirantur solos, qui in suis illis lusionibus multum valent, sapientium
studia ducunt pro nihilo, quia nec cuiusmodi sint coniectura assequuntur;
20   sic feminae deliciis, voluptatibus lasciviae dementiae addictae, eos demum
sapientissimos opinantur qui illis ipsis rebus sunt demersi quique eis tribu-
unt plurimum. Quicquid autem saniorem mentem resipit velut nugas et
amentiam magno vultus fastidio reiciunt. Stolidos et insanos amant, colunt,
suspiciunt, sapientes esse et existimant et aperte fatentur. Contra vero, sapi-
25   entes contemnunt, aversantur, stultos esse dicunt et insulsos, non aliter quam
incensi febre mellita tamquam fellea respuunt et suibus gratior caeni est odor
quam amaracini.

---

145. (Circes ... mutasse) *Hom. Od. 10, 234* // (suibus ... amaricini) *Lucr. 6, 973*

14–16 Omnia ... perhibent Γ *deest in* H // **16–17** quemadmodum Γ ut H // **17** qui
... sapiunt Γ qui per aetatem altius nil et praestantius sapiunt H // **18** lusionibus multum
valent Γ ludis dextere se gerunt H // **18–19** sapientium ... assequuntur Γ *deest in* H
// **21** sapientissimos Γ sapientes H // **21–p.190,40** qui illis ... antecelluerunt Γ qui
eiusmodi rebus plurimum valent, quicquid saniorem mentem resipit, amentiam censent, ita
eo corruptelae iudiciorum veniunt, ut stultos ament, colant, habeant in pretio, sapientes
existiment; contra vero sapientes aversentur, oderint, despuant, magno fastidio contemnant,
et stultos pronuntient velut incensi febre mellita dicunt fellea, et suibus gratius olet coenum
quam amaricinum. Quid de illis sperandum est, quarum iudicia tam turpiter sunt a vitiis
depravata? At vero puellae, quae votis vel tacitis vel etiam apertis optant eos, in quibus
aliquod ex istis exterius, seu naturae, seu fortunae dotibus, quae vulgo bona dicuntur, enitet
nec curam interiorum habent, quandoquidem nobilius et praestantius, quod in animo est
prae viliore ac despicatiore quod foris existit, contempserunt, dignae sunt quae perpetuum
sentiant dolorem et dent poenas sui errati quam diu vixerint H

that they have the instinct of the she-wolf in choosing a mate, since she is said to choose the vilest and most foul-smelling of the males that follow after her. From this characteristic the name of she-wolf has been transferred to women. Men are not easily captured by women in whom no quality of fortune or physical beauty or talent stands out. Some women love certain men simply because they think nothing is truly worthy of love, so that they care not one whit for discretion, reason, judgement or good sense. These have no influence on them and whatever they do is done under the impulse of this sickness of mind, devoid of reason, or rather totally averse to reason.

145. It cannot be estimated how great a part of our youth is corrupted by this type of—shall I call her a woman or a stinking corpse? I cannot even mention such squandering of life without a feeling of disgust. Inexperienced young men, devoid of better judgement, aspire to receive the approval of the girls they love and desire. They see that this cannot be attained except by dissociating themselves from every honorable practice and from the cultivation of talent and good morals. They make everything subservient to the tyranny of love. Thus love for that type of women is very much like the potions of that famed witch Circe, by which they say she turned men into wild beasts. Just as boys absorbed in their games, who at their age know nothing better or more elevated, have admiration only for those who excel in those games, with no appreciation of the pursuits of wise men which they cannot even imagine, so women addicted to pleasures, sexual license and madness, attribute great wisdom to those who are immersed in such pursuits and who esteem them of great importance. Whatever is redolent of a sounder mind they reject as worthless trash and madness with expressions of great disdain. They love, admire and look up to those that are stupid and insane, consider them wise and openly confess it. On the contrary they despise the wise, avoid them, say they are stupid and insipid, like people burning with fever who spit out things tasting of honey as if it were gall and as swine find the smell of mud better than that of marjoram.

144. she-wolf: 'De natura de lobas son / ciertamente 'n escoger', Pere Torroella, *Maldezir de mugeres* 3, 1-2. He was a bilingual poet (Spanish and Catalan) of the 2nd half of the 15th c. His poems appeared in the *Cancionero general*, published in Valencia in 1511 and 1514.

146. At si scirent quantum prodesse possent multis, commutata iudicandi perversitate, non tam male de illis ipse sentio, quin credam eas et in statuendo et in vita tota sapientiores fore. Ausim dicere apud adolescentes et iuvenes non perinde contionatorum omnium, parentum, magistratuum
5 recta monita atque exhortationes ad virtutem habitura esse virium quantum istarum et mentes sanas et verba mentibus sanis digna. Plurimum auctoritatis habet quicquid ab eo vel dicatur vel fiat quem ames, cui placere studeas; idque legis latorem Lacedaemoniorum sensisse Plutarchus est auctor in Lycurgo.

10 **147.** Memini narrari olim mihi peradulescentulo esse in Hispania civitatem in qua iuventus nobilitatis ex otio atque opulentia coeperit in studia sese luxus proicere, ut nihil curarent praeter convivia, saltationes, amores, lusus et alia exercitia quae minimum vel bonae mentis adferrent vel prudentiae, cum magno seniorum maerore, qui ex iis initiis grandem rei publicae
15 suae iacturam augurabantur; multique eorum noctes ac dies quomodo hisce suorum iuvenum vitiis obviam ire possent inter se consultabant, etenim se mortuis civitatem in perditissimorum hominum manus deventuram videbant. Eorum quidam consilium attulit saluberrimum. Nam cum animadvertisset amatorculos esse hos iuvenes et de voluntate ac iudiciis feminarum
20 plurimum pendere, auctor reliquis senibus fuit ut quisque filiabus suis et nuribus iisque feminis quae ad curam suam pertinerent declararet quo in discrimine sitae essent civitatis res, quae ex florenti ac felice miserrima ac perditissima esset futura, simul primum amentissimi homines administrationem illius suscepissent, feminas vero, quae nunc molliter per opulentiam
25 aetatem agerent, inversis negotiis in egestate atque inopia rerum omnium durissimam toleraturas vitam, unicum restare hisce malis remedium si illae quarum censuris iuventus tantopere tribueret ad prudentiae illos studium curamque publicae salutis exstimularent; id futurum perfacile si saltatorculos, loquaculos, ineptos, scurriles, convivatores, ludibundos aperta significatione
30 fastidii defugerent atque aversarentur; probos autem, moderatos, sobrios, in quibus nonnihil eluceret cordis, comiter ac benevole exciperent, hos laudarent tamquam futuros aliquando columen et tutelam patriae, vituperarent illos ut nequam et perditos adolescentes, nullius frugis et patriae futuros dedecori atque exitio. Placuit senibus consilium, quod et explanatum
35 feminis vehementer est ut in tam manifesto periculo approbatum idque illae acutissime exsecutae sunt. Brevi tempore iuventus ita est commutata ut e profligatissimis ac perditissimis cordatissimi viri evaserint et callentissimi publicae privataeque administrationis, atque illa civitas multo deinceps vigentior fuit sub his iuvenibus quam sub illis senibus fuerat longeque maiores
40 suos iuvenes isti ingenio et rerum usu antecelluerunt.

146. But if they knew how much good they could do for others if they changed their perverse opinions, I have no such low opinion of them as not to believe that they would be more wise in their choices and in their whole way of life. I daresay that the good advice and exhortations to virtue of all preachers, parents and magistrates would not have the same efficacy as the sound minds and words worthy of sound minds of these women. Whatever the one you love or wish to please says or does has very great authority. Plutarch tells us in his life of Lycurgus that the lawgiver of the Spartans understood this.

147. I remember that when I was very young I was told that there was a city in Spain in which the youth of the nobility in their idleness and opulence began to abandon themselves to the pursuit of pleasure to the point that they cared for nothing but banquets, dancing, love affairs, gambling and other pastimes that contributed nothing to good sense or wisdom, to the great grief of the older citizens, who in those beginnings prophesied great ruin for their republic. Many of them deliberated day and night how they could take counter-measures against the vices of these young men for they saw that when they were dead and gone the city would fall into the hands of morally depraved men. One of them had a very salutary plan. Seeing that these young men were aspiring Don Juans and put much faith in the caprices and judgement of women, he suggested to his fellow conspirators that each of them should explain to his daughters and daughters-in-law and those women charged to his care the perilous state of the republic, which from a flourishing and prosperous city would fall into utter wrack and ruin once these crazed men would take over its administration. The result would be that the women, who were then enjoying a luxurious existence in the midst of great opulence, would have to endure a very hard life when present prosperity would be turned into indigence and squalor. The only remedy left to them was that if they, to whose judgement the young men ascribed such importance, were to urge them on to the pursuit of wisdom and interest in the public good. This could easily be achieved if they were to shun the company of the would-be dancers, chatterers, misfits, clowns, banqueters and gamblers, giving open display of their contempt. As for honest, moderate, sober-minded young men, who gave some sign of good sense, they would welcome them with courtesy and kindness. They would praise them as future pillars of the state and would revile the others as worthless and depraved, of no merit, and destined to bring dishonor and ruin upon their country. The plan met with the old men's approval and it was explained to the women with great urgency and approved in view of the evident danger, and they put it into execution with all discretion. Within a short time the young men changed from profligate and debauched youth into men of great sagacity, skilled in public and private administration, and that city emerged more thriving under those young men than it had been under the old men, and in mental ability and experience they far surpassed their ancestors.

148. Miserae, quid facturae estis cum viris auro onustis, mente exhaustis? Num tu mavis maerere semper auro et serico involuta quam laetari in panno laneo aut etiam cannabaceo? Mavis haberi odio et vapulare in purpura quam diligi et in dulcissimos mariti complexus venire sub colore pullo? Si
5 illa mavis, habe quae optasti et ne quereris ea tibi contingere quae ipsa manu tua cepisti prudens ac videns, quamvis caece atque imprudenter. Quid quod maritos complures accepimus sola insania instigatos usque ad uxorum insontium necem processisse? Iustina, nobilissima Romana virgo, aetatis suae puellas forma supergressa, cum locupleti quidem sed stolido et furenti
10 viro in matrimonium esset tradita, de excellenti illa specie in suspicionem marito venit, qui candidissimae uxoris cervicem conspicatus inclinantis se ad exuendum calceum, furore ex zelotypia correptus, teneram puellam et novam coniugem obtruncavit. De quo facinore est illud epigramma:

       Immitis ferro secuit mea colla maritus
15   Dum propero nivei solvere vincla pedis,
       Durus et ante thorum quo nuper nupta coivi,
       Quo cecidit nostrae virginitatis honos.
       Nec culpa meruisse necem bona numina testor;
       Sed iaceo fati sorte perempta mei.
20   Discite ab exemplo Iustinae, discite patres,
       Ne nubat fatuo filia vestra viro.

149. Si recte praecipit Plato ut viri tamquam diligentes et industrii agricolae videant in quod arvum proiciant generosum semen ne vitio soli degeneret, quanto id est sollicitius prospiciendum feminae, nempe arvo ipsi?
25 Etenim si et semini et solo daretur sensus, non dubium quin utrumque alterum posceret bonum. Nam ex amborum commista facultate constant fruges, sed accuratius tamen ac anxius a terra ipsa, propterea quod fruges maximam partem virium a semine potius quam a terra accipiunt nec generosa equa nisi generosum equum admittit. Optari solet ut parentem

---

148. (Immitis ... viro) *Vat. lat. 1610, 58v*
149. (viri ... degeneret) *Plat. Phaidr. 276B* ∥

1–3 Miserae ... vapulare Γ Dementissima puella, mavis semper dolere in auro et serico quam laetari in aere et panno laneo? Mavis odio haberi ac vapulare **H** ∥ **4** et in dulcissimos ... pullo Γ et complecti in simplici ac vulgari colore **H** ∥ **6** ac videns ... imprudenter Γ *deest in* **H** ∥ **7** complures Γ plerosque **H** ∥ **7–8** sola insania ... processisse Γ sola stultitia usque ad uxorum necem evectos **H** ∥ **10** viro Γ iuveni **H** ∥ **10–11** in matrimonium ... venit Γ nuptum esset a parentibus data, ex sola sua pulchritudine marito in suspicionem **H** ∥ **13** obtruncavit Γ iugulavit **H** / De ... epigramma Γ Cuius est illud epigramma **H** ∥ **22**–p.196,**22** Si recte ... gener quam filius Γ *deest in* **H** *in quo legitur:* Nec solum bene consulunt liberis parentes probis et moderatis paribus illos coniungendo, sed sibi etiam. Quippe parant sibi per generos aut nurus praesidia senectutis, si illi modesti et boni sint; contra si scelerosi, hostes sibi asciscunt. De genero habemus exemplum in Evangelio:

148. You poor creatures! What will you do with men laden down with gold and deprived of any good sense? Do you prefer to be in perpetual mourning wrapped in gold and silk to a happy life clothed in wool and hemp? Do you prefer to be hated and beaten dressed in purple garments or to be loved and offer yourself to your husband's embraces dressed in drab colors? If it is the former that you prefer, take what you asked for and do not complain that you received as your lot what you choose consciously and deliberately, though blindly and imprudently. What shall we say of those husbands who, we are told, driven on solely by madness, ended up killing their innocent wives? Justina, a noble Roman virgin, the most beautiful young woman of her time, was given in marriage to a rich but stupid and raging madman. He became suspicious of his bride's exceptional beauty and when on his wedding night he caught sight of her immaculate white neck as she was bending down to take off her shoes, seized by a frenzy of jealousy, he butchered the young maiden and new bride. This epigram tells about this terrible crime:

My cruel husband my neck in sunder cut
While I was stooping to undo the fastenings
That were entwined around my snow-white foot,
Pitiless, and standing beside the bed
Where I had lain with him not long before,
And where I lost the honor of my maidenhood.
And yet I did not merit this vile death,
I call upon the gods to be my witnesses.
But here I lie, the victim of harsh fate.
Learn, fathers, from the example of Justina
Not to marry your daughter to a senseless man.

149. If Plato rightly prescribes that men, like diligent and industrious farmers, should be attentive into what field they scatter their noble seed, lest it degenerate because of a defect of the soil, how much more care should a woman take, since she is the ploughed field itself? For if feeling were given to the seed and the soil, there is no doubt that each would require the other to be good. Crops are produced from the combined powers of both, but the earth would be more careful and meticulous since crops receive most of their vigor from the seed rather than from the earth. A mare of good breeding mates only with a stallion of good breeding. It is commonly desired that

194   J. L. VIVES

soboles referat. Cuperes tu, uxor, filios patris huiusmodi similes? Aut tu,
socer, nepotes? Quae dementia est eum asciscere generum cuius si quis
similes nepotes precetur, velut exsecrationem abomineris. Quanto generosius
Aristides Locrensis, Platonis familiaris! A quo cum Dionysius inferior unam
ex eius filiabus uxorem sibi deposceret, respondit gratius futurum sibi
videre eam mortuam quam tyranno nuptam. Convictus in collocutione
situs est et communicatione fortunarum omnium. Quid colloquetur, quid
dicet stupidus et cunctarum rerum ignarus prorsus? Quae crux erit audire
asinum perpetuo rudentem? Et tanto acerbior si ipsa non careas ingenio,
quemadmodum solet dici, nullum cruciatum esse parem homini cordato
quam illi fatuum alligari.

150. Paulus Apostolus non patitur ut mulieres loquantur in ecclesia sive
docendi sive discendi gratia, sed si quid avent scire, viros suos domi rogent.
Quem rogabis, misera, si quid de pietate dubitas aut de vita? Formam scilicet
ipsam aut nobilitatem aut divitias quas expetisti in demente? Quis familiam,
quis filios instituet? Rebus prosperis moderatione est opus, rebus adversis
consolatione, in utrisque magno et valido consilio. Quis haec praebebit, cum
virum habeas a iudicio, a ratione nudum penitus ac inopem? Si transis in
mores mariti mali, fis mala; sin ei repugnas, invisa. Quae rixa! Quod odium
aeternum! Quod interdum ut vites, vel in similitudinem concedis scelerum
vel in approbationem! Ecclesia quo minus sinat Christianam barbaro aut
haeretico viro nubere vel contra virum fidelem infideli mulieri haec est causa:
ne alter contagio inficiatur alterius.

151. Considera mihi versa vice quae confabulationes sint cum ingenioso
et prudente, ut nullum suaviorem concentum inveniri posse constet sermone
hominis eiusmodi et eo magis si accedat facundia. Quae filiorum institutio!
Quae familiae descriptio viri prudentis! Quam et ad usum accommoda et ad
stabilitatem firma et ad honestatem spectabilis! Si quid cupis discere, habes
paratum magistrum; si consilio indiges, sive ut te sapienter in rebus secundis
geras sive ut in adversis fortiter, habes ad manum fontem ex quo copiose
haurias. Nec illa modo, sed praecepta, monita, exhortationes, consolationes,
ea denique omnia quibus inter has vitae tempestates per singula momenta
est opus. Cum bono quae mansuetudo! Quanta pax et tranquillitas! Quae
incrementa pietatis, adiuvante viro non praeceptis solum et inani quadam
philosophatione verborum, sed exemplo suarum actionum! Ut non maritum
contigisse tibi experiare, sed angelum caelitus missum, universae vitae tuae
ducem.

149. (Aristides Locrensis) *Plut. Timol. 6, 3–4*
150. (non patitur ... rogent) *Vulg. I Cor. 14, 34*

19 mali **WW²B** malis **V**

offspring resemble their parents. Would you, the wife, wish your children to resemble such a father? Or would you, the father-in-law, wish grandchildren who resembled him? What madness it is to adopt into one's family the kind of son-in-law that if someone were to express the wish that you would have grandchildren like him you would regard it as a curse. How much more nobly Aristides of Locri, an intimate friend of Plato, conducted himself. When Dionysius the Second asked for the hand of one of his daughters, he responded that he would be much more content to see her dead than married to a tyrant. Living together consists of talking together and sharing all fortunes. What would such a dolt, totally ignorant of everything, talk about? What a torture it will be to hear the ass constantly braying, and how much more irksome if you are not lacking in intelligence, as it is commonly said that there is no greater torment for a person of intelligence than to be stuck with one who is ignorant.

150. The Apostle Paul does not allow women to speak in church, whether it be to teach or to learn, but if they wish to know something, they should ask their husbands at home. Whom will you ask, you poor thing, if you have any doubts about piety or about religion? Will you ask this of the beauty, nobility or riches that you sought after in a demented person? Who will look after the family, who will educate your children? In prosperity there is need of moderation, in adversity, of consolation; in both cases there is need of sound and effective judgement. Who will provide this when you have a husband totally devoid of judgement and reason? If you go over to the morals of your evil husband, you become evil. If you contradict him you will be hated. What quarrels! What unending hatred! In order to avoid this at times you will acquiesce to what seem like wicked actions or will even indicate approval. The reason why the Church does not allow a Christian woman to marry a pagan or a heretic, or vice versa, a man of the Christian faith to marry an unbelieving woman, is so that neither will be tainted by the contagion of the other.

151. Consider on the other hand what conversations you will enjoy with a gifted and prudent man, such that no sweeter harmony could be found than the speech of this man, and all the more if added to that is the gift of eloquence. What training for the children! What a model of the family of a prudent man! How suited to practical realities, how unshaken in its stability, how irreproachable in its honor! If you wish to learn something, you have a teacher at your disposal; if you are in need of advice, whether it be to conduct yourself wisely in prosperity or courageously in adversity, you have at hand a fountain from which you can draw copiously. Not only this, but precepts, recommendations, exhortations, consolations, in a word, all that is necessary at any moment in the tempests of life. With a good man what mildness of manner! What peace and tranquillity! What growth in piety with the help of your husband not only by precept and idle philosophizing but by the example of his actions, so that you will find that it is not a husband that you have gained but an angel sent from heaven, a guide for your whole life.

152. Haec vera est et germana tranquillitas, gustus plane quidam aeternae illius felicitatis. Propter virum eiusmodi et uxori et liberis et universae familiae, affinibus quoque ipsis et necessariis benefaciet Dominus. Propter Abraham dedit Dominus filium Sarae; propter Isaac geminos Rebeccae. Generationem
5   iustorum curae esse Deo testatur Ipse oraculis suis non uno loco, qui toties Israeliticae genti gravissima condonavit scelera propter Abraham, Isaac, et Iacob. 'Generatio rectorum,' inquit Psalmista, 'benedicetur.' Et idem alibi: 'Iuvenis fui et senui, et non vidi iustum derelictum nec semen eius quaerens panem. Tota die miseretur et commodat et semen illius in benedictione erit.'
10 Tum Salomon in Proverbiis: 'Qui conversatur sine reprehensione in iustitia beatos filios relinquet.' Apud homines vero quae potest commendatio illi comparari: 'Optimi viri coniunx, optimi viri filius'? Evander, Arcadum rex, simul primum est Aeneam contuitus in patris Anchisae memoriam est illum complexus:

15   Ut te, fortissime Teucrum,

inquit,

        Accipio agnoscoque libens! ut verba parentis
        Et vocem Anchisae magni vultusque recordor.

153. Quid soceri? Quantum sibi parant praesidium si generi probi sint,
20 officii ac pietatis memores? Sin vero pravi, perditi, stolidi, fraudulenti, arrogantes, scelerosi, hostes sibi asciscunt. Inimicus est malus gener, non affinis; bonus, non tam gener quam filius. Socrus Petri valida febre a Domino liberata est, quod pro ea gener esset precatus. Tanti fuit illi generum habere talem quem comitem et discipulum sibi adiungere Christus non
25 dedignaretur. De nuru in libro Ruth legimus cum ex terra Moabitide Noemi revertisset in Iudaeam patriam suam marito et filiis orbata, comitatae sunt vetulam nurus duae Moabitides. Altera earum, Orpha nomine, domum reversa est ad gentem suam, Ruth vero secuta est semper socrum, quam et verbis consolata est et opera sua aluit ac fovit. Ita in Ruth et pietatem filiae
30 Noemi repperit et filii curam. Vere vidua et deserta fuisset anus si non quam Orpha erat meliorem nurum esset nacta. Sed quia Ruth habuit, non omnino

---

152. (Generatio ... benedicetur) *Vulg. psalm. 111, 2* // (Iuvenis ... erit) *Vulg. psalm. 36, 25–26* // (Qui ... relinquet) *Vulg. prov. 20, 7* // (Ut te ... recordor) *Verg. Aen. 8, 154–155*
153. (Socrus ... est) *Vulg. Luc. 4, 38* // (ex terra ... Moabitides) *Vulg. Ruth 1, 6* //

22 Socrus Petri **Γ** Socrus enim Petri **H** // **24** quem comitem et **Γ** ut **H** // **24–25** Christus non dedignaretur **Γ** dignatus sit Christus **H** // **25–27** cum ... Moabitides **Γ** cum rediisset in Iudaeam, patriam suam, ex Moabitide terra Noemi, mortuo marito, et filiis, comitata nuribus duabus Moabitidibus **H** // **28** socrum **HWW²** *om.* **BV** // **29** pietatem **Γ** amorem **H** // **30** anus **Γ** Noemi **H** // **30–31** si non quam ... esset nacta **Γ** si non Orpha meliorem nurum habuisset **H**

152. This is true and genuine tranquillity, a foretaste of eternal bliss. Because of such a husband the Lord will rain down blessings upon wife, children and the whole family, relatives too and close friends. Because of Abraham God gave a son to Sarah; because of Isaac he gave twins to Rebecca. God looks after the generation of the just as he himself testifies in his prophecies in more than one place. So many times did he pardon the grave crimes of the race of Israel because of Abraham, Isaac and Jacob. 'The generation of the righteous will be blessed,' said the Psalmist, and elsewhere he says: 'I was young, and I grew old and I did not see the just man abandoned nor his seed in search of bread. All the day he has mercy and takes pity, and his seed will be blessed.' Then Solomon in the Book of Proverbs says: 'He who dwells in justice without blame will leave his children blessed.' In human society what commendation can be compared with this: 'Wife of an excellent husband,' 'Son of an excellent father?' As soon as Evander, King of the Arcadians, saw Aeneas, he embraced him in memory of his father, Anchises:

> Bravest of the Trojan line,
> How gladly I receive and remember you,
> How you remind me of your father's speech,
> The voice and features of great Anchises!

153. What of the father-in-law? What security they provide for themselves if their sons-in-laws are men of good character, mindful of their duties and of filial piety! But if they are corrupt, morally depraved, stupid, deceitful, arrogant and wicked, then one acquires an enemy. A bad son-in-law is an enemy, not a relative. A good one is not so much a son-in-law as a son. Peter's mother-in-law was delivered from a strong fever because her son-in-law had interceded for her. It was of such profit for her to have such a son-in-law, whom Christ did not disdain to join to himself as his companion and disciple. Of the daughter-in-law we read in the Book of Ruth that when Naomi returned from the land of Moab to her native land of Judah, bereft of husband and children, two Moabite daughters-in-law accompanied the old woman. One of them, Orpah by name, returned home to her people, but Ruth continued to accompany her mother-in-law, whom she consoled with her words, nourished and watched over her. So Naomi found in Ruth both the loyalty of a daughter and the care of a son. She would have truly been a widow and an abandoned old woman if she had not had the good fortune to have a better daughter-in-law than Orpah. But since she had Ruth, she

videri potuit liberis orbata nec (quo nomine nuncupari volebat) Mara, id est, amara. Quin cum Ruth peperisset Obeth ex Booz, tam gratulatae sunt vicinae mulieres ipsi Noemi quam si illi non modo nepos esset ex filia natus aut filio, sed filii septem. Erant enim haec gratulantium verba: 'Benedictus Dominus, qui non est passus ut deficeret successor familiae tuae, et vocaretur nomen eius in Israel. En habes qui consoletur animam tuam et enutriat senectutem tuam. De nuru tua natus est quae te diliget et multo tibi melior est quam si septem haberes filios.' Hactenus quidem de sponso ipso.

154. Nunc quemadmodum quaerendus parandusque sit paucis disseram. Illud tamen ante omnia praefabor, ita homines saepenumero mutari coniugio ut quem omnes aspernabantur caelibem, hunc maritum nemo non filiae suae optaret; quemadmodum alii mutantur in peius. Dum condicio virgini prospicitur, expedire censent aliqui puellas nubiles crebro conspici in publico, eleganter ac splendide indui atque ornari, versari et confabulari cum viris, facundas esse, doctas saltare et psallere, interdum etiam amare eum quem sibi maritum destinent: sic enim fieri, ut facilius condicionem inveniant. Cui pravae opinationi poterat ex iis quae dixi in universum occurri, sed singula excutiam, ut non modo prudentibus satisfaciamus, sed etiam rudibus et inexpertis rerum. Ecquis umquam vir providus hoc consuluerit qui norit non esse mala facienda ut inde bona eveniant? Praecipue ubi mala praesentia certa sunt, bona nec certa nec omnino solita procedere. Quod si non es aliter nuptura, o virgo, nisi per has animi corruptelas et per haec discrimina pudicitiae, praestat numquam nubere aut solum habere Christum sponsum quam nubere diabolo prius, ut mox nubas viro, immo vero ut duos habeas simul maritos, vel adulterum alterum, nempe cui posterius coniuncta es, hominem scilicet. Quae sint pericula, quae mala in iis rebus omnibus explicavi antea. Itaque approbatam sententiam nostram confido esse iis quibus prima est ac potissima Christi ac pietatis cura.

155. Nunc cum iis loquamur qui, nefarie quidem ac impie, sed res mundi antiquiores rebus Christi habent. Duo esse animadverto quae maxima potest

---

153. (Mara, id est, amara) *Vulg. Ruth 1, 20* // (Benedictus ... filios) *Vulg. Ruth 4, 14–16*

2 peperisset Obeth **Γ** Isai genuisset **H** // 3 vicinae *deest in* **H** // 4 Erant ... verba **Γ** sic enim dicebant **H** // 4–7 Benedictus ... tuam **Γ** *deest in* **H** // 6 En habes **WW²B** et habeas **V** *Vulg.* // 7 diliget **HWW²** diligit **BV** *Vulg.* // 8–12 Hactenus ... peius **Γ** *deest in* **H** // 12–13 Dum condicio ... nubiles **Γ** Sed antequam huic libro extremam manum addo, respondendum est insanae cuidam puellarum, etiam matronarum et imperitae plebis persuasioni quae expedire putant puellas nubiles **H** // 16–17 Cui ... poterat **Γ** Poteram **H** // 17 occurri **Γ** respondere **H** // 19 Ecquis ... providus **Γ** Quis enim umquam cordatus vir **H** / norit **Γ** sciat **H** // 20 inde **Γ** hinc **H** // 21 solita procedere **Γ** procedere solita **H** // 24 mox **Γ** deinde **H** / ut duos **Γ** vel duos **H** // 27 confido esse **Γ** puto **H** // 28 ac potissima **Γ** *deest in* **H** // 29 quidem **Γ** *deest in* **H** / sed **Γ** *deest in* **H** // 30 Duo esse animadverto **Γ** Duo video esse **H**

did not appear to be entirely bereft of children nor did she have reason to be called Mara, which means embittered, as she wished to be called. Moreover, when Ruth bore Obed of Booz, Naomi's neighbors congratulated her so warmly that it did not seem that she had a grandchild born of her daughter or her son but that she had seven sons of her own. These were the words of those who congratulated her: 'Blessed is the Lord who has not left you this day without next of kin and may his name be renowned in Israel. You have one who will console your spirit and provide for your old age. He is born of your daughter-in-law, who loves you and who is more to you than seven sons.' So much for the spouse himself.

154. Now I shall briefly discuss how he is to be sought and acquired. I shall begin by saying that men are often changed by marriage, so that one whom everyone despised when he was single suddenly becomes one whom everyone would like for their daughters. Others, however, take a turn for the worse. When a young woman's marriage is being contemplated, some think that it is expedient that marriageable girls should be seen frequently in public, should be dressed and adorned with elegance and splendor, that they should associate and converse with men, be eloquent, skilled in dancing and playing the cithara, and sometimes even should fall in love with the man destined to be their husband, for in this way they may find a match more easily. In answer to this dangerous opinion I could cite some of the general precepts I have given, but I shall examine them one by one in order to give satisfaction not only to the wise but also to the ignorant and inexperienced. Would any sensible person ever give this advice, knowing that we should not do evil so that good may come thereof, especially when the present evil is certain and the good not certain or not at all commonly to be expected. My dear young woman, if the only way you can get married is through these corruptions of the soul and these risks to chastity, it is better never to get married or to have only Christ as your spouse rather than first marrying the devil so that you can then marry a man, or rather that you can have two husbands at the same time, the second being an adulterer, namely, the one to whom you were joined second, your mortal husband. I have previously explained what perils and what evils there are in all these things. I am confident that my views will receive the approbation of those whose first and principal care is for Christ and for piety.

155. Let us talk now with those who wrongly and impiously consider the things of the world to be more important than those of Christ. I observe that there are two things that are of most importance for a woman to bring

ad virum afferre mulier: integram pudicitiam et integram famam. Nullus
usque adeo insanit, nullus tam vel formae deditus est vel opibus vel generi,
nullus tam impurus et perditis vitae rationibus qui non ferat quamlibet
uxorem si haec duo habeat, sicuti rursum, nullus qui ferat si non habeat.
Iam quae puella integrius castitatem et nomen tuetur, quae domi sedet
clausa an quae frequens in publico? Domi nulla flagitii occasio, foris undique
scatentes innumerae multaeque ex singulis succrescentes tamquam hydrae
capita. De puella domi abdita nemo fert iudicium. De ea quae in publico
visitur unusquisque, ubi labes et facillime diversitate iudicantium aspergitur;
nec facilius usquam haeret quam in puella nec aliunde difficilius eluitur.
Utram magis admirantur viri? Utram suspiciunt et pudiciorem censent?
Quam vel raro vident vel numquam an quam ubique obviam, etiam ad
fastidium? Nec facile credunt recte servari integritatem a puella quae tam
crebro prodit in publicum. Profecto ad condicionem parandam audiri de
puella magis conducit quam eam videri, ut sunt diversa hominum ingenia
et iudicia. Puella quae spectatur aliquid vel dicit vel agit quod aut ipsi
ducturo displiceat aut alicui ex iis quos habet in consilio aut cui multum
adhibetur fidei. Ob quod unum dirimuntur plerumque coniugia, quae iam
prope cohaeserant illudque non iniuria dicit populus connubia quae multum
tractantur raro compingi.

156. Dicamus de vestibus et fuco. Si propter haec duceris, non intelligis
te odiosam fore quando sine his eris? Atqui ut hanc domi personam
aliquando ponas necesse est et verseris simpliciter ac aperte cum marito.
An illud ignoramus, ut maxime placent ea in quibus aliquod insperatum
invenimus bonum, ita maxime odio esse quae nos speratis fraudant bonis?
Si formosa videris sponso culta et picta, nec es tamen cum ille de tua
forma magnam opinionem conceperit, necesse est te oderit postquam se
falsum intellexerit. Quid quod nominare possum etiam in hac regione et in
mea puellas complures natu grandiores innuptas adhuc, quod exquisito et
sumptuoso utantur cultu? 'Tota,' inquiunt 'dos cum ipsis dotalibus donis in

1–2 Nullus usque adeo ... impurus Γ Nullus est tam stultus ac demens, nullus tam vel
formae vel opibus deditus, nullus tam sceleratus H // **4** sicuti rursum Γ *deest in* H / nullus
qui Γ et qui H // **5** integrius ... tuetur Γ integrius habet castitatem et famam H //
5–6 domi ... in publico Γ domi est crebra an quae in publico H // **7–8** multaeque ...
capita Γ *deest in* H // **8** fert iudicium Γ fert iudicium et censuram H // **8–9** De ea ...
labes Γ De ea quae est in publico, omnes ubi labes H // **10** eluitur Γ eluitur quam ex ea H
// **11** censent Γ rentur H // **14** crebro ... publicum Γ frequens est in publico H // **16**
spectatur Γ cernitur H // **17** displiceat Γ displicet H // **17–18** cui multum adhibetur fidei Γ
aut cuiquam cui habet fidem H // **18–19** iam prope cohaeserant Γ iam iam coitura H
// **19–20** illudque ... compingi Γ *deest in* H // **21** Dicamus Γ Porro H / fuco Γ forsan
fuco H // **23** ponas Γ deponas H // **25** esse Γ sunt H // **26** tamen Γ *deest in* H // **27–28**
postquam ... intellexerit Γ cum se falsum intelliget H // **29–30** quod ... cultu Γ deterritis
viris sumptuosis earum vestibus quibus utuntur H // **30** cum ... donis Γ *deest in* H

to her husband—unblemished chastity and unblemished reputation. No one is so insane, no one so much a slave of beauty or wealth or nobility, no one so vile and devoid of all principles that he would not take any woman who had these two qualities, just as no one would wish to have a woman who did not possess them. Which girl guards her chastity and her good name more irreproachably, the one who stays at home or the one who appears frequently in public? At home there is no occasion to commit wrong; outside there are innumerable occasions that crop up on all sides and multiply like the heads of the hydra. On the girl hidden away in her house no one passes judgement. On one who is often seen in public everyone has something to say, whence arises dishonor, and her reputation is easily besmirched according to the diverse opinions of her critics. There is no one more susceptible to these stains to their reputation than a young girl and no one has more difficulty in removing them. Which girl do men admire more; which do they respect and regard as more chaste, one whom they see but rarely or never, or one they run into everywhere, even to the point of annoyance? They do not easily believe that chastity can be rightly preserved by a girl who spends so much time in public. Certainly, to insure a girl's successful marriage it is of more advantage that she be heard about rather than be seen, since men's characters and opinions are so varying. A girl in the public eye will either say or do something which may displease her future spouse or one of those who counsel him or one in whom he places much trust. This one thing is sufficient to destroy many marriages that had almost been joined. There is much truth in the popular saying that marriages that are long in the making rarely come together.

156. Let us speak of dress and cosmetics. If that is why someone marries you, don't you see that you will excite his aversion when you will be without them? And yet eventually you will have to put off this mask and deal simply and openly with your husband. Are we not aware that we derive most pleasure from things in which we encounter some unexpected good and most displeasure from things that delude our good hopes? If you seem beautiful to your spouse when you are adorned and made up, but you are really not beautiful, after forming such a high opinion of your beauty, he cannot help but dislike you when he finds out that he has been deceived. I can name any number of women, no longer young, in this region and in my native Valencia, who are still unwed because of their excesses in personal adornment. They say the whole dowry and all the wedding gifts will be

vestitum unum aut monile profundenda erit.' Hic ornatus et marito est gravis
in nupta et patri in virgine. Unde est in domo maestitia illa cum filia nascitur;
videlicet quod iam tum quanti deinceps constitura sit parentes reputant.
Adde his quod nimium cultae de mentis levitate ac vanitate suspectae sunt,
modice vero, frugalem, sapientem, gravem esse iudicant et qualem quisque
matronam suam esse cuperet.

157. Iam eas quae libenter versantur cum viris, quis non aliqua sinistra
suspicione aspergit? Atalantam, Iasidis Argivi filiam, quae urbicas aspernata
delicias, silvis et venatibus dedita vixit quaeque nobilem illum Calydonium
aprum confixit prima historiae narrant virginem fuisse venatricem, sed
declamatores eius integritatem in dubium vocarunt illo argumento quod
saepe cum viris iuvenibus in silvis vagaretur. Et de pudicitia puellae nullus
est adversus rumor tam exiguus qui non velut olei macula serpat ilico ac
sese diffundat. Augetur enim sermonibus credulae in vitium turbae. Denique
quis est maritus tam patienti stomacho qui facile uxorem tolleret assuetam
semper cum viris conversari et sociare sermones, qui non malit eam quae
cum solo marito libentius sedeat et colloquatur quam cum virorum caterva,
in qua alius sollicitat forma, alius opibus, alius largitione, alius ingenio,
alius facundia, est qui nobilitate, est qui viribus corporis et robore? Nam
facundas esse puellas, hoc est garrulas (quid enim est facundia in femina
nisi garrulitas?), arguit levitatem animi et malitiam ingenii ita ut ducturus
viperam se accipere existimet, non uxorem. Loquaculam et saltatricem
et dicacem et ludibundam laudant iuvenes coram; simplicem appellant,
festivam, ingenue educatam; omnes ut facilius fallant et corrumpant, nemo
ut ducat. Omnes se potituros citius credunt tali; nullus eam uxorem libens
acceperit quam se aliis tam facilem praebere cernit. Probant in praesentia
quae illae agunt quia delectantur.

158. Miserae! si quae illi postea seorsim dimoto velo inter se colloquuntur
audirent, ibi demum cognoscerent quam ex animi sententia et laudarint et ar-
riserint et verbis ac vultu incitarint! Intelligerent, cum festivam vocant, sentire
illos lascivam; cum facundam, loquacem et garrulam; cum agilem, leviorem
animo quam corpore; perurbane educatam, inverecundam; peraulicam,

---

1 vestitum … profundenda **Γ** unam vestem aut unum monile expendenda **H** // **1–3** Hic
… reputant **Γ** *deest in* **H** // **4** Adde his … suspectae sunt **Γ** Ad haec nimium cultae leves
iudicantur et suspectae sunt **H** // **5–6** modice … cuperet **Γ** *deest in* **H** // **7** Iam **Γ** Tum **H**
// **8** aspergit **Γ** inurit **H** // **10** confixit prima **Γ** prima vulneravit **H** // **13** serpat ilico ac **Γ**
ilico serpat et **H** // **16** sociare sermones **Γ** colloqui **H** // **17** sedeat et colloquatur **Γ** sit **H**
// **18** largitione **Γ** liberalitate **H** // **19** est qui **Γ** alius **H** // **19** est qui viribus … robore **Γ**
deest in **H** // **20** femina **Γ** puella **H** // **24** fallant et *deest in* **H** // **26** acceperit **Γ** accipit **H** //
26 cernit **Γ** videt **H** // **28** colloquuntur **Γ** loquuntur **H** // **30–31** sentire … loquacem **Γ**
sentire illos loquacem **H** // **32** perurbane educatam, inverecundam **Γ** ingenue educatam,
lascivam **H**

lavished on one dress or a necklace. This finery in the case of the bride is a heavy burden for the husband and in the unmarried girl for the father. For that reason there is sadness in a household when a daughter is born, because they immediately calculate how much it is going to cost them. Add to this the fact that too much adornment makes women suspect of frivolity and vanity, whereas one who uses discretion in adorning herself is considered to be frugal, wise and dignified, the kind everyone would want as his wife.

157. As for those who freely associate with men, who does not direct some adverse criticism against her? Atalanta, daughter of Iasius, king of Argon, who spurned the pleasures of the city and lived a life dedicated to hunting in the woods and who first pierced the famous Calydonian boar with an arrow, was a virgin huntress, according to legend, but there were rhetoricians who called her chastity into question because she often wandered through the woods with young men. With regard to a girl's chastity there is no adverse rumor so insignificant that it does not spread like a spot of oil. It will be magnified in the talk of the crowd, always ready to find imperfections. Then what husband has the patience to put up with a wife who is accustomed to associate with men and join in conversations with them? Who would not prefer a woman who is content to sit and talk with her husband rather than with a crowd of men, among whom one is attractive for his beauty, another for his wealth, another for his liberality, another for his intelligence, another for his eloquence, noble birth, physical strength. When young women are eloquent, that is, garrulous (for what is eloquence in a woman but garrulity?), it is proof of levity and perverse character so that the man who intends to marry her will think he is marrying a viper, not a woman. Young men praise to her face a woman who is loquacious, skilled in dancing, witty and carefree; they call her unaffected, congenial, well-bred, but only to deceive and corrupt her, not to marry her. They all think that such a girl will be an easy conquest. No one will be willing to take a woman to wife when he sees that she makes herself so available to others. They praise what they do in their presence because they enjoy it.

158. Poor wretches! If they could only hear what these young men say to each other afterwards when they are among themselves and have thrown off their masks! Then they would know what their real sentiments were in praising them, smiling at them and exciting them by word and gesture. They would understand that when they call someone congenial, they mean of loose morals; when they call her eloquent, they mean talkative and garrulous; when they call her nimble, they refer more to lightness of mind than of body; when they call her sophisticated, they mean shameless; when they call her

---

157. Atalanta: In the Calydonian boar hunt Atalanta was the first to wound the animal but Meleager killed it. According to some versions of the myth she bore a son to Meleager but hid it in order to preserve her reputation as a virgin.

petulantem et procacem. Dixerunt simplicem et sine dolo? Fatuam subno-
tarunt et quae feminae decorum ignoret. At inveniunt istae condicionem? Fateor, nonnullae vel cura et providentia parentum aut propinquorum vel virorum imprudentia et fatuitate, sed quam multae non inveniunt! Quanto plures
nubunt et melioribus maritis et felicius quae non velut lenociniis illiciunt viros,
qui postea, cum se captos sentiunt, mala tractatione mulieres enecant? Neque
enim bono coniuge et frugi uteris umquam quem arte ac dolis circumventum
pellexeris. In summa, si quis est vel adeo demens vel adeo spurcus et nequam
ut talem mulierem malit quam solitariam, severam, cultu simplici, tacitur-
nam; ei det vicinus filiam suam, ego non darem meam. Nam necesse est levitatem amet et vitia qui ea gravitati, sanctitati, et ceteris virtutibus anteponat.

159. De amore dicenda sunt paucula; quae res maxima ex parte puellas
miserrime decipit et in mille praecipitat casus. Qui constabit non decere
puellam ne significationem quidem praebere voluntatis coniugii et amare
iuvenem ut nubat? Si illum amas antequam sit maritus tuus, quid ille ipse
suspicabitur nisi tam te facile adamaturam alium quam se, quem nondum
amatum oportebat. Utique non se solum amari credet, cum non minor sit
causa cur et alios ames; et postquam illi iuncta legitime fueris, alios quoque
adamaturam, nempe usque adeo in amores propensam. Obtegant haec
alii quibuscumque volent coloribus, mulier quae virum non maritum suum
amat, si rem habet cum eo, corpore lupa est, si non habet, animo. Nec refert
quem amet ubi nondum maritum amat. Insana, numquamne fando quidem
audisti plurimas istis amoribus intempestivis adductas ut iis obsequerentur
quos maritos sibi fore sperabant? Hos vero, ubi libidinem suam ad satietatem
expleverant, elusas illas contempsisse idque merito et sapientissime. Indignae
enim sunt quas ducant ii viri quibus eisdem ipsae declararunt posse se cum
eo qui legitimus maritus non esset concumbere. Simile et ante coniugium
facturae cum aliis procis et in coniugio cum moechis.

160. Nullus dies est quo non haec in unaquaque civitate accidant, nulla
est tam ab omni auditione eorum quae in populo agantur remota ad quam
eiusmodi non pervenerint. Audio in hac regione in qua vivo reiectos esse
a quibusdam puellis procos unicam ob causam quod nulla prius inter ipsos

---

1 petulantem et procacem Γ petulantem significare H / Fatuam Γ Stultam H // **3–4** vel
cura … fatuitate Γ *deest in* H // **4** quam multae Γ quot H // **5** illiciunt Γ captant H // **7**
bono coniuge et frugi Γ bono et frugi marito H // **8** pellexeris Γ ad te traxeris H / spurcus
et Γ *deest in* H // **9** severam Γ subtristem H // **10–11** levitatem amet et vitia Γ levitatem et
vitta amet H // **11** anteponat Γ praeferat H // **13** miserrime Γ misere H // **15** nubat Γ
nubas H // **18** illi … fueris Γ te duxerit H // **21** corpore … animo Γ prorsum scelesta
est, si non habet, animo lupa est H // **24** fore Γ *deest in* H / ad satietatem Γ *deest in* H //
27 esset Γ erat H // **28** procis Γ *deest in* H // **29** unaquaque civitate Γ omni populo H
// **31** reiectos esse Γ refutatos H // **32** puellis Γ *deest in* H // **32**–p.206,1 quod nulla …
consuetudo Γ quod nullus antea inter ipsos intercessisset amor H

polite, they mean forward and assertive. Did they say she was unaffected and guileless? What they really meant was silly and ignorant of feminine propriety. But will such girls find a marriage partner? I admit that some will, either through the efforts and foresight of their parents and relatives or because of the imprudence and stupidity of their husbands. But how many do not find a match! How many marry better husbands and more happily who do not lure them with false blandishments, who when they realize they have been captured, kill them with ill-treatment. You will never get a good exemplary husband if you win him over by wiles and cunning. In short, if there is anyone so insane, so base and depraved as to prefer such a woman over one who is shy, austere, of simple dress, silent, my neighbor may give him his daughter, I would not give mine. For if one puts frivolity and vice before dignity, holiness and other virtues, it must be those things that he loves.

159. A few things must be said about love, which miserably deceives the majority of young women and precipitates them into a thousand perils. It will be evident that a girl must not give even a sign of her desire for marriage or that she loves a young man in order to marry him. If you love him before he is your husband, what will he suspect but that you will easily fall in love with someone else other than him, to whom you should not yet have shown your love. Naturally he will think that he is not the only one loved, since there is no reason to think that you will not love others, and after you have been legitimately joined to him, you will fall in love with others, since you have such a strong inclination towards love. Let others gloss over this fact with whatever pretexts they wish, a woman who loves a man who is not her husband is a prostitute in her body if she has carnal relations with him, and in her mind if she does not. It does not matter who the man is, if she does not yet love her husband. Foolish girl! Have you never heard it said that many women have been drawn into these premature love affairs intending to surrender themselves to the ones they thought would be their husbands? But when these men had given satisfaction to their lust, they left them deluded and scorned. And they acted rightly and wisely, for these women were not worthy of marriage since they openly showed that they could lie together with a man who was not their legitimate husband. They could do the same thing with other suitors before marriage and with adulterers afterwards.

160. No day goes by without these things happening in every city. There is no woman so remote from reports of events that go on among the people as not to have heard about them. I hear that in this region where I live many suitors have been rejected by young women for the sole reason that there

intercessisset amoris consuetudo. Quippe negabant posse se cum eiusmodi maritis iucunde ac suaviter vivere quos ante coniugium nec amassent nec novissent. Idem creberrimum esse in Creta narrant, quasi vero non posset amor in coniugio coalescere. Quid opus est tales animos verbis insectari? Quos quae non videt esse impudicos, ea profecto multo impudicior est. Tu ergo non virum diliges quod ipse tibi Dei legibus, Dei iussu ac Deo velut pronubo iunctus est, sed quia eius amori ante sanctas et legitimas nuptias assueveris illiusque conversatione excalfactam libidinem ad torum affers? Hoc idem et scorta faciunt, quae eam ob causam amatores suos diligunt neque tu sane multum scortorum absimilis es. Et ita puellis eiusmodi velut ultione divina accidit ut tota amoris flamma quam in coniugio ardere conveniebat ante coniugium ardeat et inter primos nuptiarum amplexus deflagret atque exstinguatur. Unde illud vulgare verbum: 'Qui propter amores coniunguntur in maeroribus vivunt.'

161. Quippe solet in multis restincto amoris ardori maximum odium succedere. Quae res cunctae civitati magnarum saepe fabularum materiam praebet, cum ardentissimos amatores tribus aut quattuor post nuptias diebus rixatos audiunt et ad pugnos ac fustes venisse cumque adhuc ex pane in nuptiarum usum parato domi superesset, divortium fecisse. Nec mirum: durare ignis non potest qui pabulo et fomento caret, nec amor qui honestis moribus non alitur quandoquidem 'Nulla est' (ut inquit Cicero) 'firma inter malos amicitia.' Quod si amoribus non expedit conciliari connubia nec tam turpibus et fragilibus nodis sanctam illam constringi caritatem, cogitare unusquisque potest quanto minus per dissidia, rixas, lites, odia mutua, ut cum in litigio femina virum aliquem maritum esse contendit suum, e diverso vir feminam aliquam uxorem! Nihil umquam vel legi vel vidi vel audivi ineptius atque absurdius quam ut invitum et renitentem trahas ad te illum quicum individue victura es et qui, nisi te amet, misera sis futura; ceu vero cogi posset quis ut amaret. Non extorquetur amor, sed elicitur; nec umquam amicus erit qui repugnans aliquo est pertractus ubi et vinctus teneatur.

162. Quanta dementia est ab odio auspicari mysterium sacrati amoris! Servum medius fidius nolim invitum retinere, quanto minus coniugem!

---

161. (Nulla ... amicitia) *Sall. Catil. 20, 4*

1–2 cum ... vivere Γ illos amare H // 3–4 quasi ... coalescere Γ *deest in* H // 5 Quos quae non videt esse impudicos Γ Quos quae non videt esse impudicae H // 7–8 ante ... nuptias Γ prius H // 10 diligunt Γ amant H / sane Γ *deest in* H / absimilis Γ dissimilis H // 11 accidit Γ contingit H // 14 maeroribus Γ doloribus H // 16 cunctae Γ toti H / materiam Γ argumenta H // 21 moribus Γ amoribus H // 22 Quod si amoribus Γ Amoribus ergo H / conciliari connubia Γ connubia conciliari H // 24 odia mutua Γ mutua odia H // 25 in litigio Γ *deest in* H // 27 atque absurdius quam Γ ac stultius H // 29 amaret H amaretur **WW²B** amet **V** // 30 teneatur Γ tenetur H // 31 sacrati Γ sacratissimi H

was no intimacy between them beforehand. They said that they could not live a happy and pleasant life with husbands whom they had not loved or known before marriage. They say this is very common in Crete. As if love could not take root and grow in marriage! What need is there to berate such individuals with words? A woman who does not see their shamelessness is all the more shameless herself. Will you not love a man because he was joined to you by the laws of God, by God's command and with God as the godfather, as it were, but because you became used to his love before a holy and legitimate marriage? Do you approach the marriage-bed through lust awakened by being in his company? Whores do this too, and that is why they love their lovers, and you, to be sure, are not very different from them. And so it happens to girls of this type that almost by divine vengeance all the flame of love that should burn in wedlock burns before their marriage and in the first wedding embraces it dies down and is extinguished. Whence the popular saying: 'Those who marry for love live in sorrow.'

161. In many cases hatred takes the place of the extinguished love and this subject has given rise to many a story in all cities, when they hear tell that the most ardent lovers three or four days after the wedding have had quarrels and even come to blows and are divorced before all the wedding bread has been consumed. No wonder. Fire that lacks fuel and kindling wood cannot last nor can love which is not nourished by good morals. As Cicero says; 'There is no firm friendship between evil-minded persons.' But if it is not expedient that marriages be brought about by love affairs and if that holy charity cannot be secured by such dishonorable and fragile bonds, how much less so through discord, quarrels, lawsuits and mutual hatred, as when in a legal dispute a woman claims some man as her husband or a man claims some woman as his wife. I have never read, seen or heard anything more foolish and absurd than that you drag to yourself by force a person who is unwilling and reluctant, with whom you must live inseparably, and will ruin your existence if he does not love you. As if someone could be forced to love! Love is not obtained by force, but it is elicited, and one who has been dragged somewhere by force against his will, and is there held prisoner, will never be a friend.

162. What madness it is to enter upon the mystery of consecrated love out of hatred! I would not wish to keep a servant against his will, so help me God, never mind a wife! I do not merely say that a man should not

Non dico detrectantem et invitum non esse arripiendum virum, sed neque nubendum illi nisi id coniugium libens ipse et avidus expetat. Neque decet puellae patrem vel curatores rogare aut ambire, immo neque puellam offerre ultro; contra potius, virum ipsum matrimonium poscere. Sic fieret
5   nisi omnia pecunia metiretur et regeret. Nunc pecuniae nubitur, pecunia ducitur et sicut non festiviter minus quam vere Seneca dixit: 'Uxores digitis ducimus.' Propterea tam crebra connubia tristia videmus et infelicia, cum uterque coniugum pecuniae se copulatum putat, non homini; illamque velut legitimum comparem artissime uterque complectitur, uxorem vero ceu
10   paelicem maritus et maritum ceu adulterum uxor, in usum tantum libidinis, cetera alter alteri invisus atque odiosus. Qui propter divitias coniunguntur simul habitant, non simul vivunt. Qui propter voluptatem ac speciem, cum his etiam evanescit caritas coniugalis. Qui autem vero ac germano amore, hi profecto ex duobus hominibus unus animus fiunt, quae est naturalis veri
15   amoris efficacia. Qui rerum igitur naturas integras purasque conservare student nec depravatis corrumpere iudiciis, coniugium copulam quandam esse reputant amoris, benevolentiae, amicitiae, caritatis, pietatis, omnium suavium, dulcium, carorum nominum, undique stipatam fultamque. Idcirco, futurum inseparabilem socium fallacibus lenociniis non decipiunt nec aperta
20   vi rapiunt et trahunt, sed quod nomen usurpari in eo negotio solet: ducunt ac ducuntur; idque aperte, simpliciter, pure, ingenue; ne alteruter aut ambo etiam captos se fraudatosque vel vi pertractos maximo utriusque malo conquerantur, sed sancta sit inter illos et felix concordia, dulcissimum matrimonii condimentum.

---

1 detrectantem et **Γ** *deest in* **H** / arripiendum virum **Γ** virum arripiendum **H** ∥ **4** contra **Γ** *deest in* **H** ∥ **6** non festiviter minus quam vere **Γ** festiviter ac vere **H** ∥ **8** illamque **Γ** idcirco hanc **H** ∥ **10** libidinis **Γ** libidinis diligit **H** ∥ **11** odiosus **Γ** odiosus est **H** ∥ **13–15** Qui autem … efficacia *deest in* **H** ∥ **15** igitur **Γ** *deest in* **H** ∥ **16** student **Γ** volunt **H** ∥ **18** fultamque **Γ** ornatamque **H** ∥ **20** rapiunt **Γ** raptant **H** ∥ **21** ac **Γ** aut **H** ∥ **22** vi pertractos **Γ** coactos **H** ∥ **23–24** sed … condimentum **Γ** *deest in* **H**

be seized against his will in spite of his refusal, but you should not marry a man unless he gladly and eagerly desires the marriage. It is not fitting that the girl's father or guardians ask or solicit the marriage or that the girl offer herself spontaneously. On the contrary it is the man who should demand the marriage. That is the way it would be done if money did not measure and govern everything. Now the woman marries because of money and so does the man, and as Seneca said no less truly than humorously: 'We take a wife counting on our fingers.' That is why we see so many sad and unhappy marriages, when each of the spouses thinks he or she is married to money, not to a person. Each party tightly embraces it as if it were his legitimate mate; the husband regards his wife as a mistress, and the wife regards her husband as an adulterer for the purpose of lust, while everything else is hateful to them. Those who marry for the sake of riches inhabit the same house together, but do not live together. In the case of those who marry for sensual pleasure and beauty , as these disappear so does conjugal affection. Those who marry out of true and genuine love form one soul out of two persons, which is the natural effect of true love. Therefore those who wish to preserve the natural order of things pure and intact and not corrupt it with perverse opinions look upon marriage as a union of love, benevolence, friendship, charity, piety and all that is sweet, pleasant and endearing, which bolster and support it. Therefore they do not deceive with artful stratagems the person who is to be their inseparable companion, and they do not carry him off by brute force but, as is expressed in the term used for this contract, they lead and are led into matrimony, openly, sincerely, purely, honorably. Neither of them will have cause to complain that they were captured, defrauded, or dragged by force with irreparable damage to both parties. Let a holy and happy concord exist between them, the sweet condiment of marriage.

APPENDIX

38. p.54,**32**–p.56,**18** Sic Augustinus ... magistratibus **Γ** *deest in* **H**, *in quo legitur*: Nec est aliquid quo Dominus magis delectetur quam virginibus, nihil in quo angeli versentur libentius, colludant, confabulentur, nempe virgines et ipsi; cum Domino suo, qui matrem voluit habere virginem, carissimum discipulum virginem, sponsam Ecclesiam virginem, etiam reliquas virgines despondit sibi. Ad nuptias ingreditur cum virginibus et quocumque eat agnus ille sine macula, qui nos sanguine suo emundavit, centum quadraginta milium virginum eum sequuntur. In canticis scribitur: 'Soror nostra parvula est et ubera non habet,' sive vox illa est Christi sive angelorum ad animam, in qua vera sita est virginitas et Deo grata. 'Omnis enim gloria filiae Regis intrinsecus,' inquit Psalmista. Ibi est ille vestitus deauratus, ibi amictus tot virtutibus ceu gemmis distinctus ac varius. Ne efferas te, virgo, quod corpore sis integro, si animo es fracto, non quod corpus nullus attigerit vir, si animum multi viri percusserunt. Quid prodest corpus esse mundum, cum animum mentemque labe taetra horrendaque infectam geras? Exaruit animus tuus, o virgo, calore virili adustus, nec liquescis prae amore sancto, sed pinguedinem omnem deliciarum paradisi exsiccasti; idcirco virgo es fatua nec oleum habes et interim, dum ad vendentem transcurris, excluderis. Et sicut Dominus in Evangelio minatur, redeunti tibi ac pulsanti respondebitur: 'Quaenam es? Non novi te.' Dices: 'Non nosti hoc corpus clausum, intactum viris?' 'Corpus,' dicit Dominus, 'non video. Animam video viris et istis peioribus diabolis patentem et crebro pulsatam.' Intumescis, virgo, quod non est unde uterus possit intumescere, cum tumescat animus, non virili semine, sed diabolico. Audi quam placeas sponso: 'Ignoras te, o pulcherrima inter mulieres, egredere et abi post vestigia gregum tuorum et pasce haedos tuos iuxta tabernacula pastorum. Non nosti quomodo demum virginitas sit bonum; non es sponsa mea, egredere; et abi post vestigia illorum gregum quos mente alis, et quando quidem meos haedos non pascis, pasce tuos. Me pastorem unicum, summum, optimum non ita diligis. Morare iuxta tabernacula pastorum quos sequeris. Nam si me sectareris, unicus tibi notus esset pastor, non plures.' Vult nimirum ille omnia esse plana, omnia aequabilia. Non tumescit uterus nec est unde; nec tumescat animus nec sit unde. Intellige, obsecro, bona tua, virgo; aestimari non potest pretium tuum, si castitati corporis castum adiungis animum, si corpus et animum simul claudis signasque signaculis illis quae nemo aperit, nisi qui habet clavem David, sponsus ille tuus, qui sic in te quiescit, ut in templo mundissimo atque elegantissimo. An hoc parum est, incomprehensum huic mundi universitati sola te puritate capere? Quam gaudet mulier, si futurum regem utero gestet? Atqui tu iam regem non utero modo, sed quod praestabilius est, mente geris. Illum, inquam, in cuius veste adscriptus erat titulus dignitatis suae: Rex regum et Dominus dominantium; illum de quo prophetae vaticinati sunt: 'Regnum eius regnum omnium saeculorum;' illum cuius regnum finem non inventurum angelus praedixit. Tollamus nos paulo altius et in hoc pulcherrimo argumento cum Augustino philosophemur, sed ita ut nos capias et capies profecto nos melius quam nos ipsi, nempe de tuis bonis loquentes, quorum ipsa non es ignara, et id tibi indicantes, quod ipsa in te habes. Concepit Diva virgo Christum prius animo, deinde corpore, et praeclarius, nobilius, excellentius fuit animo concepisse quam corpore. Quo fit ut et tu in participatum venias excellentioris conceptionis. O te felicem, quae filii non vulgaris et admirandi non vulgariter admiranda es mater. Dominus in Evangelio suo mulieri dicenti: 'Beatus venter qui te portavit et ubera quae suxisti,' respondet: 'Immo vero beati qui audiunt verbum Dei et custodiunt illud.' Et Iudaeis nuntiantibus mane maneri eum foris a matre et fratribus: 'Quinam' rogat, 'sunt mater mea et fratres mei?' Et manum super discipulos extendens, 'Hi sunt', inquit, 'fratres mei, hi mater, et alii quicumque iussis patris mei parent.' Quocirca virgines sanctaeque omnes animae Christum spiritaliter generant. Hominem Deum unica tantum virgo corporaliter genuit, qui ceteris virginibus sponsus est et etiam pater. An hoc tibi parum videtur, o virgo, quod huic Deo et mater es et sponsa et

filia, ne nihil in eo sit quod non sit tuum? Quod non optimo tibi iure queas vindicare, nam et gignis et gigneris et nubis. Quaeris sponsum pulchrum? Huic dicitur: 'Speciosus forma prae filiis hominum, diffusa est gratia in labiis tuis.' Quaeris divitem? De hoc audis: 'Gloria et divitiae in domo eius.' Quaeris nobilem? Dei est filius et quattuordecim reges in stemmate numerat et generatio huius inenarrabilis est et antiquitas generis ante conditum mundum a diebus aeternitatis. Quaeris fortem? De hoc scribitur: 'Sapiens corde est et fortis robore.' Et in Psalmo xliiii.: 'Accingere gladio tuo super femur tuum potentissime.' Quaeris bonum? Nihil de illo audis frequentius quam quod sit optimus. Quaeris in eo magnam ditionem? De hoc legis omnia subiecta esse sub pedibus eius et, in alio psalmo, omnes reges ei servire. Et non modo illi subditos esse homines, sed angelos, sed elementa mundi et caelos ipsos; quod ipsa de se veritas testificatur, inquiens: 'Data est mihi omnis potestas in caelo et in terra.' Quaeris sapientiam? Omnia sunt nuda et aperta oculis eius, nec solum sapiens est, sed ipsa solida et vera sapientia, non Socratis, non Platonis aut Aristotelis, sed Dei, qui per illam eandem sapientiam fecit ac regit hunc mundum quem vides. Cogita nunc quanta cura margaritum hoc est servandum quod te facit similem Ecclesiae, similem Mariae, sororem angelorum, matrem Dei, sponsam Christi. Ut praeteream honores humanos, qui vel nullum vel certe postremum locum in animo Christiano habere debent, sed hi tamen velut oculos in virgine defigunt. Quam grata omnibus virgo, quam cara, quam etiam impudicis venerabilis?

I. INDEX NOMINUM

II. INDEX LOCORUM

III. INDEX VERBORUM MEMORABILIUM

SELECTED WORKS OF
J. L. VIVES

General Editor:

C. MATHEEUSSEN

1. *Early Writings,* edited by C. Matheeussen, C. Fantazzi and E. George. 1987. ISBN 90 04 07782 0

2. *Declamationes Sullanae,* I. edited by Edward V. George. 1989. ISBN 90 04 08786 9

3. *De conscribendis epistolis,* edited by Charles Fantazzi. 1989. ISBN 90 04 08896 2

4. *De subventione pauperum,* edited by C. Matheeussen. *In preparation*

5. *Early Writings 2,* edited by Jozef IJsewijn and Angela Fritsen, with Charles Fantazzi. 1991. ISBN 90 04 09223 4

6. *De Institutione Feminae Christianae.* Liber Primus, edited by C. Fantazzi and C. Matheeussen, translated by C. Fantazzi. 1996. ISBN 90 04 10659 6

ISSN 0921–0717